www.wadsworth.com

www.wadsworth.com is the World Wide Web site for Thomson Wadsworth and is your direct source to dozens of online resources.

At *www.wadsworth.com* you can find out about supplements, demonstration software, and student resources. You can also send e-mail to many of our authors and preview new publications and exciting new technologies.

www.wadsworth.com
Changing the way the world learns®

American Public School Finance

WILLIAM A. OWINGS
Old Dominion University, Norfolk, Virginia

LESLIE S. KAPLAN
Assistant Principal, Newport News Public Schools, Virginia

THOMSON

WADSWORTH

Australia • Canada • Mexico • Singapore • Spain
United Kingdom • United States

American Public School Finance
William A. Owings and Leslie S. Kaplan

Publisher: Vicki Knight
Acquisitions Editor: Dan Alpert
Development Editor: Tangelique Williams
Assistant Editor: Jennifer Keever
Editorial Assistant: Larkin Page-Jacobs
Technology Project Manager: Barry Connolly
Marketing Manager: Terra Schultz
Marketing Assistant: Rebecca Weisman
Senior Project Manager, Editorial Production: Kimberly Adams
Executive Art Director: Maria Epes
Print Buyer: Doreen Suruki

Permissions Editor: Sarah Harkrader
Production Service: Vicki Moran
Illustrator: Lotus and International Typesetting and Composition
Copy Editor: Kay Mikel
Cover Designer: Bill Reuter
Cover Images: school image, Photodisc/PunchStock; money image, Getty Images; blackboard image, Steve Cole/Getty Images
Cover Printer: Coral Graphic Services, Inc.
Compositor: International Typesetting and Composition
Printer: R.R. Donnelley/Crawfordsville

Printed in the United States of America
1 2 3 4 5 6 7 09 08 07 06 05

For more information about our products, contact us at:
Thomson Learning Academic Resource Center
1-800-423-0563

For permission to use material from this text or product, submit a request online at
http://www.thomsonrights.com.

Any additional questions about permissions can be submitted by e-mail to
thomsonrights@thomson.com.

Library of Congress Control Number: 2005920270

ISBN 0-534-64372-8

Thomson Higher Education
10 Davis Drive
Belmont, CA 94002-3098
USA

Asia (including India)
Thomson Learning
5 Shenton Way
#01-01 UIC Building
Singapore 068808

Australia/New Zealand
Thomson Learning Australia
102 Dodds Street
Southbank, Victoria 3006
Australia

Canada
Thomson Nelson
1120 Birchmount Road
Toronto, Ontario M1K 5G4
Canada

UK/Europe/Middle East/Africa
Thomson Learning
High Holborn House
50–51 Bedford Row
London WC1R 4LR
United Kingdom

We, Bill and Leslie, dedicate this book to each other, our writing and life partners; and to those who will use its perspectives and data to improve public education funding as an investment in our nation's human capital.

Brief Contents

Preface   xix

Chapter 1   Misconceptions about School Finance   1

Chapter 2   History of School Finance   45

Chapter 3   The Legal Framework for Financing
Public Education   65

Chapter 4   School Finance as Investment in Human Capital   95

Chapter 5   Taxation Issues   119

Chapter 6   Fiscal Capacity   151

Chapter 7   Fiscal Effort   183

Chapter 8   Equity and Adequacy   201

Chapter 9   The Structure of School Finance Systems   227

Chapter 10   Demographics and School Finance   253

Chapter 11   Budgeting: Applying Policy Values   289

Chapter 12   Spending and Student Achievement   315

Chapter 13   Critical and Emerging School Finance Issues   339

Name Index   373

Subject Index   377

Contents

Preface   *xix*

Chapter 1

Misconceptions about School Finance   *1*

MISCONCEPTION 1   The United States Spends More on Education
Than Any Other Country   5
  What Is Being Said   5
  What Should Be Said   6

MISCONCEPTION 2   Education Costs Have Skyrocketed in the Last Few
Years While Test Scores Have Gone Down   12
  What Is Being Said   12
  What Should Be Said   13
    Education Costs Are Up Because Enrollments Are Up!   *13*
    Education Costs Are Up Due to Greater Variance in Students'
      Needs!   *15*
    Test Scores Are Not Declining!   *16*
    Differences in National Education Spending Portray
      Misleading Sums!   *24*

MISCONCEPTION 3   Spending More Money on Education Does Not
Mean Better Achievement Results   25
  What Is Being Said   26
  What Should Be Said   27
  Summing Up School Finance Misconception 3   30

MISCONCEPTION 4   Educator Salaries Are High in Comparison with Other
Professions with Similar Qualifications   32
  What Is Being Said   32
  What Should Be Said   32

MISCONCEPTION 5   There Are Too Many School Administrators
                   Compared with 30 Years Ago   35
What Is Being Said   36
What Should Be Said   36
Summary   39
Conclusion   40
Case Study   40
Chapter Questions   42

Chapter 2

History of School Finance   45

Where and How It All Started   46
Regional Evolution of Schools and School Financing   48
The History of Federal Education Funding   50
War Years' Legislation   51
Post–World War II Legislation   54
Title I   56
Title II   56
Title III   57
Title IV   57
Title V   57
More Legislation   57
Summary   62
Conclusion   63
Case Study   64
Chapter Questions   64

Chapter 3

The Legal Framework for Financing Public Education   65

Taxation   67
Federal Control of the State's Education Function   68
Federal Contribution to Education   70
State Prerogatives   71
Property Taxes   72
Equal Protection and Taxation   73
Standards of Equal Protection   77
The Rational Relationship Test   77
The Intermediate Test   78
The Strict Scrutiny Test   79
Judicial Standards in Practice   80

State Constitutional Language and School Finance   81
Equity and Adequacy   82
Vouchers, Tuition Tax Credits, and Charter Schools   84
  History of Alternative Schools   *85*
  Vouchers   *86*
  Tuition Tax Credits   *88*
  Charter Schools   *89*
Summary   91
Conclusion   92
Case Study   92
Chapter Questions   93

Chapter 4

School Finance as Investment in Human Capital   *95*

Education as an Investment in Human Capital   96
Education Contributes to Earning Potential   98
Education Increases Employability   100
Education Increases the Quality of Life for Individuals and the Community   102
  Voting Frequency   *102*
  Health Insurance   *103*
  Volunteerism   *104*
  Charitable Contributions   *105*
  Leisure Activities   *107*
  Cultural Activities   *108*
  Childbirth and Prenatal Issues   *109*
  Incarceration Rates   *110*
  Crime Victimization   *112*
Taxing to Support Human Capital   113
Education as a Wise Investment   114
Summary   115
Conclusion   116
Case Study   116
Chapter Questions   117

Chapter 5

Taxation Issues   *119*

Understanding Taxes for Education: Some Basic Concepts   121
  Taxes Equalize Resources and Services   *121*
  Brief History of Tax Funding for Public Schools   *123*
  Flow of Production and Stock of Wealth   *123*

In Rem *and* In Personam *Taxes   124*
Proportional, Regressive, and Progressive Taxes   124
Types of Taxes Used to Generate Revenue   127
Property Taxes   127
Income Taxes   131
Sales Taxes   133
Lotteries and Gambling   133
Severance Taxes   136
Corporate Income Taxes   137
Sumptuary Taxes   138
Measuring Tax Impact   139
Marginal Utility   140
Indicators of a Good Tax   141
Fiscal Capacity: The Ability to Fund Education   143
Fiscal Effort: Putting Your Money Where You Say Your Priorities Are   143
Equity   146
Summary   147
Conclusion   148
Case Study   148
Chapter Questions   149

Chapter 6
Fiscal Capacity   151

Determining Fiscal Capacity   154
Local Fiscal Capacity Issues   156
State Fiscal Capacity Issues   161
National Fiscal Capacity Issues   168
Summary   171
Conclusion   172
Case Study   172
Chapter Questions   172
Appendix: Texas State Data   173

Chapter 7
Fiscal Effort   183

Factors Influencing Effort   184
Computing Effort   186
Relative Effort   187
Local Effort   189
State Effort   193

National Effort   193
Summary   198
Conclusion   199
Case Study   199
Chapter Questions   200

Chapter 8

Equity and Adequacy   *201*

Equality or Equity in Funding?   202
  Horizontal Equity   203
  Vertical Equity   204
  Fiscal Neutrality   205
Fiscal Equalization   206
State Aid Grants to Districts   207
  Nonequalization Grants   208
  Equalization Grants   209
Full State Funding   214
Calculating Vertical Equity   214
  Weighted Pupil Approach   214
  History of Student Weightings   215
  Florida's Model of Pupil Weighting   216
Adequacy   218
  Economic Cost Function Approach   219
  Successful School District Approach   220
  Professional Consensus Approach   221
  State-of-the-Art Approach   221
Summary   222
Conclusion   223
Case Study   223
Chapter Questions   225

Chapter 9

The Structure of School Finance Systems   *227*

Revenues and Expenditures   230
Federal, State, and Local Roles and Responsibilities   234
Advantages to Federal Financing   236
Local Equalization   238
State Equalization   239
Current School Finance Structures   241
  Flat Grants   242
  Foundation Plans   243

District Power Equalizing   *244*
Full State Funding   *246*
Accommodating Adequate Funding with Standards-Based Reform   248
Summary   249
Conclusion   251
Case Study   251
Chapter Questions   252

Chapter 10
Demographics and School Finance   253

Demographics and Instructional Issues   254
A Case Study of Demographics Changing Fiscal Planning   257
Student Demographic Profiles and Trends   258
Risk Factors Affecting School Success   261
Poverty   *262*
Second Language Learners   *265*
Transience   *266*
Low Birth Weight   *267*
Infant Mortality Rates   *267*
Single Parenthood   *269*
Grandparents as Parents   *269*
Premarital Pregnancy   *270*
Child Abuse and Neglect   *270*
Toddlers and Television   *271*
Teacher Demographics and School Finance   272
Teacher Turnover   *273*
Teacher Turnover, Teacher Quality, and Student Achievement   *275*
Alternatively Licensed Teachers   *277*
Administrator Demographics and School Finance   279
Principal Quality and School Finance   *280*
Principal, Quality, Salaries, and School Finance   *283*
School Budgets   *284*
Summary   284
Conclusion   285
Case Study   286
Chapter Questions   287

Chapter 11
Budgeting: Applying Policy Values   289

Budgets Determine Education Priorities   291
A Hypothetical Example   *291*

State Data   293
Federal Data   298
The Budget Process   300
Budget Defined   301
Educational Planning   301
Seeking Adequate Funding   303
Appropriating School Funds   304
Spending the Received Funds   306
Evaluating the Results of the Process and Program   307
Types of Budgets   308
Percentage Add-On Budgeting   308
Zero-Base Budgeting   309
Planning, Programming, Budgeting, Evaluation System   309
Site-Based Budgeting   310
Comments on Accountability   310
Summary   311
Conclusion   312
Case Study   312
Chapter Questions   313

Chapter 12

Spending and Student Achievement   315

Recent History Involving Funding and Achievement   316
The Value of Production Function Studies in Education   319
What the Research Shows about Money and Student Achievement   321
Teacher Quality   322
Professional Development   325
Reduced Class Size   326
Reduced School Size   330
Teacher Salaries   332
School Facilities   333
Summary   335
Conclusion   336
Case Study   336
Chapter Questions   337

Chapter 13

Critical and Emerging School Finance Issues   339

Maintaining Adequate School Facilities   340
Health Issues in School Facilities   343
An Interest in Interest   345

Funding Human Resources for Education   346
  Salary Schedules   346
  Interstate Salary Trends   351
  Licensing and Certification   354
  Benefits   356
  Health Care   359
  Same-Sex Benefits   362
Measuring Student Achievement   364
Emerging Issues   365
  Vouchers   365
  Federal Support for Education   367
  State Support for Education   367
  Local Support for Education   368
Summary   369
Conclusion   370
Case Study   370
Chapter Questions   371

Name Index   373

Subject Index   377

About the Authors

William A. Owings, Ed.D. is a professor and graduate program director of educational leadership at Old Dominion University in Norfolk, Virginia. He has been an elementary and high school principal, assistant superintendent, and superintendent of schools. In addition, he served 18 years on the Association for Supervision and Curriculum Development's Board of Directors and was a regional coordinator for Phi Delta Kappa. Dr. Owings has co-authored with Dr. Leslie S. Kaplan *Best Practices, Best Thinking, and Emerging Issues in School Leadership* (2003), *Teacher Quality, Teaching Quality, and School Improvement* (2002), and two Kappan monographs.

Leslie S. Kaplan, Ed.D., is an assistant principal for instruction with the Newport News, Virginia, public schools. She has been a middle and high school English teacher, counselor, and a central office director of program development. She has served five years on the Advisory Committee for the National Association of Secondary School Principals' *Bulletin* and co-edited their May 2004 issue on "Teacher Effectiveness" with Dr. Owings. In addition, she has co-authored numerous articles with Dr. Owings in professional journals on the topic of school leadership for student improvement.

Preface

As the saying goes, if you want to know the real story, "follow the money." One can easily see what people value by where they spend their resources. The same holds true for local, state, and federal government spending. This is the essence of school finance.

Most students anticipate school finance to be a rather dull and boring topic. They expect it will be a class in accounting practices, stressing credits, debits, and maintaining ledgers. Nothing could be further from the truth. As we examine local, state, and federal education spending, you will come to understand the "big picture" of school finance, deepen your appreciation for public education's contributions to our communities and nation, become competent players in the state and local finance issues arena, and develop into proactive supporters for education finance reform.

Chapter 1 deals with common misconceptions about school finance. Politicians and media loudly and often claim, "throwing money at public schools does not improve student achievement." They see little or no connection between money spent on public education and high-quality schools. Much of the general public has embraced this view but in the next breath will tell you that their own local schools are doing fine. The truth, however, is that money does have an impact on student achievement. The general public also believes education costs have been increasing exorbitantly for the past 50 years while students show flat or declining test scores. This also is untrue. SAT scores did decline for a relatively short time during the late 1960s and early 1970s, but the percentage of students taking the SAT increased dramatically during that time. Consider this analogy: if the number of individuals in the pool increases from a few expert swimmers to include many less skilled individuals, swimming competition scores are likely to fall. In essence, this is what has happened with SAT scores—many less skilled students have entered the test pool. Chapter 1 debunks five common myths about public school finance and student achievement.

Chapter 2 discusses the history of school finance in the United States. Many people believe federal funding for education began immediately after the launch of Sputnik and are quite surprised to learn that the first school compulsory education and finance laws were passed in 1642 and 1647. Moreover, our founding fathers correctly believed that the success of this new republic depended on an educated populace. To that end, federal funding for education was proposed immediately following ratification of the Constitution. This chapter traces the history of school finance in American public schools from the early Massachusetts laws to the present time and points out that the percentage of federal revenue going to local education budgets today is actually less than it was 50 years ago, despite increasing demands for student achievement.

School finance operates within a legal framework that began with ratification of the Constitution. Chapter 3 provides an overview of education legislation, including segregation, increased state responsibilities for funding, and the recent No Child Left Behind Act. Particular emphasis is placed on the evolution of legal thinking about school finance from the 1960s to the present. You will learn how and why we arrived at today's mind-set for funding education based on student-outcome accountability measures (such as annual testing) rather than on school inputs (such as the number of books in the school's library).

Chapter 4 investigates school finance as an investment in human capital. In considering business practices, we all know it is vital to invest in capital equipment. Buildings must be maintained, vehicles replaced, and machinery updated if the business is to thrive. This has been the traditional view of capital investment for years. Adam Smith's *The Wealth of Nations* first conceived of education and its investment in people—human capital—as the foundation for economic prosperity. Investing in education makes the community and the nation economically stronger and better poised for growth. In this chapter we discuss the various ways public education improves your own and your neighbor's quality of life as it also benefits society and the nation.

Chapter 5 provides an overview of taxation issues. Paying taxes, for most people, is about as rewarding as having a root canal. Indeed, some would prefer the latter. Taxes, however, have an important purpose in a democracy. They provide for the general welfare and redistribute wealth, spreading the cost of providing services over the greatest number of people possible. Without this redistribution, the few rich would get smarter and richer and the massive number of poor would get less intelligent and poorer. The chapter examines types of taxes and benefits, and their various limitations, and challenges our continued reliance on property taxes at the local level as the primary means of supporting education. We also explore why tax burdens are shifting to the local level—over the smallest group of people possible—instead of remaining at the state level where the legal responsibility for education rests.

Chapter 6 explores fiscal capacity issues. Capacity is nothing more than a measure of wealth. This chapter reviews how localities and states measure resources to fund education and how the state redistributes these resources to provide a basic level of service to each school district. Issues discussed include fairness—Is it right for the wealthy to fund educational programs for the poor?—and the methods various states use when considering capacity. A note of caution: This chapter may change the way you think and feel about measurements of wealth!

Chapter 7 addresses fiscal effort, the natural complement to fiscal capacity. Effort is a measure of how a locality and a state spend their resources in relation to their fiscal capacity—or their ability to pay. We review how the state and localities measure effort in relation to wealth. Questions for discussion include "How should effort be best measured?" and "What combination of variables at what weightings should be included in the calculation of effort?" You may be surprised to see where your state ranks in fiscal effort compared with capacity.

Chapter 8 builds on the discussion of capacity and effort and introduces the concepts of equality, equity, and adequacy. As patriotic citizens, we all believe in equality, which would mean providing the same service to every student. However, students do not come to our schools with the same abilities and life experiences. Schools cannot succeed in leaving no child behind using an equality model. Equity, simply put, means providing what students need. Some seventh grade pre-algebra students may need more time than others working with the teacher to master the content. Other students may have physical or learning disabilities. To provide a high-quality education and meet rising testing standards, school funding must consider equity. On the other hand, inequality of opportunity should be avoided. This chapter reviews issues of funding equity and equality among states and nations.

Chapter 9 brings the issues mentioned in previous chapters together in a discussion of the structure of school finance systems. Education is a state responsibility. States have a responsibility to equalize local funding based on capacity. The federal government also has a responsibility to fund federal education legislation. This chapter reviews and clarifies the political and financial relationships among the federal, state, and local governments for funding public education.

Chapter 10 focuses on demographics and changing student populations. The general public believes there are fewer students in schools today than during the baby boom. In fact, today more students are in public schools than at any other period in history. Demographic issues in education traditionally have involved simply counting the number of students enrolling each fall. Our numbers either went up or down—that was the extent of demographics for most of us. Issues of changing racial and ethnic student populations were confined to poor, decaying urban areas. Today, demographic issues have an impact on all schools. Various racial, ethnic, and economic groups have increased significantly and have a large impact on where and how education dollars should be spent—equity issues. For example, in a five-year period, some school districts have seen more than a 300% increase in students who speak English as a second language. Student risk factors associated with education issues are also discussed. The chapter ends with a discussion of teacher and principal demographics and turnover rates, teacher and principal quality, and student achievement as it affects school finance.

Chapter 11 examines the statement that where you put your money reflects what you value—even if you don't realize it! As intelligent, responsible citizens, we all try to live within our economic means. A budget in its simplest form is a snapshot of what it costs to operate an organization (home or school or large corporation) at a given time. Some keep a formal budget, and others only track the checks they write. Studying budgets shows spending patterns and the values that underlie them. This chapter outlines how budgeted monies are spent in all 50 states and includes an overview of the various types of budgets. It closes with a discussion on budgeting and accountability.

Chapter 12 brings finance to the real "bottom line"—spending and student achievement. When all is said and done, educators exist primarily to promote student achievement. Many local, state, and federal politicians love to say that money does not matter in education—that we have thrown too much money away without results, even with declining results. We have heard local politicians say that when they were in school (in the 1940s) an education meant more because the funding was so little and that we need a return to those days. School leaders need to know how to respond constructively to such uninformed beliefs. Connections do exist between school funding and student achievement. This chapter examines research that shows that increased spending makes a positive difference in student achievement—funding teacher quality, professional development, class and school size, salaries, and school facilities.

Chapter 13 examines critical and emerging issues, looking forward to what may lie ahead. Past and current school finance spending practices are the best predictors of future trends. Investment needs in the infrastructure of facilities, health-related issues in school buildings, financing school facilities, and human resource issues—salary schedules, benefits, and licensure standards—are all discussed. We also examine voucher plans and federal, state, and local support trends for education, paying particular attention to the increased costs associated with the federal No Child Left Behind legislation. If we have done our job well, you will have the foundation to knowledgably and effectively address the critical issues we see in education finance and student achievement.

ACKNOWLEDGEMENTS

We would like to acknowledge many people for their help in developing this text. First, we would like to thank Drs. Richard Salmon and David Alexander for their friendship, guidance, and instruction that helped to formulate our thinking about school finance. Second, we would like to thank our editor, Dan Alpert, for his encouragement and vision for this project. Third, thanks to Gerald Bracey for his contribution to Chapter 1 and for his even greater contribution to education. Fourth, we would like to thank Dr. Mary Hughes and her colleagues for their contribution to Chapter 8 with the ideas of equity, equality, and adequacy. Fifth, we would like to thank several Old Dominion University graduate students for reviewing the text and making suggestions that will enhance your reading and understanding. Those students are

Leo K. Akujuobi
Janet Blake-Perry
Dwayne M. Godette
James R. Kenny
Dennis M. Moore Jr.
Phyllis F. Parker
Adam A. Prater
Angela Rhodes

We also are grateful to the following manuscript reviewers for sharing so many constructive suggestions at various stages of the manuscript development process:

Katie Foley, Syracuse University
Maxwell Prof. Timothy Smeeding, Syracuse University
Dr. Sam Wright, Lewis University

Prof. Richard Wiggall, Illinois State University
Prof. Robert Riccobono, NYU
Dr. Seth Hirshorn, University of Michigan
Prof. J.D. Willardson, Brigham Young University
Dr. Cozette Buckney, Roosevelt University
Prof. Donna Lander, Jackson State University
Dr. Carlos Cruz, Texas A&M University Kingsville
Prof. Leonard Elouitz, Kean University
Prof. Jimmy Byrd, Tarleton State University
Prof. Kent Murray, The Citadel
Prof. Bradley Balch, Indiana State University
Dr. Marilyn Hirth, Purdue University
Dr. Richard Conrath, Saint Leo University
Prof. Lynda Cook, Shippensburg University
Prof. Peter Madonia, Southern Connecticut State University

Finally, we would like to thank you readers in advance for the work that you do and will do to advance our profession in promoting student achievement. We trust that you will become knowledgeable and persuasive advocates for education finance reform. May you intelligently lead various learning communities to see our country's need for investing in human capital and the powerful relationship of public education to our nation's current and future economic stability and growth. American public school finance reform is in our economic and political self-interest, from your own locality to the national and global arena.

MISCONCEPTIONS ABOUT SCHOOL FINANCE

FOCUS QUESTIONS

1. Over the past 50 years, how has our changing student population affected high school completion rates and standardized test scores?

2. How big is the American "public education business"?

3. How much does the United States spend on public education compared to the rest of the world?

4. How have the costs of public education changed since 1970?

5. Does increased spending result in increased student achievement?

6. What is the real picture of salaries in public education?

7. Has the percentage of public school administrators grown too large?

In this chapter we answer these questions and provide data for discussion about five misconceptions that pervade our culture regarding education. Many of these misconceptions persist because educators and the general public do not know the facts and how to respond to criticisms of this profession. As we discuss these issues, we hope you will develop a fundamental understanding of school finance and that you will learn how to apply analytical reasoning to fiscal issues. School leaders must be able to accurately interpret local and national education policies without bias or ideology, so parents and neighbors will continue to support our public schools, both politically and fiscally. When people have all the facts, they can make informed choices. Education leaders must thoughtfully consider public school critics' arguments and carefully evaluate them based on real data, historical accuracy, and their own experiences. Critical thinking about school finance issues is essential if tomorrow's schools are to receive the backing necessary to keep our communities thriving, both economically and culturally. For education leaders, this is a matter of no less urgency than maintaining or enhancing the standard of living in our communities.

Let's face the truth. Education has never been a highly prestigious or highly paid profession in the United States. Our founding fathers knew that an educated citizenry provided the essential foundation for their new experiment in democratic government (see Chapter 2), and recent polls indicate that Americans support education and want public schools spared from budget cuts.[1] Even though education is favored, the general public views teachers in a less flattering light. Think about characters from pop culture such as the economics teacher in *Ferris Bueller's Day Off* or Washington Irving's classic teacher Ichabod Crane–the gangly, gullible fool in *The Legend of Sleepy Hollow*. (In Hebrew *Ichabod* means "The glory is gone." Maybe Irving was an education prophet for our times.)

Critics say they are disappointed with public education today. They say schools today are not like used to be. To that, we say a hearty "Amen"! Today's public schools are more successful than they have ever been, educating a more diverse student population to higher academic standards and keeping more students in formal learning programs through high school graduation. This is not merely an opinion; the data support this view.

Consider the public schools over the past 50 years, as far back as most practicing educators have experienced firsthand. In 1950 about one-third of the population graduated from high school;[2] the graduation rate for black males was 12.6% and for black females 14.7% (about one-third the graduation rate of their white counterparts); *Brown v. Board of Education of Topeka* (1954) had not been adjudicated, leaving many minority students to attend lower quality and deliberately separated schools; and the situation worsened. Today we educate all students with an ethnic, socioeconomic, and disability diversity unmatched in other countries—or at least we try. Admittedly, not all are educated to the highest standards, and we remain challenged to increase all students' achievement.

Even though the number of students graduating has increased since the 1950s, the general public continues to hear that public schools are failing. What is happening? When we consider funding and compare it with what other countries spend (see page 7) and with what we used to spend in the "good old days," it is amazing how well our teachers and students perform today. A few of you may be old enough to remember Marshall McLuhan, once considered the "Oracle of the Electronic

---

[1]Public Education Network, "Even in Troubled Times, Quality Public Education Remains Nation's Top Priority" [Press Release], February 24, 2003.

[2]The figure for all races was 34.3%. http://nces.ed.gov/pubs2002/digest2001/tables/dt008.asp provides complete information for all races and sex.

Age."[3] He noted how we love to live in "Bonanza-land," recalling the popular 1960s and 1970s television show about a wise father and his three grown sons living on a large ranch in 19th century Nevada. People enjoy looking through the rearview mirror to a more emotionally comfortable, simpler era. McLuhan said that the "Good old days never were." To prove his point, some "old-timers" claim that when they entered the teaching profession in the 1950s and 1960s, teaching was "a calling" and a highly respected field.[4] They are living in Bonanza-land. The truth is that teaching has always been a difficult, demanding, and poorly resourced profession that has swayed in local, state, and increasingly since the 1980s, national political winds.

Federal education involvement has always been supportive although largely subject to the political agenda of the day. It wasn't until Jimmy Carter's 1976 presidency that education was reinstated as a cabinet level position. In the 1980s the Reagan White House asserted substantial negative and often false claims about public school students' behavior and achievements. Today George W. Bush's No Child Left Behind Act (2001) places federal mandates for highly qualified teachers, a national collection of approved state curricula, and high-stakes accountability into every schoolhouse in exchange for federal dollars (we address these issues throughout the book).

The importance of public education to our national agenda and to our economy makes it a logical political focus. Controversy exists about the effectiveness of our educational system. Some sincerely believe that the public education system is not working and call for vouchers and charter schools as alternatives to give parents choices about the best school environments for their children. Public school supporters, on the other hand, believe that "organized malevolence might actually be underway"[5] to undermine this valuable democratic institution. Regardless of your point of view, the data show that U.S. schools have never been asked to do more with fewer resources under a higher level of public scrutiny—and with higher expectations for all students' achievement—at any other time in our history.[6]

Education places many demands on the U.S. economy. Big budgets make big targets, and public education is a big business with a substantial budget.

---

[3]Marshall McLuhan (1911–1980) authored *The Medium Is the Message* (New York: Bantam, 1967) and was director of the Center for Culture and Technology at the University of Toronto, Canada (1963–1979), where he studied the psychic and social consequences of technologies and media, becoming a popular "guru" of media culture.

[4]We feel comfortable saying this since many of our contemporaries are retiring at this time.

[5]D. Berliner and B. Biddle, *The Manufactured Crisis: Myths, Fraud, and Attack on America's Public Schools* (New York: Longman, 1995), xiii.

[6]See G. Bracey, *Setting the Record Straight: Responses to Misconceptions about Public Education in the United States* (Alexandria, VA: ASCD) 1997 and Berliner and Biddle, *The Manufactured Crisis.*

In the 1999–2000 school year, the latest data available, the operating budgets for all public K–12 education totaled more than $373 billion,[7] employing approximately 3 million teachers.[8] This figure does not include the 1.6 million administrators, counselors, paraprofessionals, and support staff who work in schools educating the 53.2 million public school students enrolled in the fall of 2001.[9] In total, approximately 4.6 million people work with public school students. If public education were a national company, it would be more than 5 times larger than General Motors, General Electric, and IBM combined.[10]

Obviously, education is a bigger business than most realize. Education comprises almost 5% of the total United States domestic output each year. In fact, K–12 schooling expenditures are equivalent to approximately 4.3% of the gross domestic product (GDP)—the total output produced within a country during a year—down from 4.5% in 1997.[11] If school construction costs are added to this figure, the percentage of dollars going to public schools rises sharply.[12] When higher education institutions are included in budget figures, education spending as a percentage of GDP increases to 7.1%.[13]

Perhaps because of education's size or the large amount of money and influence involved, misconceptions concerning school finance abound. Since publication of *A Nation at Risk*[14] in 1983, education bashing has become

---

[7]U.S Department of Education, National Center for Education Statistics, "Revenues and Expenditures for Public Elementary and Secondary Education: School Year 1999–2000," http://www.policyalmanac.org/educationa/archive/doe_education_spending.shtml.

[8]U.S. Department of Education, National Center for Education Statistics, "Digest of Education Statistics, 2001," http://nces.ed.gov//pubs2002/digest2001/tables/dt004.asp.

[9]*America's Teacher Profile* (Washington, DC: U.S. Government Printing Office, 1999), table 45, p. 105.

[10]The total number of employees for these three companies in the year 2001 totaled 848,876. Information for these companies shows the following breakdown: General Motors, 310,000 world-wide employees (www. ge.com/annual01/financials/index.html); General Electric, 219,000 total employees (*GE Annual Report, 2001,* p. 65); IBM, 319,876 U.S employees (www.ibm.com/ibm/us/).

[11]U.S. Department of Education, National Center for Education Statistics, "Digest of Education Statistics, 2001," http://nces.ed.gov//pubs2002/digest2001/tables/dt029.asp.

[12]We cannot be certain about public school construction costs because states and localities vary in who pays these costs and how they are reported. Some school systems report debt service in their own budgets; other school systems have the municipal government pay and report these costs in their budgets; still others are reported by the state.

[13]U.S. Department of Education, National Center for Education Statistics, "Digest of Education Statistics, 2001."

[14]National Commission on Excellence in Education, *A Nation at Risk* (Washington, DC: U.S. Government Printing Office, 1983). This very political document has many errors and misrepresentations that were probably intentionally designed to promote vouchers and public support for private schools. This is discussed at length in Gerald Bracey, *Setting the Record Straight: Responses to the Misconceptions about Public Education in the United States* (Alexandria, VA: ASCD, 1997).

fashionable. In fact, since the mid-1980s, no national political candidate has been elected without an education platform that promises to change a "broken" system.

With this background, we begin this judicious study of American school finance by presenting—and challenging—the five most popular misconceptions about our public schools. First, we question whether our country does spend more on education than any other country. Second, we explore whether education costs really have recently skyrocketed. Third, we review a popular myth that spending more money on education does not mean better student achievement results. Fourth, we assess the fiction that education salaries are high in relation to other similarly trained professions. Finally, we discuss the folklore that education today employs too many administrators—what Gerald Bracey calls "the administrative blob."[15] We discuss both sides of the issue so you will be aware of what critics may say and how an education leader can effectively respond. Armed with this information, you should be able to dispel many of the education misconceptions heard in your community—especially when it is time to adopt state and local education budgets.

Misconception 1   The United States Spends More on Education Than Any Other Country

In a Nutshell: This is not true for public education (K through grade 12). It is only true if you include total dollars spent for higher education as well.

WHAT IS BEING SAID

I ask each semester's school finance graduate students if they believe that the United States spends more on public education than other countries do. More than 90% of the students every semester believe this is a true statement. It is not. If graduate students in educational leadership programs believe this to be the case, what must the general public believe? As a rule, people will believe what they hear most frequently.

Since the Reagan administration, the public has heard that we spend more on education than any other country. Two previous secretaries of education, Lauro Cavasos and Lamar Alexander, and an assistant secretary

---

[15]Bracey, *Setting the Record Straight.*

of education, Chester Finn, have made similar, frequently quoted comments. Louis Gerstner, author of *Reinventing Education,* former IBM chief, and now adviser to the New York City schools' overhaul, claimed that spending on American education is without equal in the world.[16] Let us show you how inaccurate this misconception is.

WHAT SHOULD BE SAID

The United States does not spend more on its K–12 public education than does any other country. As you can see from Figure 1.1, in total dollars the United States does spend more than any other country on public education *if* you include grades K through 12 *and* all higher education (which includes undergraduate and graduate education). This "world's highest" spending argument usually refers to K–12 public education, however, and that statement is inherently misleading.

In addition to the lack of significant differences in dollars spent on K–12 education between the United States and other developed countries, other subtle but distinct indicators show that such spending comparisons are false. First, comparing total dollars spent on education without equalizing dollars for cost of living is not comparing "apples to apples." Comparing U.S. dollars to the equivalent currency in Mexico, Poland, Hungary, or the Czech Republic is inaccurate and inappropriate. We might say that the leather coat we bought in New York was overpriced because we could have bought it in Mexico for one-tenth of the cost. But would we want to live in Mexico at the relative standard of living of those who make those leather coats? We think not!

Obtaining international comparisons of education expenditures and other education-related data informs us about international spending for public education and provides more meaning and context for our own school finances. Figure 1.1 shows the amount of money different countries spend for their primary, secondary, and postsecondary education. The horizontal lines represent expenditures per student, and the square highest on the chart represents the United States' total expenditures, kindergarten through college, grades K–16. It is important to remember, however, that virtually no other country provides a free and appropriate education to *all* of its

---

[16]Louis V. Gerstner, R. Semerat, D. Doyle, and W. Johnston, *Reinventing Education* (New York: Dutton, 1994).

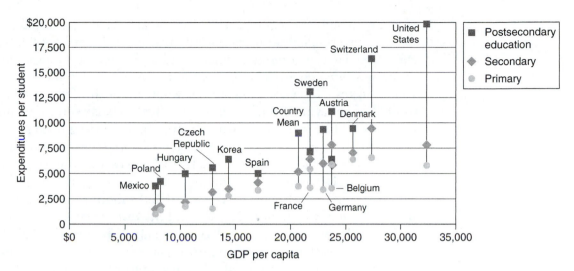

FIGURE **1.1**

Educational Expenditures per Student in Relation to GDP per Capita, by Level of Education for Selected OECD Countries, 1998

Source: U.S. Department of Education, National Center for Education Statistics, "The Condition of Education 2002, Section 6, Indicator 41."

children from kindergarten through grade 12 and from ages 2 to 22 for students with special needs. That alone greatly increases the average U.S. spending per student on a per capita basis in comparison with other countries—even if we equalize for cost of living comparisons.

It is also important to compare spending at different grade levels, and we will examine spending at the K through 12 levels. The United States does, however, outspend other nations for colleges and universities. That helps to explain why so many international students come to this country for higher education. For the purpose of this text, however, we will examine only K through 12 spending.

If we eliminate the "squares" representing postsecondary education in Figure 1.1, it is obvious that U.S. spending on education is comparable to that of other "first world" countries. In fact, our relative spending on secondary education is lower than our relative position for elementary spending compared with some other first world countries. As we examine international spending patterns, it is important to compare "apples with apples."

Next, when we consider international spending comparisons, we need to account for some equalization to provide more meaning about the value of money in different countries. Unless these dollars are equalized to account for a relative standard of living, the comparisons will not be valid. Salaries compose a large part of education expenditures, and the average educator salary in Mexico does not come close to the average educator salary in the United States.[17] To make comparisons without equalizing for cost of living would be like saying that a banker in New York City is overpaid compared, for example, to bankers in Burrundi, Africa, a developing nation.

In addition, many countries have national salary schedules whereas for the most part in the United States salary schedules are locally determined, with substantial variance based on the community's wealth and geography. The salary difference between U.S. rural and suburban secondary principals, for example, can be $17,500,[18] and the difference between a South Dakota and a New Jersey secondary principal can be nearly $57,000.[19]

Another method to weigh international education expenditures is to visualize education costs as a part of each country's total economy.[20] On the surface that would seem a fair basis for comparison. We then examine not the actual dollar amounts spent for education on a per pupil basis but the percent those dollars represent as a portion of the entire country's economy. This method shows the relative spending on education against one measure of the overall national economy.

One method of international comparisons is to match education spending as a part of the gross domestic product (GDP). GDP is the measure of a country's output of goods and services calculated by considering personal consumption, government expenditures, private investment, inventory growth, and trade balance. The GDP recognizes that business has been globalized, deregulation is increasing business activity, and relative prices for goods change quickly and dramatically. The government recalibrates

---

[17]We compare Mexico and the United States here as Mexico has one of the lowest expenditure levels whereas the United States has a relatively high expenditure level, and the two are contiguous.

[18]S. Poppink and J. Shen, "Secondary Principals' Salaries: A National Longitudinal Study," *National Association of Secondary School Principals' Bulletin* 87 (634), March 2003: 67–82, at 71.

[19]Ibid., 73.

[20]International spending comparisons can be studied by looking at a country's Gross Domestic Product or Gross National Product. GDP measures all production within a country by whoever happens to be working there; GNP measures the production of all citizens of that country, wherever they happen to be working. (Maybe you can remember the "N" in GNP stands for "anywhere.") GNP and GDP tend to be used as synonyms, but GDP is the preferred measure among economists and is gaining popularity in general conversation as well; the two measures are fairly close numerically. Comparing expenditures by GDP has advantages over GNP. GDP comparisons allow us to factor in expenditures relative to various nations' ability to finance education. Both measures place dollar amounts within a cultural context, but GDP is more narrowly focused on the goods and services produced inside the country.

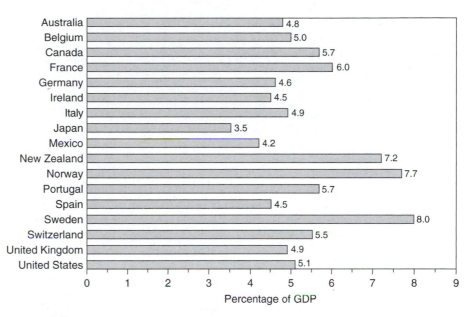

FIGURE **1.2**

Public Direct Expenditures for Education as a Percentage of GDP, Selected Countries, 1998

Note: Includes all government expenditures for education institutions.

Source: Adapted from "Total public expenditures on education," *Education at a Glance: OECD Indicators 2001 Edition.* Copyright © 2001 OECD. Used by permission.

the relative prices of these goods—and their relative importance to the economy—every year.

GDP for the United States is far ahead of that of most other countries. This indicates that our relative wealth and standard of living is high in relation to the other Organization for Economic Cooperation and Development (OECD) nations referenced in Figure 1.2. As you can see, U.S. education spending is not commensurate with our relative wealth.

The United States spends approximately 5.1% of its gross domestic product on education; that is, we rank 10th among 17 "First World" OECD countries. The mean (average) education expenditure in these 17 countries is 5.4%, so U.S. spending on education as a percentage of GDP is less than the 17-country average.

One way to view these patterns is to conclude that the United States makes an "average effort" to finance education. Because our overall national wealth (capacity) for funding education is high, however, an "average" effort

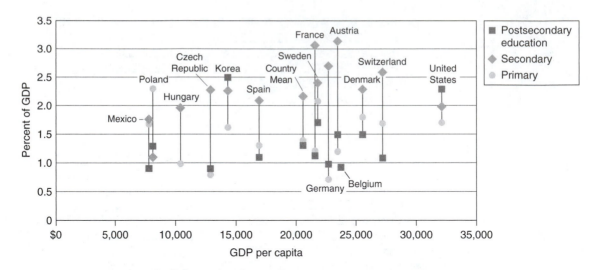

FIGURE **1.3**

Educational Expenditures as a Percentage of GDP, by GDP per Capita and Level of Education, for Selected OEDC Countries, 1998

Source: U.S. Department of Education, National Center for Education Statistics, "The Condition of Education 2002, Section 6, Indicator 41."

may appear insufficient. The United States holds very high academic expectations for all students—especially with the No Child Left Behind legislation. On the other hand, our nation also devotes substantial resources to other public areas, especially Social Security, transportation, health, and medicine. It might be said, therefore, that we are actually doing very well in our overall social and education funding patterns.[21]

At first glance Figure 1.3 resembles Figure 1.1; however, per student spending is no longer on the vertical axis. Percent of GDP is now the vertical axis. As stated previously, examining the gross domestic product is perhaps the best indicator of spending comparisons because GDP comparisons allow us to factor in expenditures relative to the ability of various nations to finance education. It shows what education dollars are actually "worth" in the society.

---

[21]Daniel U. Levine, "Educational Spending: International Comparisons," *Theory into Teaching* 33, 1994: 126–131.

According to the OECD, a positive correlation exists between a nation's per capita GDP and levels of education.[22] Wealthier countries tend to spend more per primary, secondary, and postsecondary students than do less wealthy countries. In the latest comparison year available, 1998, annual expenditures at the primary level among OECD members ranged from $863 in Mexico to $6,713 in Denmark. At the secondary level, expenditures ranged from $1,438 in Poland to $9,348 in Switzerland. U.S. spending on primary and secondary education was $6,043 and $7,764, respectively, which ranked high among OECD nations, with only Austria and Switzerland spending more.

However, in terms of spending on education as a percentage of GDP, you can see that we outspend most countries for primary education (circles), but at the secondary level (diamonds), we outpace only Poland and Mexico and virtually tie with Hungary. As measured by GDP, the United States is among the lowest in spending for secondary education on a per capita basis. In other words, we are not spending as much as most other first world countries on middle level and high school education. In this area, our financial effort is relatively low even though our financial capacity is very high. Our measure of wealth, as determined by GDP, ranks the United States highest in the comparison group.

In relative terms, however, per capita GDP spending on primary education ranged from 0.7% in Germany to 2.3% in Poland. U.S. spending on education as a percentage of GDP in this area was 1.7%—roughly the same as Mexico and Switzerland. At the secondary level, there was greater variance—from 1.1% in Poland to 3.2% in Australia. The United States spent 2% of GDP—a percentage lower than 13 OECD countries and lower than the OECD average of 2.2%.[23]

Clearly U.S. spending on K–12 education is not higher than that of any other country. In fact, some evidence shows that U.S. spending on K–12 education in equalized dollars is less than that of 16 other industrialized countries, placing our spending 9th of 16 nations—30% less than Japan.[24] An equalized comparison would show that in terms of wealth as measured by GDP, our spending places us 10th—below the average of 17 OECD countries. Only when considering higher education do we score at the top

[22]Organization for Economic Cooperation and Development, Center for Educational Research and Innovation, *Education at a Glance: OECD Indicators, 2001* (Paris, France: OECD, 2001).

[23]U.S. Department of Education, National Center for Education Statistics, *The Condition of Education, 2002*, NCES 2002-025 (Washington, DC: U.S. Government Printing Office, 2002).

[24]Berliner and Biddle, *The Manufactured Crisis*, 66–67.

of the scale. When we consider that our relative wealth places us at the top of the scale, the meaning of our educational expenditures changes substantially. In other words, our relative capacity to fund K–12 education is high; our relative effort is low.

Misconception 2   Education Costs Have Skyrocketed in the Last Few Years While Test Scores Have Gone Down

In a Nutshell: The word "skyrocketed" is inflammatory. True, costs have increased, but not to the level education critics would have the public believe. In constant dollars expenses for teachers' salaries remain almost flat. Special education expenses, increased teachers' salaries in real dollars, and smaller class sizes have been the primary reasons for increased costs since the early 1970s and 1980s. Meanwhile, Scholastic Achievement Test (SAT) scores, National Assessment of Educational Progress (NAEP) scores, and state test scores were on the rise—not falling—from the mid-1970s until the early 1990s when they leveled off. Test scores for 2003 appear to be rising again.

WHAT IS BEING SAID

When we look at what we spend and what we produce, we learn that our "output"—international achievement test scores—is low compared with that of other industrialized nations. Even worse, Japan pays less per student than the United States but has the highest math and science achievement test scores in international comparisons whereas we have the lowest.

Public education critics quote William Bennett's 1993 study relating spending and achievement on the SATs.[25] Bennett noted that some states have low per pupil spending and high SAT scores, and other states have high per pupil spending and low SAT scores. Therefore, Bennett argues, more money spent on education does not necessarily lead to higher student achievement. This deduction fits well with Eric Hanushek's earlier research in which he reviewed almost 200 studies examining school expenditures and student achievement and concluded that there was "no strong or systematic relationship between money spent and achievement."[26] Similarly, George Will noted in the *Washington Post* on August 23, 1993,

---

[25]W. Bennett, *Report Card on American Education* (Washington, DC: American Legislative Exchange Council, 1993).

[26]E. Hanushek, "The Impact of Differential School Expenditures on School Performance," *Educational Researcher* 18 (4), May 1989: 45–51, at 47.

that the five states with the highest SAT scores (Iowa, North Dakota, South Dakota, Utah, and Minnesota) were all relatively low education spenders. Conversely, he also observed that New Jersey spent most on education yet finished 39th in the SAT rankings.

Politicians, businesspeople, and the general public make similar negative comments about school spending and student achievement. Because influential people comment publicly on television, radio, and in newspapers, the community at large understandably questions education expenditures. The public is receptive to the viewpoint that spending does not equate to increased achievement. Since the now-discredited 1960s Coleman Report—which asserted that students' family backgrounds play a greater role than do schools in raising achievement—has become a solid part of popular culture, the "person-in-the-street" comfortably accepts new "proof" of the ineffectiveness of public schools. This misconception is held especially true when states and localities ask citizens to pay higher taxes to support public education.

WHAT SHOULD BE SAID

Education Costs Are Up Because Enrollments Are Up!

As seen in Figure 1.4, U.S. education costs in real and constant dollars have increased, but so have enrollments. We have also decreased class size, resulting in an increase in teachers and, subsequently, costs. When one of the authors began teaching in an affluent school division in the early 1970s, he had five eighth grade English classes with no fewer than 40 students in each section. Today many states would outlaw these numbers.

Examining school enrollment, teachers, and expenditures in billions of dollars along the vertical axis and expenses by year along the horizontal axis in Figure 1.4, you can see that the slope of each chart's lines match. In other words, the student enrollment increases match teacher increases. Likewise, these slopes match cost increases.

Teachers' salaries are often given as a significant reason for increased education expenses. Figure 1.5 refutes this allegation. It shows teacher salaries—in constant and current dollars—along the vertical axis and the school year along the horizontal axis. It is obvious that teacher salaries in real dollars have increased over the years. Paycheck numbers are higher. Salary scales pay teachers for years of service and for earning advanced degrees; many teachers today have both maturity and more academic credentials. In constant dollars, however, their purchasing power is almost flat.

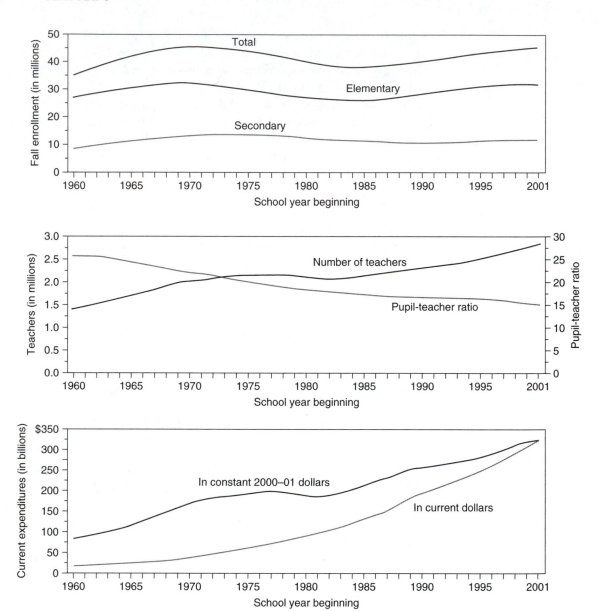

FIGURE **1.4**

Enrollment, Number of Teachers, Pupil-Teacher Ratios, and Expenditures in Public Schools, 1960–61 to 2000–01

Source: U.S. Department of Education, National Center for Education Statistics, *Statistics of State School Systems; Statistics of Public Elementary and Secondary School Systems; Revenues and Expenditures for Public Elementary and Secondary Education;* and Common Core of Data surveys.

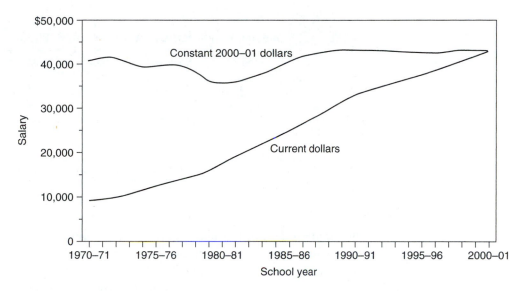

FIGURE **1.5**

Average Annual Salary for Public Elementary and Secondary School Teachers, 1970–71 to 2000–01

Source: National Education Association, *Rankings & Estimates: Rankings of the States 2003 and Estimates of School Statistics 2004,* Fig. 3.1. Copyright © 2004 by the National Education Association. Used by permission.

In other words, today's teachers may have larger numbers on their paycheck, but they can buy no more with it today than they did 30 years ago.

Because the number of teachers (and their salaries) has increased to meet class size reductions and increased enrollments, total expenditures must increase. This does not explain the whole picture, however. Changing student demographics, especially in special education, affects the larger context for increased educational expenses.

Education Costs Are Up Due to Greater Variance in Students' Needs!

We pay more money for teachers' salaries because we have more students and, subsequently, more teachers. But we also have a greater variance in the population we serve as more students with special needs enter public school classrooms.

In 1975 Congress enacted Public Law 94-142, the Education for All Handicapped Children Act, to ensure that all children with disabilities had

TABLE 1.1	SPECIAL EDUCATION ENROLLMENTS 1976–2000				
	1976–77	**1980–81**	**1989–90**	**1994–95**	**1999–2000**
Numbers served	3,694,000	4,144,000	4,631,000	5,378,000	6,195,000
Percent of total enrollment	8.32%	10.14%	11.32%	12.19%	13.22%

Source: U.S. Department of Education, Office of Special Education and Rehabilitative Services, *Annual Report to Congress on the Implementation of The Individuals with Disabilities Education Act,* various years, and unpublished tabulations, http://nces.ed.gov/pubs2002/digest2001/tables/dt052.asp; and National Center for Education Statistics, *Common Core Data Survey* (April 2001).

the right to a free and appropriate public school education. To be sure, court cases at the state and federal levels advanced the educational interests of students with disabilities before this—most notably the *Mills* decision.[27] No one would argue against children with disabilities receiving a good public education, but until 1975 public schools did not serve much of this student population and, therefore, per pupil school expenditures were lower.

From the 1976–77 school year until the 1999–2000 school year, public schools served an additional 2.5 million students with special needs (see Table 1.1). The lower student-teacher ratio and additional resources required to appropriately educate these exceptional students necessarily requires larger expenditures. Bracey[28] observed that in 1988 it cost $2,500 to educate each general education pupil and $17,600 to educate each exceptional education pupil. With 13% (and rising) of all U.S. students enrolled in special education programs, the reasons huge sums have been spent in this arena since 1975 are clear.

Test Scores Are Not Declining!

The most frequently cited misconception is that costs are increasing while test scores are falling.[29] Education's goal is to promote student achievement, and the school finance candidate's first concern should be how schools can maximize learning with the resources available. First, consider the

---

[27]*Mills v. Board of Education of District of Columbia,* 348 F.Supp. 866 (D.D.C.1972).

[28]G. W. Bracey, "Why Can't They Be Like We Were?" *Phi Delta Kappan* 73 (2), October 1991: 104–117, at 112.

[29]It is also probably the most deviously stated and, bluntly, the most stupid of the arguments. It assumes that the public will not think through these issues and understand the larger context.

argument that SAT scores have declined during a period of increased expenditures.

As noted earlier, education critics complain that we spend too much money to have declining SAT scores. Considering the idea that the states spending the least on education have the highest SAT scores and vice versa, Gerald Bracey sums up this situation best when he says,

> What neither Will nor Bennett bothered to observe, of course, was that in those high-scoring states, virtually no one takes the SAT. In the year of the study, the percentage of high school seniors taking the SAT was 5 percent in Iowa, 6 percent in North Dakota, 5 percent in South Dakota, 4 percent in Utah, and 10 percent in Minnesota. The rest of the college-bound seniors in these states are not dumb. They take the other college entrance examination battery, the ACT. Those taking the SAT are those interested in attending such institutions as Stanford and the Ivy League and Seven Sisters colleges, which require the SAT.
>
> In New Jersey, on the other hand, fully 76 percent of the senior class huddled in angst on Saturday mornings to bubble in answer sheets on the SAT. We could applaud New Jersey for encouraging three-quarters of its senior class to apply to schools that require the SAT. But, of course, when a team composed of 75 percent of the class goes up against a team made up of a 5 percent elite, the elite will always win the day.[30]

In short, looking at educational expenditures based on SAT scores in these states and making judgments about the inverse relationship between money input and student achievement output is simply invalid. We do not have a level playing field because of the vastly different student populations taking (or not taking) this particular college admissions test. To draw conclusions from these data as some critics have done is misleading at best.

Moreover, we need to examine the premise that SAT scores are decreasing. The Educational Testing Service (ETS) keeps statistics on average SAT scores by racial/ethnic groups. As shown in Table 1.2, only one of eight sub-categories decreased between 1991 and 2001. Only Mexican Americans, the fastest growing minority group in the United States, showed an SAT score decrease from 1991 to 2001: a 1 point drop in Math, and a 3 point drop in Verbal. All other groups showed an increase from 3 to 20 points in Math and a 2 to 21 point increase in Verbal. The average increase for all college-bound seniors was a 14 point increase in Math and a 7 point increase in Verbal. Clearly, SAT scores are not declining; they are rising.

---

[30]Bracey, *Setting the Record Straight*, 21–22.

TABLE 1.2   **SAT AVERAGES FOR RACIAL/ETHNIC GROUPS, 1991 AND 2001**

	Verbal			Math		
	1991	2001	Difference	1991	2001	Difference
American Indian, Alaskan Native	470	481	11	468	479	11
Asian, Asian American, Pacific Islander	485	501	16	548	566	18
African American/ Black	427	433	6	419	426	7
Mexican American	454	451	(3)	459	458	(1)
Puerto Rican	436	457	21	439	451	12
Hispanic/Latino	458	460	2	462	465	3
White	518	529	11	513	531	18
Other	486	503	17	492	512	20
All College-Bound Seniors	**499**	**506**	**7**	**500**	**514**	**14**

Source: www.collegeboard.com/press/senior01/html/pdf/table9.pdf

In addition, the SAT's history helps explain the change in scores over time. This test first appeared in 1926 as a way to distinguish among applicants for selective colleges. Test makers established norms on 8,040 students entering private colleges, mostly in the Northeast; students were 98% white, 60% male, and 40% attended private high schools.[31] This original student norming group is somewhat different from today's student demographic distribution.

Furthermore, the SAT has 138 test items: 78 Verbal and 60 Math. The scores are converted to scaled scores with a range of 200 to 800 for Math and for Verbal, making the combined range from 400 to 1,600. Converting to scaled scores can confuse the general public. For example, one incorrect answer can account for about 10 points on the test. Berliner and Biddle point out an even more significant oddity. They state that the relation of correct to incorrect answers impacts the scaled score so that "the very talented student who correctly answers all but one of the questions on the verbal part of the SAT loses fifty scale points for that one error, earning a score of 750 rather than 800."[32]

---

[31]http://www.collegeboard.com/about/newsat/history.html.

[32]Berliner and Biddle, *The Manufactured Crisis*, 16.

As a benchmark of student achievement, SAT math scores rose 14 points between 1991 and 2001.[33] This increase appears in spite of the fact that minorities, who traditionally score lower than white students, made up more than one-third of all SAT takers in the class of 2001.[34]

To complain about the SAT decline in scale score points on 138 items when gauging the value of 12 years of schooling, and when one wrong answer can account for a 10 to 50 point difference, seems a bit ridiculous—especially when a larger and more diverse group of students is taking the test! Given these data, it is unreasonable to believe scores are decreasing or that schools all over the country are doing a poor job meeting students' academic needs.

Can we determine whether achievement scores are really going down? Each state is developing its own testing program required for No Child Left Behind funding. Some of these state tests closely correlate with national tests, and others do not. In states that have implemented high-stakes testing programs, test scores have risen, especially for disadvantaged and minority students. To an extent, test scores have increased because school districts and classroom teachers have consciously aligned their curricula and instruction with the test content.

In addition, teachers must assure that *each* child passes these external assessments for students to receive diplomas and for schools to earn accreditation and meet adequate yearly progress (AYP) guidelines. The greater the opportunity students have to learn assessed content, the better they will perform on tests measuring knowledge of that content. Minority test scores are increasing as seen in the reduction of the achievement gap noted by Kati Haycock.[35] Figure 1.6 shows what a dramatic difference effective teaching can make in reducing the achievement gap.

Likewise, the National Assessment of Educational Progress (NAEP, "The Nation's Report Card") scores from 1971 to 1999 show that student scores have not fallen. They are rising (see Table 1.3). Keep in mind that these are scaled scores and that the trend is an upward one—it is not declining.

---

[33]www.cp;;egebpard.com/press/senior01/html/pdf/table9.pdf. Only the Mexican American group showed a decrease in math SAT scores over the 10-year period. The range of increases was from 3 points for Hispanic/Latinos to 20 points for those designated "Other." The next largest increase was shared between White and Asian, Asian American, and Pacific Islanders.

[34]www.collegeboard.com.press/senior01/html/pdf/graph8.pdf. Whites comprised 66% of those tested; African Americans, 11%; Asian Americans, 10%; Mexican Americans, 4%; Other, 4%; Other Hispanic, 4%; and all other categories each at 1%.

[35]See K. Haycock, C. Jerald, and S. Huang, "Closing the Gap: Done in a Decade," *Thinking K-16*, Vol. 5 (Washington, DC: Education Trust, 2001), 2. Kati Haycock is the Director of the Education Trust, Inc. in Washington, D.C.

Data: NAEP 1998
Effective Teaching & Minority Achievement

• Grade 8 Writing:	• Grade 8 Writing:
– African American students:	– Latino students:
– 146 points – Texas	– 146 points – Virginia
– 121 points – Arkansas	– 106 points – Mississippi
**A 25-point difference worth 2½ years of learning	**A 40 point difference worth 3–4 years of learning.

FIGURE **1.6**

Effective Teaching and Minority Achievement Using 1998 NAEP Data

Source: K. Haycock, C. Jerald, and S. Huang, "Closing the Gap: Done in a Decade."
Thinking K–16 5(2). (Washington, DC: Education Trust, Spring 2001), 3–22.

TABLE **1.3**   **NAEP AVERAGE STUDENT PROFICIENCY IN READING BY AGE, 1971–1999**

	1971	1980	1990	1999	Change
9-year-olds	207.6	215.0	209.2	211.7	4.1
13-year-olds	255.2	258.5	256.8	259.4	4.2
17-year-olds	285.2	285.2	290.2	287.8	2.6

Source: http://nces.ed.gov/pubs2002/digest2001/tables/pdf/table112.pdf.

Other critics point to the Third International Math and Science Study (now known as the Trends in International Mathematics and Science Study), which also ranks U.S. students as low achieving. TIMSS assesses the math and science proficiency of U.S. students in comparison with their international peers at the 4th, 8th, and 12th grades. In 1995 (the latest analysis to date), U.S. 4th graders performed well in the math and science assessments compared to other nations.[36] Unfortunately, U.S. 12th graders scored below the international average on these tests and rather low in other areas.

Figure 1.7 illustrates the international comparisons by relating countries scoring significantly higher, not significantly different, and significantly

---

[36]For a detailed chart, see http://nces.ed.gov//pubs2002/digest2001/ch6.asp and click on tables 405, 406, 407, and 408.

Fourth grade (in most nations)	End of secondary education
Average scores significantly higher than the United States	Average scores significantly higher than the United States
Singapore Korea Japan Hong Kong (Netherlands) Czech Republic (Austria)	(Netherlands) (Norway) (Austria) Sweden (France) (Slovenia) (Denmark) New Zealand (Germany) Switzerland (Australia) Hungary (Iceland) (Canada)
Average scores not significantly different from the United States	Average scores not significantly different from the United States
(Slovenia) Canada Ireland (Israel) (Hungary) (Australia)	(Italy) (Russian Federation) (Lithuania) Czech Republic
Average scores significantly lower than the United States	Average scores significantly lower than the United States
(Latvia) Norway Portugal Scotland New Zealand Iceland England Greece Iran, Islamic Republic Cyprus (Thailand) (Kuwait)	(Cyprus) (South Africa)

FIGURE **1.7**

Average Mathematics Performance of Other Countries Compared with the United States, 1995

Note: Nations not meeting international guidelines are shown in parentheses.

Source: U.S. Department of Education, National Center for Education Statistics, *Pursuing Excellence: A Study of U.S. Fourth-Grade Mathematics and Science Achievement in International Context,* 1997, and *Pursuing Excellence: A Study of U.S. Twelfth-Grade Mathematics and Science Achievement in International Context,* 1998.

lower than the United States in mathematics. As you can see, U.S. fourth grade students did much better than students at the end of the secondary level in math when compared to students in other countries.

Figure 1.8 details the average science achievement on the TIMSS. Here the United States scores rather well at the fourth grade level but less well at the end of the secondary level.

In the 1999 TIMSS assessment, U.S. eighth graders scored well, exceeding 38 other nations in math and in science. In math, eighth grade students in the United States outscored peers in 17 nations, scored below peers in 14 nations, and scored about even with 6 nations.[37] In science, our eighth

---

[37]For a detailed chart, see http://nces.ed.gov//pubs2002/digest2001/ch6.asp and then click on table 399.

Fourth grade (in most nations)	End of secondary education

Average scores significantly higher than the United States
  Korea
	Average scores significantly higher than the United States
	  Sweden (Canada) (Austria)
	  (Netherlands) New Zealand (Slovenia)
	  (Iceland) (Australia) (Denmark)
	  (Norway) Switzerland

Average scores not significantly different from the United States
  Japan
  (Austria)
  (Australia)
  (Netherlands)
  Czech Republic
	Average scores not significantly different from the United States
	  (Germany) (Italy)
	  (France) Hungary
	  Czech Republic (Lithuania)
	  (Russian Federation)

Average scores significantly lower than the United States
  England   Hong Kong   Iceland
  Canada   (Hungary)   Greece
  Singapore   New Zealand   Portugal
  (Slovenia)   Norway   Cyprus
  Ireland   (Latvia)   (Thailand)
  Scotland   (Israel)   Iran, Islamic
                      Republic (Kuwait)
	Average scores significantly lower than the United States
	  (Cyprus)
	  (South Africa)

FIGURE **1.8**

Average Science Performance of Other Countries Compared with the United States, 1995

Note: Nations not meeting international guidelines are shown in parentheses.

Source: U.S. Department of Education, National Center for Education Statistics, *Pursuing Excellence: A Study of U.S. Fourth-Grade Mathematics and Science Achievement in International Context*, 1997 and *Pursuing Excellence: A Study of U.S. Twelfth-Grade Mathematics and Science Achievement in International Context*, 1998.

graders scored better than 18, lower than 14, and even with 5 nations.[38] It appears that U.S. students have been improving in international comparisons since the rankings' inception. The general public hears and believes otherwise.

It is important to remember that many of the countries with higher scores do not open public education to all students—including students with special needs—as the United States does. Furthermore, most Western European countries track students into early career decisions and apprenticeships and out of college preparatory education; many of these less

---

[38]For a detailed chart, see http://nces.ed.gov//pubs2002/digest2001/ch6.asp and then click on table 401.

academically able students are not tested for these international comparisons. In comprehensive U.S. schools, on the other hand, all students can be tested. Results, therefore, do not compare apples with apples.

In addition, the content of these international tests do not closely match what most students learn in U.S. classrooms. Not all students in this country are top-flight and university bound as are most international high school students. Our teachers, therefore, are less likely to teach the content and skills that these instruments assess. Without the opportunity to learn, the mismatch between student knowledge and test content becomes greater and the test scores lower. These realities plus the greater variance in the pool of U.S. high school students taking the tests contribute to our disappointing final scores in international comparisons. This perspective does not excuse U.S. students' poorer performance in international comparisons, but it does place these results in a more accurate context.

One could correctly infer that school expenditures do not correlate directly with academic output; other variables are more important. Reasons for the relatively poor U.S. academic results on international achievement tests might also include the following cultural differences:

1. European and Asian students have a longer school day (average 6 hours to our 5.2 hours) and school year (200 to 225 days compared to our 180 days).
2. A growing underclass and at-risk population is present in U.S. public schools (about 40% of students qualify for free or reduced price lunch; student drug addiction, student violence, gang activity, and teenage pregnancy are higher in the United States than in all other industrialized nations).
3. The breakdown of the American family (more than 50% of U.S. students live with a single head of household).
4. Television's influence (U.S. students average 3.5 hours of daily TV viewing).
5. The U.S. teaching force for the neediest students is less stable and experienced than for the least needy students. A large proportion of U.S. teachers quit the profession, especially in the first 5 years (about 50%, most frequently in urban school districts), so teachers in other industrialized nations have, on average, considerably more experience and more effectiveness producing student learning gains than less experienced U.S. teachers.
6. Many European nations have a national education system (and a consistent school finance structure). A national education system attempts to spend the same amount per child. When Norway, for

example, spends the equivalent of $5,000 per child, this reflects the true spending per child—not an average of spending within the nation. In the United States, however, we have a wide variance in school spending within and among states, with the neediest students often receiving the fewest resources essential to learn and score well.

Differences in National Education Spending Portray Misleading Sums!

Education costs in the United States may be so variable as to insufficiently support many of the neediest students, leaving them less prepared to perform well on rigorous tests. Figure 1.9 indicates state average per pupil education expenditures along the vertical axis. The variance ranges from a high of more than $9,500 per pupil in the four highest spending states to a low of $4,001 to $4,500 per pupil in Utah. Comparisons within states frequently show even greater variance than state comparisons. All states attempt to compensate for the impact of local wealth and education spending (much more will be explained later in the book), but wealthier school districts usually outspend poorer school districts by a wide margin. The poorer school districts tend to be urban poor and isolated rural districts, which have great demands and few available resources. These inequalities tend to have a "savage" impact on the neediest students.[39]

State education websites usually list expenditures per locality. Obtain the figures for your state and discuss ideas such as local wealth and average per pupil expenditure. Which localities spend the most per child? Which school districts have the greatest need? Do the neediest school districts have the greatest funding on a per pupil basis? Should they? A range of local per pupil spending within many states reflects at least a factor of 4 (lowest to highest spending local education agencies).

Education costs in real dollars have increased over the past several decades, but contrary to popular argument, test scores have not uniformly declined. Many state and national test scores have risen. These increased costs, however, are associated with increased enrollments, lowered student-teacher ratios, higher teacher salaries, a greater variance in the public served, and the extra learning needs that students bring to school. The public schools are currently serving 2.5 million more students with disabilities than they did

---

[39]With all due apologies for the pun to Jonathan Kozol. For an excellent read detailing these impacts, see his book, *Savage Inequalities: Children in America's Schools* (New York: Crown, 1991).

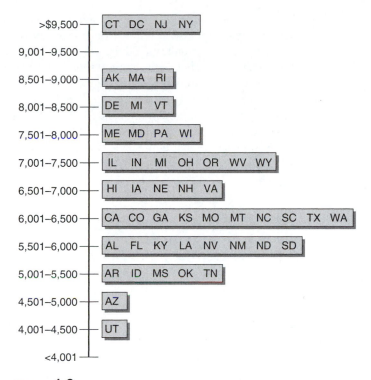

FIGURE **1.9**

Per Pupil Expenditures for Elementary and Secondary Schools, 1999–2000

Note: Current expenditures include salaries, employee benefits, purchased services, and supplies, but exclude capital outlay, debt service, facilities acquisition and construction, and equipment. Dollar amounts for states and the District of Columbia are grouped in $500 ranges (e.g., $8,501–$9,000).

Source: U.S. Department of Education, National Center for Education Statistics, Common Core Data, "National Public Education Financial Survey" School Year 1999–2000.

---

in 1976. This has all been accomplished with teacher salaries remaining relatively flat—a testimony to U.S. educators' commitment and effectiveness.

Misconception 3   Spending More Money on Education Does Not Mean Better Achievement Results

In a Nutshell: Money matters! More money usually means decreasing class size, improving facilities, hiring quality teachers with adequate resources and support services, and providing up-to-date equipment. Spent correctly, money makes a big difference in student achievement.

Of course, not all public school funds are spent correctly. In the vast majority of school districts, however, public funds are used efficiently.[40] An Alabama Department of Education study, for example, showed a positive relationship between money spent and student achievement.[41] Moreover, a Harvard study showed money spent to reduce class size and to hire experienced teachers resulted in higher student test scores.[42] Critics argue that money is not related to achievement. A closer analysis of Hanushek's research, which was critical of the money–achievement connection, shows that money does matter to student achievement.[43] We will spend some time on this misconception as it is at the heart of financing schools.

WHAT IS BEING SAID

Admittedly, fewer federal officials today are saying that we should spend less on education—that money does not mean better results. In fact, Congress and the national education bureaucracy are calling for increased education spending for the No Child Left Behind legislation. Conservative think tanks, such as the Hoover Institution at Stanford University, claim that spending will not necessarily increase student achievement.[44] Likewise, critics assert that most state funds are not used appropriately. Therefore, spending more money will only be throwing good money after bad, continuing the established but wasteful trend.

At the state and local levels, however, many politicians and activists have not gotten on the federal bandwagon. Many state and local politicians are still quoting Bill Bennett's comments (Misconception 1) as reasons to cut local and state budget requests. If we follow his argument to its logical conclusion, however, eliminating all education expenditures would result in the highest possible student achievement scores.

---

[40]Teachers buy many classroom supplies each year out of their own pockets. Although admirable, when this is not accounted for in school budgets, an inaccurate picture of the real cost of education results.

[41]R. Lockwood and J. McLean, "Educational Funding and Student Achievement." Paper presented at the Mid-South Educational Research Association, New Orleans, November 10–12, 1993.

[42]R. Ferguson, "Paying for Public Education: New Evidence on How and Why Money Matters," *Harvard Journal on Legislation* 28 (2), 1991: 465–498.

[43]K. Baker, "Yes, Throw Money at the Schools," *Phi Delta Kappan* 72 (8), April 1991: 628–630.

[44]See http://www-hoover.stanford.edu/publications/digest/024/skandera.html.

What Should Be Said

Those who say that increasing educational spending will not increase student achievement are wrong. Increasing educational spending positively impacts student achievement. The mistaken notion that schools do not make a meaningful difference in student achievement is part of our recent history. In 1966 the federal government released the Coleman Report.[45] The report said, "Schools bring little influence to bear on a child's achievement that is independent of his [sic] background and general social context."[46] In this view schools had little impact on student learning, and much depended on the child's family background. The rich would get smarter, and the poor would learn but never as much as their more affluent classmates. This naïve belief—seeming logical at the time and well before 1990s research data on teaching effectiveness appeared—greatly influenced the public culture about the effectiveness of schools.

Given this perspective and political posturing for tax cuts, the public has come to believe that increased funding will not increase achievement in public schools. School success or failure, they believe, results from students' family background and not the schools' interventions. As Berliner and Biddle stated, academic success was best predicted by "the choice (students) made of their parents at birth."[47] For many, this was a rationalization not to spend more for schools in lower socioeconomic areas because it would simply do no good.

Misconception 2 references Hanushek's study, which notes that there "was no strong or systematic relationship between school expenditures and student performance."[48] Larry Hedges and others reexamined Hanushek's data and found, instead, overwhelming evidence that school funding had a "positive" impact on student achievement.[49] Moreover, Hedges stated that if a school district spent $500 more per pupil wisely, students would gain an average of 25 percentile points on achievement tests.[50]

---

[45]J. S. Coleman, E. Q. Campbell, C. J. Hobson, J. McPartland, A. M. Mood, F. D. Weinfeld, and R. L. York, *Equality of Educational Opportunity* (Washington, DC: U.S. Government Printing Office, 1996).

[46]Ibid., 325.

[47]Berliner and Biddle, *The Manufactured Crisis*, 71.

[48]Hanushek, "The Impact of Differential School Expenditures on School Performance," 47.

[49]L. Hedges, R. Laine, and M. McLoughlin, "Does Money Matter? A Meta-Analysis of Studies of the Effects of Differential School Inputs on Student Outcomes," *Educational Researcher* 23 (3), 1994: 5–14.

[50]Ibid.

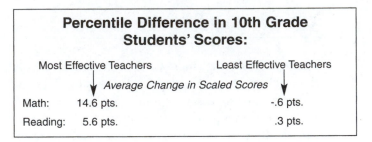

FIGURE **1.10**

Student Math Achievement and Effective Teachers

Source: K. Haycock and S. Huang, "Are Today's High School Graduates Ready?" *Thinking K–16,* 5 (1) (Washington, DC: The Education Trust, 2001), 14.

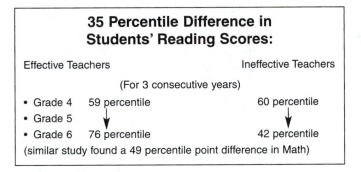

FIGURE **1.11**

Student Reading Achievement and Effective Teachers

Source: J. Archer, "Students' Fortune Rests with Assigned Teacher." *Education Week* (February 18, 1998), cited in K. Haycock, "Good Teaching Matters. How Well Qualified Teachers Can Close the Gap," *Thinking K–16,* 3 (2) (Washington, DC: The Education Trust, Summer 1998), 1–14. Available at: http://www.edtrust.org.

To know if schools are spending money wisely, we need to collect evidence that such expenditures increase student achievement. Teacher quality is a key predictor of student success.[51] Many research studies now show the measured impact of effective teaching practices on student learning. One study (see Figure 1.10) found that after one year 10th grade students with the most effective teachers showed an increase in achievement test scaled scores of 14.6 points in math and 5.6 points in reading as compared to a less than

---

[51]For a more detailed discussion of teacher quality, see L. Kaplan and W. Owings, *Teacher Quality, Teaching Quality, and School Improvement* (Bloomington, IN: Phi Delta Kappa, 2003).

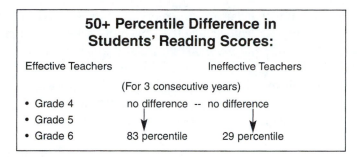

FIGURE **1.12**

Student Math Achievement and Effective Teaching

Source: W. Sanders and J. Rivers, *Cumulative and Residual Effects of Teachers on Future Student Academic Achievement* (Knoxville: University of Tennessee, Tennessee Value Added Assessment System, TVAAS, November 1966).

1 point decrease in math and in reading for students with the least effective teachers.

Similarly, a Texas study (see Figure 1.11) found an estimated 35 percentile point difference in reading achievement scores for students after three consecutive years with an effective versus an ineffective teacher. These students started out at approximately the same achievement level. The impressive resulting achievement difference came from students working three consecutive years with a "quality" teacher.

Likewise, a Tennessee study (see Figure 1.12), using a format similar to the Texas study, found more than a 50 percentile point estimated difference in math scores for students after three consecutive years with an effective teacher versus an ineffective one. Both of these studies followed students identical in achievement at the end of third grade through fourth, fifth, and sixth grade.

It is fair, therefore, to conclude that investing monies in quality teachers with instructional expertise has a measurable benefit for student achievement.[52] A study of more than 1,000 school districts concluded that every

---

[52]A question remains about how to attract quality teacher candidates into the profession in the first place. One common misconception is that students majoring in education tend to have lower SAT scores than those entering other fields of study, such as business. Those who actually do enter the field, as measured by those who pass the Praxis II exam, have scores comparable to or slightly higher than the overall population taking the SAT. Furthermore, teachers score one standard deviation higher on the National Adult Literacy Survey than does the general population. Additionally, teachers were more likely to score at the highest levels on the literacy scales. Only 3% of the population scored at the highest level (5) for literacy, but 10% of teachers scored at this level. Approximately half of U.S. teachers scored at levels 4 and 5 of the literacy scale while only a fifth of the total population scored at those levels. Apparently the teacher crop entering the harvest of work is as good as what is coming from the other fields.

additional dollar spent on more qualified teachers nets greater improvements in student achievement than any other school resource.[53] "Wealthier districts tend to spend more on education, and when all else is held constant, districts with lower spending have lower test scores."[54] Obviously, there is a point at which spending must be tightened when accounting for public monies; however, spending to improve the instructional quality is positively related to student achievement. Money does appear to matter.

Quality teachers are essential to quality learning. The quality of learning rarely exceeds the quality of teaching, and quality costs money. At the state level, full certification and a major in the field of teaching is the most significant predictor of student achievement, whereas the lack of certified teachers is the best predictor of a lack of student achievement.[55] In a 50 state study, Linda Darling-Hammond points out that teacher preparation accounts for 40% to 60% of the variance in student achievement after accounting for student demographics.[56] In spite of what we know about the links between teacher preparation, teaching quality, and student achievement, in times of teacher shortages politicians in many states now call for alternative, shorter, and less rigorous licensure routes instead of increased salaries to attract the ablest candidates to the profession.

SUMMING UP SCHOOL FINANCE MISCONCEPTION 3

First, decreased class size has increased school expenses. Reducing class size was necessary (see Figure 1.4). No teacher could effectively teach the 40 students in each class, considering both the diverse range of students' abilities and learning needs in each classroom today linked with the higher accountability levels of state standards and the No Child Left Behind legislation. The diverse learner needs in today's classrooms do not allow for the pupil-teacher ratios of 30 years ago.

Second, the critics who say that increased teacher salaries are one source of increasing education costs are partially correct. Average salaries

---

[53]R. F. Ferguson, "Paying for Public Education: New Evidence on How and Why Money Matters," *Harvard Journal on Legislation* 28 (2), Summer 1991: 465–498.

[54]"Quality Counts," *Education Week* 16, January 22, 1997: 54. Available at: http://www.edweek.org/sreports/qu97/indicators/res-n2.htm.

[55]L. Darling-Hammond, "Teacher Quality and Student Achievement: A Review of State Policy Evidence," *Educational Policy Analysis Archives* 8 (1), January 2000.

[56]Ibid.

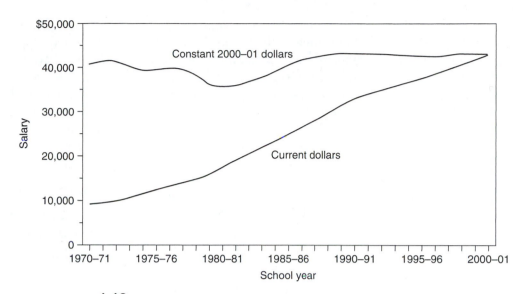

FIGURE **1.13**

Average Annual Salary for Public Elementary and Secondary School Teachers, 1970–71 to 2000–01

Source: National Education Association, *Rankings & Estimates: Rankings of the States 2003 and Estimates of School Statistics 2004,* Fig. 3.1. Copyright © 2004 by the National Education Association. Used by permission.

in current dollars have increased, but their purchasing power has remained relatively flat. Controlled for inflation, therefore, educators' salaries have not increased significantly in spite of the professional longevity and accumulated education degrees that boost paychecks over years of service. Given the cost of living changes, although teachers' salaries may be higher today, the dollars do not buy much more than they did 30 years ago.

Third, some have estimated that a significant increase in spending is due to an aging teaching population. This is true. We are reaching a point where more educators as a percentage of the population are retiring or are within a few years of retirement than we have ever seen. Most U.S. teacher salary scales are built around seniority and professional credentials held. Many teachers are at the top of their salary scales now. This means higher salaries. However, in constant dollars, the *average* wages remain relatively flat as seen in Figure 1.13 in spite of the educators' career maturity.

Fourth, critics say that decreased student enrollments during the 1970s through the 1990s coupled with decreased class size prove that money has been thrown at the schools with little or negative achievement results. This decrease in student enrollment (Figure 1.4) occurred during a time of rapid social and school change. Special education court rulings culminating with the 1975 Education for All Handicapped Children Act required reducing class size and increasing the number of teachers for children with special needs.[57] Not only did schools hire additional teachers for reduced class size, schools also needed more classrooms and different learning materials. In retrospect, it is obvious why costs increased while enrollments decreased. We began to educate a segment of society never adequately addressed before, and public education needed resources to accomplish this important task.

Misconception 4   Educator Salaries Are High in Comparison with Other Professions with Similar Qualifications

In a Nutshell: Educator salaries are not high in comparison with other professionals with the same level of training and responsibility.

WHAT IS BEING SAID

We have all heard it said before. Teachers only work 9 months a year, and then only from 9 to 3 o'clock. For that they earn a full-time salary that is higher than most other people make in our community.

WHAT SHOULD BE SAID

Let's address one issue at a time. First, teachers do not only work 9 months out of the year. For the most part, teachers in the United States work a 200-day contract—or 10 months. They work the same months—plus a week or so on each end—that students attend schools.

Second, teacher work hours include more than the time spent actually teaching in their classrooms. In reality, teacher work hours also include preparing lessons, setting up laboratory or other learning activities, grading students' papers, working after school tutoring students, and studying for their own professional development. A study by the University of Wisconsin–Milwaukee found that U.S. teachers work an average of 10.25 hours per day,[58] and Darling-Hammond asserts that teachers work

---

[57]Public Law 101-46, 104 Stat.1103 (1975).

[58]As reported in http://weac.org/News/1998-99/mar99/workday/htm.

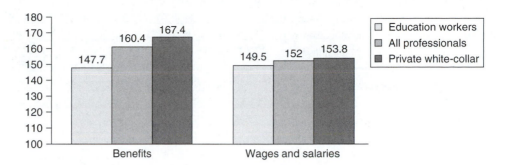

FIGURE **1.14**

Employment Cost Index in 2001 for Education Workers, White-Collar Workers, and Professional Workers

Source: American Federation of Teachers, *Survey & Analysis of Teacher Salary Trends 2001,* Fig. II-9, available at www.aft.org/research. Copyright © 2002 AFT. Reprinted by permission.

10 to 12 hours per day.[59] That is 2 1/4 hours longer than the average 8-hour workday. By itself, 2 hours and 15 minutes may not sound like much. However, if we add those extra hours to the 40-week contract, it becomes an extra 500 hours. That figure divided by 40 (a regular work week), is equal to 12.5 weeks of work. The 40-week contract plus the 12.5 weeks worth of "overtime" equals a work year of 52.5 weeks.

The Department of Labor reports that the average salary in manufacturing in 2000 (latest data available) was $44,778.[60] The average teacher salary for the same year was $42,929,[61] or $1,849 less than the average salary in manufacturing. Darling-Hammond believes teacher salaries are "twenty-five percent less than other professionals with similar levels of education."[62]

Moreover, cost indices for workers provide a different view of their earnings. A cost index shows the relative cost of all wages and benefits for various employee classifications. A lower number represents a lower cost of employing an individual. A higher number shows a higher cost. Figure 1.14 shows the relative cost index for education workers compared with private sector white-collar workers and all professional workers. It is obvious that salaries and benefits for education workers are lower than those for professional

---

[59]See http://www.pbs.org/onlyateacher/today2.html.

[60]K. Hovey, and H. Hovey, *CQ's State Fact Finder: 2000* (Washington, DC: CQ Press, 2002), 46.

[61]Ibid., 209.

[62]See http://www.pbs.org/onlyateacher/today2.html.

FIGURE 1.15

Entry Level Salary Comparisons in Education and Other Fields

Source: American Federation of Teachers, *Survey & Analysis of Teacher Salary Trends 2001,* Fig. III-5, available at www.aft.org/research. Copyright © 2002 AFT. Reprinted by permission.

workers in other categories. Individuals with the same education as teachers can enter careers that pay higher salaries initially and over their careers, offer periodic monetary bonuses, provide better financial and health benefits, and offer other "perks" teachers don't receive.

The cost index for education workers is lower than that of their counterparts. In addition, examining educators' starting salaries compared with those from other professions that require an entry-level bachelor's degree shows low teacher entry-level salaries compared with those of their former college classmates. Figure 1.15 illustrates this relative comparison.

It is not just entry-level salaries that put teachers financially behind their professional peers. Changes in salaries should also be compared when addressing the argument that teachers make too much money in comparison with other professions. Figure 1.16 shows the change in salaries from 1991 to 1996 and from 1996 to 2001 for various professions. In the past 10 years, teachers' starting salaries have increased by less than 20% whereas salaries for other liberal arts graduates increased by 25%, for engineers by 30%, for accountants by 38%, and for statisticians by 50%. Teachers' salaries start lower and increasingly fall behind those of other professionals over the years.

Between 1990 and 1996, the growth in beginning teacher salaries matched beginning salary growth in other fields. Since 1996, however, beginning teacher salaries increased just 20.8%, the slowest rate of any field. Salaries in all other fields grew approximately twice as fast (41.3%) as teaching. Over the entire decade, beginning teacher salaries lost ground to beginning salaries in every field except chemistry.

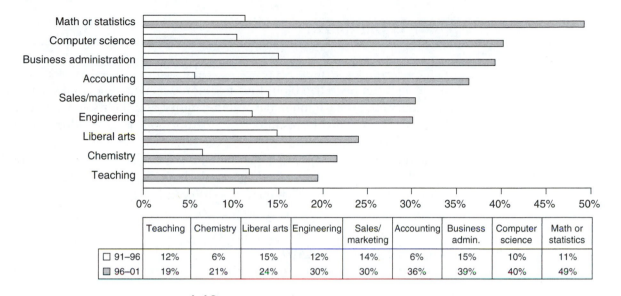

	Teaching	Chemistry	Liberal arts	Engineering	Sales/ marketing	Accounting	Business admin.	Computer science	Math or statistics
☐ 91–96	12%	6%	15%	12%	14%	6%	15%	10%	11%
▨ 96–01	19%	21%	24%	30%	30%	36%	39%	40%	49%

FIGURE **1.16**

Changes in New Teacher Salaries Compared to Salary Offers in Other Fields

Source: American Federation of Teachers, *Survey & Analysis of Teacher Salary Trends 2001,* Fig. III-4, available at www.aft.org/research. Copyright © 2002 AFT. Reprinted by permission.

Administrator salaries are another matter. Granted, educational administrators earn higher salaries than most teachers. Principals' salaries have been, on average at least 50% more than the average teacher salaries since the 1987–88 school year.[63] The variance in principals' salaries depends on the school's size and location (rural, suburban, or urban). Nevertheless, salaries for administrators, controlled for inflation, have increased only 6.8% in the 12 years between 1987–88 and 1999–2000.[64]

Misconception 5   There Are Too Many School Administrators Compared with 30 Years Ago

In a Nutshell: There are more administrators per student than existed 50 years ago. In comparison with other industries, however, education is a management-lean organization.

---

[63]S. Poppink and J. Shen, "Secondary Principals' Salaries: A National, Longitudinal Study," *NASSP Bulletin* 87 (634), March 2003: 67–82.

[64]Ibid., 69.

WHAT IS BEING SAID

William Bennett, former Secretary of Education, accused education of having an "administrative blob" that smothered its personnel ranks. Critics say public schools have too many administrators, and their salary and benefit costs drain valuable resources away from educating children. Some also say that administrators are "good ole boys" who know nothing about instruction and came up under the wing of one of the system's influential power brokers. To be fair, some "good ole boys" have come through the system undeservedly, and schools have suffered for it.[65]

WHAT SHOULD BE SAID

First, it is true that public schools employ more administrators today than they did 50 years ago, as can be seen by Table 1.4. Virtually all other industry sectors, however, can say the same thing.

Today's schools have more leadership and management responsibilities than ever before. For example, today's administrators oversee transportation and school safety with more frequency and more intensity than in the past. With public schools serving increasingly diverse student groups from a range of neighborhoods, administrators must now organize and monitor school buses delivering and returning students from their homes as well as to and from special pullout magnet or vocational programs. Likewise, principals spend more time assuring a safe and orderly learning environment in the building. They must deal with errant students and high-maintenance parents. Principals also observe and conference with teachers. In addition, principals continually meet with school and community leaders to review and use student achievement data in the school improvement planning process.

Moreover, the number of school management tasks has increased geometrically. Principals and assistant principals spend much time and expertise coordinating and addressing the special education referral, identification, annual and triennial review processes, writing individual education plans

---

[65]We hope the educational leadership program in which you find yourself will prepare you to work on improving instruction. Even though our subject is school finance, the end goal of school finance is to provide you with information to advocate for better funding to enhance the teaching and learning process for students.

TABLE 1.4   STAFF EMPLOYED BY FUNCTIONAL AREA, 1949–2000

School Year	District Office School District Administrators	Selected School Instructional Staff (Does not include all categories) Total	Principals & Assistant Principals	Teachers	Teachers' Aides	Guidance	Support Staff Total
Full-Time Equivalents							
1949–50	33,642	963,110	43,137	913,671	—	—	303,280
1959–60	42,423	1,457,329	63,554	1,353,372	—	14,643	589,531
1969–70	65,282	2,859,573	107,061	2,184,216	57,418	63,973	1,229,929
1979–80	78,784	2,859,573	107,061	2,184,216	325,755	63,973	1,229,929
1989–90*	75,868	3,051,404	127,417	2,398,169	395,959	79,970	1,366,804
1999–2000*	93,916	3,810,308	133,011	2,906,554	621,385	95,697	1,713,173
Percentage Distribution							
1949–50	2.6	74.1	3.3	70.3	—	—	23.3
1959–60	2.0	69.8	3.0	64.8	—	.8	28.2
1969–70	1.9	68.0	2.7	60.0	1.7	1.5	30.1
1979–80	1.9	68.6	2.6	52.4	7.8	1.2	29.5
1989–90*	1.7	67.9	2.8	53.4	8.8	1.1	30.4
1999–2000*	1.7	67.8	2.4	51.7	11.1	1.7	30.5
Pupils per Staff Member							
1949–50	746.4	26.1	582.1	27.5	—	—	82.8
1959–60	829.3	24.1	553.6	26.0	—	2,402.7	59.7
1969–70	697.7	19.9	502.8	22.6	793.3	934.1	45.1
1979–80	518.9	14.3	381.8	18.7	125.5	639.0	33.2
1989–90*	543.3	13.5	323.5	17.2	104.1	515.5	30.2
1999–2000*	498.9	12.3	352.3	16.1	75.4	489.6	27.4

Note: We have condensed this chart and omitted several categories. In addition, we have included only 10-year benchmark data, not yearly data. Due to variation in data collection instruments, some categories are only roughly comparable over time.

*Data not comparable with figures prior to 1985.

Source: http://nces.ed.gov/pubs2002/digest2001/tables/dt082.asp; adapted from U.S. Department of Education, National Center for Education Statistics, *Statistics of State School Systems,* Common Core of Data surveys, and unpublished estimates, February 2001.

(IEPs), and conducting manifestation determination hearings (to decide whether an identified student with special needs who broke school conduct rules did so knowingly or as a by-product of the handicapping condition)—all of which did not even exist in 1950. These events, alone, can take days out of every week for a principal or assistant principal.

Finally, coordinating the school's standardized testing function is also a major management task today. In the past, schools administered one or perhaps two tests a year to students in select grade levels. Today, with No Child Left Behind and state high-stakes testing programs, it is not unusual for most students to be tested several times each year. In short, schools employ more administrators today because schools have many more administrative tasks to accomplish to meet the community's accountability and achievement demands.

Table 1.4 highlights three distinct areas: full-time equivalents, percentage distribution, and pupils per staff member. The number of principals and assistant principals increased from 43,137 in the school year 1949–50 to 133,011 in the 1999–2000 school year. The percentage distribution, however, dropped from 3.3 percent of employees to 2.4 percent. The number of principals or assistant principals per student also dropped from 582.1 to 352.3. The number of principals and assistant principals has increased, but so have the number of teachers and students. As a result, the number of principals as a percentage of all employees has decreased.

The column marked School District Administrators includes superintendents, school board staff, and instruction coordinators. Likewise, their numbers have increased while their percentage of total employees and per pupil numbers have decreased.

Following the same trend is the category of Teachers. The total number of teachers has increased from 913,671 in the 1949–50 school year to 2,906,554 in 1999–2000. The percentage of teachers as total members of the education workforce decreased from 70.3 percent to 51.7 percent in the same time frame. In terms of teachers on a per pupil basis, the numbers dropped from 27.5 to 16.1 in the identical time frame.

The number of instructional aides (teachers' aides) has increased in numbers, percent of the population, and on a per pupil basis. School counselors have increased in numbers and as a percentage of the education workforce. They have decreased, however, on a per pupil basis.

Jerry Bracey puts the "administrative blob" issue into perspective: Central office personnel account for only 1.6 percent of all staff in school districts. If they were all fired, the resulting savings would allow teachers a 5% salary increase and a class size reduction of 1 student.[66]

Finally, we can compare the number of school administrators in relation to the number of people employed per executive, administrator, or manager in other industries. Robinson and Brandon report that elementary and

---

[66]Bracey, *Setting the Record Straight*, 171.

secondary schools have approximately 14 persons employed for each "manager" compared to 9 in transportation, 8 in food products, 7 in manufacturing, 6 in utilities and construction, 5 in printing/publishing and mining, 4 in communications, and 3 in public administration.[67] In other words, building level school administrators supervise more than twice the number of personnel as do the typical managers in manufacturing and almost four times the number in public administration.

Where is this administrative blob? The research indicates that it does not exist. Moreover, as we deal with school administrators, the comment is made all too often that workload and responsibility are increasing much too rapidly.

Summary

School finance misconceptions are part of the popular culture. In fact, education finance is both the context and the driver for many contemporary cultural issues. Knowledgeable school leadership candidates can critically challenge these myths and enlist greater community support for public schools and for their appropriate funding.

Data reveal that U.S. schools have been asked to do more with fewer resources under a higher level of public scrutiny—and with higher expectations for all students' achievement—than at any other time in our history. The facts do not support the five mistaken ideas most often cited about education finance.

First, the United States does not spend more on education than any other country unless one includes costs for kindergarten through all higher education. Virtually no other country provides a free and appropriate education to *all* of its children from kindergarten through grade 12 and from ages 2 to 22 for students with special needs. In addition, comparing total dollars spent on education without equalizing dollars for cost of living is not comparing "apples to apples."

Second, recent education costs have not skyrocketed while achievement has declined. Costs have increased in constant dollars, but teachers' salaries have remained almost flat. Increased student enrollments, special education expenses, increased teachers' salaries in real dollars, and smaller class sizes have increased costs since the early 1970s and 1980s. Meanwhile, scores on several national standardized tests have been rising.

---

[67]G. Robinson and D. Brandon, *Perceptions about American Education: Are They Based on Facts?* (Arlington, VA: Educational Research Service, 1992).

Third, educational spending does have an impact on student achievement. Data show that spending to decrease class size, improve facilities, hire quality teachers, and provide adequate resources and support services makes a big difference in student achievement.

Fourth, education salaries are not high in relation to other similarly trained professions. Teachers' actual work hours include hours outside the classroom: preparing lessons, setting up laboratory or other learning activities, grading students' papers, tutoring students after school, and studying for professional development. Some researchers have found that the average teacher salary is 25% less than that of other professionals with similar levels of education.

Finally, although public schools do employ more administrators than they did 50 years ago, today's schools have more leadership and management responsibilities. In fact, the number of principals as a percentage of all educational employees has decreased. Building level school administrators supervise more than twice the number of personnel as do typical managers in manufacturing and almost four times the number in public administration.

CONCLUSION

People hold many incorrect ideas about public schools, which lead them to resent and resist funding schools to the levels needed. Educational leaders need to understand these mistaken beliefs and effectively challenge them if we are to gain meaningful community support as advocates for school finance reform.

CASE STUDY

You are the retiring principal of a 75-year-old high school. Your career has spanned 25 years in that position. The school board has hired a new principal for the recently completed 2,000-student high school in Suburbia County School District, a once-rural school system that has become a bedroom community for the large Urbana City School District just to the south. Student enrollment has increased from 2,500 students 10 years ago to 6,500 students today. Several new elementary schools have been built and other remodeling has taken place to accommodate middle school students.

As a life-long resident, you have seen much change in Suburbia County. Many of the more affluent citizens have moved from Urbana to Suburbia over the last decade because of Urbana's increasing crime, high tax rates, and their schools' declining test scores. The latest residents are evenly divided among the younger families and the empty nesters who have either retired or will retire in the next 10 years. The county's growth has caused real estate values to rise and strains the municipality for water, sewer, and road maintenance as well as for schools and social services.

Voters passed the bond referendum for the next high school by a rather slim margin: 52% to 48%. The younger parents, ages 24 to 40, voted strongly in favor whereas the remaining demographic voted strongly against the new school and the associated debt payments. Almost no one was neutral on this issue. The vote caused much controversy in the county and left many bitter feelings. The school board soundly favored the proposed school, and the nine-member board of supervisors passed the motion to fund the school by one vote. In 2 months an election will determine the seats of two supervisors whose terms expire. They both voted for the school construction and are seen as strong supporters for education.

A taxpayers association has recently started meeting in Suburbia County in reaction to what some see as the beginning of higher taxes to fund public schools—which they say is a bottomless pit. The association's members say that Suburbia's schools were fine before the influx of current students, and that the per pupil spending levels then are adequate for the students now.

The school board is presenting its coming year's budget, which includes a spending increase from $7,000 to $7,700 per pupil—still $400 less than the state average. The rise will cover salary increases to attract quality new teachers to the district, hire additional special education and gifted education teachers, and increase curricular offerings at the middle and high school levels. For example, the existing salary schedule places Suburbia teachers below the state average. The school board wants to raise salaries to the state average. Currently, the high school offers only one foreign language, Spanish. The school board has placed two additional foreign languages, Latin and Chinese, in the budget. There is also an increase in middle school teachers to implement interdisciplinary teams at that level.

The taxpayers association has come out as strongly opposed to the school budget, putting forward two fresh candidates who oppose any increase in per pupil funding for the board of supervisors. In fact, the new candidates want a full investigation into possible areas that might be cut from the school board budget.

The two board of supervisors members whose terms expire are running to keep their seats, but they face very strong opposition. In fact, polls indicate that they are already 20 percentage points behind the taxpayers association candidates. The taxpayer candidates are running on a platform of no new taxes, especially for the schools. They cite new parents demanding new programs for their children that were not needed in the past. Test scores have not increased in spite of increased funding. The taxpayer candidates want to freeze property taxes at the current rate and require a three-quarters majority approval of a referendum if taxes are to be raised.

In 2 weeks, the candidates will debate in the old high school auditorium. The superintendent and the school board have called you in, quietly, to help get the school board's budget passed. The superintendent and school board were shrewd enough not to ask you to serve as the education adviser to the incumbent supervisors' campaigns, but they left you knowing what they wanted and needed you to do for the students' sake. Since they may have to work with the candidate they did not endorse, the current board could not publicly take a position in the election, making a difficult situation worse. Your job is to advise the incumbents on these issues:

- Why the public needs to support the education budget.
- Why spending on education provides a return to the community.
- Why cutting spending will harm the long-term health of the community.
- Why it is difficult to increase test scores when enrollment is increasing and the community is changing.
- Why it is important for the community's long-term health to vote for candidates who have pro-education platforms.

Additionally, you will propose to the incumbents a plan for communicating education's importance to the community members who are life-long residents. How will you proceed, and what facts and figures will you provide for the incumbents?

CHAPTER QUESTIONS

1. State three reasons it is inappropriate to say that the United States spends more on K–12 education than any other country. Provide factual explanations to back up your reasoning.
2. Explain in a letter to the editor of your local paper why national education costs have increased out of necessity (within the 250 word limit imposed by the editor of the paper).
3. Locate a website showing per pupil expenditures in your state and note the five lowest socioeconomic status (SES) school districts and the five highest SES districts. Determine the mean per pupil expenditure

for these two groups and whether the lower SES students receive
spending comparable with the higher SES group.

4. Explain the factors associated with an increase in education spending
   and show that teacher salaries in constant dollars have remained relatively flat over time.

5. Administrative salaries in your school district have lagged behind
   teacher salaries for the last few years. In fact, teacher salaries have
   had an annual 5% increase in the last 4 years, but administrators have
   had only a 3% salary increase in that same time period. Prepare a
   written statement to the school board advocating a larger percentage
   salary increase for administrators than for teachers this year.

HISTORY OF SCHOOL FINANCE

FOCUS QUESTIONS

1. What are the roots of public education financing?
2. How did regional differences in approach and philosophy in the financing of education come about?
3. What has been the historical impact of federal financing in education?
4. How did World Wars I and II influence education finance?
5. What is the history of the "Title Programs" in education (for example, Title I in reading and math for disadvantaged students)?

This chapter traces the history of education finance from settlement to present. Regional differences in philosophy and approach to funding schools are examined. The strong federal role and the historical impetus for education funding are discussed.

WHERE AND HOW IT ALL STARTED

From the earliest days, the governing American colonists valued education enough to pay for it. The first American school finance law was the Massachusetts Act of 1642, requiring parents and masters to attend to the educational duties of the colony's sons and servants. George Martin, a historian of the Massachusetts school system, states, "the child is to be educated, not to advance his personal interest, but because the state will suffer if he is not educated."[1]

According to Ellwood Cubberley, the General Court (the colonial legislature) empowered "certain chosen men"[2] of each town to ascertain, from time to time, if the parents and masters were attending to their educational duties; if the children were being trained "in learning and labor and other employments . . . profitable to the Commonwealth."[3] "Profitable" meant that sons and male servants learned to read and understand religious principles while they received training in "learning and labor." Women stayed at home and learned household tasks and embroidery—an obvious Title IX violation today.

The law also authorized the Selectmen to impose fines on those who were not educating their children. If that were not enough, the General Court ordered that all youth between the ages of 10 and 16 would also be schooled in "ye exercise of arms, as small guns, halfe pikes, bowes & arrows" and the like.[4] Colonial education was both idealistic and pragmatic.

Within 5 years, the 1642 law failed, and the Massachusetts colony legislators enacted the famous "Ye Olde Deluder Satan" law. Religiously motivated, the law presumed that those who could read and understand the Bible couldn't be tempted to follow Satan's wiles (and possibly offend God or harm their neighbors). Varying requirements existed for different sized settlements. For every town of 50 or more households, the law required that towns appoint a reading and writing teacher and pay him (only men needed to apply) what compensation the citizens deemed appropriate. For settlements of 100 or more households, the community taxed property owners to provide a grammar school that prepared students for eventual university attendance.

Towns not meeting this educational requirement faced a financial penalty of 5 pounds, which was later increased to 20 pounds (probably out of necessity), and those who violated the ordinance endured public humiliation in the

[1]As cited in Ellwood Cubberley, *The History of Education* (Boston: Houghton Mifflin, 1920), 366.
[2]Also known as Selectmen or Councilmen.
[3]Cubberley, *The History of Education,* 364.
[4]Ibid.

stocks. Local government taxed property because land was considered to be a valid measure of wealth. The well-to-do owned property and made money from that land through farming, manufacturing, selling goods, or other means. From earliest days, therefore, the founding fathers believed property was a proxy for wealth and that taxes on property, as a measure of that wealth, should fund education.

The 1647 law represented a distinct step forward in public education without precedent. "Not only was a school system ordered established— elementary for all towns and children, and secondary for youths in the larger towns—but for the first time among English-speaking people, there was an assertion of the right of the State to require communities to establish and maintain schools, under penalty if they refused to do so. It can be safely asserted, in light of later developments, that the two laws of 1642 and 1647 represent the foundations upon which our American state public-school systems have been built."[5] These two legislative actions established the state's right to tax citizens to provide public education.

Massachusetts's precedent—establishing property taxes as the basis for funding public schools—quickly caught on in other New England colonies. In 1650 Connecticut enacted school laws similar to those of Massachusetts but that added greater strength to the law. The Connecticut legislation had provisions to remove children and servants from families who did not comply with the act and place them with masters who would "more strictly look unto and force them to submit unto government, according to the rules of this order, if by fair means and former instructions they will not be drawn unto it."[6]

In fact, taxing property to fund education remains a tradition to this day. Property taxes still pay the greatest percentage of local school board budgets. Taxing property evolved somewhat differently, however, in various regions of the country. The middle and southern colonies subsidized very basic public schools (small facilities, limited curriculum, few students attending) and churches and parents primarily financed further education.

A century later, the United States Constitution's framers seriously debated education's importance to their new nation's future. They believed public education essential to maintaining a republican form of government. Rousseau noted in 1758 that "public education . . . is one of the fundamental rules of popular or legitimate government."[7] In other words, this American *people's*

---

[5]Ibid., 366.

[6]Ellwood Cubberley, *Readings in Public Education in the United States* (Boston: Houghton Mifflin, 1934), 19–20.

[7]Jean Jacques Rousseau, "A Discourse of Political Economy, 1758," in *The Social Contract and Discourses,* translation and introduction by G. D. H. Cole (London: J. M. Dent & Sons, 1973), 149.

government, very different from anything in Europe, required an educated general populace for its survival as a democratic republic.

Following the Declaration of Independence in 1776, the Articles of Confederation, and other nation-building documents, attention turned from federal law to state constitutions. Leaders vigorously debated whether to control the United States at the national or the state level. After all, the new country was called the *United States* of America. Politics, at its best, is the art of the possible. Accordingly, representatives compromised to appease both state's rights advocates and federalists. Issues such as education that did not appear in the first 10 Amendments to the United States Constitution fell under the state's purview, so education became a state function by default. Both sides could live with this trade-off. This compromise has far-reaching legal and financial effects today; state's rights issues continue to be a discomforting national concern with keen impact on educational policy and practices.

REGIONAL EVOLUTION OF SCHOOLS AND SCHOOL FINANCING

The evolution of schools in the new republic differed among the various geographic regions. Cubberley wrote that the New England settlers fled religious persecution in England.[8] In England, laws barred them from reading and interpreting the Bible for themselves. In their new land, therefore, they established a schooling system unlike anything they had left behind. Uniquely, their colony became the first English-speaking settlement requiring that children learn how to read.[9] Although religious in inspiration and scope (students would be able to interpret the Bible for themselves and save their immortal souls), knowing how to read and comprehend also enabled individuals to think for themselves on many issues and to act without offense or injury to others.

The Virginia settlement contrasted with that of New England. The earliest Virginia settlers were from the same class as those who settled in New England. However, the former were not dissenters from the Church of England; they adhered to the National Church and had come to America to make their fortunes. The regional differences in crops and the economics of plantations led to the introduction of indentured servants and slaves,

---

[8]Cubberley wrote what is arguably the best history of education in our country up to 1920. For a detailed reading, see Cubberley, *The History of Education*.

[9]Ibid., 364.

which led to the development of distinct societal classes. This social construct was in contrast to the small New England town with democratic town meetings. New England was developing a new society whereas Virginia remained similar to England in spirit and practice.[10]

Cubberley described the developing country's four basic schooling practices: good school conditions, mixed conditions, pauper and parochial schools, and the "no action" group.[11] Under *good school conditions*, citizens generally valued education and saw its worth for the "entire" populace—if you happened to be a white male. States in this category included Maine, Vermont, New Hampshire, Massachusetts, Connecticut, New York, and Ohio. These states developed rather high-quality and relatively progressive education programs in comparison with the rest of the country.

Mixed conditions described diverse settlements where people held conflicting ideas about what public education should be and what it should provide for children. These regions showed wide variance in education quality. Indiana and Illinois were such states.

The *pauper and parochial* school conditions existed mostly in the middle and southern colonies. Emigrants in these regions, for the most part, did not flee England's religious persecution. Instead, they left their homeland on good terms. Many arrived in the colonies with or seeking their fortunes and enhanced or found them. As a result, these newcomers did not abandon their traditional English ideas about education: high-quality schooling was for the elite. Therefore, the privileged sent their children to church-sponsored (parochial) schools in England or to those newly established in America. Similarly, in these "pauper and parochial" states, community leaders believed that the poor, the paupers, deserved a minimal level of education lasting only a few years. States in this category included Pennsylvania, New Jersey, Delaware, Maryland, Virginia, Georgia, South Carolina, and Louisiana.

Finally, Cubberley characterized the *no action* group as the religious freedom and antigovernment states. Philosophically, these colonists believed that "government" should play little role in citizens' or community affairs. Individuals held responsibility for their own actions and well-being, including providing for their children's education. Subsequently, these regions took little or no action about establishing public education in their early days. Such states included Rhode Island, Kentucky, Tennessee, North Carolina,

---

[10]Ibid., 371–372.

[11]Elwood Cubberley, *Public Education in the United States: A Study and Interpretation of American Educational History* (Cambridge, MA: Houghton Mifflin, 1947), 97–105. This, along with Cubberley, *The History of Education*, provides an excellent overview of the development of schools in the United States.

Mississippi, and Alabama. Not all states appear in Cubberley's listing, and several states reflect an amalgam of people and ideas not fitting one distinct pattern.

Regardless of how a state began its educational evolution, the good school conditions model offered its eligible children the best learning opportunities. As discussed in Chapter 1, and again in Chapters 4 and 12, education has a positive economic impact on the individual and society. States must invest as heavily in education as their capacity allows if they want future economic prosperity for all their citizens.

THE HISTORY OF FEDERAL EDUCATION FUNDING

Even though the U.S. Constitution made education a state responsibility, the federal government did not abandon involvement with public schools or leave their financing solely to the states. On the contrary, the federal government heavily promoted and financed education even before ratifying the Constitution. After all, the founding fathers deemed an educated populace a matter of national security. Although federal financial involvement in education is somewhat complex, certain themes emerge.[12]

In 1778, shortly after the revolution and before ratifying the Constitution, Congress eagerly sought ways to generate revenues for the new country and to pay its war debts. One method involved selling claims to the western territories. After much debate in the Continental Congress, federal legislators enacted the Land Ordinance of 1785. Legislators decided that new Congressional townships in the western territories should be 6 miles square (or 36 square miles). The 6 miles square would be surveyed and divided into 36 lots, each of 1 square mile. The law reserved 4 of these 1-square-mile lots—numbers 8, 11, 16, and 19—for future sale. Towns could set aside the proceeds from lot number 16 to finance their public schools. This section came to be known as the "sixteenth section" of the Ordinance of 1785, or the first land ordinance. Clearly, the federal government provided for public education in this first ordinance while recognizing the new states' (or territories') control of that function.

The Northwest Ordinance of 1787, the second land ordinance, authorized land grants to establish education and was filled with magnificent rhetoric but little guidance to carry it out. This ordinance included the rather famous provision in its third article, saying, "religion, morality, and knowledge being

---

[12]For a chronological listing of federal legislation, go to http://nces.ed.gov//pubs2002/digest2001/ch4.asp.

necessary to good government and the happiness of mankind, schools and the means of education shall be forever encouraged." The Northwest Ordinance also established the requisite conditions for territories to become states and included a provision that each state have an education stipulation within its basic laws.

In the same year the Ordinance of 1787, the third land ordinance, conveyed approximately 5 million acres to land speculators. Later, in 1802, the fourth "wave" of federal policy governing granting lands clarified the "sixteenth section's" township intent with the new state of Ohio, *requiring* monies from this section's sales be spent for public schools. Additionally, in 1802 when Ohio became a state, a debate arose as to whether or not states could tax the federal properties within the state's borders. Parties reached a compromise that gave states "a 5 percent" portion of public land sales. For that 5%, states agreed that federal lands within states would be exempt from state taxes. These revenues added to monies available to establish public schools. By this time, the federal and state roles in establishing education had been clarified. States then developed their public education structures at varying rates of speed and effectiveness.

Under Andrew Jackson's presidency, a move to decentralize the federal government began. With decentralization, Congress did not need as much money as it had collected. On the other hand, the states needed more. Realizing this funding discrepancy, in 1836 the Surplus Revenue Deposit Act gave $28 million of federal funds to the states. Much of this windfall was spent for public schools.

Looking beyond basic literacy and numeracy to its own national survival needs, the federal government took a different major role in financing U.S. education. In 1802 Congress enacted legislation establishing the U.S. Military Academy. Forty-three years later, in 1845, Congress established the Naval Academy and founded the Coast Guard Academy in 1876. The Merchant Marine Academy began in 1936, and the United States Air Force Academy opened its doors in 1954. This direct investment in schooling illustrated the federal government's commitment to assure its own national security through education.

WAR YEARS' LEGISLATION

Somewhat later, despite preoccupation with the Civil War, in 1862 Congress established the Morrill Act, which authorized the states to use public land grants to establish and maintain agricultural and mechanical colleges. This federal education investment assured the country's economic security by producing knowledgeable managers and planners trained at these new colleges for the nation's growth. Twenty-eight years later, in 1890, Congress passed the second Morrill Act, authorizing funds to support teaching in the colleges that the first Morrill Act established.

In 1867, two years after the Civil War, Congress enacted legislation to establish the United States Department of Education. This advanced public education to a leadership and policy position in the federal government. But a year later, in 1868, the department was "downgraded" to the Office of Education. In 1953 the Office of Education became part of the Department of Health, Education, and Welfare (HEW), where it remained until reestablished as a department with a cabinet chair in October 1979 under Public Law 96-88.

Wars bring changes to any society, and education was no exception. During World War I, necessity forced rapid changes in the United States. The military faced war on a scale and horror not seen before—including chemical weapons. We began this "War to End All Wars" with horses and wagons and ended it with machinery. The United States was recognized as a world power. America had entered the Industrial Age, and there was no turning back. Workers needed different skill sets as the agrarian lifestyle gave way to urbanization.

The government faced large numbers of returning soldiers who needed specific workplace skills. Congress also felt obligated to train people in specific areas of expertise. Hence, the 1917 Smith-Hughes Act provided states with grants to support vocational education. The national government directed the state's role in administering this program according to federal standards and funds—a model followed in future federal education grants.

At the same time, Congress also confronted the problem of what to do with returning injured soldiers who required further workplace training. In 1918 Congress passed the Vocational Rehabilitation Act, providing funds to rehabilitate World War I veterans. In 1919, to assist states and school programs, Congress passed the Act to Provide for Further Educational Facilities, which authorized the federal government to sell surplus machine tools to schools for 15% of their original purchase price—enabling schools to acquire the equipment needed for "real world" training. In 1920 the Smith-Bankhead Act authorized grants for the states to provide vocational rehabilitation programs.

Following World War I, life progressed agreeably for most middle-class families and especially well for the upper class until October 1929. With the Great Depression in full swing by 1932, Congress and the executive branch desperately sought a quick fix to save the crashing economy. There were significant social and political ramifications for elected officials. Picture millions of families waiting for food in bread lines and soup kitchens. Think of the elementary-aged children dropping out of school to work solely to help put meals on the family table. Not immune to that tableau, in 1935 Congress passed the Agricultural Adjustment Act, setting up what we know today as the School Lunch Act—providing food to schools. In 1946 the National School Lunch Act enhanced and expanded this assistance to schools.

With World War II, Congress recognized the need for workforce technology and technology skills to an even greater extent than following WWI. Again, public schools played an important role in filling the need. In 1941 Congress passed the Amendment to the Lanham Act of 1940, providing federal aid for the construction, maintenance, and operation of schools located in federally impacted areas (where U.S. military families lived and worked on government-owned land and facilities that paid no state or local property taxes). Congress continued this financial support under various Public Law statutes.

In 1943 disabled veterans began returning home, and political pressure resulted in another Vocational Rehabilitation Act, Public Law 78-16. This, like the one after World War I, assisted disabled veterans. In 1944 the federal government enacted legislation for returning military service workers with the Servicemen's Readjustment Act, Public Law 78-346. Known as the GI Bill, this act provided education benefits to military returnees as they reentered civilian life.

This remarkable legislation had far-reaching consequences for U.S. democracy, education, and the scope and quality of middle-class life at midcentury and beyond. First, World War II brought the United States out of the Great Depression, admirably gearing up its war machine. With thousands of servicemen returning to the civilian workforce after the war, the economy, in all probability, could not have supported the worker surplus. By providing an attractive education alternative, the GI Bill delayed many of the returning veterans from flooding the labor market, creating massive unemployment, and stalling the economic recovery.

Second, the GI Bill enabled an educational investment in U.S. infrastructure by enhancing the workforce's job skills. The world had changed during the war, moving into the Nuclear Age. Many recognized the need for enhanced workforce knowledge and skills, and the GI Bill provided just such an incentive.

Third, the GI Bill offered a living stipend while veterans attended school, effectively transitioning the potential labor glut into a student cohort earning their living while learning a new skill set. Finally, less than half of the U.S. population graduated from high school prior to World War II. The

GI Bill effectively supplied a massive education infusion to citizens, raising the education bar, and expanding learning horizons, career, and lifestyle opportunities for future generations.

Many returning servicemen took advantage of the GI Bill's educational benefits. Schools and colleges felt a bit overwhelmed with the newfound demand for their services, straining their resources. Congress helped states and localities in 1949 with the Federal Property and Administrative Services Act, Public Law 81-152. This act allowed the national government to donate surplus federal property to educational institutions. Congress effectively recognized the financial burden that localities and states faced and spread that financial burden over the entire country by taking equipment bought with federal (your and my tax) dollars and donating them to schools. In Chapter 5 we propose that a good tax is one that spreads the burden for payment out over the largest possible number of people.

POST–WORLD WAR II LEGISLATION

After World War II, the national economy thrived. Colleges and universities bristled with activity. Levittowns and other planned suburban communities sprang up, offering home ownership to thousands of families. Americans believed they were part of the world's most powerful military and economic nation. Following Sputnik in 1957, however, the nation confronted a wrenching reality check. With the Russians becoming the first country to send someone into outer space, serious national questions arose about whether public schools had enough direction and resources to keep our global superiority.

As a result of this wake-up call, public education received a massive infusion of federal dollars in 1958 with the National Defense Education Act, otherwise known as NDEA, Public Law 85-864.[13] Congress viewed math and sciences education as essential to protect our national security in an era of superpower rivalry for control of outer space. The NDEA provided economic assistance to states and individual school systems to "beef up" science and math instruction, foreign language learning, and other "critical" subjects. NDEA also supplied states with resources for improved services including statistical reporting, guidance and counseling, and testing. It also supplied higher education student loans and fellowships and foreign language study

---

[13]If these events had occurred in the past 15 years, one wonders whether politicians might have chosen to scrap the public schools rather than provide a massive capital infusion as they did with the NDEA.

and training. For the first time, the national government looked at ways to enhance teaching and learning through media such as television. NDEA infused massive funding for vocational and technical programs deemed necessary to America's defense.

Also passed in 1958, although overshadowed by the NDEA fanfare, was the Education of Mentally Retarded Children Act, Public Law 85-926, which offered groundbreaking legislation for students with disabilities.[14] Earlier federal legislation for the disabled focused on injured veterans returning from World War I or World War II. Recognizing a severe national need, Congress passed this bill to train teachers to work successfully with students with disabilities. Prior to this time, only a few states distributed funds to localities to supplement programs for such students. Most families with children with disabilities had to find their own help. Unfortunately, not until the 1971 *Pennsylvania Association of Retarded Citizens* federal district court case did real change begin.[15]

In 1972, moving forward with special education initiatives, the *Mills* case in the District of Columbia[16] (where plaintiffs estimated that 18,000 students in that jurisdiction did not receive educational services) resulted in the 1975 Education for All Handicapped Children Act (EAHCA), Public Law 101-46. This legislation originally intended that the federal government pay 40% of the funding necessary for special education services, with the remaining portion to paid by the state and the locality.[17] Today, the federal government pays only 17% of special education costs.

In 1965, under President Lyndon Johnson's leadership, Congress passed Public Law 89-10, the Elementary and Secondary Education Act (ESEA). ESEA is the parent of today's No Child Left Behind 2001 legislation. This "Great Society" legislation of 1965 was arguably the most important congressional action to fund education programs up to that time. An offshoot of the Civil Rights Act of 1964, ESEA contained five title categorical aid programs specifically designed to finance education for certain student populations. Let's look at each of them briefly.

---

[14]For an excellent historical and legal overview of the rights of people with disabilities, see Kern Alexander and M. David Alexander, *American Public School Law*, 6th ed. (Belmont, CA: Wadsworth, 2005).

[15]*Pennsylvania Association for Retarded Citizens v. Commonwealth*, 334 F.Supp. 1257 (E.D.Pa.1971), 343 F.Supp. 279 (E.D.Pa.1972).

[16]*Mills v. Board of Education of the District of Columbia*, 348 F. Supp. 866 (D.D.C.1972).

[17]Unfortunately, federal government funding has never reached this goal. According to the National Education Association, funding remains at less than 20%, far below the 40% goal (see http://www.nea .org/specialed/index.html). This places a great burden on localities and states to fund special education appropriately and undermines spreading the cost out over the largest possible population.

Title I

Title I provides supplemental school program grants for children of low-income families. This program was intended to help economically disadvantaged students succeed in the regular school program by improving their basic and advanced skills and by helping them achieve grade-level proficiency. The program could include supplemental or schoolwide activities encouraging intensive parent involvement. The government distributes these funds in two ways—through basic grants and concentration grants.

Most Title I funds are basic grants that flow through the State Education Agency (SEA) to localities based on a formula involving the school district's number of eligible students and the average state per pupil expenditure.

Concentration grants represent a smaller percentage of the overall funding within this statute. Concentration grants are designed for localities with a high number of eligible students—more than 6,500 students or more than 15% of all students eligible for Title I funding. This is particularly useful for school districts with a student population containing a high percentage of disadvantaged students. As both economic and learning factors impact students' learning, these localities face daunting challenges in addressing children's educational needs. Interestingly, the annual amount of funds allocated for Title I varies from year to year, depending on political and fiscal decisions. A critical provision, however, requires school divisions to receive not less than 85% of its previous year's funding share.

Title I funding decreased in the 1980s, and when accounting for inflation on a per pupil eligible basis, funding actually remained lower in 1990 than it was a decade earlier. Reviewing annual changes in inflation-adjusted dollars from 1979–80 through 1993–94, the annual mean change was .56% while serving almost half a million more students. In other words, Title I money had less buying power in the 1990s but was expected to support learning interventions for more children.

Title II

This section has several titles as it consolidated 29 original federal categorical programs. Title II of ESEA also provides grant monies for school library resources, textbooks, and other instructional materials, including audiovisual equipment. Called the Dwight D. Eisenhower Mathematics and Science Education Act,[18] it resembled the 1958 NDEA and was intended to strengthen the country's economic competitiveness and national security. Other parts of

---

[18]20 U.S.C 2981.

Title II provide presidential awards for outstanding teaching, funds for magnet schools, monies for talented and gifted programs, funds for women's educational equity, grants for drug abuse prevention and dropout prevention, bilingual education, and other programs.

Title III

Title III provides funds for supplementary education centers and services to public and private schools. This block grant has changed over the years to eventually include a variety of special needs programs.

Title IV

Title IV allocates funds for regional educational research and training laboratories. The 10 Mid-Continent Research for Education and Learning (MCREL) labs, Appalachian Education Laboratory, the Far West Lab, and others provide valuable resources for the operation of public schools. MCREL, for example, and its primary researcher Robert Marzano, has intensively studied the teaching and learning process and has published numerous books that show classroom teachers "what works" to increase student learning and achievement.

Title V

Finally, Title V provides funds for strengthening state departments of education (otherwise known as State Education Agencies—SEAs). Prior to this legislation, as many as 15,000 school districts reported directly to the federal Department of Education. This statute provided funds for states to establish one reporting agency per state, the State Education Agency. The streamlined efficiency potential this brought to the federal department was staggering. Most states refer to this consolidated reporting, advising, and compliance organization as their State Department of Education. Others, such as Texas, refer to it as the State Education Agency, more closely paralleling the statute's language.

MORE LEGISLATION

The following brief overview of legislation passed from the 1960s to the present, although not a comprehensive list, represents some of the major school finance legislation.

In 1967 Congress passed the Public Broadcasting Act, creating the Corporation for Public Broadcasting (CPB), which assumed a major role in routing federal monies to noncommercial radio and television stations. The CPB began program production groups and started Educational Television (ETV) networks. Additionally, the CPB was responsible for awarding construction grants for educational radio and television facilities. Many of today's new teachers were raised on programming that the CPB started, including *Sesame Street, The Electric Company,* and others that have played an important part in children's developing lives.

In 1968 the Handicapped Children's Early Education Assistance Act, Public Law 90-576, was passed. This act authorized states to provide preschool and early education programs for children with disabilities. In 1975 Public Law 94-142, the Education for All Handicapped Children Act, directed that all children with disabilities have a free, appropriate public education to meet their learning needs. At the time, Congress's stated goal was to pay 40% of the program's cost.

In 1970 many federal legislative actions reflected the time's social changes. The National Commission on School Finance was established under the Elementary and Secondary Education Assistance Programs Extension, Public Law 91-230. Additionally, this year was the beginning of *Brown v. Board of Education II,* mandating school desegregation. As a result, the Office of Education Appropriation Act, Public Law 91-380, provided emergency school assistance to desegregating local school districts and schools.

The Environmental Education Act, Public Law 91-516, established an Environmental Education Office to develop curriculum and start environmental education programs in elementary and secondary schools, help distribute information about environmental education, and provide training for teachers dealing with the environment and ecology. The Drug Abuse Education Act of 1970, Public Law 91-527, gave funding for the development, demonstration, and evaluation of materials dealing with aspects of drug abuse.

In 1974 the Education Amendments of 1974, Public Law 93-380, consolidated several programs, but most important this act established the National Center for Education Statistics. Additionally in that year, the Juvenile Justice and Delinquency Prevention Act, Public Law 93-415, authorized technical assistance, research, resources, and training to develop and implement programs to keep elementary and secondary students in school.

In 1977 the Career Education Implementation Incentive Act established a federal career education program for elementary and secondary schools. It emphasized the infusion of functional career education and life skills into general education classes.

The Office of Education was separated from HEW and reestablished as a department with a cabinet chair in 1979 under Public Law 96-88. This "promotion" may have reflected education's importance to Congress and the executive branch. Its increased visibility may also have signaled that political insiders suspected federal education spending would decrease over the next few years and a seat at the cabinet table might help influence spending.[19] Raising the office to a department could bring political advantage as holding a cabinet seat brings education officials more influence with the executive branch and with Congress.

In 1981 the Education Consolidation and Improvement Act, Public Law 97-35, consolidated 42 different programs into 7 that were funded under block grants. Federal funding for education fell more than 20% between 1980 and 1985, and grant consolidation made the funding reduction more politically invisible.

In 1984 the Education for Economic Security Act, Public Law 98-377, provided funds for the addition of new elementary and secondary schools science and math programs.[20] These new programs included magnet schools, equal access programs, and excellence in education programs. Also in that year, the reauthorized Carl Perkins Vocational Education Act continued federal financial assistance for vocational education programs. States received funding to make vocational programs available to all persons, including individuals with disabilities and those from financially disadvantaged backgrounds.

In 1986 the Handicapped Children's Protection Act, Public Law 99-372, became law. This allowed parents of students with disabilities to collect the attorney fees in cases brought under the Education of the Handicapped Act. Redress became a reality for parents of special needs children.

In 1988 Public Law 100-297, the Augustus F. Hawkins–Robert T. Stafford Elementary and Secondary School Improvement Amendments reauthorized many major programs through 1993 including Chapter 1, Chapter 2, Bilingual Education, Math-Science Education, Magnet Schools, Impact Aid, and other smaller programs.

In 1990 the Americans with Disabilities Act, Public Law 101-336, became law. Also known as ADA, this far-reaching legislation prohibited discrimination against persons with disabilities in a variety of ways. Unlike the Rehabilitation Act of 1973, Section 504, the ADA covers all employees in

---

[19]Federal spending for elementary and secondary education actually decreased 21% between 1980 and 1985. See Robert Reich, "What Is a Nation?" *Political Science Quarterly* 106 (2), 1991.

[20]Funding was also included for postsecondary math and science programs.

public or private companies who employ 15 or more people. The act covers most areas of employment and treatment in society including transportation, communications, accommodations, and more. This act brought important classroom and school protections for students with special physical or learning needs not met through special education.

Also in 1990, the School Dropout Prevention and Basic Skills Improvement Act was passed. This act continued funding for dropout prevention programs and provided funding for improvement of secondary school programs related to basic skill development.

The following year, 1991, saw creation of the National Institute for Literacy, the National Institute Board, and the Interagency Task Force on Literacy. These organizations were formed as the result of the National Literacy Act of 1991.

In 1993 the NAEP Assessment Authorization, Public Law 103-33, authorized use of the National Assessment of Educational Progress, otherwise known as the "Nation's Report Card," for making state-by-state comparisons of student performance. Country-by-country comparisons had already been made public.

In 1994, Goals 2000: Educate America Act, Public Law 103-227, established a federal partnership through a system of grants to states and local communities to reform education systems. This legislation formalized the national education goals and established the National Education Goals Panel. It also provided a mechanism for voluntary national certification of state standards and assessments.

Also in that year the Safe Schools Act of 1994, part of Public Law 103-227, authorized awarding competitive grants to local education agencies with serious crime problems to implement violence prevention strategies. These strategies included conflict resolution and peer mediation.

The original Elementary and Secondary Education Act (ESEA) legislation, reauthorized in 1994 with the Improving America's Schools Act, is also known as Public Law 103-382. This reauthorization included Title I, the largest federal program providing assistance to disadvantaged students. The act also contained provisions for professional development and technical assistance programs, safe and drug-free school provisions, and provisions to promote school equity.

In 1996 states and localities, frustrated with federal legislation requiring them to take certain actions that required money without providing the financial resources to cover the costs, pressured Congress. The Contract With America: Unfunded Mandates, Public Law 104-4, was passed in an attempt to curb the practice of imposing federal mandates on states and localities without the federal dollars to pay for them. This legislation also applied to tribal governments.

In 1997 the Individuals with Disabilities in Education Act Amendments, Public Law 105-17, went into effect. Originally known as the Education for All Handicapped Children Act (EAHCA) and renamed in 1990 as Individuals with Disabilities Education Act (IDEA), this legislation revised the original IDEA provisions and extended the authorization of appropriation for 5 years (through fiscal year 2002). It provided additional protections to special needs students and their parents.

In 2000 a new program, the Consolidated Appropriations Act 2001, created assistance for school repair and renovation, addressing the needs for capital improvements to facilities. The act also reauthorized the ESEA of 1965, providing credit enhancement initiatives to help charter schools with site acquisition, construction, and repair of facilities. It also reauthorized the Even Start program and enacted the Children's Internet Protection Act.

In 2001 President George W. Bush passed legislation reauthorizing the ESEA funds called *No Child Left Behind*. The act, signed into law on January 8, 2002, has arguably had the most far-reaching impact on public education in the last 50 years. Basically, No Child Left Behind legislation increases accountability for states and local school districts in return for continued federal financial support under the act. The most significant changes from the ESEA involve school accountability.

Every state is required to develop a comprehensive system of standards and assessments in language arts, math, and science. Students will be tested almost yearly to measure school accountability. States will adopt criteria for improving test scores on a yearly basis, called adequate yearly progress (AYP), to increase all students' proficiency and to close the achievement gap. Achievement for all students is monitored, and school and school district averages are examined along with the scores for four subgroups: minorities, English language learners (ELL), special education students, and students receiving free and reduced price lunch. Students in all of these categories must make AYP in the overall reporting figures.

The stair-step progress must increase yearly as an average and for all the individual subgroups. Should AYP not be made, consequences begin to accumulate on an escalating basis. According to the legislation, all subgroups must pass 100% of the state standards' assessments by school year 2013–14. Additionally, all schools must have highly qualified teachers in place for core area subjects by the end of the 2005–06 school year.

Today the federal government funds approximately $50 billion for education purposes at the elementary and secondary levels. Figure 2.1 shows

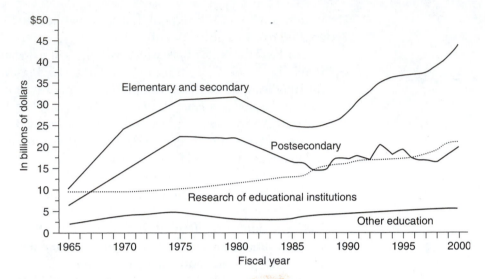

FIGURE **2.1**

Federal On-Budget Funds for Education, 1965 to 2000

Note: In constant fiscal year 2000 dollars

Source: U.S. Office of Management and Budget, *Budget of the U.S. Government,* fiscal years 1967 to 2001; National Science Foundation, *Federal Funds for Research and Development,* fiscal years 1967 to 2000; unpublished data.

federal spending on education from 1965 to 2001, represented in constant 2001 dollars. The federal government has invested more than $1 trillion in elementary and secondary education in that 36-year period—an average of more than $27.7 billion per year.[21] The federal moral and financial commitment to public education continues to shape education policy at the state and local levels.

SUMMARY

Our founding fathers strongly believed that their new democracy's health depended on its people's virtues as right, honorable, ethical, and knowledge-able citizens. They wanted a population that was both good and smart. They

---

[21]We say invested purposefully; see Chapter 4 for our discussion on this issue.

believed public education was essential to maintaining a republican form of government. This new concept of education for everyone would require the government to collect and spend public monies to reach and teach the widest range of students. Because the first 10 Amendments to the U.S. Constitution do not mention education, schooling became a state function. This compromise has far-reaching legal and financial effects today.

In colonial days, towns raised local "provisions" that established schools where sons and male servants learned to read and understand religious principles while they received training in "learning and labor." Women stayed home. Eventually, local governments taxed property because they considered land to be a valid measure of wealth.

Different regions evolved different types of schools. Some regions' citizens valued education for the "entire" (white male) populace, and they gave public financial support to educate large numbers of students. Other states showed wide variance in their willingness to fund local public schools.

Even though the Constitution made education a state responsibility, the federal government heavily promoted and financed education while recognizing the states' (or territories') control. Financing the various military academies directly showed the federal government's commitment to its own security through education. Likewise, the Morrill Act authorized the states to use public land grants to establish and maintain agricultural and mechanical colleges, assuring the country's economic security by producing knowledgeable managers and planners for the nation's growth.

Throughout the years, the federal government invested heavily in education to benefit its national security, citizens' quality of life, and continued representative democracy. After World War I, Congress passed the Smith-Hughes Act to train people in specific areas of expertise. Other national programs invested in vocational rehabilitation and workplace training for returning soldiers and citizens, providing food to schools so it could feed students (because their families might not be able to), and supporting education of its most vulnerable students.

Conclusion

Financing schools has historically been a local matter, but the federal government initially required localities to educate their children and continues to contribute significant funds to implement its vision for America and to for pay for its citizens' education.

CASE STUDY

The evolution of American public education began in the colonies as a local act in the Massachusetts Bay Colony. Other colonies followed suit, and education remained largely a local provision. The founding fathers began discussing the importance of education to the continuance of the new country's democratic republic form of government. In the 20th century the evolution continued and compulsory attendance laws were enacted. Recent views have emerged that do not espouse compulsory education and fly in the face of the direction education has taken for more than 200 years. For example, Milton Friedman, a Nobel-winning economist, has said, "Like most laws, compulsory attendance laws have costs as well as benefits. We no longer believe the benefits justify the costs."[22]

Has the cost of education exceeded its benefits? On which side of this issue do you stand? Defend that position.

CHAPTER QUESTIONS

1. Not all states appear in Cubberley's original listing of school conditions. Several states reflect an amalgam of people and ideas, not fitting one distinct pattern. Make a case for the school conditions under which your state was established and discuss whether your state still fits in this category. If it has changed, under what school conditions do you believe your state operates now? Why do you think this is true?
2. Rank the five most influential federal acts affecting education prior to 1870, and explain your reasons for placing these acts in the order you did.
3. Rank the five most influential federal acts affecting education after 1870, and explain your reasons for placing these acts in the order you did.
4. Take a position as to whether the federal role in education has changed for the better or worse in the last 20 years and defend this position.
5. How has the No Child Left Behind act changed financial allocations in your school district? How much additional federal funding has your district received? How much additional money was raised locally to meet these provisions? What challenges still lie ahead for your school district?

---

[22]Milton Friedman and Rose Friedman, *Free to Choose* (New York: Harcourt Brace Jovanovich, 1980), 161–163.

The Legal Framework for Financing Public Education

Focus Questions

1. Considering the strong federal influence and concern for education, who is ultimately responsible for education and why?

2. When, where, why, and how was the first law in education?

3. If education is a state function, how can the federal government become involved in education and use tax monies to fund education projects it deems necessary?

4. Why does our county rely primarily on property taxes to fund education? Why may this not be the best source of revenue for schools?

5. How has the Equal Protection clause of the U.S. Constitution influenced the practice of education?

6. What do the issues of equity and adequacy have to do with financing education?

7. What have the courts said about vouchers, tuition tax credits, and charter schools? What impact have these alternative schooling concepts had on public education?

This chapter traces the legal framework for how public education is financed in the United States.[1] We begin by examining the historical development of education's importance to the founding fathers. The federal and state constitutional provisions for education are discussed. Foundational issues of equity and adequacy are introduced, and court rulings on vouchers, tuition tax credits, and charter schools are reviewed.

---

[1] For a thorough and scholarly examination of this topic, see K. Alexander and D. Alexander, *American Public School Law*, 6th ed. (Belmont, CA: Wadsworth, 2005), which provides an outstanding overview of the legal framework surrounding education finance.

Chapter 2 provided a historical overview for the development of school finance in the United States. The founding fathers valued education as essential for our democratic republic government's survival. That value was seen in the early federal funding initiatives for public education, which included the various land ordinances, including the sixteenth section, and myriad congressional acts and appropriations. This chapter deals with the legal framework surrounding the operation of school finance.

Although education is a state responsibility,[2] the federal government has a lengthy precedent of providing the states with education programs and funds. Without this federal intervention, many education initiatives might not have been undertaken, and many injustices would have continued longer. Consider *Brown v. Board of Education of Topeka* (desegregation), *Brown II* (more desegregation), the Kentucky Education Reform Act (finance equity), Title IX (gender discrimination), Public Law 94-142 (special education), and many others; every one reflects federal initiatives to improve educational opportunities for all citizens.

If the federal government is controlling more education practice, as the No Child Left Behind legislation demonstrates, and if federal involvement in education has positively influenced education in general, some may wonder why we do not have a national education system similar to the one in Germany or the United Kingdom. The answer is simple.

The first 10 amendments to the U.S. Constitution are known as the Bill of Rights. The Tenth Amendment says that the powers that the Constitution does not delegate to the federal government or prohibit altogether are reserved for the states. As stated previously, education is not mentioned and became a state function by default. The framers made this compromise to balance the interests of those who wanted a strong federal government and those who wanted to preserve states' rights. Today that dynamic tension still exists: States are not willing to surrender their control of education, and the federal government wants greater accountability in the form of student achievement for its dollars but can't afford to pay its promised share.[3]

The Tenth Amendment's compromise gives each of the 50 states plenary power over education.[4] That is, each state is responsible for setting up an educational system and may pass laws it considers desirable toward that

---

[2]Actually, there are 46 U.S. states and 4 commonwealths: Kentucky, Massachusetts, Pennsylvania, and Virginia.

[3]The federal government intended to pay 40% of special education costs with the implementation of 94-142. Congress has never met even half of that targeted percentage.

[4]Many years ago after a graduate school law class, our 6-year-old daughter overheard a conversation about plenary power and asked what that meant. She summarized my lengthy answer by saying it meant "plenty of power"—a good paraphrase.

end as long as those laws do not conflict with the state or federal constitutions. The courts can only intervene if a party with legal standing raises a challenge based on a legitimate controversy concerning the state's practice and the state or federal constitution or its application. Over the past decades, federal powers have somewhat reduced the plenary nature of the states' control of education.

Each state's constitution has language that forms the legal framework for organizing the state's education function.[5] All states except Hawaii (and the District of Columbia) delegate much of the authority for education to local school boards, coordinated through the State Department of Education, also known as the State Education Agency (SEA). Hawaii has a single system of education, and education in the District of Columbia is a federal function. All other states have local school districts or school divisions, also known as the Local Education Agency (LEA). The state constitution's language about education and the states' Department of Education policies and regulations control the parameters under which each local school district operates.

Financing education is arguably the most critical issue facing states and the federal government. Increasingly, federal courts are ruling against states in cases involving their education funding formulae, challenging equity and adequacy, a topic discussed later in this chapter and fully in Chapter 8. This chapter focuses on the historic and legal perspectives for funding American public education. Specifically, we review the guiding principles regarding taxation, equal protection, state constitutional language, equity and adequacy, and finally vouchers, charter schools, and tuition tax credits.

TAXATION

Chapter 5 deals more fully with taxation issues; here we examine taxation only from a legal perspective. School revenue from federal, state, and local governments comes from taxes. From what source do the federal, state and local governments derive the power to tax? What are the precedents for taxes to fund education initiatives? A long history of federal taxing and spending to pay for education services exists. The first public school laws were in place before the Revolutionary War and involved the Massachusetts Bay Colony taxing citizens to raise the necessary funds for education services, Ye Olde Deluder Satan laws of 1647.

---

[5]This may be a good time to examine the education language in your own state's constitution.

Moving ahead more than 125 years in time, Section 8 of Article 1 of the U.S. Constitution gives Congress the right to tax and spend. The article, in part, reads, "The Congress shall have Power to lay and collect Taxes, Duties, and Imports and Excises, to pay the Debts and provide for the common Defense and General Welfare of the United States."[6] A rather substantial constitutional debate ensued originally about what the General Welfare clause actually meant.

Some, like James Madison, held a narrow interpretation. He believed that "general welfare" referred only to those powers mentioned in the same section (Section 8) of the Constitution. Alexander Hamilton and others believed the clause gave Congress broad and substantial power to tax and spend for purposes that would enhance the new nation's general welfare. The Supreme Court finally sided with Alexander Hamilton's broader idea, giving Congress wide-ranging powers to tax and spend for the general welfare of the United States.[7] That interpretation seems rather simple now, but it was a contentious issue for the new government.

At the state level, the Supreme Court has ruled that states have taxing power "to resort to all reasonable forms of taxation in order to defray government expenses."[8] Further, the Court said, "Unless restrained by provisions of the Federal Constitution, the power of the state as to the mode, form, and extent of taxation is unlimited."[9]

FEDERAL CONTROL OF THE STATE'S EDUCATION FUNCTION

Many ask how the federal government can intrude into education when it is clearly a state function. The federal government derives its authority to enter the states' education purview from three sources: (1) the states' agreement in accepting federal grants provided under the authority that the General Welfare clause gives the Congress; (2) congressionally authorized standards and regulations within the Commerce clause; and (3) Court constrained actions enforcing federal constitutional provisions protecting individual rights and freedoms.[10] In other words, the federal government can only become involved with the states' education programs under certain conditions.

---

[6]Article 1, Section 8, cl. 1.

[7]*United States v. Butler,* 297 U.S. 1, 56 S. Ct. 312 (1936).

[8]*Shaffer v. Carter,* 252 U.S. 37 (1970).

[9]Ibid.

[10]Alexander and Alexander, *American Public School Law,* 6th ed., 68.

First, the federal government has standing when the state has accepted a federal grant (for example, for No Child Left Behind or for Drug Free Schools) and the grant's provisions require the state to comply with certain federal guidelines if it accepts the grant monies. Should states and localities not comply, the federal government can become involved and force compliance or withdraw grant monies.

Second, federal involvement with local school issues could occur if states take action that affects the Commerce clause as in the case of *United States v. Lopez*.[11] In this case, the U.S. Congress made it a federal crime to have a gun within a defined geographic area known as a school zone. A Texas high school student brought a loaded pistol to school and was charged under state law with possessing a firearm on school property. The next day, the state dismissed the charges and instead charged the student with violating the federal Gun-Free School Zone Act of 1990.[12] Initially the student was found guilty, but the appellate court reversed the lower court decision. On further appeal, the U.S. Supreme Court affirmed the appellate court's ruling. The Supreme Court explained that charging the student under a new federal law was not allowed because Congress exceeded its authority in tying the gun-free zone to the Commerce clause.[13]

Third, federal involvement can occur if an action restricts rights or freedoms guaranteed in the U.S. Constitution as in *Tinker v. Des Moines Independent Community School District*.[14] In this case, the school administration heard that a group of students were planning to wear black armbands to school to protest the Vietnam War and hastily wrote a policy that wearing black armbands was a suspendable offense. The school then suspended the offending students when they showed up at school with their black armbands. When the suit eventually reached the Supreme Court, it ruled that a school policy cannot outweigh a fundamental right, such as the freedom of expression (speech), without reasonable knowledge that such an act of expression would have foreseeably caused a substantial disruption to the school process.

---

[11]*United States v. Lopez,* 131 L.Ed.2d 626, 115 S. Ct. 1624 (1995). This case should not be confused with *Goss v. Lopez,* which required procedural due process for temporary suspensions.

[12]18 U.S.C. Section 992(q)(1)(A)(1988 ed., Supp.V).

[13]Congress passed the gun-free school zone law under the Commerce clause, which gives Congress the authority to regulate and protect interstate commerce and those activities that substantially affect interstate commerce. Congress argued that commerce would be adversely affected if schools were not safe and students did not feel comfortable and safe in their learning environments. Having guns in and near schools would make them less safe and subsequently less effective in producing good citizens. The Supreme Court said that Congress went too far with this act as it essentially regulated schools, which was not the intent of the Commerce clause.

[14]*Tinker v. Des Moines Independent Community School District,* 393 U.S. 503, 89 S.Ct. 733 (1969).

Obviously, fundamental rights such as those in the Bill of Rights apply in all 50 states. Other provisions apply in states only when grant funds are accepted and the terms of the grant include acceptance of certain provisions.

FEDERAL CONTRIBUTION TO EDUCATION

How much money does the federal government contribute to state and local education agencies in education grants to gain some degree of control over the state function? Historically the federal government contributes, on average, about 10% of total education spending. Figure 3.1 shows the revenue figures from federal, state, and local sources from 1970 through 2000. The federal share of school revenue is rather constant at 10%, which is a substantial sum even though it is not a majority of school budgets. Surprisingly, state and local revenues show little variance over that time. The federal share has remained relatively constant, and the state and local ratios have fluctuated somewhat. Recently, there has been a trend for the states to reduce education spending, leaving localities with the choice of reducing services or increasing local taxes for education.

The federal government's 10% figure includes educational spending not only from the Department of Education (ED) but also from other federal agencies, such as the Department of Health and Human Services for the Head Start program and the Department of Agriculture for the School Lunch program. Subtract these other department dollars, and the Department of Education contributes only 6% of total K–12 education spending. To keep the federal dollars spent on education in perspective, the $63.2 billion appropriation for the Department of Education is only 2.9% of the federal government's nearly $2.2 trillion budget in fiscal year 2003.[15] The remaining education dollars come almost equally from state and local revenues.[16]

The federal portion of revenue, even at approximately 10%, provides sizeable revenue to the overall education function. By accepting these federal funds, states and localities surrender some of their power to operate the schools in their state or locality as they want. As the federal government places restrictions on funding, states lose some of their plenary power over education and adopt more of a federal policy perspective.

---

[15]http://www.ed.gov/about/overview/fed/role.html?src=ln

[16]http://nces.ed.gov/programs/digest/d02/ch_2f.asp#figure11

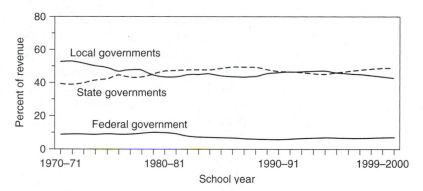

FIGURE 3.1

Sources of Education Revenue, 1970 to 2000

Source: U.S. Department of Education, National Center for Education Statistics, *Statistics of State School Systems; Revenues and Expenditures for Public Elementary and Secondary Education;* and Common Core of Data surveys.

STATE PREROGATIVES

States may tax what they wish as long as it does not conflict with federal provisions or with the state's constitution. School districts have no inherent capacity to tax unless the state's constitutional language specifically permits such taxing authority. A robust legal precedent exists for state constitutional language to be strong and clear about when a state, through legislative action, delegates the taxing authority to school boards.[17]

Some states have enacted legislation whereby school districts have the legal authority to levy taxes for school budgets. Other states do not provide school districts with the authority to levy taxes for schools. In these states, the districts must wait for a governing body to approve a school budget as one part of a city or county budget. The governing body must then set the tax rate, levy taxes, and apportion those funds to the local school district. This issue has been contested as recently as 1993 in Florida.[18] In this case, the Florida Supreme Court ruled that the School Board of Sarasota County

---

[17]In *Marion and McPherson Railway Co. v. Alexander,* 64 P. 978 (Kan. 1901), the Kansas Supreme Court ruled that the authority to levy taxes is an extraordinary one and should never be left to implication. Further, the court ruled that taxing authority must be clearly found by an act of the legislature.

[18]*Florida Department of Education v. Glasser,* 622 So.2d 944 (Florida, 1993).

required legal authorization by the state legislature to levy school taxes. Absent the specific authorization, the school board could not direct the county tax collector to collect and remit school taxes.

Not all states operate in the same manner regarding taxation for public schools. To complicate matters, some states' constitutional language prohibits taxing certain items. For example, some states do not have a state income tax. Others do not have a state sales tax. Some states tax all purchases, and others exempt food and medicines from taxes. Pennsylvania has a unique legislative provision called the "Tax Anything Act," which takes the idea of state prerogatives to an unsurpassed level. In spite of the states' taxing prerogative, virtually all states rely on one historical primary revenue source to finance public school operations—property taxes—dating back in our country to the Massachusetts law of 1647.

Property Taxes

Taxing property has precedent that goes back much further than Ye Olde Deluder Satan Act in Massachusetts. Property taxes to fund education date back to ancient Greece. In Athens, the Greeks taxed land and houses. Later, the Roman government taxed people and property. Early Europeans taxed land, homes, and livestock. Therefore, taxing property owners for education in the Massachusetts Bay Colony was not a new idea but rather an extension of prior practice.[19]

In the United States, taxing property became the established vehicle for funding schools during the 1800s. In the early 19th century, governing bodies imposed property taxes differently than is common practice today. Then, localities taxed land at different rates if it were cleared, uncleared, or cultivated. As the century continued, taxing agencies saw livestock and equipment as additional sources of taxable property. Taxing property and equipment at different rates became increasingly complex for localities.

For example, Farmer Brown and Farmer Jones both own 40 cleared acres for planting. Farmer Brown's land produces 100 bushels of wheat per acre, but Farmer Jones's land only produces 50 bushels per acre. Should both parcels be taxed at the same rate just because they are both cleared? What if hard-working Farmer Brown is a better farmer than lazy Farmer Jones who knows little about agriculture? If both 40-acre parcels are taxed

---

[19]See Ellwood Cubberley, *History of Education* (Boston: Houghton Mifflin, 1920). This book provides a thorough overview of the history of education.

at the same rate, is one farmer penalized for being a knowledgeable, hard-working farmer? Is one benefiting from being lazy? Would income produced from the property be a better vehicle for taxation?

Extending this example, both farmers bought their plows and disks at the same time. Farmer Brown keeps his equipment in good working order, but Farmer Jones never maintains his equipment. Should Farmer Jones pay lower taxes on his equipment because it is in poor condition? Does that practice reward Farmer Jones for being a poor caretaker of his machinery? Should the equipment be taxed on its value or just on a flat fee?

This complexity led to a uniform general property tax based on a percentage (or millage) of the land's worth. This provided for taxation based on the property's value, not on whether the land was cleared or wooded. In this case, the government assesses and taxes land and property at a set rate according to its market value. If Farmer Brown's land were worth more than Farmer Jones's land, Farmer Brown would pay more property taxes on that land. The tax rate, however, would be uniform throughout the state or locality. Personal work habits would not factor into the land's worth.

EQUAL PROTECTION AND TAXATION

Once governing bodies establish a revenue source, for example, in property taxes at a uniform rate and under strict state constitution language, they must decide how to distribute that revenue to school districts. The Fourteenth Amendment provides guidance in how to apply these laws and regulations. The Fourteenth Amendment, ratified in 1868, reads as follows:

> Section 1. All persons born or naturalized in the United States and subject to the jurisdiction thereof, are citizens of the United States and of the State wherein they reside. No State shall make or enforce any law which shall abridge the privileges or immunities of citizens of the United States; nor shall any State deprive any person of life, liberty, or property, without due process of law; nor deny to any person within its jurisdiction the equal protection of the laws.

> Section 5. The Congress shall have power to enforce, by appropriate legislation, the provisions of this article.

The Civil War had ended 3 years earlier, and the country was trying to decide how to legally and civilly accommodate the newly freed slaves. Clearly, this amendment attempted to legislate civil rights following the war.

The Fourteenth Amendment's ramifications, however, were very far-reaching, affecting law to this day.

The Supreme Court took a leading role in defining "equal protection" of state taxation issues.[20] In 1890 the Supreme Court described the equal protection clause as a limitation on state revenue. Here the Court determined that the equal protection clause established a minimum standard of uniformity to which state legislation must adhere. The Court devised a "test" to determine the constitutionality of state taxation. As stated by Justice Jackson,

> Equal protection does not require identity of treatment. It only requires that classification rest on real and not feigned differences, that the distinction have some relevance to the purpose for which the classification is made, and the different treatment be not so disparate, relative to the difference in classification, as to be wholly arbitrary.[21]

The Court ruled that states required a credible rationale for spending collected tax dollars differently for different groups of people. In other words, once a state has collected taxes, if it spent the monies differently for different groups of people, the state must make a good faith effort to link those spending differences to a legitimate purpose for which they were raised. After this ruling, most states provided language in their state constitutions regarding equal protection provisions for their citizens.

Moving ahead in time, the Civil Rights Act of 1964 contained groundbreaking language regarding race and discrimination under equal protection auspices.[22] This time, the law linked the equal protection clause to federal spending. In 1965 Congress wrote that education was a constitutionally protected right of all citizens that should be provided to all citizens on equal terms. Following that logic, if a state gave fewer dollars to poor school districts, the state denied those children equal protection under the law.[23] Because the Supreme Court had already ruled that it was unreasonable to classify people on the basis of poverty, occupation, or home site, it held that a state could not base educational quality on a state or local taxing system where a locality's wealth determined the education level.[24]

---

[20]*Bell's Gap Railroad Co. v. Pennsylvania*, 134 U.S. 232, 10S.Ct533 (1890).

[21]Ibid.

[22]Notice that the Civil Rights Act of 1964 was 10 years after *Brown v. Board of Education*.

[23]See "Is Denial of Equal Educational Opportunity Constitutional?" *Administrator's Notebook* 13, 6, February 1965.

[24]See *Griffin v. Illinois*, 351 U.S. 12, 76 S.Ct. 585 (1956); and *Baker v. Carr*, 369 U.S. 186, 82 S.Ct. 691 (1962).

Following this logic and legislation, plaintiffs litigated two court cases under the Fourteenth Amendment's Equal Protection Clause and education spending: *McInnis v. Shapiro,* in Illinois, and *Burruss v. Wilkerson,* in Virginia.[25] Both cases argued that education was a fundamental right and a state responsibility. Both cases challenged the constitutionality of state education spending across the various school districts under the Equal Protection clause, citing large disparities in the districts' ability to fund education within their respective states. This funding disparity resulted in wealthy school districts spending more to meet student needs than did poorer districts that had greater educational need than the affluent districts. They both argued that spending was based on local wealth and not on educational need.

The appellate court affirmed the lower courts' rulings against the parents and for the existing funding practices in Illinois and Virginia, saying that the Fourteenth Amendment did not require equal expenditures. Moreover, the plaintiffs could not define a court-requested reasonable standard to assess and measure educational need. At that time, little consensus or research existed to answer the court's questions about measuring need. Because the court could not address these ideas concerning educational need, it refused to declare the states' finance systems to be unconstitutional. In *McInnis,* the court stated that there were "no discoverable and manageable standards by which a court can determine when the Constitution is satisfied and when it is violated."[26] The U.S. Supreme Court affirmed both cases without offering an opinion or statement. This vagueness left many legal and finance scholars unclear about the Court's rationale in the decisions.

Soon after these two cases, a California Supreme Court case challenged the California school funding formula in *Serrano v. Priest.*[27] Here, the court first determined that education was a fundamental interest. Second, it determined that the California funding model's basic state aid did tend to equalize among the disparate school districts. Third, the court determined that the state funding model generated combined state and local funds in such a manner that it created substantial disparities in school revenue—proportional to the property wealth of the individual school. The court found property wealth to be a suspect classification. In other words,

---

[25]See *McInnis v. Shapiro,* 293 F.Supp. 327 (N.D.III.1968) affirmed sub nom; *McInnis v. Ogilvie,* 394 U.S., 89 S.Ct. 1197 (1969); and *Burruss v. Wilkerson,* 310 F.Supp. 572 (W.D. Va.1069), affirmed 397 U.S. 44, 90 S.Ct. 812 (1970).

[26]*McInnis v. Shapiro,* op. cit.

[27]*Serrano v. Priest,* 5 Cal.3d 584, 96 Cal.Rptr. 601, 487 P.2d 1241 (1971), appeal after remand, 18 Cal.3d 728, 135 Cal.Rptr.345, 557 P.2d 929 (1976), cert. Denied, 432 U.S. 907, 97 S.Ct.2951 (1977).

when a group of people is treated unequally without a compelling reason, that group of people may be identified as a suspect classification.

The law remained mostly silent on the issue of race until the *Brown v. Board of Education of Topeka Kansas* decision in 1954.[28] Brown made race a suspect classification. In *Serrano v. Priest,* the Supreme Court ruled that the California funding model gave a greater share of funding to the wealthier school districts and less money to the poorer districts. The Court stated that the funding model discriminated against people with lower property values and determined that property wealth was a suspect classification. After careful deliberation, the Court declared the California funding model to be unconstitutional under the Equal Protection clause.

These school funding cases prepared the way for the *San Antonio Independent School District v. Rodriguez* case—perhaps the most famous Supreme Court school finance litigation.[29] Following the logic and ruling of *Serrano v. Priest,* a Texas court concluded that the Texas finance model denied equal protection of the law to the plaintiffs. Several Mexican American parents from the Edgewood Independent School District sued regarding the Texas education funding system. The plaintiffs argued that the Texas education funding model made educational quality a function of the local property tax base and that state funding was insufficient to correct the inherent inequalities.

The three-judge panel declared that education is a state function and that the quality of education should not be determined by the locality's wealth but by the state's overall wealth. The panel of judges determined that the Texas funding model assumed incorrectly that property wealth in the school districts was sufficiently equal to allow for comparable spending throughout the state. The Texas Supreme Court then declared the Texas model of education funding unconstitutional under the Equal Protection clause. The panel's ruling meant that the quality of education should not be based on a district's wealth. Instead, it should be based on the state's wealth.

The U.S. Supreme Court overturned the three-judge panel's ruling. On appeal, in 1973, the U.S. Supreme Court heard the *Rodriguez* arguments and decided that the Texas funding formula's wide disparities did not violate the Fourteenth Amendment's Equal Protection clause. It reversed the lower court decision and allowed the Texas funding model to stay as it had been. Justice Powell wrote that education could not be considered a fundamental right as had been assumed from the *Brown v. Board of Education*

---

[28]*Brown v. Board of Education of Topeka,* 347 U.S. 483, 74 S. Ct. 686 (1954).

[29]*San Antonio Independent School District v. Rodriguez,* 411 U.S. 1, 93 S.Ct. 1278, rehearing denied, 411 U.S. 959, 93 S.Ct. 1919 (1973).

case.[30] For that reason, the case did not warrant "strict scrutiny" in its review. The Court would defer to the legislatures' wisdom in such matters. For all intents and purposes, litigation for school finance reform under the Equal Protection clause umbrella ended with *Rodriguez.*

STANDARDS OF EQUAL PROTECTION

How do courts rule whether a government's different treatment of individuals is constitutional? How do courts decide if government actions that treat individuals differently for any reason violate the Equal Protection clause? Clearly, people can be treated differently under the law.

Over time, judicial reasoning has developed a rationale regarding litigating cases under the Equal Protection clause. This rationale includes three conditions.[31] First, the action must affect a suspect discrete class of deprived persons. Second, the actions must deny benefits to these deprived individuals that are available to others. Third, the act of denial must adversely affect a fundamental right. The U.S. Supreme Court ruled that these three conditions were not present in *Rodriguez,* allowing the Court to rule that the Texas funding system was constitutional.

Clearly, the government can act in ways that treat people differently. What tests do the courts use to determine the constitutionality of the government's action that treats individuals differently? Three judicial tests exist to answer this question: the rational relationship test, the intermediate test, and the strict scrutiny test.

The Rational Relationship Test

This test asks if the government had a rational reason for treating individuals differently that does not violate the Constitution. Using this test, the court recognizes that it has no greater institutional capability to assess the different treatment's "reasonableness" than the legislative body that wrote the law authorizing it. The court asks only if a reasonable basis exists for the different treatment that bears a sensible relationship to why people are receiving different treatment.

---

[30]*San Antonio Independent School District v. Rodriguez,* 411 U.S. 1, 93 S.Ct. 1278 (1973).

[31]K. Alexander and R. Salmon, *Public School Finance* (Needham Heights, MA: Allyn and Bacon, 1995), 31.

With the rational relationship test, the court usually upholds the state's action. The court is not looking for scientific data to substantiate the claim. They are looking only for a rational relationship between the state's action and the reason for taking it. Here, the court almost always presumes that the government's action is constitutional.

For example, under increasing pressure to provide more state funds to high poverty school districts, a state adopts a new equalization funding formula for distributing monies to the various school districts so that the poorer districts get more state monies than they had in the past. The new action also provides for fewer state dollars to the richer school districts than they had received in the past. Plaintiffs, unsatisfied that the legislation goes far enough, challenge the state's new funding formula in court as unconstitutional under the Equal Protection clause. They argue that the funding model continues to allow for an excessive disparity in per pupil spending for education. Moreover, they maintain that the funding model does not equalize spending sufficiently to provide enough funding for the state's poorest school districts.

Under the rational relationship test, the court would ask the state to explain its rationale for establishing the funding formula in the manner it did. Using the rational relationship test, the court accepts that the judicial body does not have the knowledge, the means, or the authority to understand or develop a superior funding model as long as the state has a rational explanation for taking the action it did.[32] As long as the state has a logical reason or explanation for its actions, the court would find the funding formula is constitutional because the state had a sensible explanation for its action.

The Intermediate Test

The second test "ratchets up" the government's reasoning for treating individuals differently. This test does not presume constitutionality. Instead of requiring the state's treatment to be based solely on a rational relationship or explanation, the court asks for evidence of some substantial government interest for taking the action. Courts have applied this test to sex discrimination cases and used it to overturn many policies that treated women differently from men.[33] The intermediate test has also been used in Equal Protection clause cases.

---

[32]*McInnis v. Shapiro,* 310 F. Supp. 572 (W.D.Va.1969), affirmed, 397 U.S. 44, 90 S.Ct. 812 (1970).

[33]Allan Odden and Lawrence Picus, *School Finance: A Policy Perspective,* 3rd ed. (Boston, MA: McGraw-Hill, 2004), 30.

Applying the intermediate test, the court would review the state's rationale for the action, for example, in implementing the new funding formula described in the rational relationship test. The court would provide more inquiry about whether or not the state's action advances a substantial government concern. If the funding formula shows a large portion of monies flowing from wealthy school districts to poorer ones, the state will have to prove that this new funding formula is meeting an important state interest.

Using the intermediate test, courts examine the state's action more closely than in the rational relationship test. If the courts are to uphold it, the state must give evidence of a greater level of government interest in taking a particular action that treats individuals differently. The intermediate test is not as stringent, however, as the third test, strict scrutiny.

The Strict Scrutiny Test

Using the strict scrutiny test, the government assumes the greatest burden for justifying treating individuals differently. At this highest level of judicial analysis, the government must show a compelling or overriding state interest in treating individuals differently; and the government must prove that no less discriminatory manner exists to accomplish this prevailing interest.

Courts only invoke strict scrutiny in two circumstances: (a) when it affects a fundamental right and (b) when the government action creates a suspect classification of individuals. In strict scrutiny, unlike the rational relationship test, the court will not defer to the legislative body's ability or understanding for taking the action. The *Rodriguez* case from Texas referred to these terms. In that case, the Supreme Court determined that education was not a fundamental right and did not warrant strict scrutiny review.

Because the courts invoke strict scrutiny when cases affect fundamental rights or when the government creates a suspect classification of individuals, understanding these terms will be helpful.

Fundamental Rights   The first instance invoking strict scrutiny involves fundamental rights—or *fundamentality*. Fundamental rights are those civil liberties that the U.S. Constitution guarantees under the Equal Protection clause. Briefly, these are the rights contained in the Bill of Rights: freedom of speech, freedom of the press, the right to substantive and procedural due process, and others. Denying fundamental rights requires a higher and stricter level of judicial examination.

Suspect Classification   The second case involving strict scrutiny is when a government's action creates a suspect classification of individuals. The

Constitution prohibits unequal treatment of individuals under the law based on different classifications. Religion is one of these classifications. The Constitution is silent on some other classifications.

For example, the 1954 U.S. Supreme Court decision, *Brown v. Board of Education,* made race a suspect classification. The *Brown* ruling on school segregation found that state laws denied equal protection under the law to a group of people. The laws, known as "separate but equal" provisions, were inherently *un*equal. With the *Brown* decision, unequal protection under the law based on race as a suspect classification became illegal. The Civil Rights Act of 1964 added other suspect classifications.

In another strict scrutiny example, if a state's current school funding formula did not provide sufficient money for the poorest school districts, the government would have to withstand strict scrutiny by the courts to allow the funding formula to stand. Not deferring to any other branch of government's decision, the court would examine the formula and require the government to plainly demonstrate that keeping the old formula achieves a compelling state interest to such a degree that by doing so it justifies the limitation of fundamental rights.

Judicial Standards in Practice

These three judicial standards (rational relationship, intermediate, and strict scrutiny) affected two cases previously reviewed—*Serrano* and *Rodriguez.* In *Serrano v. Priest,* the California Supreme Court examined the school finance issue carefully. They applied the strict scrutiny standard in evaluating the situation for two reasons. First, the state supreme court determined that education was a *fundamental right* based on judicial language in the 1954 *Brown v. Board of Education* case. Second, the California Supreme Court also decided that property wealth created a *suspect classification* of individuals. Applying the strict scrutiny standard, the court found the California finance model to be unconstitutional. In *San Antonio Independent School District v. Rodriguez,* the Texas court arrived at the same conclusion.

When this issue came to the United States Supreme Court by way of the *Rodriguez* case, however, the highest court did not see the issues in the same light. The U.S. Supreme Court reversed the *Rodriguez* decision. Justice Powell, writing for the Court majority, maintained that education was not a fundamental right afforded by the Constitution under the Equal Protection clause as the Texas Supreme Court presumed from *Brown*. Powell further said that "within the limits of rationality the legislature's efforts to tackle the problems should be entitled to respect."[34] This perspective forced the Court to revert to a lower standard for examining the case—the rational relationship test instead of strict scrutiny.

STATE CONSTITUTIONAL LANGUAGE AND SCHOOL FINANCE

Each state constitution has language that frames how it will treat education. This language is generally known as the state's education clause. The state's education clause wording is important philosophically as well as legally. In fact, state education clauses have been the basis for many legal challenges to state school finance models. The constitutional wording has been responsible for an entire state redesigning how its schools operate and receive funding. In that light, state constitutional wording is extremely important.

Historically, many New England states use the word "cherish" in their education clauses. By referencing this as the "cherish clause," legislators affirmed education's value to society and to those who govern them. By historical precedent and legal wording, education is important to the civic good.[35]

Likewise, states use various adjectives in their constitutions' education clauses that suggest the framers' intentions and may have an impact on how courts determine legal challenges. Some states describe education as a "system." Other states use words such as "effective," "thorough," or "uniform" to describe their education organization. In 1989 the Kentucky Supreme Court referenced the words "efficient system of common schools" in its state constitution's education clause as a basis to invalidate the entire public school structure.[36]

In the *Rose* case, Chief Justice Stephens wrote that the Kentucky General Assembly had fallen short of its responsibility to provide for an efficient system of common schools. He wrote that the common schools

---

[34]*San Antonio Independent School District v. Rodriguez*, 411 U.S. 1, 93 S.Ct. 1278 (1973).

[35]Massachusetts enacts the idea of "cherish" in its constitution more than most other states. The Massachusetts Constitution contains the following statement under the duties of the legislators and magistrates. ". . . it shall be the duty of legislatures and magistrates, in all future periods of this commonwealth, to cherish the interests of literature and the sciences, and all seminaries of them; especially the university of Cambridge, public schools and grammar schools in the towns . . ." Massachusetts Constitution, Part 2, Chapter V, Subsection 11: The Encouragement of Literature, Etc.

[36]*Rose v. The Council for Better Education, Inc.*, 790 S.W.2d 186 (1989).

system in Kentucky was constitutionally deficient and that the General Assembly was required to re-create and reestablish a system of common schools in conjunction with the parameters the Court outlined.[37]

In this instance, the word "efficient" in the state constitution affected a legal decision and an entire state's education system. The resulting legislation is known as the Kentucky Education Reform Act, or KERA. In defining "efficient," Chief Justice Stephens referenced earlier discussions that would serve as the basis for "efficient." He writes,

> The fundamental mandate of the Constitution and Statutes of Kentucky is that there shall be equality and that all public schools shall be nonpartisan and nonsectarian. Uniformity does not require equal classification but it does demand that there shall be a substantially uniform system and equal school facilities without discrimination as between different sections of a district or a county.[38]

Justice Stephens's discussion about efficient and equality actually addresses a concept called *equity*. Education does not strive for equality. As educators we do not treat all of our clients in the same manner. Instead, educators provide the services students need. For example, no effective fourth grade teacher would say that he or she were going to teach the unit on "Skin, Muscles, and Bones" even if all the students already knew all the material. That would be a waste of time. Similarly, providing all students with one hour of reading instruction each day may not be what everyone needs. Some may require more, and others may have need of less. Equity addresses the means to bring all students to high achievement levels by meeting different learning needs in ways that promote success for each student.

EQUITY AND ADEQUACY

Ironically, equality, although an important legal issue, is not a school finance issue. With wide diversity regarding students' learning needs, educational and cultural backgrounds, and community resources to support schooling, students should not be treated equally. Each need requires a different

---

[37]For more on this, research various state constitutional language provisions and relative fiscal state effort to determine whether stronger constitutional language is associated with increased fiscal effort for schools.

[38]Cited in K. Alexander and D. Alexander, *American Public School Law*, 5th ed. (Belmont, CA: Wadsworth, 2001), 39–40.

treatment to support students' success. Different treatments have dissimilar costs. It would be neither professional nor ethical to instruct the student with severe learning disabilities in a resource class with the same professional practices as the honors student in an Advanced Placement classroom. Instead, school finance focuses on equity and adequacy. Equity involves giving students what they need to be successful. Adequacy involves giving students enough of what they need to be successful.

Equity in school finance comes in two forms—horizontal and vertical equity. Horizontal equity states that people who are alike should receive equal funding shares. People who are equal should receive equal treatment. In other words, students on one side of a county should have roughly the same student-teacher ratios, roughly the same resources, and similar funding as the students on the county's opposite end. Likewise, the high schools on the wealthy side of the town or city should receive the same level of resources as the high schools on the poorer side of town.

Vertical equity states that the treatment of unequals requires appropriate unequal treatment. Not everyone is equal, so everyone should not be treated equally. For instance, most people accept that a special needs classroom is more expensive to operate than a regular classroom. Lower student-teacher ratios and teaching assistant availability increase the cost. A special needs student and a regular needs student should be treated differently—their learning needs require different teaching styles and education costs.

In this case unequal treatment should exist. These cost differentials, however, should be relatively consistent throughout the school system. Likewise, the self-contained classrooms for emotionally disturbed students on the north and west ends of the town should have the same basic resources as their counterparts on the south and east sides of town. In short, once a school district identifies a learning need requiring unequal resources, these programs must be funded at a consistent level throughout the district. Treating unequals equally is a most unfair thing to do.

In sum, equity involves giving people what they need to succeed. This concept can be quantified and measured objectively. Adequacy, however, involves providing *sufficient* funding for the education program. This concept is less neutral and more subjective than the equity issue. Both equity and adequacy, nevertheless, have profound school finance implications.[39]

A major school finance litigation case dealing with state constitutional language and school finance involved equity. In Kentucky the *Rose v. The Council for Better Education, Inc.* plaintiffs filed challenges asserting that

---

[39]Equity and adequacy are discussed more fully in Chapter 8.

the state's education provisions were not in line with the state's constitutional language. The court agreed and overturned Kentucky's entire education system. This decision required the General Assembly to develop a new schooling organization that would receive constitutional approval and adequate funds. "Adequate" school funding in the courts as a school finance issue started here. In fact, Chief Justice Stephens's written opinion used the word "adequate" in one form or another at least 14 times. He penned the word "sufficient" at least 7 times.[40]

Later cases, continuing through the present, increasingly deal with "adequacy." In reviewing the "adequate" education litigation, four goals consistently appear: (1) prepare students to be citizens and economic participants in a democratic society; (2) relate to contemporary, not archaic educational needs; (3) anchor educational standards to more than a minimal level; and (4) focus on providing opportunity rather than outcome.[41]

The adequacy issue is perhaps one of the major sources of education finance reform. Of the 31 lawsuits involving the issue of adequacy, 15 have dates of 2000 or later. Of those 31 cases, courts found 20 state funding formulae to be unconstitutional. In these 31 cases, verdicts required substantial additional state funding for programs or facilities. Chapter 8 deals extensively with the concepts of equity and adequacy.

VOUCHERS, TUITION TAX CREDITS, AND CHARTER SCHOOLS

Vouchers, tuition tax credits, and charter schools are essentially political issues that involve parents' and taxpayers' dissatisfaction with the current public school system and their desire for the state to pay for some alternative, preferred form of education. Basically, these issues reflect parents' and politicians' desire for increased public school choice.

Vouchers are receipts or documents that the state issues that can be used to pay tuition at another school. Funds generally involve state monies that parents can use at public or private schools. In 2002 the United States Supreme Court ruled that vouchers could be used to pay for tuition at private religious schools.

---

[40]*Rose v. The Council for Better Education, Inc.*

[41]M. A. Rebell, "Education Adequacy, Democracy, and the Courts," in *Achieving High Educational Standards for All: Conference Summary*, T. Ready, C. Edley, and C. E. Snow, eds. (Washington, DC: National Academy Press, 2002), 218–268.

Tuition tax credits permit parents who send their children to nonpublic schools to reduce their tax liability by taking deductions for private school tuition and related expenses from their income taxes.

Charter schools are alternative schools whose operation is defined in the state constitution. Usually specialty schools, charter schools operate with fewer state restrictions and constraints than regular public schools. The charter, or state contract, stipulates how the school will function and assess student achievement. If the school does not keep the charter's measures, the state may revoke the charter.

History of Alternative Schools

Dissatisfaction with the direction of public schools and the attempt to fund or operate alternative schools, rather than being a new agenda, has a lengthy history.

> By 1750 the change in religious thinking had become quite marked. . . . New secular interests began to take the place of religion as the chief topic of thought and conversation. Secular books began to dispute the earlier monopoly of the Bible. . . . These changes manifested themselves in many ways in the matter of education. . . . New textbooks, containing less of the gloomily religious than the *New England Primer,* and secular rather than religious matter, appeared and began to be used in the schools.[42]

This move to increased public school secularism affected both those who wanted to keep the past emphasis on the Bible and religious instruction and others who pressed for more progressive educational changes. By 1820 education had evolved from a concern "left largely to private individuals, churches, incorporated school societies, and such state schools for the children of the poor as might have been serviced by private or state funds" to a loosely organized school district public system of more secular interest.[43] Cubberley referred to this looming conflict as the Battle for Free State Schools.[44]

Not only did people who simply did not want to pay taxes for public schools join this controversy, but also conservative Protestant ministers entered the debate, arguing that public schools would injure religious schools' attendance, thereby reducing their influence and thus retarding the progress

---

[42]Ellwood Cubberley, *Public Education in the United States* (Boston: Houghton Mifflin, 1934), 59–63.

[43]Ibid., 111.

[44]Ibid., see chap. 6.

and welfare of the churches.[45] Clearly, conflict arose about the public schools' mission. Disagreement about school funding could not be far behind.

The Massachusetts Act of 1827 became the most significant event bringing the cultures of education for religion and secularism to the front. This act declared that School Committees should "never direct to be used or purchased in any of the town schools any school books which were calculated to favor the tenets of any particular sect of Christians."[46] As a result, for the first time in American public school history, some called the public schools "Godless."[47] Publications and sermons attacked the Massachusetts Secretary of the Board of Education, Horace Mann, asserting that the "increase in intemperance, crime, and juvenile depravity in the State was due to the 'Godless schools' they were supporting."[48]

Defending public schools' religious outlook, the *Princeton Review* wrote: "The people of each school district have the right to make the schools as religious as they please; and if they cannot agree they have the right severally of withdrawing their proper proportion of the public stock of funds."[49] In other words, if taxpayers did not agree with how the public schools were run, it was argued that they should be allowed to have that portion of school taxes returned so those funds could be used to provide an education more closely resembling parents' wishes.

Taking their stock of public funds and using the monies to establish schools more to their liking is essentially what contemporary vouchers, charter schools, and tuition tax credits advocates try to effect. Today's calls for tax credits were actually first referenced before 1850.

Vouchers

Parents can use a voucher to pay their child's tuition at an alternative school that the child would either choose to attend at parents' expense or not normally attend without the extra money required for enrollment fees and related costs. Vouchers are not new. In 1869 Vermont adopted a tuition statute trying to ensure that students in urban and rural school districts could receive a quality secondary education. In towns too small to support a local school, the state paid students' tuition to attend another

---

[45]Alexander and Alexander, *American Public School Law*, 6th ed., 159.

[46]Cubberley, *Public Education in the United States*, 233.

[47]Ibid., 233--234.

[48]Ibid., 234. Sound familiar?

[49]Ibid., 235, note 1.

public school or a private, nonsectarian school. This provision included sending students and Vermont monies to public schools outside Vermont. In 1961 the state legislature banned religious schools from receiving public voucher monies.

In 1903 Maine enacted legislation to provide all students a high school education. The state paid tuition to any schools the parents chose. As with Vermont, this voucher provision included paying tuition to schools outside of Maine. In 1980, however, the U.S. Department of Education enacted provisions to end tuition payments to attend parochial schools in towns where public high schools exist. In 1999 the Maine Supreme Court ruled in *Bagley v. Raymond* that the 1980 ban on religious schools is not unconstitutional.[50] At the same time the state court heard the *Bagley* case, federal court heard the same issue in *Strout v. Albanese*.[51] Both courts delivered the same opinion— the state could ban religious schools from receiving voucher funds.

More recently, Milton Friedman, a 20th century U.S. economist, made vouchers a topic of serious discussion.[52] He submitted that the public should pay for education but not administer schools. He advocated using tax dollars paying for schooling but providing a voucher system giving parents a certain sum each year to pay for approved schooling for their children. Public schools could compete for students in an open marketplace with private and parochial schools. By taking this action, Friedman suggests the states could provide parents with increased freedom of choice and increased school quality through competition while eliminating the public schools' educational monopoly.

In 1990 Milwaukee enacted a Parental Choice program. This legislation provided for up to 1% of the Milwaukee Public Schools' economically disadvantaged students to obtain a voucher for the state's share of public school costs to attend a participating nonsectarian private school. Five years later, the program for Milwaukee students was expanded to include participating religious schools. This action was challenged in *Jackson v. Benson* (1998).[53] The Wisconsin Supreme Court did not allow the program's expansion into religious schools but allowed the program to include nonsectarian schools.

---

[50]*Bagley v. Raymond School Department*, 728 A 2d 127 (ME, 1999).

[51]*Strout v. Albanese*, 178 F. 3d 57 (ME, 1999).

[52]See Milton Friedman, "The Role of Government in Education," in *Economics and the Public Interest*, Robert Solo, ed. (New Brunswick, NJ: Rutgers University Press, 1955).

[53]*Jackson v Benson*, 570 N.W. 2d 407 (Wis. App 1997, rev'd 578 N.W. 2d 602 (1998), cert. Denied 119 S.Ct. 466 (1998).

In 1997 the Wisconsin legislature expanded the school choice voucher program. On remand, a district court ruled it unconstitutional. Appealed to the Wisconsin Supreme Court in 1998, the court upheld publicly funded vouchers used to send students to private religious schools, stating it did not violate the Establishment clause. On further appeal, the United States Supreme Court declined to hear the case.

Similarly, in 1995, the Ohio state legislature enacted two educational assistance programs for parents of children in the struggling Cleveland Public Schools—tuition scholarships and tuition assistance grants. The voucher funds could be used to pay tuition at eligible private schools in the Cleveland Public School District area or at participating public schools in adjacent districts. In 1999 the Ohio State Supreme Court overturned the program on a technicality. An injunction stopped the overturn ruling. The case, *Simmons-Harris v. Zelman,* was appealed to the federal court, which ruled the program unconstitutional.[54]

On appeal to the Sixth Circuit Court of Appeals, a three-judge panel rejected the Ohio voucher plan, ruling that it violated the First Amendment separation of church and state provision. On appeal to the United States Supreme Court, the Court ruled the Cleveland voucher program constitutional, saying that it did not infringe on the separation of church and state. The 5–4 decision finally cleared a thick fog of legal opinion regarding vouchers to private religious schools.

In effect, the legal conflict has been resolved between parents who believed the Massachusetts schools had failed by becoming more secular in curriculum and pedagogy and the more progressive legal and educational writers of the early to mid-1800s. Public funds can pay tuition at private—even religious—schools. The philosophical discussion, however, will continue.

Tuition Tax Credits

As mentioned earlier, tuition tax credits and vouchers are closely associated. With tuition tax credits, instead of receiving a "chit" for tuition at an alternative school, parents receive a tax credit if they send their school-aged children to nonpublic schools. This reduces the parent's tax liability. At the national level, Senators Patrick Moynihan (NY) and Robert Packwood (OR) first proposed tuition tax credits. The Reagan and George H. W. Bush presidential administrations advocated tuition tax credits repeatedly and unsuccessfully.

---

[54]*Simmons-Harris v. Zelman,* 54 F. Supp. 2d 725 (N.D. Ohio 1999).

Tuition tax credits at the state level have a more interesting legal history. Minnesota passed a law in 1955, amended in 1976 and 1978, allowing state taxpayers to deduct certain expenses incurred in educating their children—regardless of the type of school attended. The deduction was limited to $500 per student in grades K–6 and $700 per student in grades 7–12.

In *Mueller v. Allen,* the United States Supreme Court ruled that state tax deductions (tuition tax credits) allowed to the parents of parochial school children did not violate the First Amendment's Establishment clause.[55] The court reasoned that because parents of both public and parochial school-children could receive the tax deduction, the law did not violate the First Amendment. Further, the deduction involved a state tax—not federal taxes.

Charter Schools

Charter schools gained in popularity during the 1990s as a school choice issue. As previously stated, charter schools are alternative schools whose operations are defined in the state constitution, and they operate with fewer state restrictions and constraints than regular public schools. The charter, or contract with the state, stipulates how the school will operate and what accountability measures will gauge student achievement. If the charter's measures fails to enact the contract, the state may revoke the charter.

The idea of charter schools as a vehicle to circumvent the prohibition against using public monies to support sectarian schools may have originated from a concept mentioned by Supreme Court Justice White in the *No. 1 v. Allen* (1968) case.[56] In this case, the Supreme Court found that loaning textbooks to parochial school students did not violate the First Amendment's Establishment clause. Basically, the Court decision required local school boards to purchase textbooks and lend them without charge to students residing within that district who attended private schools that complied with compulsory attendance laws in grades 7–12. In this case, Justice White stated that the parochial schools did an acceptable job of providing a secular education to students. Some speculate that charter school advocates believed it was easier to evade the constitutional proscription against using public funds to support religious education by suggesting that the parochial schools' secular aspects were so substantial that they justified receiving public funds.[57]

---

[55]*Mueller v. Allen,* 463 U.S. 388, 103 S.Ct. 3062 (1983).

[56]Alexander and Alexander, *American Public School Law,* 6th ed., 43. See *Board of Education of Central School District No. 1 v. Allen,* 392 U.S. 236, 88 S.Ct. 1923 (1968).

[57]Alexander and Alexander, *American Public School Law,* 6th ed., 44.

Under the Clinton administration, the charter school concept changed dramatically. Clinton's education advisers proposed that charter schools should exist as public schools and not as private or parochial schools. In 1994 federal legislation redefined charter schools providing that they have the following characteristics: [58]

- Exempted from state and local regulations that inhibit flexible management;
- Operated under public supervision and direction;
- Designed with specific educational objectives;
- Nonsectarian in programs, admissions, policies, employment practices;
- Not affiliated with a sectarian school or a religious institution;
- Free of tuition and fees;
- In compliance with federal civil rights legislation;
- Open to admission of students by lottery;
- In compliance with federal and state financial audit requirements;
- In compliance with federal, state, and local health and safety requirements; and
- Operated in compliance with State law.

In 1993 Michigan challenged the charter school concept.[59] Michigan adopted a charter schools act with provisions similar to the 1994 federal legislation. The Michigan State Supreme Court had to decide if the charter schools act was constitutional and if charter schools constituted aid to religious schools. In 1994 the trial court declared Michigan's charter school act unconstitutional. The court of appeals affirmed the lower court's ruling.

After some lawmaking wrangling by the Michigan legislature and subsequent judicial review, the Michigan State Supreme Court held that since the legislature declared the charter schools to be public schools, they were subject to the State Board of Education's leadership and supervision. In that light, charter schools must comply with all applicable laws, and the State Board maintains control as evidenced by authorizing funding for some and not others. Further, the Supreme Court held that the Michigan Charter School Act did not constitute state aid to religious schools.

School finance's legal aspects are complicated. One chapter is insufficient to provide all the necessary information to fully understand all the issues involved. This chapter introduced you to the complex history of school finance and the direction toward which this issue may be headed.

---

[58]20 U.S.C.A. Section 8061 to Section 8066.

[59]*Council of Organizations of Others for Education about Parochiaid v. Governor,* 455 Mich. 557, 566 N.W. 2d 208 (1997).

SUMMARY

Education finance is arguably a critical issue facing states and the federal government. Although education is a state responsibility, the federal government has a lengthy precedent of providing the states with education programs and funds. Each state is responsible for setting up an educational system and may pass laws toward that end as long as they do not conflict with its own state or the federal constitution.

The courts can intervene only if a party with legal standing raises a challenge based on a legitimate controversy concerning the state's practice and the state or federal constitution or its application. Increasingly, federal courts are ruling against states in cases involving state education funding formulae.

The federal government can enter the states' education purview only when (1) states agree to accept federal grants provided under Congress's General Welfare clause; (2) Congress authorizes standards and regulations within the Commerce clause; or (3) courts constrain state actions enforcing federal constitutional provisions protecting individual rights and freedoms.

School revenue from federal, state, and local governments comes from taxes. The federal government contributes, on average, about 10% of the total United States education spending. By accepting federal funds, states and localities surrender some of their power to operate their schools as they choose. States may tax what they wish as long as it does not conflict with federal provisions or with the state's constitution. Not all states tax the same way to support public schools. School districts have no inherent capacity to tax unless the state's constitutional language specifically permits such taxing authority.

Legal interpretation of the Equal Protection clause places a limitation on state revenue, requiring a minimum uniform standard and a credible rationale for spending collected tax dollars differently for different groups of people. The Civil Rights Act of 1964 linked the Equal Protection clause to federal spending. In 1965 Congress said education was a constitutionally protected right to be provided to all citizens on equal terms; states that gave fewer dollars for poor school districts denied those children equal protection under the law. Cases including *McInnis*, *Burruss*, *Serrano*, and *Rodriguez* challenged the constitutionality of state education spending under the Equal Protection clause.

Judicial rationale has developed a three-pronged test to decide Equal Protection clause cases: The action must have an impact on a suspect discrete class of deprived Persons; the actions must deny benefits to these deprived individuals that are available to others; and the act of denial must adversely affect a fundamental right. Likewise, courts use three tests to determine the constitutionality of government actions when it treats individuals differently: the rational relationship test, the intermediate test, and the strict scrutiny test. Each test requires an increasingly greater degree of evidence to justify different treatment.

Each state constitution has language describing its education such as "uniform," "efficient," or "effective"—the state's education clause—that has underpinned many legal challenges to state school finance models. Likewise, school finance equity and adequacy are becoming grounds for challenging school funding practices.

Finally, vouchers, tuition tax credits, and charter schools are political issues involving parents' and taxpayers' dissatisfaction with the current public school system and their desire for the state to pay for a preferred, alternative education. Voucher, tuition tax credit, and charter school cases in several states have ruled that public funds can pay tuition at private—even religious—schools.

CONCLUSION

Through national legislation and judicial proceedings, school funding issues have given the federal government entree into the states' education arena, effecting changes from the outside. Some school finance issues under federal scrutiny remain subject to serious debate and litigation, but federal initiatives against state practices have also protected citizens against constitutional violations of language or human rights.

CASE STUDY

You are the education consultant on the legal team that has successfully argued and won the *Serrano v. Priest* California court case. You are now working with the same legal team in the *San Antonio ISD v. Rodriguez* court case in Texas. You believe that the U.S. Supreme Court will overturn the Texas Supreme Court's decision that declared the Texas model of education funding unconstitutional under the Equal Protection clause unless you can make a more compelling case. If the U.S. Supreme Court overturns the state supreme court, this means that the quality of education should not be based on a state's wealth. Instead, education funding should be based on the locality's wealth. How will you legally argue to make a better case that education should be based on the overall wealth capacity of the state rather than the disparate wealth of localities?

CHAPTER QUESTIONS

1. What exactly does the education clause say in your state constitution? Do you believe that the intent of the clause is in effect in your state's public school system? Explain your answer.
2. If there have been court cases dealing with finance over the last 10 years in your state, explain what they were about and what their final impact was on schools.
3. Explain your state's position on vouchers, charter schools, and tuition tax credits. If they exist in your state, explain how they are being implemented. Has there been resistance or support for these concepts? Explain your answer.
4. How has the state changed its funding of public education in your state over the last 20 years? How would you design a better system of funding public schools? Defend your answer.
5. What federal funding changes have happened in your state since implementation of the No Child Left Behind legislation of 2001? Has the funding been adequate for the requirements? Explain and justify your answer.

SCHOOL FINANCE AS INVESTMENT IN HUMAN CAPITAL

FOCUS QUESTIONS

1. How does Adam Smith's idea about human capital in the *Wealth of Nations* affect the practice of education?

2. How does an increased level of education for the general public contribute to the overall economy of the United States?

3. How do low levels of education hurt the U.S. economy and individual citizens?

4. How can increased levels of education decrease expenditures for social service programs?

Education is a significant investment in human capital that has clear benefits for the individual, the economy, and society at large. Increased levels of education result in higher incomes, increased taxes, increased participation in the arts, decreased social service costs, and decreased levels of childbirth complications. Instead of thinking of education as a cost to taxpayers, think of education as a long-term investment that pays significant dividends.

EDUCATION AS AN INVESTMENT IN HUMAN CAPITAL

The idea that educating everyone would benefit the community is relatively new. For much of our history, the idea that educating everyone to his or her potential could enhance community well-being represented thinking "outside the box." To be sure, the founding fathers saw education as an important component of their new form of government. Few beyond those initial patriots, however, had the vision to believe that educating all citizens would benefit the society's overall economy, safety, and quality of life. Classical economists considered labor as one of three factors of production—in addition to land and capital—but they viewed workers as a constant, essential but less important. For the most part, local and state government limited education to the elite. Labor, the working classes and the poor, remained largely under- and uneducated.

Early civilizations valued sheer numbers of people for protection, hunting, and gathering. Developing societies, however, prized individuals for what and how well—and later for how much—they could produce. Brick masons and arrow smiths, carpenters and wheat grinders earned community respect for the usefulness, quality, and quantity of their goods. Later, investing in the fixed capital of making bricks, arrows, and gristmills became a primary economic concern. Until Theodore W. Schultz's 1960s work on investment in human capital gained popular acceptance, society had valued labor primarily for its physical rather than its intellectual attributes.[1]

Adam Smith's *The Wealth of Nations* (1776) included human capital in the fixed capital equipment of manufacturing goods.[2] He discussed society members' acquired abilities as part of the predetermined resources. A revolutionary concept for the time, this belief followed naturally from the founding fathers' discussions about a literate society's importance to their democratic republic government. Smith may have adopted the founding fathers' vision for an educated general public. Given his era, however, Smith viewed this investment in human capital in a limited way, only as providing workers with vocational training related to production. His original concept, however, provided an early first step toward the larger context of educated workers' contributions to the economy and to society at large.

It took 200 years to advance the human capital concept to its present maturity. Addressing the broader intellectual and social perspective, Theodore

---

[1]Theodore W. Schultz, "Investment in Human Capital," *American Economic Review* 51, March 1961, 1–17.

[2]Adam Smith, *The Wealth of Nations*, rev. ed. (New York: Modern Library, 1937).

Schultz's 20th-century work articulated the belief that investing in the goods-and-services producers' minds held economic worth for the larger community.[3] His theory of investing in human capital won the 1979 Nobel Prize for Economic Science and became the basis for considering investment in education as a significant contributor to a society's economic development. Using this premise, the Organization for Economic Cooperation and Development (OECD) and the World Bank have quantified the predominant impact of investing in human capital. These and other findings clearly show that public investment in education explains the sustained development of many countries and the lack of economic, political, and social progress in others.[4]

Today, workforce managers realize that an educated populace makes better employees. Moreover, an educated citizenry has a substantial positive impact on society. More than any other social investment, education raises the standard of living by increasing employability and disposable income and reducing community social service costs, thereby increasing revenue to support even more education—creating a dynamic synergy. In addition, a good public education system is a major drawing card for local business development and expansion. Furthermore, education enhances the quality of life, not just for the educated individuals but for the entire community as well.

This chapter presents convincing data to support the belief that public education increases a community's economic well-being, safety, and overall quality of life as expressed by the following factors:

- Earning potential
- Employability
- Voting rates
- Percent of individuals with health insurance
- Charitable contributions
- Leisure and cultural activity participation
- Childbirth and prenatal issues
- Incarceration rates
- Crime rates

---

[3]Schultz, "Investment in Human Capital."

[4]The World Bank Report, *World Development Report, 1991, The Challenge of Development* (Oxford: World Bank and Oxford University Press, 1991), credits education for economic growth. In "Where Tigers Breed: A Survey of Asia's Emerging Technologies," *Economist* 321 (7733), 1991, the *Economist* also credited education with economic growth. Many of the reports written in the *Economist* making such statements were reported, however, before the Pacific Rim's economic collapse.

Education is a community's investment in its own best interest. Although taxes fund education as a public service, not every educational leader or taxpayer sees the "big picture." Educational leaders must be able to articulate to all stakeholders—teachers and staff, parents, business, and the community—that education's investment in human capital provides substantial paybacks for the individual, the locality, the state, and the nation. This chapter provides educational leaders with the data to argue convincingly for investment in education by detailing the relationship between education and standard of living in our communities. The question then becomes "How do we pay for this human capital investment and increased living standard?"

Generally, most people view education favorably, but they regard taxes somewhat less favorably. Unless taxpayers have children or grandchildren currently enrolled in public schools, many cannot see how paying monies to support public education benefits them directly. Using the following data, an educational leader can assure stakeholders of the importance of investing in education.

EDUCATION CONTRIBUTES TO EARNING POTENTIAL

Education is a major contributor to our economy's financial health. As a rule, citizens with higher levels of educational achievement earn more money, give more tax dollars to support government services (including funding schools), add more to the general consumer economy to enhance their lifestyles, and draw fewer resources from society than do those with less education.

Education, therefore, has a direct impact on our personal living standard by influencing how much people earn. Figure 4.1 shows that for those ages 25 and over, employed full time, relative yearly mean earnings increase with education. These are individuals who have likely completed their formal schooling and have spent several years in the workforce. Higher levels of education are associated with greater individual worker's earnings.

Although disparities exist between men's and women's earnings, it is clear that education level is closely associated with increased income. An individual with a bachelor's degree, on average, will earn annually about two and one half times the income of a high school dropout. Higher level degrees predict even higher income levels.

When these earning differences compound over a working lifetime, the effects of education become even more pronounced. Assume that these

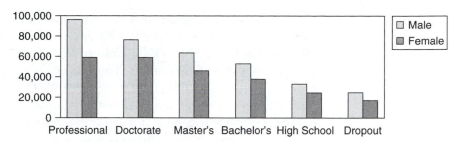

FIGURE 4.1

Mean Earnings per Person in the United States, Age 25 and Over, in Full-Time Employment, 2000

Source: U.S. Department of Commerce, Bureau of the Census, Current Population Reports, Series P-60, "Money Income of Households, Families, and Persons in the United States," "Income, Poverty, and Valuation of Noncash Benefits," various years; and Series P-60, "Money Income in the United States," various years. (Prepared April 2001.)

dollar figures remain constant and that two 25-year-olds work for 40 years before retiring. High school dropouts, earning approximately $20,000 per year, will make $800,000 over their working life. If they pay a federal tax rate of 10% of those funds, they will have contributed $80,000 in federal taxes.[5] This leaves them with an income minus federal taxes of $720,000 over their working lifetime.

On the other hand, if the college graduates earn approximately $50,000 per year for the 40 years of their working life, they will earn $2 million. If the graduates pay a federal tax rate of 20% of those funds, they will have contributed $400,000 in federal taxes.[6] This will leave them with income (minus federal taxes) of $1.6 million over their lifetime. Obviously, the $2 million lifetime earners will not only pay more in taxes, they will also invest more, spend more, and probably donate more to charities than will the $800,000 lifetime earners. The highly educated earner spends and contributes significantly more to the economy than does the less educated earner.

---

[5]Paying federal taxes of $2,000 (10% of $20,000) per year for 40 years, the total federal tax contribution would be $80,000. This is admittedly low, and the 10% figure is used as a minimum level to make a point.

[6]Paying federal taxes of $10,000 (20% of $50,000) per year for 40 years, the total federal tax contribution would be $400,000. This, too, is low but consistent with the minimum level used earlier for the dropout.

To extend this argument further, if individuals with a master's degree earn $60,000 per year over the 40 years of working life, they will earn $2.4 million.[7] If they pay a federal tax rate of 25%, they will have contributed $600,000 in federal taxes. This leaves them with income (minus federal taxes) of $1.8 million over their lifetime. These individuals have even more discretionary income available to stimulate the economy and further contribute to the tax base. Over their lifetime, these individuals with a master's degree will pay in federal taxes almost the equivalent of the high school dropout's lifetime gross earnings. Examined in this light, education dividends are even more evident.

Education acts as an economic stimulus. With increased earnings, wealthier individuals pay increased taxes. The enlarged tax revenues then finance increased education and related services that, in turn, further fuel economic growth. Education has a synergistic impact on the economy. Specifically, when people can support themselves with their own labor, they are less likely to depend on public assistance or to steal from their neighbors. As a result, education reduces the need for expensive safety net social programs and law enforcement services that can strain a community's economic resources. This reality illustrates an even greater return on the education investment.

EDUCATION INCREASES EMPLOYABILITY

Education also increases employability. Individuals with lower education levels are more likely to be unemployed and underemployed than those with higher educational attainment. The unemployment rate in 2000 for those who had not completed high school was 6.4%, compared with high school graduates at 3.5%, and college graduates at 1.7%.[8]

In addition, individuals with higher educational levels are more likely to remain employed. Figure 4.2 shows that, over time, educational attainment levels have an even more distinct effect on those who participate in the workforce. About 70% of individuals ages 20 to 24 who have not completed high school participate in the workforce. By age 25 only 43% of these high school dropouts continue to participate in the workforce. Of those

---

[7]Obviously, these are not the salaries of teachers in most of America's communities.

[8]U.S. Department of Education, National Center for Education Statistics, "Digest of Education Statistics, 2001." Available at: http:nces.ed.gov//pubs2002/digest2001/ch5.asp. Of course, we all hope our children are not in that 1.7% when they graduate from college, which necessitates that they move back in with us.

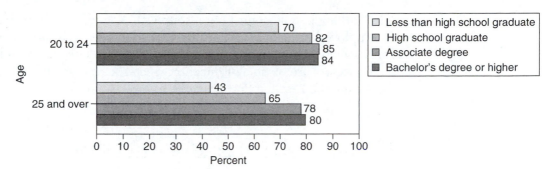

FIGURE 4.2

Labor Force Participation by Age and Highest Level of Education, 2000

Source: U.S. Department of Labor, Bureau of Labor Statistics, Office of Employment and Unemployment Statistics, *Current Population Survey, 2000.* See http://nces.ed.gov/programs/digest/do3/tables/dt378.asp.

who have completed high school, however, the figure drops from 82% of those aged 20 to 24 to 65% of those over the age of 25. Better educated persons have longer, more stable working careers.

As the data indicate, individuals with less education and fewer employable skills have difficulty finding employment in an information and service economy; they also have difficulty keeping their jobs over time as the economy changes. Too frequently they lack the intellectual skills, knowledge, and work habits to keep a steady job or to adapt successfully and learn new skills. Clearly this lack of employability has a serious impact on social service agencies, tax revenues, and overall economic spending.

We have shown both unemployment rates and labor force participation rates, but the two indicators are not equivalent. Unemployment rate statistics are sometimes misleading as they include only those who work or are actively seeking employment. These figures do not count individuals who are able to work but who, after seeking employment unsuccessfully, no longer seek jobs and drop out of the potential workforce. Unemployment rate statistics, therefore, tend to make the labor market picture look rosier than it actually is. A better indicator is people who are actually participating in the workforce. Eighty percent of adults with bachelor's degrees or higher participated in the workforce in 2000 compared with 65% of persons with only a high school diploma and 43% of individuals who did not complete high school.[9]

---

[9]U.S. Department of Education, National Center for Education Statistics, "Digest of Education Statistics, 2001," chap. 5.

Working people contribute resources to society, locally and nationally. Unemployed individuals—unless independently wealthy—draw resources from society. The greater benefits that educated citizens provide for the larger society are obvious. Education creates a synergy with the economy, increasing the revenue flow available to society.

EDUCATION INCREASES THE QUALITY OF LIFE FOR INDIVIDUALS AND THE COMMUNITY

Education increases the quality of life for individuals and for society at large in a variety of ways:

- Voting frequency
- Health insurance coverage
- Volunteerism
- Charitable contributions
- Leisure activity participation
- Cultural activity participation
- Childbirth in marriage versus out of wedlock
- Prenatal care
- Incarceration rates
- Crime victimization rates

Now let's take a closer look at how increased education affects each of these issues and enriches our communities.

Voting Frequency

Our democratic form of government depends on an educated citizenry voting wisely for those who will represent us. Individuals with higher levels of education vote more frequently than do individuals with less education.[10] Table 4.1 shows the voting records and educational level of those ages 25 to 44 who voted between 1964 and 1994. Although voting percentages have decreased somewhat over time, voting rates increase with education level.

---

[10]Obviously, it is a goal of public education to perpetuate our democratic republic form of government.

TABLE 4.1	VOTING BEHAVIOR BY EDUCATIONAL ATTAINMENT, AGES 25 TO 44, FOR ELECTIONS BETWEEN 1964 AND 1994		
Type of Election and Year	**1 to 3 Years of High School**	**4 Years of High School**	**4 Years of College and Beyond**
Congressional			
1974	24.7%	41.9%	59.3%
1994	12.9%	30.6%	57.0%
Presidential			
1964	60.5%	75.5%	86.2%
1984	29.0%	49.1%	74.7%
1992	27.0%	49.8%	78.5%

Source: National Center for Educational Statistics, "The Condition of Education, 1996, Indicator 37, Voting Behavior by Educational Attainment." Available at: http://nces.ed.gov/pubsold/ce96/c9637a01.html.

In the 1984 presidential election, individuals with a college degree and higher went to the polls at a rate two and one-half times that of high school dropouts. Persons with additional education more actively influence their elected government's direction and policies than do persons with less education. Furthermore, this trend accelerates over time. While the voting participation rate decreased by almost half for high school dropouts in congressional elections between 1974 and 1994, the rate for those with college degrees and higher only decreased by 2 percentage points.

Sadly, recent voting participation appears to be dropping at every education level except in the 1992 presidential election. The smallest drop, however, appears in those with 4 years of college and beyond. The lowest participation rate appears with high school dropouts where approximately 1 in 4 voted in the 1992 presidential election compared with almost 3 in 4 for those with a college degree.

Health Insurance

Access to affordable health care is another important "quality of life" arena where having more education makes a difference. Individuals with higher education levels tend to have health insurance as compared with those with lower education levels. Table 4.2 shows that in 1999 high school dropouts were 300% less likely to have health insurance than those with a college degree or higher. In addition, persons with health insurance tend to maintain their health with regular checkups and wholesome lifestyles. Their regular attention to wellness also places fewer burdens on social service networks

TABLE 4.2	PEOPLE WITHOUT HEALTH INSURANCE FOR THE ENTIRE YEAR, 1999
Education Level	**% without Health Insurance**
No high school diploma	26.7%
High school graduate, only	17.6%
Some college, no degree	15.2%
Associate degree	12.9%
Bachelors degree or higher	8.2%

Source: U.S. Census Bureau, Current Population Survey, March 2000. Available at: http://www.census.gov/prod/2000pubs/p60-211.pdf.

and public hospitals than do their less educated neighbors, thus reducing the costs for public social service agencies. Moreover, one recent study shows that almost half of bankruptcy filings are due to high medical bills.[11]

In addition, current research is finding biological proof of education's protective effect on a person's health. A recent study finds a correlation between years of education and Alzheimer's disease symptoms of dementia. Scientists autopsied brains from members of a religious order who had an average of 18 years of formal education and found the more years of formal schooling, the better the brain could tolerate the accumulation of the disease.[12] People with 22 years of formal education showed less clinical evidence of Alzheimer's while living, even though their brains showed classic Alzheimer's pathology. With more years of education, the same number of physical brain changes from the disease had less effect on their cognitive test scores.

Volunteerism

Volunteers bring extra resources to a community, helping those in need and contributing to the local quality of life. Persons with higher education levels tend to volunteer more frequently than those with lower education levels. Table 4.3 shows that 67% of the college graduate population performed

---

[11]http://money.cnn.com/2005/02/02/pf/debt/health_bankruptcy.reut/

[12]D. A. Bennett, R. S. Wilson, J. A. Schneider, D. A. Evans, C. F. Mendes de Leon, S. E. Arnold, L.L. Barnes, and J. L. Bienias, "Education Modifies the Relation of AD Pathology to Level of Cognitive Function in Older Persons," *Neurology* 60, June 2003, 1909–1915. Available at: http://www.neurology.org/cgi/content/abswtract/60/12/1909.

TABLE 4.3	PERCENT OF ADULT POPULATION DOING VOLUNTEER WORK, 1998	
Educational Attainment	**% Volunteering***	**Average Hours/Week**
Elementary school	29.4%	—
Some high school	43.0	3.9
High school graduate	43.2	2.8
Trade, technical, or business school graduate	53.5	3.5
Some college	67.2	4.8
College graduate	67.7	3.1

Note: *Volunteers are persons who worked in some way to help others for no monetary pay during the previous year. Activities include education, human services, religion, youth development, and work-related organizations.

Source: S. K. E. Saxon-Harrold, Murray Weitzman, and the Gallup Organization, Inc. *Giving and Volunteering in the United States: 1999 Edition* (Washington, DC: Independent Sector, 2000). Available at: http://landview.census.gov/prod/2002pubs/ statab/sedc12.pdf. Reprinted with special permission of INDEPENDENT SECTOR. www.independentsector.org

some sort of volunteer work during the year compared with about 30% to 43% for high school dropouts. Volunteers provide important services to neighbors and their children that would otherwise either go undone or would have to be paid for through increased taxes or fees. Obviously, volunteer work within a community has many benefits that are difficult to quantify and compile. Many would argue that volunteering enhances the individual's life as well.

Charitable Contributions

Giving money and materials through charitable contributions also increases a community's quality of life. Charitable contributions and higher education levels are related. Many households across the education spectrum donate money to help the less fortunate. Table 4.4 shows that those with lower levels of income tend to donate fewer total dollars but a larger percentage of their income to charities. As income rises, the percentage donated decreases, but the amount increases.[13] These data reflect dollars donated both in cash and in-kind.

---

[13]A note of caution: We were unable to find data detailing charitable contributions and level of education. These data reflect income level and charitable contributions from federal tax returns. We are making the assumption (and you know what assuming can do) that the increased levels of income are associated with the levels of education. Contribution percentages cannot be directly related to education level. We feel comfortable, however, in saying that education affects income and that income affects charitable contributions.

TABLE 4.4   CHARITABLE CONTRIBUTIONS BY HOUSEHOLD INCOME, 1998

Household Income	All Contributing Households		Contributors and Volunteers	
	Average Amount (in dollars)	% of Household Income	Average Amount (in dollars)	% of Household Income
Under $10,000	$329	5.2%	$419	6.3%
$10,000–19,999	495	3.3	633	4.2
$20,000–29,999	552	2.2	650	2.6
$30,000–39,999	734	2.1	886	2.5
$40,000–49,999	951	2.1	1,073	2.4
$50,000–59,999	1,041	1.9	1,189	2.2
$60,000–69,999	1,696	2.6	1,948	3.0
$75,000–99,999	1,394	1.6	1,748	2.0
$100,000 & over	2,550	2.2	3,029	2.6

Source: S. K. E. Saxon-Harrold, Murray Weitzman, and the Gallup Organization, Inc., *Giving and Volunteering in the United States, 1999 Edition* (Washington, DC: Independent Sector, 2000). Available at: http://landview.census.gov/prod/2001pubs/statab/sec12.pdf. Reprinted with special permission of INDEPENDENT SECTOR. www.independentsector.org

TABLE 4.5   CHARITABLE CONTRIBUTIONS BY TYPE OF CHARITY, 1998

Type of Charity	% of Households	Average Contributions (in dollars)
Arts, culture, humanities	11.4%	$221
Education	12.6	382
Environment	12.4	194
Health	20.8	234
Human services	27.3	250
Public, societal benefit	11.1	134
Youth development	21.4	174

Source: Virginia Hodgkinson, Murray Weitzman, and the Gallup Organization, Inc., *Giving and Volunteering in the United States, 1992 and 1996 Editions* (Washington, DC: Independent Sector, 1992 and 1996); S. K. E. Saxon-Harrold, Murray Weitzman, and the Gallup Organization, Inc., *Giving and Volunteering in the United States, 1999 Edition* (Washington, DC: Independent Sector, 2000). Available at: http://landview.census.gov/prod/2001pubs/statab/sec12.pdf. Reprinted with special permission of INDEPENDENT SECTOR. www.independentsector.org

People donate their money to a wide range of causes—the arts, human services, the environment, education, and other areas. Table 4.5 shows the types of charities receiving donations as reported on federal tax returns. The highest average contribution ($382) goes toward education, yet the highest percentage

TABLE 4.6 **PERCENTAGE OF PARTICIPATION IN VARIOUS LEISURE ACTIVITIES, 1997**

	Attendance at . . .		Participation in . . .		
Level of Education	**Movies**	**Sports Events**	**Exercise Programs**	**Charity Work**	**Home Improvement**
Grade school	14%	13%	46%	20%	40%
Some high school	52	25	66	31	59
High school grad	62	38	74	36	65
Some college	78	48	81	50	71
College graduate	82	59	87	55	76
Graduate school	81	55	88	67	73

Source: U.S. National Endowment for the Arts, *1997 Survey of Public Participation in the Arts, Research Division Report No. 39*, December 1998. Available at: http://landview.census.gov/prod/2001pubs/statab/sec12.pdf.

of households donate to human services (27.3%), youth development (21.4%), and health (20.8%) before donating to education (12.6%). Regardless, donations help further the mission and impact of an organization. Many charitable contributions are tax deductible, and donations become a tax issue as donors channel monies toward programs that fit their vision. People give money to those organizations they believe deserve and need external funding.

Leisure Activities

Increased education also buys leisure time and the resources to enjoy it. How individuals spend their leisure time partly defines their quality of life. Table 4.6 provides data about attending leisure activities and education levels. Well-educated people can afford lifestyles that seek and bring free time activities to their locales. They also work at maintaining and improving their own homes. Leisure time spending stimulates the economy, increases home assessments and subsequently local tax revenues,[14] and provides more jobs and employment—and improves the quality of life—for neighbors locally and across the country.

Closely associated with participation in leisure activities is the spending related to these pursuits. Table 4.7 details education level and sporting

---

[14]Tax revenues are increased by home improvement activities in three ways. First, home improvements increase the value and tax base of a home. Second, purchases in most states are subject to sales tax, which generates revenue. Third, home centers provide jobs that generate further tax revenues.

TABLE 4.7 PERCENTAGE OF CONSUMER PURCHASES OF SPORTING GOODS BY CONSUMER EDUCATION LEVELS, 1998

Household Head's Education Level	Footwear and Equipment				
	Jogging Shoes	Camping	Exercise	Golf	Skate-boarding
Less than high school	3.2%	6.0%	5.0%	1.0%	.3%
High school	13.7	20.0	18	13	23.9
Some college	32.9	37.0	36.0	35.0	36.4
College graduate	50.2	37.0	41.0	51.0	39.4

Source: The Sporting Goods Market in 1999 (Mt. Prospect, IL: National Sporting Goods Association, 2001), Available at: http://landview.census.gov/prod/2001pubs/statab/sec07.pdf. Used with permission.

goods purchases by their related activity. Individuals with more education spend more time in sporting and leisure activities and consequently spend more on the consumer goods (specialized clothes, equipment, fees) related to their hobbies. This leisure spending helps to stimulate the economy. Additionally, the activities listed in Table 4.7 are exercise-related and involvement brings the consumer direct health benefits. Whether educated individuals exercise to stay healthy or whether these folks have the time and money to participate in sports is a chicken-and-egg question for a statistics or a logic class. Suffice it to say that higher levels of education are associated with spending in leisure activities that stimulate both the economy and the cardiovascular system.

Cultural Activities

Individuals with more education participate in a wide array of cultural activities, as detailed in Table 4.8. Again, the higher the education, the more the cultural involvement. Arts bring music, theater, dance, and graphic arts to a community. Having many free-time choices provides increased opportunities for social and intellectual enjoyment. Moreover, going to a play, concert, or gallery exhibit often means a day "on the town," with people typically boosting the local economy by patronizing restaurants near the entertainment venue, purchasing gasoline for the trip, buying new clothes to wear for these occasions, as well as providing employment for artists and service providers. Many of these cultural activities are found in cities that also benefit from the use of urban buildings and from the sales tax revenues received from ticket sales.

TABLE 4.8	PERCENTAGE ATTENDANCE RATES FOR VARIOUS CULTURAL LEISURE ACTIVITIES, 1997

| Household Education Level | Attendance at Least Once in Prior 12 Months at . . . | | | | | |
	Jazz	Opera	Musical Play	Nonmusical Play	Ballet	Art Museum
Grade school	2%	—	6%	3%	2%	6%
Some high school	3	2	13	7	2	14
High school grad	7	2	16	9	4	25
Some college	15	5	28	19	7	43
College graduate	21	10	44	28	11	58
Graduate school	28	14	50	37	14	70

Note: In percent for individuals 18 years and over, performances at elementary and high schools are excluded.

Source: U.S. National Endowment for the Arts, "1997 Survey of Public Participation in the Arts," *Research Division Report No. 39,* 1998. Available at: http://landview.census.gov/prod/2001pubs/statab/sec07.pdf.

Childbirth and Prenatal Issues

Along with economic and cultural benefits, higher education levels bring major long-term social benefits. Table 4.9 shows women's marital status by education level at the time of their first child's birth. Almost two-thirds of first births for high school dropouts were premarital. The issue of "children having children" and the myriad social and educational ramifications associated with this situation are beyond this text's scope. The social impact and costs are, however, substantial.

Fewer than 10% of first births occurred before marriage for those with a college degree or higher. In contrast, only about 25% of the children born to high school dropouts were conceived after marriage, whereas more than 87% of children born to college educated individuals were postmaritally conceived.

These childbearing statistics have significant implications for the community and its education and social services budgets. Two-parent families tend to form more stable environments to raise children. Typically, two-parent families have more money and other resources to meet their children's and their own personal, health, social, and educational needs. In addition, they are more likely to raise children to value education, have fewer special learning needs requiring expensive interventions, develop good work habits, prepare for well-paying careers, and contribute to their community. This also reduces federal and state aid to social service agencies, freeing additional dollars for other community needs.

TABLE 4.9 MARITAL STATUS OF WOMEN 15 TO 44 YEARS OLD AT FIRST BIRTH BY EDUCATION LEVEL, 2001

Years of School Completed	Number of First Births (per 1,000)	Percent of First Births	
		Premarital	**Postmaritally Conceived**
Not a high school graduate	1,304	63.6%	25.9%
High school graduate (includes GED)	2,612	38.9	47.1
Some college, no degree or associate degree	2,192	30.8	56.9
Bachelor's, graduate, or professional degree	1,751	7.0	87.4

Source: U.S. Census Bureau, *Current Population Reports.* Available at: http://landview.census.gov/prod/2001pubs/statab/section02.pdf p. 41.

In a related area, prenatal care is also associated with education level. Table 4.10 shows the mother's education level and when prenatal care began in the pregnancy. The higher the mother's education level, the more likely she is to seek medical care during pregnancy. Receiving adequate prenatal care affects the baby's birth weight. We know that birth weight and the overall health of the child are closely related. Healthier babies have fewer learning problems (costing less to educate) and make fewer demands on educational and social service agencies.

Incarceration Rates

Most people agree—prevention is better than cure. Money is better spent on education than on prisons. The notion of spending money on education to reduce incarceration rates is not new. Victor Hugo, the famous 19th century writer, said that the person who opens a school closes a prison. In fact, a 2001 study by Lochner and Moretti concludes that many indicators suggest that education reduces crime.[15] Specifically, incarceration rates are significantly lower for those with higher levels of education than for those who have not completed high school. Furthermore, a significant part of lower

---

[15]L. Lochner and E. Moretti, "The Effect of Education on Crime: Evidence from Prison Inmates, Arrests, and Self-Reports," *Joint Center for Poverty Research, Policy Brief* 4 (5), 2001, 26.

TABLE 4.10   PRENATAL CARE AND MOTHERS' EDUCATION LEVEL, 1991 TO 1995

Education Level	Months Pregnant When Prenatal Care Began		
	Less than 3 Months	3 to 4 Months	5 Months or More or No Prenatal Care
No high school diploma or GED	78.9%	6.9%	14.3
High school diploma or GED	88.5%	6.3%	5.2%
Some college, no bachelor's degree	94.5%	3.0%	2.5%
Bachelor's degree or higher	93.8%	2.3%	3.9%

Source: U.S. National Center for Health Statistics, "Fertility, Family Planning, and Women's Health: New Data from the 1995 National Survey of Family Growth, Vital and Health Statistics," Series 23, No. 19, 1997.

incarceration rates results from the higher wages high school graduates earn as compared to high school dropouts (see Figure 4.1). Through a rather complex formula, they estimate that a 1% increase in the high school graduation rate would save the United States as much as $1.4 billion per year in reduced crime costs.[16] Lochner and Moretti state, "It is difficult to imagine a greater reason to develop policies that prevent high school drop out."[17]

Some politicians favor increased police spending as the way to reduce incarceration rates. Lochner and Moretti show that hiring one police officer at an approximate cost of $80,000 per year would reduce the annual crime costs by $200,000. To generate equivalent social savings from raising education levels requires that 100 additional students graduate from high school who would have dropped out. The one-time cost for this would be approximately $600,000 in school expenditures. The authors also state that such an education effort would then raise human capital by more than 40% (or $800,000).[18] Lochner and Moretti conclude that increasing police forces is a cost-effective policy, but increasing high school graduation rates offers far greater benefits when both crime reduction and productivity are considered.[19]

---

[16]Ibid., 27.

[17]Ibid.

[18]Ibid.

[19]Ibid.

TABLE 4.11   VICTIMIZATION RATE BY VIOLENT CRIME TYPE BY FAMILY INCOME

Household Income	Victims per 1,000 Persons			
	All Crimes	Robbery	Assaults	Personal Theft
Less than $7,500	65.5	6.5	54.2	1.7
$7,500–$14,999	51.1	5.8	41.0	1.8
$15,000–$24,999	40.7	3.6	33.5	1.3
$25,000–$34,999	43.1	6.9	28.1	1.6
$35,000–$49,999	33.3	3.1	28.1	1.6
$50,000–$74,999	33.1	2.8	28.5	1.1
$75,000 or more	34.1	2.9	29.0	1.0

Source: U.S. Bureau of Justice Statistics, *Criminal Victimization,* Annual; and *Criminal Victimization 1998, Changes 1997–98 with Trends 1993–98,* Series NCJ-176353 (Revised August 25, 1999). Available at: http://landview.census.gov/prod/2001pubs/statab/sec05.pdf.

The lack of education has specific negative effects on individuals and society. Those who do not graduate from high school earn less money than all other groups, vote less frequently, go to jail at much higher rates, and use social services at higher rates than does the general public or high school or college graduates.

Crime Victimization

Finally, those with higher levels of education and higher incomes are less likely to be crime victims.[20] Table 4.11 indicates victimization rates for individuals by household income and shows some dramatic decreases by income level. For those earning $60,000 per year (the average salary for an individual with a master's degree, see Figure 4.1), about one-third have been victims of a crime. Compare that to what happens to high school dropouts in the lowest two income categories: between one-half and almost two-thirds have been crime victims.

Not being a crime victim certainly contributes to quality of life by anyone's measure. Quality of life has to do with where and how we live. Being able to afford to live in a nicer and safer neighborhood means that those with higher levels of education are less likely to reside near or associate with

---

[20]Again, because income and education are related, we examine income level and infer its association with education level.

individuals who commit crimes and consequently are less likely to become victims. If higher education and greater income help individuals live in nicer and safer neighborhoods, they contribute to an increased quality of life.

Taxing to Support Human Capital

Education is a community's investment in its own best interest. Although taxes fund education as a public service, one of educational leaders' most important responsibilities is helping every local taxpayer see the "big picture" and understand that investment in human capital through education provides substantial paybacks for the individual, the locality, the state, and the nation. All of the factors discussed in the previous section have a significant impact on everyone's quality of life and are important dimensions for the community's well-being. When public education becomes widely valued, adequate funding will become an easier challenge.

Basically, taxes redistribute wealth (see Chapter 5 for much more on taxation issues). People do not naturally want to give their money away. In the United States we hold a moral and legislative imperative that wealth must be redistributed, in part, to promote equity of educational opportunity and democratic citizenship. Without this resource reallocation, poverty and ignorance would spiral, lowering general well-being, increasing deprivation, and fomenting civil unrest. Taxation, therefore, perpetuates our democratic government, permits our comfortable lifestyles to continue, and allows all educated individuals—regardless of race, ethnicity, gender, age, or creed—to invest their own human capital and participate in "the good life."

A basic taxation tenet is that the tax burden should be spread over as large a group as possible. Each state has established a minimum "floor of educational services" that localities must provide. Wealthy localities may have no problem meeting this standard. Poor localities, on the other hand, may be unable to meet that level. The state, therefore, has a legal responsibility to help redistribute monies—or equalize funding—to help less wealthy localities meet this educational benchmark.

Legal and moral reasons require equalization of funds. For example, dispersing education's tax bill over the entire state allows smaller, remote, or economically disadvantaged localities with little local wealth to provide a quality education for their citizens. Moreover, if a regional economic downturn occurs, the entire state can help the affected area shoulder the financial burden for services. For example, in a state with a relatively healthy economy, a locality's largest employer, a textile plant, closes. The many recently out-of-work local residents can no longer afford to maintain their schools to minimum state standards. Nevertheless, the local children can still receive a strong education when the entire state helps pay the schooling costs.

The courts have ruled that states must provide a method to equalize education spending based on a locality's ability to pay. The entire state benefits economically from an educated population that works and provides higher income tax revenues, requires less public assistance, has lower incarceration rates, and gives to charitable causes at higher rates, to name a few advantages. Therefore, it seems logical—not just legal—that all state taxpayers contribute toward education costs.[21]

EDUCATION AS A WISE INVESTMENT

Education is an important investment in human capital. An educated citizenry substantially improves the society in which those individuals live. Education, more than any other social investment, raises the standard of living by increasing employability and income level, thereby increasing tax revenue to support even more education. The interaction between education and economic health is synergistic. Education increases quality of life not only for the educated individuals themselves but also for others throughout the entire community. In turn, an educated public creates support for more education.

Increasingly, local and state governments are having financial difficulty meeting their citizens' needs and demands while complying with federally required unfunded and partially funded mandates. There are only four ways to meet financial mandates. First, as seen in this chapter, the economy can be "grown" to meet needs by investing in human capital. As that economy grows, the tax base expands, providing revenue for services. The second option is to cut costs by reducing or eliminating services. The third option is to raise taxes, which is becoming increasingly difficult to do. The fourth option is to borrow money and incur debt. Of all the options, clearly the investing in human capital through education is most proactive and appealing for the long term.

Despite these facts, educational funding issues invite both strong advocates and critics with competing agendas. Taxpayers want lower taxes, and different government agencies hold different ideas on how to spend tax

---

[21]It would be interesting to speculate on how the founding fathers may have changed the Constitution had they anticipated the complications of state versus federal education funding and the impact that would have on public school operations today.

dollars. Interest groups, such as those pursuing parental choice, tuition tax credits, or school voucher programs, complicate educational funding decisions still further and potentially draw money away from public schooling and its investment in human capital in its broadest sense.[22] Informed educational leaders can use the human capital investment information provided here to effectively advocate for the needed financial resources to support education in their own district and state. The money spent for education pays clear dividends in human capital that any financial analyst would envy in a long-term investment portfolio.

SUMMARY

Education plays an important part in raising the standard of living in a community. In fact, the very viability of communities rests in the quality of education available to its next generation. Simply put, education creates a synergy with the economy. Likewise, a lack of education creates a slow but sure atrophic impact on an economy.

The founding fathers believed educating all citizens would benefit society's overall economy, safety, and quality of life. In this way, too, our country was unique. Historically, governments limited education to the elite. Labor, the working classes and the poor, remained largely uneducated.

Theodore Schultz's 20th century ideas that investing in the goods-and-services producers' minds held economic worth for the larger community became the basis for establishing the investment in education as a significant contributor to a society's economic development. Education, more than any other social investment, raises the standard of living by increasing employability and disposable income, reducing a community's social service costs, drawing business development and expansion, and enhancing the entire community's quality of life.

Data support the positive results of investing in education. Higher levels of education are associated with greater individual workers' earnings. Those who do not graduate from high school earn less than all other groups, vote less frequently, go to jail at much higher rates, and use social services at higher rates than do high school or college graduates. Individuals with lower education levels are more likely to be unemployed and underemployed than those with higher educational attainment, and better educated persons have

---

[22]Mark Walsh, "New Year Shaping Up as Pivotal for Vouchers," *Education Week,* 9, September 1998, 7.

longer, more stable working careers. Working people contribute resources to society, locally and nationally. Unemployed individuals—unless independently wealthy—draw resources from it.

In addition, data show that increased education benefits both individuals and communities in a variety of ways, including increasing voting frequency, access to health insurance, volunteerism, giving charitable contributions, and increasing leisure and cultural activity participation. More education also increases the rate of childbirth in marriage versus out of marriage, raises the probability of securing prenatal care to keep babies and children healthy, and reduces the likelihood of being a crime victim.

Education is a community's investment in its own best interest. Educators need to help their taxpaying community see the many ways their school funding benefits them directly.

Conclusion

Education is an investment in the future of a community. By investing in the human capital of the next generation, a community avoids problems associated with blighted and decaying communities and creates the conditions for a continued high quality of life that attracts businesses and citizens with a low need for social support programs.

Case Study

Your school district has an excellent reputation for providing quality education. In the past several years, however, a small group of individuals who used to pass through the area as migrant workers have now settled permanently in your area. They bring with them some of the disadvantages of poverty—poor study skills, poor language and writing skills, and a lack of employability skills other than what has been referred to as "stoop labor." In fact, most of the parents do not see a need for their children to continue their education beyond age 16. There is some animosity in the community about "these people" coming to live here on a permanent basis.

Your school board sees the importance of providing the programs these students need to be successful in today's world and has requested additional funding for programs to meet these students' needs. The local taxpayers association is campaigning against this increased funding for your local school district. They have placed ads in the local newspaper asking that local residents contact their elected officials and reduce the proposed education budget—especially in the area of dropout prevention and after school homework help programs. Their slogan is "Why Throw Good Money Away Needlessly?" They see no need to help struggling students who, as they put it, don't want to be and don't need to be in school anyway. The taxpayer group believes these individuals will go on to work in low-wage jobs at the local factory and really don't need all that much of an education.

Because you have grown up in the area, gone to the local schools, graduated from college, and come back home to teach, you have been asked by the superintendent to speak at the next budget meeting about the need for communities to invest in education and why these new programs are in the long-term best interests of the community.

Your talk at the public input section of the meeting is limited to 5 minutes. Prepare your speech and deliver it convincingly to a partner before speaking in public. Prepare a written text of your speech and speakers' notes to aid you in your presentation.

CHAPTER QUESTIONS

1. Explain the cycle of association between a high-quality school system and increased earnings and employability within a community.
2. What is the link between education, prenatal care, and special education services in schools? How can increasing the quality of education reduce long-term community costs?
3. What are some of the social service costs in your school district? How much does it cost to provide these services? How could your school district partner with a social service agency to provide educational programs that help to prevent social service needs instead of providing for these needs on a remedial basis?
4. How would this country have been different had we developed a public education system that was elitist instead of inclusive or encouraged school conditions Cubberley described as pauper and parochial?

TAXATION ISSUES

FOCUS QUESTIONS

1. How do taxes equalize resources and services for citizens?

2. What are the differences between proportional, regressive, and progressive taxes?

3. How are property tax rates determined?

4. How do states compare in rankings of per capita property taxes, income taxes, and sales taxes?

5. In addition to property, income, and sales taxes, what other sources of revenue do states have?

6. What are the indicators of a good tax?

7. How is tax effort determined?

This chapter investigates taxation issues. The concept of equalization is explained. Sources of state revenue for education combined with the idea of comparative effort to fund programs are explored in detail.

Clearly, education is an important investment in human capital, but taxpayers want lower taxes and government agencies hold diverse ideas on how to spend their funds. Interest groups, such as advocates for parental choice, tuition tax credits, or school voucher programs, complicate educational funding decisions still further and potentially draw money away from public schooling and its investment in human capital.[1] Informed educational leaders can use this chapter's information to help their community understand taxation issues and to effectively support the needed financial resources to sustain education in their district and state.

Reluctance to finance public education is not only a recent phenomenon, although it has become more pronounced since the 1983 publication of the politically charged report, *A Nation at Risk*.[2] In all probability, the 1647 New England colonists resented paying taxes for their sons' and servants' education. The founding fathers, however, realized education's importance to their new democratic republic better than many do today. Education is a state responsibility that requires public funds. With these public monies come public scrutiny and public comment. Therein lies the rub. Most people believe the correct taxation level is somewhat less than what they currently pay, and the level of service they want is somewhat higher than currently exists. In turn, many politicians build platforms based on tax reduction and education reform.

In the public service "business" of education, operating revenues come from the community mainly in the form of property taxes. As noted in Chapter 2, we no longer fund public schools by user fees or by tuition. In fact, the courts have repeatedly stated that public education must be tuition free.[3] Consumers do not buy education services based on economist-derived price points. As a state function, states are responsible for funding education. To this end, many states rely on local property tax revenue as the major funding source to support public schools.[4]

Increasingly, however, U.S. taxpayers are rejecting using property taxes to pay for their schools. On June 6, 1978, California taxpayers voted "Yes" to Proposition 13 to amend the state constitution by limiting local property

---

[1]Mark Walsh, "New Year Shaping Up as Pivotal for Vouchers," *Education Week* 9, September 1998, 7.

[2]National Commission on Excellence in Education, *A Nation at Risk: The Imperative for Educational Reform* (Washington, DC: U.S. Government Printing Office, 1983).

[3]*Randolph County Board of Education v. Adams*, Supreme Court of Appeals of West Virginia, 467 S.E. 2d 150 (1995); *Cardiff v. Bismark Public School District*, 263 N.W.2d 105 (1978); *Hartzell v. Connell*, Supreme Court of California, In Bank 35 Cal.3d 899, 201 Cal. Rptr. 601, 679 P.2d 35 (1984).

[4]The tradition of funding education started with the Massachusetts law of 1647 and remains today.

tax rates and making increasing other taxes more difficult.[5] This reduced local revenues by 23%. The loss to local California school districts was estimated to be $3.5 billion. This taxpayer revolt spread to other states in an antitax, anti–big government platform.

As evidenced by the Proposition 13 vote, many taxpayers resent property taxes—taxing a stock (rather than a flow) of wealth to fund state services. In fact, a national survey conducted one year after Proposition 13 was implemented showed a dramatic countrywide reduction in tax revenue at the state level.[6] The trend continues more than 25 years later. With the recession following the 9/11 tragedy, this antitax mentality strains the allocation of tax dollars for services.

UNDERSTANDING TAXES FOR EDUCATION: SOME BASIC CONCEPTS

Public education depends on tax dollars for funding. Schools do not operate as for-profit companies designed to generate dividends and increase stock prices for shareholders, as do IBM, General Electric, and General Motors. Neither are schools professional fee-for-service organizations as are dental practices or physicians' offices. Schools are a public service provided on a scope and scale unlike anything else in our society—or for that matter, in the world. The key question is, "What is the best way to generate political support and fiscal resources for our large and expensive public education service investing in human capital?"

Taxes Equalize Resources and Services

The purpose of a tax is to pay for a government function. In legal terms (see Chapter 3), a tax should be "equalized"—that is, the government should have a formal mechanism to calculate a lower cost for those who

---

[5]According to Kern Alexander and Richard Salmon, *Public School Finance* (Boston: Allyn and Bacon, 1995), Proposition 13 had four provisions: (1) property taxes were limited to 1% of full cash value plus the rate needed to service bond obligations approved prior to 1978-79; (2) assessed property values were rolled back to 1975-76 levels with increases of only 2% annually; (3) statutes to increase state taxes had to be approved by two-thirds of each of the state houses with a provision for no new ad valorem, sales, or transaction taxes on real property; and (4) special local taxes and taxes on real property had to be approved by two-thirds of a local vote.

[6]The Editor's Page, "The Spirit of 13 Continues to Sweep the Country," *Phi Delta Kappan,* October 1979, 84.

can least afford the service and a higher cost for those who can most afford the service. This equalization tends to make the most needed services more affordable to those who are least able to pay. In essence, taxes have the effect of redistributing wealth at the local, state, or federal level. This equalization tends to level the playing field as we invest in the human capital of each succeeding generation.[7]

A major taxation tenet is that taxes should be spread out—redistributed—over as large a population as possible. In other words, the funding base for a service should be as large as the population being served. Funding a federal service, therefore, such as defense, should be spread out over the entire country. Funding a state service, such as education, should be extended over the entire state. Funding a local service, such as a city or county park, should be distributed over the entire locality.

Likewise, each state has established a minimum "floor of educational services," which localities must provide. In this way, the state requires that each student living within its boundaries complete a basic series of courses and competencies to be promoted to the next grade or to graduate from high school. With the No Child Left Behind (NCLB) legislation of 2001, the federal government is attempting to "ratchet up" that floor level, increasing the number and intellectual rigor of courses that each student must complete.[8] Moreover, students at certain grades must now pass high-stakes reading, language, math, and science assessments to demonstrate their mastery and confirm their school's accountability.

Wealthy localities may have no problem meeting these standards. Often these communities are already providing the extra courses and highly qualified teachers, and almost all students pass their tests. Poor localities, on the other hand, face challenges in offering extra courses and finding highly qualified teachers.[9] Within a state, therefore, not all localities have the same ability to prepare their students to meet the required levels of increasing academic progress, or AYP (adequate yearly progress). The state has a legal responsibility to help redistribute monies—or equalize funding—to help less wealthy localities meet these educational benchmarks.

---

[7]It must be noted that perfect equalization does not exist. Inequities exist at every level in spite of equalization's goal.

[8]There is certainly controversy about whether NCLB is increasing the intellectual rigor of schooling or increasing test preparation and test taking strategies. This obviously varies by state and by what the local practice prior to NCLB had been.

[9]As a result of litigation, some poorer localities spend more per pupil than wealthier districts as in, for example, New Jersey.

Brief History of Tax Funding for Public Schools

The history of paying for U.S. public schools goes back to the country's early days. The first public school finance law was the Massachusetts Law of 1647. Town elders used property owners' taxes to hire a teacher in towns of 100 or more to educate the community's sons and servants. Having to learn to read the Bible, the elders reasoned, would keep educated youth and adults from falling prey to Satan's temptations.

Property was taxed because it was the means by which most people generated income. A farmer made his living by growing crops or animals on his land—his property. Once sold, the crops or livestock created his income. Likewise, a merchant operated a store (above which she usually lived) and derived her income from the profits of selling merchandise on her property. A furniture maker derived income from property—in the shop behind his house—selling handcrafted chairs or cabinets. Not all these transactions, however, were cash sales. Individuals bartered or traded many items, using exchange of goods as a money substitute to secure desired products or services.

It was logical, therefore, for government to tax property because that property was the basis for making one's income. At that time, property was a realistic proxy for income. Unfortunately, this is no longer the case. Today, very few of us derive our income from our property. We earn our income from our place of employment. For most of us today, our homes represent more of a revenue drain than a revenue source. Our homes represent a stock—rather than a flow—of accumulated wealth. We do not realize any financial gain from our property until we sell it.

Flow of Production and Stock of Wealth

Taxes fall into two broad categories: taxes levied on the flow of production or services and taxes levied on a stock of wealth. Taxes may be based on a flow of production derived from purchases, such as income, and sales. These taxes include personal income taxes, corporate income taxes, and retail sales taxes, to name a few. As money moves along the production or service process, it is taxed as it flows from one individual to another or from one company to another.

Alternatively, taxes may be based on a stock or accumulation of wealth. A stock of wealth has ceased to move in the flow of production. It does not involve building, making, selling, or servicing anything or anyone. Instead, it has become an individual's or a company's asset. Property, as measured in our home valuation is, therefore, a stock of wealth. Taxing property is taxing an individual's or a company's portion of wealth. This is known as an *ad valorem* tax. Property taxes are ad valorem taxes because a portion of the home's assessed value is taxed to support a service. In the same locality, the owner of a house valued at $200,000 pays twice the tax of the owner of a $100,000 home because the former home's value is twice the latter's.

In Rem *and* In Personam *Taxes*

Another tax classification includes in rem and in personam taxes. *In rem* taxes are those imposed on "things" such as machinery, cars, and houses. In some areas these taxes are known as *personal property* taxes, and they are based on the value of the "thing" being assessed. In rem taxes do not consider whether an individual owns the "thing" free and clear or whether the "thing" is bought entirely on credit. A disadvantage of in rem taxes is that individuals may pay taxes on items they do not really own, and they cannot claim their full and outright ownership as an asset. Although they "have" the taxable item, the item may not actually be theirs—the bank may hold the title and the majority of the item's equity.

In personam taxes are imposed on people. The best example of in personam taxes are those imposed on people's earned income—an income tax. In personam taxes account for equity in the value of the income derived. In other words, personal income determines the amount of tax to be paid. In rem taxes do not account for the equity in property; they assess the entire value of a "thing" whether or not the individual owns the property or has a mortgage on it.

Each of these types of taxes is used to generate funding for public services such as education. It is important for educators to know what types of taxes support their school's funding and what taxes tend to be more popular with the public. Different types of taxes can have different effects on taxpayers and generate varying levels of support. The effects of these taxes are discussed next.

Proportional, Regressive, and Progressive Taxes

Politicians often talk about the *regressive* nature of one tax versus the *progressive* nature of another tax. Very infrequently, however, does the public hear discussion of *proportional* taxes. Informed educational leaders should be able to discuss the advantages and disadvantages of each.

The sales tax is a proportional tax; each person pays the same percentage. For example, everyone in Virginia pays a 5% sales tax on purchased items that are not exempt from sales tax. Because everyone pays 5%, this is considered a proportional tax. Although a proportional tax initially seems fair, it taxes poorer persons more heavily than it does richer ones. Although the percent taxed on any item is the same dollar amount for each person, this amount represents a larger share of the less well-off person's financial resources.

For example, buying groceries for a family of four (two teenagers) might cost $200 each week. A sales tax of 5% on a grocery bill of $200 would amount to $10. Over a period of one year (assuming the cost of groceries were constant), the sales tax on groceries alone would total $520. For a family with an income of $100,000 that represents .52% of their income—about one-half of one percent. For a similar family with the same eating habits earning an income of $50,000 per year, the sales tax on groceries as a percentage of their income represents 1.04% of their income—or about 1% of their gross income.

Although a proportional tax may have a regressive effect on those with lower incomes, some argue that those who earn more tend to spend more, eventually paying more in sales tax. To make this kind of tax more fair, some states do not tax food, or tax it at a lower rate, and do not tax prescription drugs or patent drugs.

A regressive tax allows individuals with higher incomes to pay a lower percentage of their income in taxes. Virtually no tax is intentionally designed to be regressive although some taxes become regressive. An example would be what most think of as the Social Security taxation system. It is more accurately known as the Federal Insurance Contributions Act, or FICA.

At the beginning income levels, all individuals pay 7.65% of their income in FICA tax.[10] FICA taxes, however, are not collected after one's income reaches $90,000.[11] Higher income individuals, therefore, pay a lower percentage of their overall income than do lower income individuals—making FICA a regressive tax. In other words, an individual earning $90,000 would pay $6,885 each year in FICA taxes. An individual earning twice that amount, or $180,000, would pay the same amount to Social Security (plus

---

[10]Self-employed individuals pay both the employer and employee share of the 7.65%, or a total of 15.3%.

[11]As of 2005, under the Federal Insurance Contributions Act, 12.4% of one's earned income up to $90,000 must be paid into Social Security and an additional 2.9% must be paid into Medicare. There are no income limits on Medicare taxes, so even if one's income is above the $90,000 limit for Social Security taxes, one still owes Medicare taxes. A wage or salaried employee pays only one-half the FICA bill (6.2% for Social Security and 1.45% for Medicare for a total of 7.65%). These taxes are automatically withheld for salaried employees with the employer contributing the other half. For most employees 7.65% is withheld and the employer pays another 7.65%. Self-employed individuals are expected to pay employee and employer shares of FICA.

TABLE 5.1	FEDERAL TAX BRACKETS, 2004 TAXABLE INCOME	
Joint Return	**Single Taxpayer**	**Rate**
$0–$14,300	$0–$7,150	10.0%
14,301–58,100	7,151–29,050	15.0
58,101–117,250	29,051–70,350	25.0
117,251–178,650	70,351–146,750	28.0
178,651–319,100	146,751–319,100	33.0
319,101and up	319,101 and up	35.0

Source: Internal Revenue Service. Available at: www.irs.gov/forumspubs/article/0,,id+133625,00.html.

1.45% for Medicare), with an effective tax rate of 4.55%, a little more than half that of the $90,000 earner. In this way, the FICA tax has the effect of being a regressive tax.

Finally, progressive taxes are those that increase as a percentage along with income. Federal income taxes are designed to be progressive.[12] Currently, the lowest income wage earners are taxed at 10%. As income rises, the percentage of tax owed increases, and the highest income earners are taxed at a rate of 35%. Table 5.1 shows the intended progressive nature of the federal tax structure.

Table 5.2 shows each of the three tax classifications at three income levels. Generally, "good" taxes are considered to be progressive whereas "bad" taxes are considered to be regressive. Progressive taxes require those who can pay more to do so, whereas regressive taxes require those who can afford less to pay more.

Under proportional taxation each income group pays the same percentage rate of tax—10%. In the regressive tax structure, lower income individuals pay a greater percentage of their income in taxes than do upper income individuals. In the progressive scenario, the lower income individuals pay a lower percentage of their income in taxes than do upper income individuals. In other words, as income increases, so does the percentage of taxes paid.

Poorer people tend to spend a greater percentage of their income on basic living costs in contrast to those at the higher income levels. The spending habits of two families with incomes of $50,000 and $75,000 may

---

[12]The thought of federal income taxes as progressive here excludes IRS tax loopholes that may have the potential for making these taxes regressive if higher income individuals actually use options to reduce their tax liability significantly.

TABLE 5.2	PROPORTIONAL, REGRESSIVE, AND PROGRESSIVE TAXES		
Individual	**Income**	**Taxes Paid**	**% of Income**
Proportional Tax			
1	$10,000	$1,000	10
2	50,000	5,000	10
3	100,000	10,000	10
Regressive Tax			
1	10,000	500	5
2	50,000	2,000	4
3	100,000	3,000	3
Progressive Tax			
1	10,000	300	3
2	50,000	2,000	4
3	100,000	5,000	5

not be significantly different. Life's basic necessities—bread, milk, and butter, for example—differ little in quantity purchased by a family of four at these income levels. However, a family at the $319,101 level (the highest tax bracket level referenced in Table 5.1) pays a lower percentage in sales taxes related to these basic necessities of life. A proportional tax tends to have a regressive effect on lower income individuals.

TYPES OF TAXES USED TO GENERATE REVENUE

States have three major sources of tax revenue—property, income, and sales taxes. In this section we discuss these major sources of tax revenue, some other minor tax sources, and another relatively new tax source—lottery and gambling funds.

Property Taxes

As mentioned previously, property taxes are the primary revenue source for financing education. Property taxes are an ad valorem tax because it taxes a portion or a percentage of the property's value. Property taxes are frequently expressed in "mills," which is a unit of monetary value equal to

	Variable Rate		Fixed Rate	
Assessed Value	**Tax Rate**	**Tax Bill**	**Tax Rate**	**Tax Bill**
$100,000	$1.50 @ $100	$1,500	$1.50 @ $100	$1,500
$200,000	$1.25 @ $100	$2,500	$1.50 @ $100	$3,000
$300,000	$1.00 @ $100	$3,000	$1.50 @ $100	$4,500

TABLE 5.3 REAL ESTATE TAXES BASED ON 100% OF FAIR MARKET VALUE AT FIXED AND VARIABLE TAX RATES

Note: We are assuming the fair market value is the assessed value. We recognize that this may not be the case all of the time.

$0.001 of a dollar—or one-tenth of one cent. The method for determining the tax rate is as follows:

$$\frac{\text{Amount of Tax Revenue to Be Raised}}{\text{Tax Base or the Value of Property}} = \text{Rate}$$

If the total assessed value of real estate in a locality is $500 million, and the locality needs to raise $5 million in taxes for services, the formula would look like this:

$$\frac{\$5,000,000}{\$500,000,000} = 1.0\% \text{ or } 10 \text{ mills}$$

Today, for the most part, only tax professionals or doctoral students specializing in school finance calculate the millage rate. Most frequently the tax rate is based on 100% of the home's assessed value. This rate is expressed as a certain dollar figure per $100 of assessed value.[13] Therefore, homeowners are most accustomed to seeing that the tax rate is, for example, $1.50 per each $100 of assessed value of the home. Table 5.3 shows the various scenarios associated with tax rates.

Sometimes, the public resents paying property taxes. Shannon, in a classic work, cites two reasons for this unpopularity.[14] First, people consider property taxes as a threat to the American dream of home ownership.

---

[13]It is important to compare assessments at 100% of fair market value of the home. A tax rate of 75 cents would appear low compared to $1.50 until we knew that the 75 cent assessed rate was based on each $25 of assessed value, making the tax rate in this case twice what it would be at $1.50 per $100 of assessed value.

[14]John Shannon, "The Property Tax: Reform or Relief?" in *Property Tax Reform,* George E. Peterson, ed. (Washington, DC: Urban Institute, 1973), 26-27.

Second, taxing a home's value is taxing unrealized profits—the owner would have to sell the home to get the assessed monetary value versus the price originally paid for the house. The home's value is only a paper profit until the home is sold, and yet the taxes are based on its current value. Many of us have grandparents, for instance, who must sell their homes because they are living on a fixed income. The value of their home has increased so much that they can no longer afford to pay the property taxes. We can picture ourselves in that predicament and begin to resent the idea of property taxes.

Additionally, property taxes are difficult and costly to administer. Fair market value is sometimes arbitrary, and the cost of administering property tax programs can be expensive. Furthermore, property tax bills usually arrive once a year—making payment difficult for those who have not budgeted for this.

Consider the many municipal departments and employees a locality needs to manage property taxes. First, a system to inventory and organize all the locality's property and improvements on that property is needed. Second, specialized personnel must make periodic physical assessments of the property. States vary on how often they must make these physical assessments. Third, an appeals system must be available for contesting valuation. Fourth, tax bills must be sent out and collected (an accounts payable and receivable system), requiring additional staff. Fifth, a system must be established to collect delinquent taxes, and the list goes on.

Furthermore, a home's fair market value is sometimes difficult to calculate. Realtors use a comprehensive market analysis (CMA) to determine a home's correct selling price. A three bedroom, two bath brick rancher on a half acre lot on one side of town may have a greater value than the same house across town, and subjectivity often comes into play. As a result, comparing real estate tax assessments generally confuses and angers homeowners. Why does one house's assessment increase by 15% while another goes up only 3%? Moreover, although people want their home's value (and their personal wealth) to increase, they do not want to pay the resulting higher taxes on that unrealized position. Because property taxes primarily support schools, it is logical for taxpayers to associate and voice frustration with the schools over their growing real estate tax bills.

Table 5.4 shows the amount of property tax collected by local and state sources on a per capita basis for the year 1999 (latest data available), including relative state rankings. Income taxes are the states' second major source of tax income, and income may be a better measure of wealth today than is property. The federal government and most states collect income taxes.

TABLE 5.4   PROPERTY TAXES PER CAPITA BY STATE

State	Property Tax Per Capita	Rank	State	Property Tax Per Capita	Rank
Alabama	$273	50	Montana	$1,009	13
Alaska	1,174	9	Nebraska	941	15
Arizona	750	32	Nevada	697	33
Arkansas	550	40	New Hampshire	1,677	2
California	767	31	New Jersey	1,761	1
Colorado	842	23	New Mexico	338	49
Connecticut	1,577	3	New York	1,361	4
Delaware	462	44	North Carolina	569	38
Florida	920	18	North Dakota	784	29
Georgia	696	34	Ohio	829	25
Hawaii	502	42	Oklahoma	369	48
Idaho	651	35	Oregon	771	30
Illinois	1,163	10	Pennsylvania	805	26
Indiana	871	21	Rhode Island	1,297	5
Iowa	873	20	South Carolina	637	36
Kansas	797	28	South Dakota	842	22
Kentucky	421	46	Tennessee	489	43
Louisiana	371	47	Texas	938	16
Maine	1,235	7	Utah	559	39
Massachusetts	1,182	8	Vermont	1,289	6
Maryland	801	27	Virginia	838	24
Michigan	893	19	Washington	1,001	14
Minnesota	934	17	W. Virginia	449	45
Mississippi	502	41	Wisconsin	1,052	12
Missouri	604	37	Wyoming	1,089	11
All 50 states	$880				
District of Columbia	$1,309 (would rank number 5 if it were a state)				
Total United States	$881				

Source: K. Hovey and H. Hovey, *Rankings across America: CQ's State Fact Finder, 2002* (Washington, DC: Congressional Quarterly Press, 2002), 146.

Income Taxes

Taxing income has been practiced in the United States for more than a century. The first federal tax experience came after the Civil War to pay for war debts. This tax expired, but Congress revived it in the late 1800s to aid in antimonopoly and antitrust reform efforts. In 1894 Congress passed a flat 2% personal and corporate income tax. The U.S. Supreme Court found the tax unconstitutional in 1895.[15] In other words, a federal income tax could not be levied until the U.S. Constitution was amended. The Sixteenth Amendment, ratified in 1913, allowed the federal government to collect taxes on income. It states:

> The Congress shall have power to lay and collect taxes on incomes, from whatever source derived, without apportionment among the several states, and without regard to any census of enumeration.

Federal taxation was challenged again at the U.S. Supreme Court level, but due to the addition of the Sixteenth Amendment, the issue of a federal income tax was found to be constitutional.[16]

At the state level, Wisconsin had already initiated a rather progressive state income tax in 1911. The tax proved to be rather lucrative for the state. It was so well devised and administered that it served as the basis for other states' income tax model.

It is important to keep the idea of federal and state income taxes separate. Federal taxes provide approximately 7% of state school budgets. State taxes (including income taxes) provide a much larger share of school budget dollars.[17]

Table 5.5 shows the per capita personal income by state for the year 2000 (latest data available). These data show personal income relative to population and serve as a measure of each state's affluence. In fact, these data are so well suited to measure wealth that the federal government uses this gauge to determine the percentage of each state's Medicaid costs it pays.

You can see that there is a wide variance in per capita income across our country. Connecticut has the highest per capita income at $40,870. Mississippi has the lowest per capita income at $20,856. The range is $20,014 for every man, woman, and child in the state. Obviously, wealth as measured by income is disparate across the country. How that income is

---

[15]*Pollock v. Farmers' Loan and Trust Co.*, 157 U.S. 429 and 158 U.S. 601 (1895).

[16]*Brushhaber v. Union Pacific R.R. Co.*, 240 U.S. 1 (1916).

[17]K. Hovey and H. Hovey, *Rankings across America: CQ's State Fact Finder, 2002* (Washington, DC: Congressional Quarterly Press, 2002), 40.

TABLE 5.5   PER CAPITA PERSONAL INCOME, 2000

State	Per Capita Personal Income	Rank	State	Per Capita Personal Income	Rank
Alabama	$23,460	43	Montana	$22,541	46
Alaska	29,597	14	Nebraska	27,658	25
Arizona	24,991	37	Nevada	29,551	15
Arkansas	21,945	47	New Hampshire	33,042	6
California	32,225	8	New Jersey	37,112	3
Colorado	32,441	7	New Mexico	21,883	48
Connecticut	40,870	1	New York	34,502	4
Delaware	31,074	12	North Carolina	26,842	31
Florida	27,836	21	North Dakota	24,780	38
Georgia	27,790	23	Ohio	27,914	20
Hawaii	27,819	22	Oklahoma	23,582	42
Idaho	23,640	41	Oregon	27,649	26
Illinois	31,842	10	Pennsylvania	29,533	16
Indiana	26,838	32	Rhode Island	29,158	17
Iowa	26,376	33	South Carolina	23,952	40
Kansas	27,408	28	South Dakota	25,993	34
Kentucky	24,057	39	Tennessee	25,878	35
Louisiana	23,041	45	Texas	27,722	24
Maine	25,399	36	Utah	23,364	44
Maryland	33,621	5	Vermont	26,904	30
Massachusetts	37,710	2	Virginia	31,065	13
Michigan	29,071	18	Washington	31,129	11
Minnesota	31,913	9	West Virginia	21,767	49
Mississippi	20,856	50	Wisconsin	28,066	19
Missouri	27,186	29	Wyoming	27,436	27
All 50 states	n/a				
District of Columbia	$38,374 (would rank number 2 if it were a state)				
Total United States	$29, 451				

Source: K. Hovey and H. Hovey, *Rankings across America: CQ's State Fact Finder, 2002* (Washington, DC: Congressional Quarterly Press, 2002), 40.

taxed at the federal and state levels is a source of concern for all public service sectors—especially schools.

Sales Taxes

Table 5.6 shows sales tax revenues (from all sources, not just retail sales) generated almost $291 billion in the United States in 1999 (latest data available). Some states have no direct sales taxes on purchases; however, states also tax gasoline, utilities, telephone and 911 services, and other items that qualify as a sales tax. Sales tax revenue provides income for states to fund educational services. The impact of sales tax revenue comes from visitors and tourists as well as from residents of the locality and the state. Tourism plays an important part in many state and local budgets.

State and local sales taxes generate a great deal of funding for education. It is interesting to note how per capita income (see Table 5.5) and the state and local sales taxes vary. Connecticut has the highest per capita income level, but ranks 24th in state and local sales tax as a percentage of personal income. Mississippi, on the other hand, has the lowest per capita income level and the 6th highest level of state and local sales taxes as a percentage of personal income.

Lotteries and Gambling

Government-sponsored lotteries are a legal form of gambling. In this form of revenue collection, the government sells chances to win some prize. A government-sponsored lottery may be considered a voluntary tax. When a lottery winner claims the prize, the state and federal governments collect income taxes. For our purposes, we will not consider gambling's moral issues but only its function as revenue sources for education.

Some states, Nevada and New Jersey particularly, sponsor gambling. Other states sponsor or regulate racing of horses or dogs. Regardless of the source of income, gambling enhances state revenue. Legal gambling in the United States grossed more than $50 billion in 2000. That amounts to $180 for every man, woman, and child in the country. Table 5.7 details this revenue.

If we continue to compare Connecticut and Mississippi, Connecticut ranks 28th in terms of revenue from these sources. Mississippi, on the other hand, ranks 4th in terms of revenue from legal lotteries and gambling. These comparisons show that states must generate revenue from whatever sources they can to fund education and other state-related services that its citizens demand.

TABLE 5.6   STATE AND LOCAL SALES TAXES AS A PERCENTAGE OF PERSONAL INCOME, 1999

State	Percent of Personal Income	Rank	State	Percent of Personal Income	Rank
Alabama	4.56%	15	Montana	1.64%	47
Alaska	1.66	46	Nebraska	3.44	35
Arizona	4.86	13	Nevada	6.42	3
Arkansas	5.06	9	New Hampshire	1.47	48
California	3.92	25	New Jersey	2.89	43
Colorado	3.70	30	New Mexico	6.47	2
Connecticut	3.93	24	New York	3.63	32
Delaware	1.26	49	North Carolina	3.67	31
Florida	5.19	8	North Dakota	4.78	14
Georgia	4.38	18	Ohio	3.38	37
Hawaii	6.30	4	Oklahoma	4.19	19
Idaho	3.78	28	Oregon	0.98	50
Illinois	3.42	36	Pennsylvania	3.17	40
Indiana	3.19	39	Rhode Island	3.34	38
Iowa	3.60	33	South Carolina	3.79	27
Kansas	4.17	20	South Dakota	4.52	16
Kentucky	4.06	21	Tennessee	5.34	7
Louisiana	6.12	5	Texas	4.92	11
Maine	3.96	23	Utah	4.98	10
Maryland	2.70	44	Vermont	3.06	41
Massachusetts	2.36	45	Virginia	2.95	42
Michigan	3.55	34	Washington	6.57	1
Minnesota	3.88	26	West Virginia	4.91	12
Mississippi	5.59	6	Wisconsin	3.72	29
Missouri	4.06	22	Wyoming	4.40	17
All 50 states	3.94				
District of Columbia	4.75 (would rank number 14 if it were a state)				
Total United States	3.94				

Source: K. Hovey and H. Hovey, *Rankings across America: CQ's State Fact Finder, 2002* (Washington, DC: Congressional Quarterly Press, 2002), 148.

TABLE 5.7 **LEGAL GAMBLING REVENUE BY STATE, 2000**

State	Gross Revenue ($ in millions)	Per Capita Revenue	Rank by Revenue
Alabama	$58	$13	41
Alaska	54	86	42
Arizona	196	138	33
Arkansas	52	19	43
California	2,629	78	6
Colorado	869	202	18
Connecticut	418	123	28
Delaware	576	735	22
Florida	1,618	101	10
Georgia	1,063	130	16
Hawaii	0	0	na
Idaho	45	34	44
Illinois	2,680	216	5
Indiana	2,049	337	8
Iowa	1,004	343	17
Kansas	127	47	36
Kentucky	507	125	25
Louisiana	2,194	491	7
Maine	104	81	38
Maryland	747	141	19
Massachusetts	1,347	212	12
Michigan	1,706	172	9
Minnesota	422	86	27
Mississippi	2,685	944	4
Missouri	1,262	226	13
Montana	302	335	29
Nebraska	120	70	37
Nevada	9,632	4,820	1
New Hampshire	158	128	35
New Jersey	5,451	648	2
New Mexico	161	89	34
New York	2,739	144	3

Continued

TABLE 5.7   CONTINUED

State	Gross Revenue ($ in millions)	Per Capita Revenue	Rank by Revenue
North Dakota	76	119	39
North Carolina	8	1	47
Ohio	1,199	106	14
Oklahoma	62	18	40
Oregon	607	178	21
Pennsylvania	1,134	92	15
Rhode Island	298	285	30
South Carolina	422	105	26
South Dakota	275	364	31
Tennessee	0	0	na
Texas	1,364	65	11
Utah	0	0	na
Vermont	34	57	45
Virginia	523	74	24
Washington	659	112	20
West Virginia	525	290	23
Wisconsin	241	45	32
Wyoming	8	16	46
All 50 states	$50,411	$179	
District of Columbia	$117	$205 (would rank number 38 if it were a state)	
Total United States	$50,528	$180	

Source: K. Hovey and H. Hovey, *Rankings across America: CQ's State Fact Finder, 2002* (Washington, DC: Congressional Quarterly Press, 2002), 69.

Severance Taxes

The term "severance taxes" may be new to some. The Department of Commerce defines this as "taxes imposed distinctively on removal of natural products—e.g., oil, gas, other minerals, timber, fish, etc.—from land or water and measured by value or quantity of products removed or sold."[18]

---

[18]"State Government Tax Collections" (Washington, DC: U.S. Department of Commerce, Bureau of the Census, November 1992), 48.

TABLE 5.8	PER CAPITA SEVERANCE TAX REVENUE FOR SELECTED STATES				
State	**Per Capita Revenue**	**Rank**	**State**	**Per Capita Revenue**	**Rank**
Alaska	$856.33	1	Missouri	$00.01	50
Wyoming	$604.76	2	Illinois	$00.02	49
New Mexico	$244.71	3	Indiana	$00.09	48
North Dakota	$218.01	4	Tennessee	$00.19	47
Louisiana	$110.13	5	Virginia	$00.23	46
U.S. Total	$ 14.69				

Source: www.census.gov.govs/www/statetax02.html.

This tax is quite lucrative for some states, but overall it accounts for less than 1% of all state revenues. Some states collect no revenue from severance sources, and others collect a substantial amount. Fifteen states have no severance taxes.[19] Table 5.8 shows per capita severance tax revenue for the top and bottom five states that generate revenue through this means.

Alaska generates a significant level of revenue from severance taxes—most notably from the oil pipeline—but the majority of states generate relatively small levels of funds from these sources. Again, comparing Connecticut and Mississippi in terms of revenue generated from these sources indicates that Connecticut generates no income from this source whereas Mississippi generates $11.11 per capita. One must wonder about the cost effectiveness in Missouri of collecting one penny per person for the severance tax![20]

Corporate Income Taxes

The corporate income tax began at the federal level in 1909 when Congress levied an excise tax for the privilege of doing corporate business. The corporate income tax at the state level can be traced to Wisconsin in 1911. You will remember from earlier in this chapter that Wisconsin passed an individual income tax that same year that served as a model for many other states.[21] Corporate income taxes once generated approximately one-fourth

---

[19]These states include Connecticut, Delaware, Georgia, Hawaii, Iowa, Maine, Maryland, Massachusetts, New Hampshire, New Jersey, New York, Pennsylvania, Rhode Island, South Carolina, and Vermont.

[20]Does it cost more to collect this tax than the tax brings to the state in revenue?

[21]See Alexander and Salmon, *Public School Finance*, 104-105, for a more detailed discussion of corporate income tax.

of all federal revenue. Today, they account for less than 10% of federal revenue.[22]

Corporate income taxes are calculated on sales revenue less production costs, interest or rent payments, depreciation on capital equipment and facilities, as well as any state or local taxes that are paid. This tax has an impact on the price of many stocks and pension plans. As such, the ramifications of corporate income taxes are rather broad. Generally, they are seen to be popular with the public at large and unpopular with business owners and executives.

Corporate income taxes, however, do have many critics. To some it is seen as a "double taxation" system. Others see corporate income taxes as increasing the final cost of goods and services to the end consumer. Still others see these taxes as taking money from investors in the form of dividends or stock appreciation, which has an impact on John Q. Babyboomer who has a retirement portfolio that includes stocks. He may feel better positioned for retirement with lower corporate income taxes, which could result in a higher yield on his investments.

The issue is complicated and beyond the scope of this text. Suffice it to say that where there are thriving businesses, people are employed and paying income taxes, purchasing and maintaining homes that generate property taxes, and buying goods and services that generate sales taxes. This is a healthy cycle for a local economy that will result in greater capacity to fund public education. Funding education appropriately keeps that healthy cycle turning.

Sumptuary Taxes

Governments impose sumptuary ("sin") taxes on alcohol and tobacco, for example, to help regulate or limit activities seen to be not in the public's best interest. Legislatures attempt to regulate these "bad" behaviors by taxing them at varying rates above and beyond the sales tax. The revenue generated by the "sin tax" on alcohol, for example, is an attempt to regulate alcohol sales by increasing its price. Lawmakers reason that if a product's sale and use are not in the public interest, the additional tax should be used to benefit various other state functions.

Similarly, many states received millions of dollars from the recent federal court settlements against the tobacco industry. Some states elected to

---

[22]Richard King, Austin Swanson, and Scott Sweetland, *School Finance: Achieving High Standards with Equity and Efficiency* (Boston: Allyn and Bacon, 2003), 93.

use most of their tobacco settlement monies to fund schools. Other states used the tobacco settlement funds to balance their state budgets by placing these monies in the state's general fund.

"Sin taxes" present a conundrum for educators. We receive some of our operating revenue from the sale of substances we teach our students are harmful to them. Without this extra money, however, our already too low funding would be even further reduced. At what point do these taxes have a substantial negative impact on tobacco farmers and vineyards? This is an interesting topic for class discussion.

MEASURING TAX IMPACT

All citizens are concerned about the impact of the tax structure. The public often hears elected officials' divergent rhetoric on the subject; politicians voice opposing ideas and devote entire platforms to taxation issues. The divide between lawmakers favoring tax cuts (while continuing high spending) and those wanting to raise taxes to support more government services is regrettably becoming wider. Our public school students may be the ones who fall into this opening chasm.

Education funding should be a national priority. The tax impact to fund education needs to be equitable. In a climate of high-stakes testing and high levels of accountability for educators, resources are sorely needed in our classrooms. The No Child Left Behind legislation, which has not been fully funded as of this writing, requires adequate yearly progress (AYP) standards to be in full effect by 2014—that is, all students must pass the high-stakes state tests to graduate. If politicians and legislators do not recognize that requiring all students to meet AYP standards requires additional funding for professional development, supplies, and remediation for students—especially in poor urban schools—the public schools will probably fail in this important legislative mandate of leaving no child behind.

Students in educational leadership must measure the tax impact of education on the local and state constituency. The impact of taxes must be coupled with positive results in the schools. If local and state school boards ask that more public funds enter the education stream, then educators must and will be held accountable for results. These results include higher levels of student achievement, increased satisfaction with the public school system, and customer friendly places for students and the community.

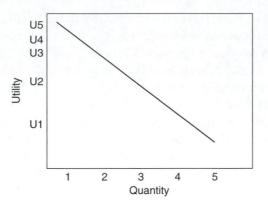

FIGURE **5.1**
Diminishing Marginal Utility

Marginal Utility

Economists discuss a concept called diminishing marginal utility (see Figure 5.1). For clarity purposes we can consider that "utility" means the same as "satisfaction." The basic idea is that consumers try to maximize their satisfaction (or utility) through their income by purchasing goods and services.

This is best explained with an example. When I was growing up in Baltimore with its hot and humid summers, my parents' home did not have air conditioning. When I started to work as a teenager, it brought great satisfaction (or utility) to me to purchase a window air conditioner for my bedroom. I hated those hot and muggy Baltimore summers, and the new room air conditioner was loved. It was not long before my parents bought a window unit for the living room, and then one for their bedroom. That first air conditioner was novel and brought great relief on hot days and nights. There was a great deal of satisfaction with that initial purchase. Going from no air conditioning to my room having air conditioning had great utility to me. The second unit brought utility to the main living area of the house—nice, but not as important to me. The third window unit brought utility to my parents' bedroom—which had little utility for me (but probably much for them). Other areas of the house could have been air conditioned, but the rooms were used less often and the expense would have brought diminishing utility to everyone in the house. As you can see from Figure 5.1, the utility does not decrease to zero. Purchasing more window units would have taken away from available dollars to purchase other items that were wanted or needed that would have brought more utility.

The same concept of diminishing marginal utility can be brought to taxes. There is some point at which people see the utility in paying taxes. They see the new roads and the new schools. They are proud of the accomplishments of the school district. They see how much easier the commute is to work with the new road. They see their children learning more in school.

As taxes rise, however, and consume a larger percentage of income, the utility or satisfaction with paying taxes tends to decrease unless citizens see that the cost brings utility for them in some significant way. This is an important concept for the student of educational leadership to keep in mind. People will only be willing to pay taxes for schools as long as they see it has utility for them. It is the job of all educators to make certain that the tax-paying public sees this educational utility in a personal way that makes sense to them.

Indicators of a Good Tax

Coinciding with this idea of diminishing marginal utility is the idea of a good tax. When tax structures are too complicated to understand or when loopholes allow individuals or companies with high capacity to pay little or nothing, people become frustrated about all taxes. The following ideas are generally agreed upon principles of a good tax system, discussed in alphabetical order.[23]

Adequacy of Yield The cost of administering a tax should not exceed the revenue generated by that tax. In other words, if a bridge were built and a toll were placed on the bridge to pay for the construction, the toll should pay for the bridge and for the means to collect the toll (personnel, management, audits, and so forth) in a reasonable time frame. The adequacy of the yield should be such that it makes sense to collect the tax or toll on the bridge. Using the idea of adequacy of yield, some must wonder about the severance tax in Missouri that generates one penny each year per person in the state. Is the yield adequate to continue the tax?

Administration Costs The cost of administering and collecting the tax should be low. The income tax is collected with much greater efficiency than is the property tax. In essence, the company for which you work deducts your income tax and sends it to the proper authority. There is a minimum number of personnel involved. Property taxes, on the other hand,

[23]These come from a variety of sources, including Vera Brimley and Rulon Garfield, *Financing Education in a Climate of Change* (Boston: Allyn and Bacon, 2002); and King, Swanson, and Sweetland, *School Finance*.

as mentioned earlier, require a much more personnel-intensive operation for collection.

Convenience of Payment   A good tax is convenient for the citizen to pay. If the public must stand in line for hours, shuffle from one office to another, and face arrogant and rude government workers, any utility for the tax is lost. If a tax can be paid through the mail or electronically, it should be done for the convenience of the taxpayer.

Economic Neutrality   Ideally, taxes should leave individuals in the same relative position after taxes as before paying taxes. Neutrality is much more easily said than done. One way that we approach neutrality is through diversification of taxes. As taxes are diversified through income, property, sales, lottery, sumptuary, and the like, we lessen the impact of any one tax.

Everyone Pays Something   All citizens enjoy the benefits of government. Police protect. Teachers teach. Firefighters fight fires. Soldiers defend. Roads transport. And so it goes. In a good tax system all citizens contribute something to the common good for the benefit of having these services.

Fairness of the Tax System   Fairness is sometimes judged in the eye of the beholder. Basically, however, a fair tax structure has a greater burden on the rich than on the poor. If a tax system has the greater burden fall on the poor, it may be said to be an unfair one. Some politicians and economists argue that a tax is not fair unless it is progressive. Others argue about the relative merits of a proportional tax. Virtually all, however, agree that a regressive tax system is unfair.

Visibility of Benefit   A highly visible benefit to the public is another indicator of a good tax. Many of us see road signs during construction saying something like "Your tax dollars at work." When a new school opens, the public has a visible anchor of utility on how their tax dollars were spent. Each time the school is used for a community benefit and the school is well maintained, the community sees the benefit of the school.

A good exercise at this point is to examine the taxes that support education and discuss whether they meet the criteria for good taxes. How could they be improved? How could we as educational leaders advocate for reform in these areas? If you were to become the superintendent of schools in your state, the governor of your state, or president one day, how would you campaign to restructure the funding of education in a more fair and equitable manner using the principles of good taxes?

FISCAL CAPACITY: THE ABILITY TO FUND EDUCATION

Capacity, or the ability to pay for goods and services, is discussed more thoroughly in Chapter 6, but it is important to introduce the concept here in relation to taxes. The United States has approximately 15,000 school systems, and community wealth varies widely throughout the country. The community's wealth—or tax base—to finance each of these school systems is known as its fiscal capacity.

Personal income is one good indicator of ability to pay the taxes to fund education. Taxes from real estate assessments, sales taxes, and corporate income taxes also contribute to an area's wealth and ability to fund education. Capacity varies from locality to locality, state to state, and region to region. The variance in per capita income by state is rather substantial (see Table 5.5). To equalize these variances, Table 5.9 adjusts state per capita income for cost of living. In other words, we know that it costs more to live in Massachusetts, New York, or California than it does to live in North Carolina or Montana. The cost of living has a direct effect on the amount of money left over from each paycheck after paying monthly bills to spend on additional taxes.

FISCAL EFFORT: PUTTING YOUR MONEY WHERE YOU SAY YOUR PRIORITIES ARE

The level to which the locality chooses to support education to the fullest capacity that it can afford speaks to its "effort." Capacity, or a measure of wealth reflecting the locality's ability to fund education, is only one side of the proverbial coin. A state or locality can have a great deal of capacity to fund education and may choose not to do so (that is, lack effort). Conversely, a state or locality may have limited capacity and apportion a great deal of effort into funding education. Effort will be introduced here and explained more thoroughly in Chapter 7.

Many factors determine the level of fiscal effort the public is willing to provide for education. Some of these factors may not be related to the quality of the schools in the locality or state. History of effort, attitudes toward taxes, the overall tax structure, the percentage of students attending public versus private schools in the area, the education level of the community, the perceived satisfaction level with the public schools, and the percentage of the population with school-aged children or grandchildren in the area all affect the level of effort that will be expended on education.

TABLE 5.9   STATE PER CAPITA INCOME ADJUSTED FOR COST OF LIVING, 1998

Rank	State	Income	Cost of Living Index	Income Adjusted for Cost of Living
1	Connecticut	$37,700	1.124	$33,541
2	Maryland	30,023	0.975	30,793
3	New Jersey	33,953	1.139	29,809
4	Minnesota	27,667	0.945	29,277
5	Delaware	29,932	1.031	29,032
6	Massachusetts	32,902	1.140	28,861
7	Illinois	28,976	1.004	28,861
8	Virginia	27,489	0.956	28,754
9	Colorado	28,821	1.006	28,649
10	New York	31,679	1.134	27,936
11	Texas	25,028	0.911	27,473
12	Michigan	25,979	0.948	27,404
13	Florida	25,922	0.947	27,373
14	Georgia	25,106	0.918	27,349
15	Nevada	27,360	1.004	27,251
16	California	27,579	1.013	27,225
17	Washington	28,066	1.035	27,117
18	New Hampshire	29,219	1.085	26,930
19	Kansas	25,049	0.935	26,790
20	Wisconsin	25,184	0.952	26,454
21	Nebraska	24,786	0.938	26,424
22	Missouri	24,447	0.930	26,287
23	North Carolina	24,122	0.922	26,163
24	Ohio	25,239	0.981	25,728
25	Iowa	24,007	0.934	25,703
26	Pennsylvania	26,889	1.048	25,657
27	Tennessee	23,615	0.929	25,420
28	Indiana	24,302	0.964	25,210
29	Oregon	24,775	0.984	25,178
30	Rhode Island	26,924	1.108	24,300
31	Wyoming	23,225	0.958	24,243
32	South Dakota	22,201	0.920	24,132

TABLE 5.9	CONTINUED			
Rank	State	Income	Cost of Living Index	Income Adjusted for Cost of Living
33	Kentucky	21,551	0.919	23,450
34	Vermont	24,217	1.037	23,353
35	North Dakota	21,708	0.930	23,342
36	Arizona	23,152	1.000	23,152
37	Alabama	21,500	0.929	23,143
38	South Carolina	21,387	0.925	23,121
39	Louisiana	21,385	0.930	22,995
40	Alaska	25,771	1.127	22,867
41	Oklahoma	21,056	0.924	22,788
42	Arkansas	20,393	0.912	22,361
43	Idaho	21,080	0.951	22,166
44	Maine	23,002	1.050	21,907
45	Hawaii	26,210	1.231	21,292
46	West Virginia	19,373	0.910	21,289
47	Montana	20,247	0.954	21,223
48	Utah	21,096	0.999	21,117
49	Mississippi	18,998	0.906	20,969
50	New Mexico	20,008	0.974	20,542
	United States	$26,482	1.000	$26,482

Source: Bureau of Economic Analysis; Kennedy School of Government. Available at: www.stateok.us/osfdocs/budget/table7.pdf.

Effort may be defined as the level to which a governmental entity uses its capacity to support the needs in public education. A simple formula for determining fiscal effort is as follows:

$$\text{Fiscal Effort} = \frac{\text{Revenue Collected for Education}}{\text{Overall Tax Base (or Capacity)}}$$

Effort in this equation is defined as a ratio. This ratio indicates the level and the willingness of the public or the government to fund education. It is one way to determine the level to which a government uses its resources to support the needs of education. This ratio or index can be computed at the local, state, or national level.

Effort is a measure that equalizes or compensates for capacity in comparing expenditures. It would not be fair to compare localities, states, or nations with others by education expenditures alone and draw any conclusions other than how wealthy that locality, state, or nation is. Determining the ratio for effort equalizes for capacity and allows for fair comparisons in how much is spent on developing the human capital within the government boundaries (local, state, or nation). In other words, effort is a vehicle to determine how much of a fiscal priority is placed on education within some jurisdiction.

EQUITY

Equity is introduced here and developed much more fully in Chapter 8. Equity is one of the more difficult concepts in school finance. Sue Books states, "Because little consensus exists, even among educational researchers, either about what equity means or about how it ought to be measured, it is difficult to answer the seemingly straightforward question: How equitable is school funding? It depends."[24]

Equity has been at the core of school finance reform efforts and court decisions since 1976 and the *Serrano v. Priest* decision of the California Supreme Court.[25] Basically, the court found that California's system for financing education did tend to equalize funding among the school districts, but the system also generated revenue proportional to the wealth of the school and the school district. Although such funding violated the idea of equity, it was permissible under the Equal Protection clause of the Fourteenth Amendment. Following the *Serrano* decision, educational equity funding issues would have to look to each state's constitution for redress.

Equity can be defined as a fairness issue for both students and taxpayers. (We deal with the former more than the latter.) Equity should not be confused with equality. In its essence, equity is providing the services students actually need whereas equality is providing the same services for all students without considering the individual needs of the students or the locality. Most people believe students should be treated equally. The difference between equality and equity explains why equity, much more than equality, is a basic tenet of our school finance system.

Consider the following scenario. Two relatively similar school systems have roughly the same level of capacity to fund education and the same

---

[24]S. Books, "School Funding: Justice v. Equity," *Equity and Excellence in Education,* December 1999, 54.

[25]*Serrano v. Priest,* 5 Cal.3d 584, 96 Cal. Rptr.601, 487 P.2d 1241 (1971), appeal after remanded 18 Cal.3d 728, 135 Cal. Rptr. 345, 557 P.2d 929 (1976), cert. Denied 432 U.S. 907, 97 S.Ct. 2951 (1976).

TABLE 5.10	EQUALITY VERSUS EQUITY			
School System	Average Family Income	State Revenue	Local Revenue	% Eligible for Special Education
A	$65,000	$3,500	$6,500	8%
B	$64,500	$3,450	$6,550	20%

number of students, about 10,000. Both receive approximately the same amount of funding from the locality and the state. Both school systems draw from upper-middle-class neighborhoods where parents expect their children to go on to college. In school system A, 8% of the students have been identified as eligible to receive special education services—somewhere near the national average. In school system B, about 20% of the students are eligible to receive special education services—much higher than the national average (see Table 5.10).

If we look solely at the issue of equality, both school systems have the funds they need. If we look at the equity issue, however, the needs of students in school system B are greater than those in school system A. School system B must spend more money to meet the identified special education population's learning needs than does school system A. Equal funding for these school systems might seem fair at first—until we consider the student population's needs. Because of varying student needs and associated costs, treating the two systems equally on a financial basis would not be fair or equitable. Because education is a state function, each state has a method for equalizing school funding to help achieve equity. These concepts are discussed fully in Chapter 8.

SUMMARY

Taxation invested in critical social institutions such as schools perpetuates our democratic government, permits our comfortable lifestyles to continue, and allows all educated individuals—regardless of race, ethnicity, gender, age, or creed—to participate in the "good life."

Using taxes to pay for public education is both controversial and critically important. A tax's purpose is to pay for a government function. Education, as a public service "company," depends on operating revenues from the community in the form of taxes. States are responsible for funding their citizens' education because education is a state function. States rely on property tax revenue for the majority of their income to operate schools in the United States. Many U.S. citizens, however, reject paying property taxes to support public schools. Nevertheless, our country holds a moral and legislative imperative to redistribute wealth, in part, to promote equity of educational opportunity and democratic citizenship. A dynamic tension arises from these conflicting views.

A tax should be "equalized"—that is, the government should have a formal mechanism to calculate a lower cost to those who can least afford the service and have a higher cost to those who can most afford the service. This equalization tends to make the most needed services more affordable to those who are least able to pay. In effect, taxes redistribute wealth.

Each state has established a minimum "floor of educational services" that localities must provide. In this way, the state requires that each student living within its boundaries complete a basic series of courses to be promoted to the next grade or to graduate from high school.

States have three major tax revenue sources: property, income, and sales taxes. Lotteries, legal gambling, corporate taxes, and "sin" taxes all contribute revenues to fund schools. All present opportunities and difficulties.

Fiscal capacity is the ability of a group to fund education. Effort involves whether or not the locality sees education as a fiscal priority.

Equity means providing the services students actually need; equality is providing the same services for all students without considering the individual needs of the locality. Until recently, this complex idea had placed equity at the core of school finance reform efforts and court decisions for decades.

Conclusion

It is important for educators to know what types of taxes support their school's funding and what taxes tend to be more popular with the public. Different types of taxes can have different effects on taxpayers and generate varying levels of support.

Case Study

You have been selected by the governor to design a two-page (front and back) brochure that will be mailed to all state residents explaining how your state funds education. Your directions are to make the brochure understandable to someone reading on the ninth grade level. You are to include in your letter the following information:

- Sources of major tax revenue to the state
- The major expenditures and why education ranks as such a major state expenditure
- How the state equalizes funding so localities with greater capacity receive fewer state dollars and localities with less capacity receive more state dollars
- The reason for any special programs initiated by the governor and how they relate to the No Child Left Behind Act of 2001

Include graphs and charts to make your illustrations clear to the public. You may include any other information you deem relevant to the explanation.

CHAPTER QUESTIONS

1. What is the relative fiscal capacity of your state to fund education? Show this in terms of state per capita income, property values, and sales tax compared with surrounding states. Based on that capacity, how much effort (per pupil expenditure) does your state put into education?
2. Describe the differences among proportional, regressive, and progressive taxes. What efforts has your state made to make the tax structure as progressive as possible? What tax structures appear to have a regressive impact on citizens?
3. How could a proportional tax have the impact of being regressive? Cite examples from your state. How would you recommend that these taxes be improved?
4. Discuss the concept of equity as it relates to school finance.

FISCAL CAPACITY

FOCUS QUESTIONS

1. Is it possible for a high-wealth district (high capacity) to commit few of its resources for education (low effort)?

2. What factors are associated with capacity?

3. How can national, state, and local capacity be measured?

4. Can these capacity measurements be compared?

5. How is efficiency associated with capacity?

6. It costs more to live in Manhattan, New York, than it does in Manhattan, Kansas. Can adjustments be made to calculate these cost-of-living differences in terms of capacity?

7. How does equalization compensate for variance in capacity?

In this chapter we discuss the idea of fiscal capacity—the financial resources available to fund services. We discuss the factors associated with capacity, and how those factors are measured and compared from a national, state, and local perspective. Finally, adjustments to capacity to allow for variance in cost of living are shown.

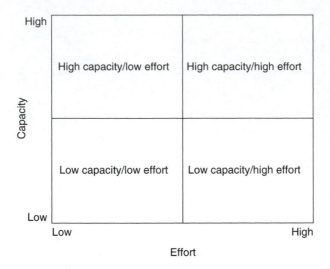

FIGURE **6.1**
Relative Fiscal Capacity and Effort

Chapter 5 introduced the idea of fiscal capacity—or the measurement of wealth. Capacity reveals the ability of a locality, state, or nation to fund those services it deems important. Fiscal capacity can be defined as the tax base of a locality, a state, or a nation as measured by some form of economic income or wealth. Capacity can be measured using various methods. For example, a county's fiscal capacity might be measured by the per capita property value of residents. At the state level, fiscal capacity may be represented by per capita income for state residents. As a nation, we can examine fiscal capacity by comparing our GDP to that of other nations. These examples display widely varying levels of capacity based on different criteria: property, income, and GDP.

This chapter deals with the concept of capacity; Chapter 7 addresses the other side of the same coin—effort. We examine various issues concerning local, state, and national fiscal capacity and methods for determining capacity. Is one method better than another? Is a combination of methods best? In what proportion should a combination of methods be employed?

It is helpful to think of capacity and effort as a two-axis construct (see Figure 6.1). On the vertical axis, capacity ranges from low to high. On the horizontal axis, effort ranges from low to high. This yields four quadrants

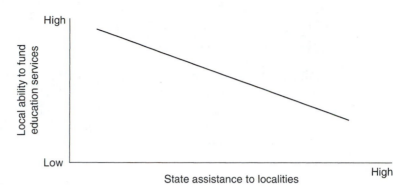

FIGURE **6.2**

Equalization for Capacity

within which various education systems may fall. For example, government entities may possess or have access to a great deal of capacity, yet elect not to fund education commensurate with that capacity. On the other hand, localities may have moderate or low capacity but choose to put more effort into funding education programs.

Obviously, not all localities within a state have the same fiscal capacity. Some localities are relatively wealthy while others struggle to keep the lights on in the Municipal Administration building. Yet with the No Child Left Behind legislation, all school divisions must make adequate yearly progress to the same high state standards. Struggling localities, however, cannot be expected to bring the same level of resources to the table as wealthy localities do.

As discussed in Chapter 3, states must equalize for this variance in capacity between school districts by providing greater financial resources to low-capacity localities and fewer state resources to high-capacity systems. In other words, high-capacity systems must fund a greater share of education with local dollars. Conversely, lower capacity systems are funded to a greater level with state funds to make up for their lack of ability to raise funds at the local level.

Figure 6.2 shows that low-capacity systems pay some of the cost of education whereas high-capacity systems pay most—but usually not all—of the cost. As a rule, the poorest locality will always pay something, and the richest locality will always receive something. What they pay and what they receive is calculated by a formula that determines the slope of the diagonal line in Figure 6.2.

Determining Fiscal Capacity

Initially, the idea of fiscal capacity and how state and federal governments equalize for capacity seems relatively simple: Low-capacity states and localities receive a greater share of funds from respective federal and state treasuries to operate the schools to "level the playing field" for educational opportunity. The richer help the poorer. As we know, however, sharing scarce resources turns out to be much more complex. Most localities use property taxes as the primary source of school funding. As previously noted, the value of one's home as measured by the property tax may not the best measure of capacity to fund schools. Income may be a better measurement of wealth in today's world. Moreover, a combination of measurements may be the best overall indicator of capacity.

With this in mind, several questions beg answers. To what relative level should both personal property and income be calculated to determine capacity? Furthermore, what role should commercial and industrial property value play in the overall equalization equation? Should sales tax revenue be calculated in this formula? If so, what should be taxed, and how should it be applied?

Taxing groceries and medicines tends to have a regressive effect on poorer people. To that end, should high-end foods and elective medicines be taxed and the rest untaxed? Determining a working formula for fiscal capacity is not simple. What factors determine capacity? And what political factors come into play that ultimately shape the algebraic slope of the equalization formula line? This is the stuff of equity court cases.

Let's consider two school district scenarios (Table 6.1). Both school districts have the same per capita residential property value.[1] School district A, however, has virtually all of its property wealth in residential property value. School district B, on the other hand, has approximately one-half of its property wealth in residential sites with the other half evenly divided between commercial and industrial sites. Both school districts have the same per capita income. We have not addressed agricultural values here, but many localities have a great deal of capacity in agricultural land values.

Do both districts have the same capacity to fund schools? Unlike residential property owners, commercial and industrial property owners can transfer their tax burden to other users through higher prices. What do the

---

[1]You would need to know how much residential property value was generated in each district and not just the per capita value. For example, there could be only 20 houses in one locality and 20,000 in another locality. Even though the per capita values are similar, the revenue generated from these properties would vary greatly.

TABLE 6.1 COMPARISON OF TWO DISTRICTS		
	School District A	**School District B**
Number of pupils	10,000	10,000
Per capita residential property value	$50,000	$50,000
Per capita commercial property value	$0	$25,000
Per capita industrial property value	$0	$25,000
Per capita income	$50,000	$50,000

higher prices of products have to do with local capacity if the tax burden is shifted to the consumer from commercial or industrial property owners? This table provides a simplified overview of several factors associated with school district funding to demonstrate the complexity of computing capacity. The sales taxes generated by the commercial sites are not included, nor have we indicated the number or diversity of the industrial sites. Are the localities and their economies in a growth mode or in decline? In addition, the per capita income and property values are averages. Are there one or two very large, wealthy businesses or homes with the rest of the properties at poverty levels? Extreme factors, or outliers in the equation, tend to distort the mean, or per capita data. These are all concepts that must be considered. As always, the devil is in the details.

Which school district is better able to fund schools? Initially, it would appear that school district B is the obvious choice. To make that determination, however, requires more data than is provided.[2] It is obvious that not all school districts have the same ability to fund education to state standards. To have each district—poor and wealthy—fund education on its own would require very little effort for the wealthiest communities and an almost impossible effort for the poorest (see Chapter 7). This is the reason states are required to equalize funding based on the districts' ability or capacity to fund those services. Localities have varying levels of capacity, as do states and nations.[3] Many factors must be considered in determining ability to fund schools.

---

[2]Even though the per capita residential property values and income are the same for both districts, school district B could have several mansions worth tens of millions of dollars while the rest of the area held modest homes. The distribution of income could fall along the same lines—several with extremely high income and most on the free and reduced-price lunch program.

[3]It is important for educators to understand that using capacity to fund education is not only a moral obligation for the next generation but also provides a significant investment human capital, as discussed in Chapter 4.

LOCAL FISCAL CAPACITY ISSUES

Traditionally, a locality measured its fiscal capacity as a ratio of the district's property valuation divided by the number of pupils within the system, which provides a property value amount on a per pupil basis. On the surface, this seems like a fair means of comparing local capacity.

This calculation method lacks an important education component—the students' needs. A high-poverty school district will have greater proportional needs than virtually any other school district. Students who come to school well fed and already possessing basic literacy and numeracy skills do not have the same educational needs as those who come to school hungry and without years of reading and arithmetic experiences at home.

In addition, all other factors being equal, a school district with 20% of its students identified as eligible to receive special education services will have a greater need than the district with 10% of its students receiving special education services. Moreover, an isolated, rural school system has different needs from those of an affluent, suburban district close to a great city's cultural and intellectual advantages. To have each district fund education independently based primarily on property wealth puts a far greater burden on the poor than on the rich and jeopardizes students' educational equity. Relying solely on local property value to fund education does not meet the legal criterion of education as a state function.

Thankfully, states have more sophisticated methods for determining capacity, and most states now include the district's and state's income and sales tax measurements as a way to equalize assessments. Constitutional exceptions and variations exist regarding how each state measures fiscal capacity.[4]

How school districts measure capacity is the hinge pin for determining how each state equalizes education funding. Scholars have known for years that wide disparities existed in fiscal capacity within states and that a single measurement of wealth (such as property) only exacerbates the problem. They know that taxation needs to be equalized at the state level to accommodate district variances. In 1906 Ellwood Cubberley wrote, "any attempt at the equalization of opportunities for education, much less any attempt at equalizing burdens, is clearly impossible under a system of exclusively local taxation."[5]

---

[4]As you remember from Chapter 3, education is a state function. As such, its method for equalizing the funding of education services depends largely on the state's constitution.

[5]E. Cubberley, *School Funds and Their Apportionment* (New York: Teachers College Press, Columbia University, 1906), 28.

How these funds are equalized today is the fodder of state constitutional challenges and Supreme Court cases.

When discussing capacity, it is important to consider the size of school districts and the number of school districts within states as Kern Alexander and Richard Salmon, two distinguished finance scholars and researchers, note:

> Recent studies in a number of states have indicated a range in fiscal capacity for county units and other large school district states, from less than 10 to 1 to about 20 or 25 to 1 for small district states . . . it is apparent that a considerable difference exists among the districts in their ability to finance educational programs. If no state aid were provided in these states, the low fiscal capacity districts would have to make 10 to 25 times the fiscal effort made by their high-capacity peers to finance an equitable program of educational opportunity. The situation in the states that maintain large numbers of very small school districts is of course much more serious, with the range often exceeding 100 to 1.[6]

In other words, it is easier for states to fund programs with large school districts than to fund them for many small school districts. In Virginia, for example, small, rural, isolated Highland County has approximately 375 students. Fairfax County, one of the largest school districts in the country, located outside the nation's capital, has approximately 166,000 students. The per capita tax base is much larger in Fairfax than in Highland. Resources are more available, the schools have an efficiency of size, administrative costs are controlled by economies of scale, and salaries higher than the state average (although lower than the average county income) provide Fairfax County with certain financial advantages over Highland County. (The Appendix at the end of this chapter provides an opportunity for you to examine Texas state data based on this same issue.)

In general, larger school divisions reach a point of efficiency. The cost of all services is spread out over a larger student base, reducing per pupil costs. For example, a school with 400 students and another with 600 students may have the same number of administrators, secretaries, librarians, and nurses, but the larger school may have four or five more teachers. If the cost of operating the school on a per student basis is spread out over all of the students, it is more cost effective to run the school with 600 students than the one with 400 students. Larger districts have the ability to organize schools more efficiently than do smaller school districts.

In this light, it is wise to look at the number of students in each state and the number of school districts in each state and compute the average

---

[6]K. Alexander and R. Salmon, *Public School Finance* (Boston: Allyn and Bacon, 1995), 166–167.

NUMBER OF SCHOOL DISTRICTS AND PUPILS PER DISTRICT BY STATE, 2002

TABLE 6.2

State	Districts	Pupils/District	State	Districts	Pupils/District
Alabama	128	5,760	Montana	453	335
Alaska	53	2,535	Nebraska	576	495
Arizona	410	2,249	Nevada	17	20,989
Arkansas	310	1,451	New Hampshire	178	1,162
California	985	6,344	New Jersey	604	2,221
Colorado	176	4,217	New Mexico	89	3,598
Connecticut	166	3,435	New York	703	4,086
Delaware	19	6,082	North Carolina	120	10,961
District of Columbia	1	75,392	North Dakota	230	461
Florida	67	37,321	Ohio	662	2,766
Georgia	180	8,170	Oklahoma	554	1,123
Hawaii	1	184,546	Oregon	197	2,799
Idaho	115	2,144	Pennsylvania	501	3,636
Illinois	894	2,317	Rhode Island	36	4,390
Indiana	295	3,377	South Carolina	90	7,679
Iowa	374	1,299	South Dakota	176	725
Kansas	304	1,547	Tennessee	138	6,703
Kentucky	176	3,718	Texas	1,040	4,003
Louisiana	78	9,376	Utah	40	12,117
Maine	282	729	Vermont	288	351
Maryland	24	35,860	Virginia	135	8,615
Massachusetts	349	2,788	Washington	296	3,409
Michigan	734	2,358	West Virginia	55	5,143
Minnesota	415	2,052	Wisconsin	431	2,040
Mississippi	152	3,247	Wyoming	48	1,836
Missouri	524	1,736	United States	14,859	3,192

Note: We divided the number of students by the number of districts to obtain the average number of pupils per district. Hawaii and the District of Columbia were omitted from the final calculation as each has only one district. Errors in total calculations are due to rounding.

Source: The data for number of school districts were obtained from http://nces.ed.gov/pubs2003/digest02/tables/dt087.asp. Data for number of students per school district were obtained from http://nces.ed.gov.nationsreportcard/states/profile.asp.

number of students in each school district. Remember that there will be significant variance in the size of the school districts—as in Highland and Fairfax counties. Table 6.2 shows the number of local education agencies for each state in 2002 (latest data available), the number of districts in that state, and the average number of pupils per district.

As shown in Table 6.2, the United States educates its more than 47 million public school students in almost 15,000 school districts. At first glance, it may appear that Hawaii and the District of Columbia have relatively large school districts. In fact, they have only one school district each. The numbers represent their total student enrollments. Florida and Maryland have sizeable average school districts with 37,321 and 35,860 pupils per district, respectively. Montana and Vermont, on the other hand, have the lowest average number of pupils per district with 335 and 351, respectively. Consider the building costs, the administrative overhead, and the State Department of Education costs amortized over the small school districts as compared to those of larger districts.

Another important variable at the local level is the number of residents and the per capita income. Let's say school district A has 1,000 students. The locality has only 4,000 residents with a per capita income (PCI) of $35,000. School district B has 2,000 students in a total local population of 10,000 residents with the same per capita income of $35,000. Using our formula for determining capacity by property values, Table 6.3 shows the relative capacity of these two systems.

School district A has $140,000 of per capita income per student. School district B has $175,000 of per capita income per student. On this basis, School district B has a greater capacity to fund services. Clearly, where there is a greater ratio of residents to students, there exists greater capacity.

How does your locality "measure up" compared to other localities in your state? How does the state equalize funding for education in your locality? Most important, what standards has your state accepted with the No Child Left Behind requirements? It will take money to achieve adequate yearly progress (AYP) toward the end goal of the year 2014. Does your state have the capacity to fund the programs needed to truly leave no child behind? Does your locality have the capacity?

A case study to clarify this concept is in order. The Appendix at the end of this chapter lists all Texas counties alphabetically with total county population (tax base relative to student enrollment), per capita income, per capita property values, total public school enrollment, number of schools in the county, and number of school districts in the county. Texas is somewhat different from many states in that a county may have more than one school district. Each school district may have its own superintendent and central office staff.

TABLE 6.3	RELATIVE CAPACITY BY PER CAPITA INCOME (PCI)

School District A

$$\frac{4{,}000 \text{ residents} \times \$35{,}000 \text{ PCI}}{1{,}000 \text{ students}} = \$140{,}000 \text{ PCI per student}$$

School District B

$$\frac{10{,}000 \text{ residents} \times \$35{,}000 \text{ PCI}}{2{,}000 \text{ students}} = \$175{,}000 \text{ PCI per student}$$

Examining the data provides some interesting contrasts. For example, in the Coastal Bend Region, Kenedy County has a total population of 414 residents with 78 students enrolled in one school (with only one district). Its per capita income is not much different from the state average. Its per capita property value, however, is significantly higher than the state average at $1,083,787. If you take the total property value in Kenedy County (total population multiplied by the per capita property value) totaling $448,687,818 (414 population multiplied by $1,083,787) and divide that figure by the number of students (78) you have a figure of $5,752,407 of property value per student in Kenedy County available to fund services.

Compare that with Coryell County in the Central Region. Using the same calculation method, there are 74,978 residents in the county with a per capita property value of $17,956. This gives a total county property value of $1,346,304,968. Divided by the number of pupils (10,632) gives a property value per student of $126,627. The per pupil property value in Kenedy County is more than 45 times greater than that of Coryell County.

In addition, Coryell County has 21 schools in five school districts. The cost of amortizing the administrative overhead in Coryell County is much higher than in Kenedy County. On top of that, the property revenue basis is less than that in Kenedy County.

These figures can be examined in terms of per capita income as well. In Kenedy County, there is a total income of $10,739,160 (total population multiplied by the per capita income). That number divided by the total school enrollment provides income of $137,681 per pupil. Coryell County has a total income of $1,245,384,580 (74,978 residents times $16,610 per capita income). That number divided by the 10,632 pupils in the county provides income of $117,135 per pupil. On the sole basis of total income per pupil, Coryell County compares favorably with Kenedy County: $117,135 to $137,681. It is only when the entire picture is clear that the glaring differences in capacity become evident.

Clearly, states need to intervene with an equalization formula to help the lower capacity school districts meet the same high academic standards that the states hold for the highest capacity school districts. Determining capacity can be a difficult concept to measure—especially when deciding how much money one district will receive from the state as compared with another.

STATE FISCAL CAPACITY ISSUES

Just as localities have differences in their ability to raise funds for services, states also vary in their capacity. For example, the pictures President Lyndon Johnson showed in the mid-1960s of family poverty in the Deep South bore no resemblance to anything that most Connecticut families had seen in their state. In truth, most comfortable Americans could not relate to that type of abject poverty. If that level of deprivation existed in homes, what types of schools did these children attend? What resources did their teachers have? How much money was the PTA able to raise for these schools?

Variance exists in the fiscal capacity of states. Just as in the late 19th century when capacity was measured as property values, per capita property values by state can be calculated. Likewise, it is possible to calculate per capita income, and also to adjust for cost-of-living standards across states. Each of these pieces of information provides part of the puzzle in determining state capacity.

Variance also exists in how state capacity is measured. Some states measure capacity on a capita or total population basis. Other states calculate capacity on a per student enrolled in public school basis. In the first instance, it is argued that government services must be provided for all the population—not just for public school students. In the second instance, it is argued that for education purposes the number of students enrolled in public schools should be the measure of capacity. Clearly this can be a point of contention. State population demographics vary. Florida, for example, as a United States retirement haven, has a relatively low ratio of students to the overall population. Generally, the preferred method for computing capacity uses the number of public school students as the denominator.

Table 6.4 shows the per capita personal income for individuals on a statewide basis. Over time the rankings may change. One cautionary note in using income indicators: Per capita income can change rapidly. If a statewide downturn occurs and a great portion of the population becomes unemployed, income will decrease rapidly and not reflect the overall picture accurately.

Furthermore, costs of living vary. It is more expensive to live in New York City than it is to live in upstate New York, and it is more expensive to live in

TABLE 6.4   PER CAPITA PERSONAL INCOME BY STATE

State	1980	1990	1995	2000	2001	2002
Alabama	$7,465	$14,899	$19,683	$23,521	$24,477	$25,128
Alaska	13,007	20,887	25,798	29,642	31,027	32,151
Arizona	8,854	16,262	20,634	24,988	25,878	26,183
Arkansas	7,113	13,779	18,546	21,995	22,750	23,512
California	11,021	20,656	24,496	32,149	32,655	32,996
Colorado	10,143	18,818	24,865	32,434	33,455	33,276
Connecticut	11,532	25,426	31,947	40,702	42,377	42,706
Delaware	10,059	19,719	25,391	31,012	32,166	32,779
District of Columbia	12,251	24,643	33,045	38,838	40,539	42,120
Florida	9,246	18,785	23,512	27,764	29,048	29,596
Georgia	8,021	17,121	22,230	27,794	28,523	28,821
Hawaii	10,129	20,905	25,584	27,851	29,034	30,001
Idaho	8,105	15,304	19,630	23,727	24,506	25,057
Illinois	10,454	20,159	25,643	31,856	32,990	33,404
Indiana	8,914	16,815	21,845	26,933	27,522	28,240
Iowa	9,226	16,683	21,181	26,431	27,225	28,280
Kansas	9,880	17,639	21,889	27,374	28,432	29,141
Kentucky	7,679	14,751	19,215	24,085	24,878	25,579
Louisiana	8,412	14,279	19,541	23,090	24,454	25,446
Maine	7,760	17,041	20,240	25,380	26,853	27,744
Maryland	10,394	22,088	26,896	33,482	35,279	36,298
Massachusetts	10,103	22,248	28,051	37,704	38,864	39,244
Michigan	9,801	18,239	23,975	29,127	29,629	30,296
Minnesota	9,673	18,784	24,583	31,935	33,059	34,071
Mississippi	6,573	12,578	17,185	20,900	21,653	22,372
Missouri	8,812	17,407	22,094	27,206	28,221	28,936
Montana	8,342	14,743	18,764	22,518	24,044	25,020
Nebraska	8,895	17,379	22,196	27,630	28,861	29,771
Nevada	10,848	20,248	25,808	29,506	30,128	30,180
New Hampshire	9,150	20,231	25,008	33,169	33,969	34,334
New Jersey	10,966	24,182	29,277	37,118	38,625	39,453
New Mexico	7,940	14,213	18,852	21,931	23,081	23,941
New York	10,179	22,322	27,721	34,689	35,878	36,043

TABLE 6.4	CONTINUED					
State	**1980**	**1990**	**1995**	**2000**	**2001**	**2002**
North Carolina	7,780	16,284	21,938	26,882	27,308	27,711
North Dakota	8,642	15,320	19,084	24,708	25,798	26,982
Ohio	9,399	17,547	22,887	27,977	28,699	29,405
Oklahoma	9,018	15,117	19,394	23,650	24,945	25,575
Oregon	9,309	17,201	22,668	27,660	28,222	28,731
Pennsylvania	9,353	18,884	23,738	29,504	30,752	31,727
Rhode Island	9,227	19,035	24,046	29,113	30,256	31,319
South Carolina	7,392	15,101	19,473	24,000	24,840	25,400
South Dakota	7,800	15,628	19,848	25,958	26,566	26,894
Tennessee	7,711	15,903	21,800	25,946	26,808	27,671
Texas	9,439	16,747	21,526	27,752	28,472	28,551
Utah	7,671	14,063	18,858	23,436	24,033	24,306
Vermont	7,957	17,444	21,359	26,848	28,756	29,567
Virginia	9,413	19,543	24,456	31,120	32,338	32,922
Washington	10,256	19,268	23,878	31,230	31,976	32,677
West Virginia	7,764	13,964	17,913	21,738	22,862	23,688
Wisconsin	9,364	17,399	22,573	28,100	29,196	29,923
Wyoming	11,018	16,905	21,514	27,372	29,587	30,578
United States	**9,494**	**18,667**	**23,562**	**29,469**	**30,413**	**30,941**

Note: Per capita personal income was computed using midyear population estimates of the Bureau of the Census.

Source: U.S. Department of Commerce, Bureau of Economic Analysis, *Survey of Current Business.* Available at: www.bea.doc.gov/bea/regional/spi/.

San Francisco than it is to live in Bakersfield. Another way to examine the capacity of per capita income is to adjust it for a cost-of-living index, which allows a better computation of capacity. Table 6.5 shows per capita income adjusted for inflation for the year 2000. The first column shows the state (and the District of Columbia). The second major column shows the Per Capita Income for the year 2000. Beneath that major column are four other columns. The first shows the rank for that state's per capita income.

For example, Virginia had the 14th highest nonadjusted per capita income for 2000, at $31,162. Considering the cost-of-living index of 0.954 in Virginia, that income was the equal of $32,595. That adjusted income based on the lower cost of living moved Virginia up in the rankings from 14th in actual income to 6th in adjusted income. Conversely, Connecticut had the highest actual per capita income, at $40,640, yet due to the high cost-of-living index

TABLE 6.5   PER CAPITA PERSONAL INCOME ADJUSTED FOR INFLATION

State	Per Capita Income, 2000				Cost of Living	
	Rank	Actual (not adjusted)	Rank	Cost-of-Living Adjusted	Rank	Index 1999
United States (mean)		$29,676		$29,676		1.000
District of Columbia	3	$37,383	1	$35,813	11	1.042
Connecticut	1	$40,640	2	$35,682	5	1.122
Maryland	6	$33,872	3	$34,753	24	0.974
Minnesota	11	$32,101	4	$33,706	31	0.950
Massachusetts	2	$37,992	5	$32,597	2	1.142
Virginia	14	$31,162	6	$32,595	27	0.954
Colorado	8	$32,949	7	$32,587	16	1.011
Illinois	10	$32,259	8	$32,162	19	1.003
New Jersey	4	$36,983	9	$31,916	3	1.137
California	9	$32,275	10	$31,597	15	1.021
Michigan	18	$29,612	11	$31,093	32	0.950
New Hampshire	7	$33,332	12	$30,499	8	1.085
Texas	26	$27,871	13	$30,407	49	0.909
Delaware	13	$31,255	14	$30,317	14	1.030
Nevada	15	$30,529	15	$30,285	17	1.008
Georgia	25	$27,940	16	$30,259	46	0.917
Washington	12	$31,528	17	$30,235	12	1.041
New York	5	$34,547	18	$29,987	4	1.132
Florida	24	$28,145	19	$29,749	33	0.943
Kansas	28	$27,816	20	$29,680	36	0.933
Wisconsin	22	$28,232	21	$29,587	29	0.952
Nebraska	27	$27,829	22	$29,554	34	0.938
Missouri	29	$27,445	23	$29,394	38	0.929
North Carolina	31	$27,194	24	$29,370	44	0.920
Ohio	20	$28,400	25	$28,968	22	0.980
Oregon	21	$28,350	26	$28,662	21	0.989
Iowa	34	$26,723	27	$28,487	35	0.934
Wyoming	30	$27,230	28	$28,346	26	0.959
South Dakota	36	$26,115	29	$28,204	45	0.920
Tennessee	35	$26,239	30	$28,154	40	0.927
Pennsylvania	19	$29,539	31	$28,151	10	1.047

TABLE 6.5 CONTINUED

| State | Per Capita Income, 2000 | | | | Cost of Living | |
	Rank	Actual (not adjusted)	Rank	Cost-of-Living Adjusted	Rank	Index 1999
Indiana	32	$27,011	32	$28,010	25	0.963
North Dakota	39	$25,068	33	$26,798	37	0.931
Alaska	16	$30,064	34	$26,637	6	1.114
Rhode Island	17	$29,686	35	$26,509	7	1.107
Kentucky	41	$24,294	36	$26,310	47	0.917
South Carolina	40	$24,321	37	$26,194	42	0.923
Vermont	33	$26,901	38	$25,933	13	1.036
Arizona	38	$25,578	39	$25,476	18	1.004
Idaho	42	$24,180	40	$25,365	30	0.951
Oklahoma	44	$23,517	41	$25,351	43	0.922
Alabama	45	$23,471	42	$25,184	41	0.927
Louisiana	46	$23,334	43	$25,014	39	0.928
Maine	37	$25,623	44	$24,367	9	1.049
Arkansas	48	$22,257	45	$24,260	48	0.910
West Virginia	50	$21,915	46	$23,931	50	0.908
Utah	43	$23,907	47	$23,835	20	1.003
Montana	47	$22,569	48	$23,607	28	0.954
Mississippi	51	$20,993	49	$23,008	51	0.904
New Mexico	49	$22,203	50	$22,714	23	0.977
Hawaii	23	$28,221	51	$22,097	1	1.217

Source: Derived from *The Federal Budget and the States*, Fiscal Year 1999, 24th ed., Table C-2. Taubman Center for State and Local Government, Kennedy School of Government, Harvard University; and Office of Senator Patrick Moynihan, United States Bureau of Economic Analysis, "2000 Personal Per Capita Income by State."

(1.122), Connecticut moved to 2nd place. The cost of living has an impact on a state's ability, or capacity, to fund governmental services.

Given this information, it is possible to compare the rankings of per capita state government expenditures for education with the measure of capacity in Table 6.5. Keep in mind that this is only one relatively simple measure of capacity and spending. Table 6.6 shows the relative ranking of income adjusted for cost of living with per capita state expenditures for education.

If measuring wealth solely as income, it would be natural to expect the state with the highest per capita income to have the highest per capita spending on education. Obviously, this is not the case. From the data in Table 6.6,

TABLE 6.6 COMPARATIVE RANKINGS, INCOME ADJUSTED FOR COST OF LIVING AND STATE PER CAPITA SPENDING, K–12 EDUCATION

State	Spending on Education, 1999		Per Capita Income, 2000 (cost-of-living adjusted)	
	Rank	Per Capita	Rank	Income
Alaska	1	$1,882	34	$26,637
New Jersey	2	$1,584	9	$31,916
New York	3	$1,579	18	$29,987
Wyoming	4	$1,436	28	$28,346
Michigan	5	$1,394	11	$31,093
Wisconsin	6	$1,388	21	$29,587
Minnesota	7	$1,337	4	$33,706
District of Columbia	8	$1,324	1	$35,813
Vermont	9	$1,308	38	$25,933
Connecticut	10	$1,281	2	$35,682
Pennsylvania	11	$1,259	31	$28,151
Washington	12	$1,239	17	$30,235
Maine	13	$1,232	44	$24,367
Massachusetts	14	$1,214	4	$33,706
Rhode Island	15	$1,211	35	$26,509
Texas	16	$1,205	13	$30,407
Delaware	17	$1,195	14	$30,317
United States		**$1,177**		**$29,676**
Oregon	18	$1,172	26	$28,662
Illinois	19	$1,168	8	$32,162
Iowa	20	$1,160	27	$28,487
Nebraska	21	$1,149	22	$29,554
Georgia	22	$1,139	16	$30,259
Maryland	23	$1,138	3	$34,753
Ohio	24	$1,137	25	$28,968
Montana	25	$1,123	48	$23,607
Colorado	26	$1,131	7	$32,587
New Hampshire	27	$1,126	12	$30,499
Indiana	28	$1,125	32	$28,010
Virginia	29	$1,123	6	$32,595
California	30	$1,122	10	$31,597
Oklahoma	31	$1,121	41	$25,351

TABLE 6.6 **CONTINUED**

| State | Spending on Education, 1999 | | Per Capita Income, 2000 (cost-of-living adjusted) | |
	Rank	Per Capita	Rank	Income
Nevada	32	$1,101	15	$30,285
West Virginia	33	$1,093	46	$23,931
New Mexico	34	$1,087	50	$22,714
Kansas	35	$1,082	20	$29,680
South Carolina	36	$1,078	37	$26,194
Utah	37	$1,077	47	$23,835
Idaho	38	$1,065	40	$25,365
North Dakota	39	$1,043	33	$26,798
Missouri	40	$1,036	23	$29,394
South Dakota	41	$1,035	29	$28,204
North Carolina	42	$994	24	$29,370
Florida	43	$992	19	$29,749
Louisiana	44	$983	43	$25,014
Alabama	45	$967	42	$$25,184
Arkansas	46	$962	45	$24,260
Arizona	47	$957	39	$25,476
Tennessee	48	$922	30	$28,154
Mississippi	49	$912	49	$23,008
Kentucky	50	$891	36	$26,310
Hawaii	51	$818	51	$22,097

Source: Derived from Table 6.5 and from *Rankings and Estimates: Rankings of the States 2001 and Estimates of School Statistics 2002,* National Education Association, Washington, D.C., 2002.

the District of Columbia, the locality with the highest per capita adjusted income of $35,813, does not have the highest per capita spending. It ranks number eight, at $1,324. This is not the best example, however, because school funding for this district comes from the federal government.

A better example is to compare Connecticut and Maryland, the number two and three states in adjusted income. Their adjusted per capita income stands at $35,682 and $34,753, respectively. Their per capita spending on education, however, ranks them 10th and 23rd, respectively. Income is probably a better proxy for wealth than property, but a mixture of variables is probably best. Remember Kenedy, Texas? Their per capita property values were significantly higher than other areas, yet their per capita income was relatively average.

Measuring capacity is not a simple process. Local and state governments may attempt to measure wealth in simple terms, but knowledgeable citizens and educators appreciate the issue's complexity.

NATIONAL FISCAL CAPACITY ISSUES

Some national and international issues are of concern to education finance. Addressing national fiscal capacity in detail is beyond the scope and responsibilities of most U.S. educators, but we will provide a brief overview here. Just as states and localities have difficulty measuring capacity, so do nations. This problem is seen in the various measurements that come in and out of favor to measure wealth and productivity. Many ways exist to compute a nation's wealth. Gross National Product (GNP) includes the total economic value of all the goods and services produced by a country during a given year. Gross Domestic Product (GDP) includes the total output a country produces, including either public or private factors, regardless of where production occurs, within a given year. GDP is now a more favored indicator than GNP.

GDP is a fair proxy for a nation's capacity. Natural resources were once considered the primary focus for developing wealth or capacity. We now know that human capital development plays an integral role in how nations develop.

In *The Work of Nations*,[7] Robert Reich sees a future in which national resources are the skills and developed human capital of the workforce. Consider Reich's comments in light of two countries—Japan, a natural resource poor country, and the United States, a country rich in natural resources. Before the Pacific Rim stock market collapse, Japan's economy was touted in journals, books, and newspapers because its per capita GNP had overtaken that of the United States.[8] Japan has virtually no natural resources of its own, and it must import almost everything used in the manufacturing process.

---

[7]R. Reich, *The Work of Nations* (New York: Alfred A. Knopf, 1991). Notice the difference from Adam Smith's work in *The Wealth of Nations,* Edwin Cannan, ed. (London: Methuen, 1904). (Originally published 1776).

[8]In 1988 the Japanese per capita GNP exceed that of the United States, $21,400 to $19,700 according to the World Bank's 1992 *World Tables*, published by Johns Hopkins University Press.

TABLE 6.7	GDP PER CAPITA FOR THE POOREST COUNTRIES, 2003

Rank	Country	Per Capita GDP
1.	Luxembourg	$44,000
2.	United States	$36,300
3.	Bermuda	$34,800
4.	San Marino	$34,600
5.	Norway	$31,800
6.	Switzerland	$31,700
7.	Cayman Islands	$30,000
8.	Canada	$29,400
9.	Belgium	$29,000
10.	Denmark	$29,000
11.	Ireland	$28,500
12.	Japan	$28,000
13.	Austria	$27,700
14.	Iceland	$27,100
15.	Australia	$27,000
	Monaco	$27,000
16.	Netherlands	$26,900
17.	Germany	$26,600
18.	Finland	$26,200
19.	France	$25,700
20.	Sweden	$25,400
21.	United Kingdom	$25,300
22.	Hong Kong	$25,000
23.	Italy	$25,000

Source: http://www.odci.gov/cia/publications/factbook/fields/2004.html.

On the other hand, the United States is the world's most powerful country with resources that other nations envy. We have an educated workforce with a high level of productivity. Our system of higher education is superior to that in any other country, and our military resources are unequaled. In spite of these strengths, the United States is not the wealthiest nation on a per capita basis. Obviously, the natural resources of a country must now include how the skills and human capital of the workforce are developed. Table 6.7 shows the rankings for countries with a per capita GDP of $25,000

TABLE 6.8	GDP PER CAPITA FOR THE POOREST COUNTRIES, 2003	

Rank	Country	Per Capita GDP
1.	Sierra Leone	$500
2.	Somalia	$550
3.	Democratic Republic of Congo	$590
4.	Burundi	$600
	Mayotte	$600
5.	Tanzania	$610
6.	Malawi	$660
7.	Ethiopia	$700
8.	Comoros	$710
9.	Eritrea	$740
10.	Afghanistan	$800
11.	Niger	$820
	Yemen	$820
12.	Mali	$840
	Nigeria	$840
13.	Madagascar	$870
	Zambia	$870
14.	Mozambique	$900
	Guinea-Bissau	$900
15.	North Korea	$1,000
	Tokelau	$1,000

Source: http://www.odci.gov/cia/publications/factbook/fields/2004.html.

or more equalized on purchasing power parity with U.S. dollars as the basis of comparison (as of March 2003).

Table 6.8 lists the world's poorest countries with a per capita GPD of $1,000 or less per year. The disparity in nations' wealth is large. One must wonder what will happen to the world economy as the countries that develop their human capital advance while other countries go without the resources even to bury their dead. Many believe that unless the United States uses the fiscal capacity it has to promote public education, other countries will surpass us in many wealth measures on a per capita basis. Chapter 7, which deals with effort, examines these capacity figures in relation to spending on education, or effort, and what that means for the United States.

These poorest countries face devastating problems including disease, starvation, and civil war. Survival needs trump education needs, but most of these developing countries realize the potential for education to elevate physical and economic circumstances and cure the ills they face. Many countries look to the United States for our education system—both public education and higher education. They realize that education develops human capital and that expenditures for schools are an investment in their country's future.

SUMMARY

Determining fiscal capacity is complex. Capacity, as a measurement of wealth, reveals the ability of a locality, state, or nation to fund those services it deems important. States and localities have different abilities to raise funds for services. Two interacting factors—capacity and effort—influence a government's decision about how to fund educational programs. How school districts measure capacity is the basis for determining how each state equalizes education funding.

Economically struggling localities cannot be expected to commit the same resource level to funding their public schools as do wealthy localities. States must equalize for the variance in local capacity by providing greater financial resources to low-capacity districts and by providing fewer state resources to high-capacity systems. High-capacity systems must fund a greater share of education with local funds. Most states now include the district's and state's income and sales tax measurements as a way to equalize assessments.

Constitutional exceptions and variations exist in how each state measures fiscal capacity. Measuring local fiscal capacity as a ratio of the district's property valuation (the numerator) divided by the number of pupils within the system (the denominator) does not consider all essential variables. A high-poverty school district will have greater needs than a high-wealth school district. Large numbers of special needs students and isolated rural districts also have increased needs. The school district's size and the number of school districts within a state also affect capacity. At the local level, the number of individuals, the per capita income, and the cost of living affect capacity. Some states measure capacity on a capita or total population basis. Other states calculate capacity on a per student enrolled in public school basis.

Nations, too, have difficulty measuring capacity. Various measurements—in and out of favor—measure wealth and productivity. GDP is now a more favored indicator than GNP.

CONCLUSION

Unless localities, states, and the nation use the fiscal capacity they have to promote public education and invest in human capital, those localities, states, and countries may never realize their potential wealth measures on a personal, local, state, or national basis. The impact on the lives of those who do not use their capacity wisely will result in a much poorer quality of life than for those who do.

CASE STUDY

Each state uses some formula to determine a locality's capacity to fund education and then has an equalization formula to determine the amount of state aid the locality will receive. Examine and understand your state and local measurements of capacity, analyze them, and evaluate the measurement of capacity. Which localities do you see as being substantially similar yet are receiving different levels of state funding? Once you have evaluated the situation in your state, make recommendations for changes based on your findings.

CHAPTER QUESTIONS

1. What is fiscal capacity? How does your state rank in terms of fiscal capacity to support the schools? Use single measures first, and then use multiple measures to determine your answers.
2. What factors are used in your state to measure fiscal capacity to equalize the state funding formula?
3. How does an education system benefit from efficiency of size in its operation of schools?
4. Using multiple measures as you examine the Texas state data in the Appendix, which locality has the greatest capacity to fund its schools? Which locality has the least capacity to fund its schools? Explain your answer.

APPENDIX **TEXAS STATE DATA**

	Total County Population	Per Capita Income	Per Capita Property Value	Total Public School Enrollment	Number of Schools in County	Number of School Districts
Alamo Region						
Atascosa	38,628	$18,286	$36,774	8,353	24	5
Bandera	17,645	$18,286	$36,774	3,020	6	2
Bexar	1,392,931	$23,918	$63,006	260,862	336	12
Comal	78,021	$28,880	$66,225	17,011	25	2
Frio	16,252	$15,285	$39,931	3,170	8	2
Gillespie	20,814	$24,996	$105,045	3,271	9	3
Guadalupe	89,023	$22,317	$42,610	16,433	30	4
Karnes	15,446	$15,465	$36,262	2,542	10	4
Kendall	27,743	$26,957	$87,622	6,130	12	2
Kerr	43,653	$26,632	$60,015	6,947	17	5
Medina	39,304	$19,012	$41,433	8,479	19	5
Wilson	32,408	$21,594	$43,941	7,052	18	4
Capital Region						
Bastrop	57,733	$20,934	$47,196	11,785	19	4
Blanco	8,418	$23,470	$149,586	1,546	6	2
Burnet	34,147	$22,244	$60,901	6,584	10	2
Caldwell	32,194	$20,018	$36,350	6,388	13	3
Fayette	21,804	$24,501	$94,724	3,699	13	5
Hays	97,589	$22,970	$53,956	20,201	29	4
Lee	15,657	$19,501	$69,893	3,029	8	3
Llano	17,044	$21,354	$115,195	1,817	5	1
Travis	812,280	$35,094	$74,572	114,205	157	7
Williamson	249,967	$29,822	$62,629	65,430	92	11
Central Region						
Bell	237,974	$26,612	$29,342	50,760	87	9
Bosque	17,204	$20,840	$36,882	3,196	14	8
Brazos	152,415	$20,033	$36,882	20,982	32	2
Burleson	16,479	$18,112	$60,591	3,198	10	3
Coryell	74,978	$16,610	$17,956	10,632	21	5
Falls	18,576	$17,374	$30,937	3,093	10	4
Freestone	17,867	$18,400	$95,839	3,172	12	4

Continued

	Total County Population	Per Capita Income	Per Capita Property Value	Total Public School Enrollment	Number of Schools in County	Number of School Districts
Grimes	23,552	$17,233	$62,517	4,237	12	4
Hamilton	8,229	$22,533	$67,210	1,577	6	2
Hill	32,321	$19,686	$40,119	6,109	24	12
Lampasas	17,762	$18,446	$46,802	3,478	5	2
Leon	15,335	$20,729	$85,703	2,971	12	5
Limestone	22,051	$20,051	$60,415	4,167	10	3
Madison	12,940	$19,242	$41,721	2,376	6	2
McLennan	213,517	$22,878	$32,265	39,054	95	18
Milam	24,238	$21,536	$55,818	4,750	14	6
Mills	5,151	$20,509	$79,546	978	6	4
Robertson	16,000	$17,525	$77,908	3,325	14	5
San Saba	6,186	$19,062	$112,207	1,115	7	3
Washington	30,373	$27,330	$69,435	5,163	9	2
Coastal Bend Region						
Aransas	22,497	$24,796	$53,584	3,337	6	1
Bee	32,359	$14,890	$25,754	5,039	13	4
Brooks	7,976	$16,775	$78,089	1,746	4	1
Calhoun	20,647	$22,388	$175,391	4,248	7	1
DeWitt	20,013	$20,627	$47,556	4,533	15	6
Duval	13,120	$14,690	$59,008	3,079	12	4
Goliad	6,928	$18,383	$111,418	1,377	3	1
Gonzales	18,628	$22,557	$54,897	3,894	11	3
Jackson	14,391	$23,572	$92,710	3,196	11	3
Jim Wells	39,326	$18,766	$26,828	8,877	22	5
Kenedy	414	$25,940	$1,083,787	78	1	1
Kleberg	31,549	$18,618	$39,685	5,972	17	4
Lavaca	19,210	$22,674	$76,279	2,141	10	6
Live Oak	12,309	$16,670	$89,276	1,906	7	2
McMullen	851	$27,448	$529,779	172	1	1
Nueces	313,645	$24,013	$40,518	60,996	105	12
Refugio	7,828	$26,514	$82,305	1,497	8	3

APPENDIX CONTINUED

	Total County Population	Per Capita Income	Per Capita Property Value	Total Public School Enrollment	Number of Schools in County	Number of School Districts
San Patricio	67,138	$20,110	$40,405	15,437	34	7
Victoria	84,088	$26,533	$45,697	15,467	27	3
Gulf Coast Region						
Austin	23,590	$25,237	$75,593	5,272	12	3
Brazoria	247,767	$24,723	$61,815	48,405	69	8
Chambers	26,031	$24,938	$166,716	5,309	18	3
Colorado	20,390	$22,849	$77,068	3,747	11	3
Fort Bend	354,452	$29,395	$54,942	77,597	98	5
Galveston	250,158	$26,564	$52,967	66,985	88	9
Harris	3,400,578	$35,268	$53,804	665,012	766	20
Liberty	70,154	$18,931	$38,672	14,607	32	7
Matagorda	37,957	$20,630	$77,787	7,884	20	5
Montgomery	293,768	$29,406	$46,345	62,446	75	6
Walker	61,758	$16,951	$23,945	7,514	12	2
Waller	32,663	$19,887	$53,339	7,371	14	3
Wharton	41,188	$23,212	$46,599	8,489	18	5
High Plains Region						
Armstrong	2,148	$19,999	$80,639	366	2	1
Bailey	6,594	$24,157	$43,186	1,479	5	2
Briscoe	1,790	$20,170	$59,330	249	1	1
Carson	6,516	$27,586	$95,093	1,261	7	3
Castro	8,285	$29,103	$61,492	1,885	6	3
Childress	7,688	$16,599	$25,361	1,192	3	1
Cochran	3,730	$22,667	$86,351	941	5	2
Collingsworth	3,206	$21,013	$71,155	702	4	2
Crosby	7,072	$18,346	$44,118	1,524	8	3
Dallam	6,222	$29,646	$70,906	1,661	5	2
Deaf Smith	18,561	$25,986	$42,486	4,133	9	2
Dickens	2,762	$20,822	$54,612	433	2	2

Continued

APPENDIX **CONTINUED**

	Total County Population	Per Capita Income	Per Capita Property Value	Total Public School Enrollment	Number of Schools in County	Number of School Districts
Donley	3,828	$18,627	$62,137	681	1	2
Floyd	7,771	$25,248	$46,284	1,756	7	2
Garza	4,872	$19,373	$84,743	1,183	4	2
Gray	22,744	$24,493	$45,836	3,930	9	4
Hale	36,602	$21,758	$34,654	7,937	20	5
Hall	3,782	$19,457	$41,836	803	5	2
Hansford	5,369	$38,649	$80,208	1,274	7	3
Hartley	5,537	$33,021	$85,766	301	2	2
Hemphill	3,351	$32,213	$229,461	755	4	4
Hockley	22,716	$19,821	$68,527	4,870	16	6
Hutchinson	23,857	$22,382	$71,927	4,711	12	4
King	356	$20,588	$560,411	85	1	1
Lamb	14,709	$22,029	$67,782	3,408	13	6
Lipscomb	3,057	$25,691	$124,290	713	5	4
Lubbock	242,628	$24,459	$34,641	41,752	82	8
Lynn	6,550	$20,313	$49,840	1,463	8	4
Moore	20,121	$22,475	$71,935	4,584	10	2
Motley	1,426	$18,299	$83,241	184	1	1
Ochiltree	9,006	$29,301	$64,531	2,024	5	1
Oldham	2,185	$26,023	$76,020	492	4	3
Parmer	10,016	$25,185	$51,721	2,434	11	4
Potter	75,000	$23,897	$40,113	31,951	58	4
Randall	19,783	$25,480	$42,506	7,547	12	1
Roberts	222	$18,537	$300,098	156	1	1
Sherman	1,075	$46,027	$144,696	816	4	2
Swisher	2,279	$26,912	$42,151	1,743	8	3
Terry	3,717	$21,712	$47,278	2,509	7	3
Wheeler	1,804	$28,090	$96,140	945	7	5
Yoakum	2,804	$20,587	$199,606	1,843	7	2
Metroplex Region						
Collin	491,675	$41,086	$83,992	98,506	140	14
Cooke	36,363	$23,542	$50,800	6182	20	8

	Total County Population	Per Capita Income	Per Capita Property Value	Total Public School Enrollment	Number of Schools in County	Number of School Districts
Dallas	2,218,899	$36,553	$59,674	407,836	549	15
Denton	432,976	$31,004	$60,538	74,128	112	11
Ellis	111,360	$25,589	$52,874	25,250	44	10
Erath	33,001	$22,067	$47,737	5,416	15	7
Fannin	31,242	$19,659	$34,552	5,276	21	8
Grayson	110,595	$23,400	$41,360	20,384	49	13
Hood	41,100	$29,148	$53,051	7,335	15	3
Hunt	76,596	$21,102	$31,990	14,263	40	10
Johnson	126,811	$22,775	$34,880	26,533	53	9
Kaufman	71,313	$24,123	$42,831	17,924	35	7
Navarro	45,124	$20,831	$40,184	9,033	20	7
Palo Pinto	27,026	$21,370	$50,181	4,932	12	6
Parker	88,495	$25,618	$49,267	16,645	34	8
Rockwall	43,080	$33,613	$68,293	10,992	15	2
Somervell	6,809	$28,932	$333,280	1,652	4	1
Tarrant	1,446,219	$30,110	$50,915	277,176	378	16
Wise	48,793	$24,092	$52,527	8,467	25	7
Northwest Region						
Archer	8,854	$23,728	$55,002	1,957	8	4
Baylor	4,093	$20,004	$61,446	676	2	1
Brown	37,674	$20,307	$41,049	7,177	24	7
Callahan	12,905	$20,635	$38,277	2,795	12	4
Clay	11,006	$20,492	$57,371	2,024	8	5
Coleman	9,235	$20,206	$55,345	1,590	9	4
Comanche	14,026	$20,438	$52,045	2,466	9	4
Cottle	1,904	$23,097	$77,174	301	2	1
Eastland	18,297	$20,866	$39,030	3,108	13	5
Fisher	4,344	$18,923	$66,158	712	5	2
Foard	1,622	$22,496	$60,076	319	2	1
Hardeman	4,724	$20,687	$61,434	841	5	2
Haskell	6,093	$20,066	$56,593	1,042	5	4

Continued

	Total County Population	Per Capita Income	Per Capita Property Value	Total Public School Enrollment	Number of Schools in County	Number of School Districts
Jack	8,763	$17,964	$74,895	1,612	6	3
Jones	20,785	$15,309	$24,572	3,012	14	5
Kent	859	$21,797	$427,886	146	1	1
Knox	4,253	$20,665	$45,105	897	7	4
Mitchell	9,698	$15,213	$46,086	1,361	6	3
Montague	19,117	$20,433	$47,551	3,326	7	15
Nolan	15,802	$20,416	$45,807	3,093	10	4
Runnels	11,495	$18,955	$45,351	2,346	11	4
Scurry	16,361	$21,177	$47,013	2,973	9	3
Shackelford	3,302	$23,121	$100,927	704	3	2
Stephens	9,674	$21,555	$57,534	1,736	5	1
Stonewall	1,693	$21,727	$98,329	257	3	1
Taylor	126,555	$24,487	$33,995	22,968	43	5
Throckmorton	1,850	$22,237	$110,126	345	3	2
Wichita	131,664	$25,309	$35,133	22,527	47	5
Wilbarger	14,676	$22,197	$43,067	2,715	7	3
Young	17,943	$24,602	$47,165	3,396	10	3
South Texas Border Region						
Cameron	335,227	$14,906	$24,803	83,527	115	9
Dimmit	10,248	$14,015	$57,098	2,481	7	1
Edwards	2,162	$15,589	$202,869	726	5	2
Hidalgo	569,463	$13,344	$24,701	149,915	201	15
Jim Hogg	5,281	$16,718	$79,621	1,200	3	1
Kinney	3,379	$15,822	$94,502	657	3	1
La Salle	5,866	$15,372	$71,258	1,270	5	1
Maverick	47,297	$12,092	$24,935	12,778	22	1
Real	3,047	$17,514	$114,063	297	1	1
Starr	53,597	$9,740	$24,244	15,278	23	3
Uvalde	25,926	$18,986	$40,851	6,180	14	4
Val Verde	44,856	$16,711	$24,956	10,293	15	2
Webb	193,117	$15,114	$35,519	52,603	65	4
Willacy	20,082	$13,551	$33,896	4,678	12	4

	Total County Population	Per Capita Income	Per Capita Property Value	Total Public School Enrollment	Number of Schools in County	Number of School Districts
Zapata	12,182	$12,674	$88,680	3,087	6	1
Zavala	11,600	$11,873	$43,542	2,475	7	2
Southeast Texas Region						
Angelina	80,130	$22,236	$37,679	15,973	33	6
Hardin	48,073	$22,264	$36,532	10,561	21	5
Houston	23,185	$22,724	$46,711	3,678	15	5
Jasper	35,604	$20,914	$55,433	7,108	15	5
Jefferson	252,051	$24,441	$55,457	43,654	71	6
Nacogdoches	59,203	$20,445	$38,191	10,096	25	9
Newton	15,072	$14,854	$51,586	2,560	9	3
Orange	84,966	$22,574	$46,847	16,631	27	5
Polk	41,133	$24,304	$47,661	6,840	16	6
Sabine	10,469	$22,158	$43,202	1,579	5	2
San Augustine	8,946	$18,729	$38,502	1,451	5	2
San Jacinto	22,246	$19,819	$42,447	3,561	8	2
Shelby	25,224	$21,032	$33,577	4,801	16	6
Trinity	13,779	$17,998	$44,964	2,305	9	4
Tyler	20,871	$17,068	$40,852	3,732	15	5
Upper East Texas Region						
Anderson	55,109	$17,446	$36,063	8,440	24	7
Bowie	89,306	$22,392	$35,549	16,150	39	13
Camp	11,549	$26,370	$38,736	2,195	4	1
Cass	30,438	$22,208	$43,076	6,029	22	8
Cherokee	46,659	$22,116	$33,919	7,972	17	5
Delta	5,327	$20,666	$32,399	1,224	5	2
Franklin	9,458	$22,029	$71,205	1,474	4	1
Gregg	111,379	$27,065	$47,784	23,233	47	7
Harrison	62,110	$20,666	$54,492	12,529	29	6
Henderson	73,277	$21,400	$43,310	10,101	26	8
Hopkins	31,960	$21,224	$44,769	6,258	16	7

Continued

	Total County Population	Per Capita Income	Per Capita Property Value	Total Public School Enrollment	Number of Schools in County	Number of School Districts
Lamar	48,499	$22,484	$44,382	8,992	22	5
Marion	10,941	$16,315	$51,214	1,437	4	1
Morris	13,048	$21,368	$49,492	2,494	8	2
Panola	22,756	$20,886	$106,718	3,691	8	3
Rains	9,139	$17,240	$39,312	1,440	3	1
Red River	14,314	$18,537	$40,806	2,699	12	4
Rusk	47,372	$20,626	$54,528	7,464	23	8
Smith	174,706	$27,421	$46,926	30,854	60	8
Titus	28,118	$20,995	$67,844	6,110	13	4
Upshur	35,291	$20,162	$37,866	6,664	22	7
Van Zandt	48,140	$20,501	$40,689	9,399	27	7
Wood	36,752	$19,032	$50,180	5,940	16	6
Upper Rio Grande Region						
Brewster	8,866	$22,327	$58,106	1,435	7	4
Culberson	2,975	$43,708	$87,312	700	3	1
El Paso	679,622	$18,535	$29,827	158,469	201	9
Hudspeth	3,344	$15,219	$97,085	878	3	3
Jeff Davis	2,207	$16,723	$136,608	392	3	2
Presidio	7,304	$13,973	$41,550	1,957	6	2
West Texas Region						
Andrews	13,004	$17,455	$101,287	3,083	7	1
Borden	729	$12,945	$366,377	165	1	1
Coke	3,864	$19,839	$84,833	835	6	2
Concho	3,966	$18,818	$82,255	468	3	2
Crane	3,996	$17,233	$171,086	986	3	1
Crockett	4,099	$14,986	$248,748	848	4	1
Dawson	14,985	$21,132	$46,411	2,832	9	4
Ector	121,123	$19,558	$37,025	26,918	39	1
Gaines	14,467	$19,999	$152,329	2,959	9	3
Glasscock	1,406	$18,130	$298,658	333	2	1
Howard	33,627	$21,404	$38,616	5,513	16	3

	Total County Population	Per Capita Income	Per Capita Property Value	Total Public School Enrollment	Number of Schools in County	Number of School Districts
Irion	1,771	$18,663	$134,822	346	2	1
Kimble	4,468	$74,664	$121,091	737	3	1
Loving	67	$33,566	$2,277,504	0	0	0
Martin	4,746	$16,857	$93,473	1,029	4	2
Mason	3,738	$17,443	$152,530	601	2	1
McCulloch	8,205	$18,891	$66,826	1,625	7	3
Menard	2,360	$15,948	$133,948	430	3	1
Midland	116,009	$30,681	$42,428	22,254	38	2
Pecos	16,809	$13,910	$118,037	3,032	9	3
Reagan	3,326	$14,058	$135,784	837	3	1
Reeves	13,137	$14,643	$31,669	2,894	8	2
Schleicher	2,935	$15,197	$115,782	639	4	1
Sterling	1,393	$15,845	$201,203	285	3	1
Sutton	4,077	$17,676	$144,182	917	3	1
Terrell	1,081	$21,887	$307,722	201	3	1
Tom Green	104,010	$23,453	$32,871	18,706	44	6
Upton	3,404	$18,460	$197,385	772	5	2
Ward	10,909	$17,621	$69,446	2,170	7	2
Winkler	7,173	$17,456	$72,579	1,675	6	2

FISCAL EFFORT

FOCUS QUESTIONS

1. What is fiscal effort?

2. What factors influence effort?

3. How can effort be calculated?

4. Can levels of effort be compared?

5. If effort is a function of capacity, are there different methods for determining effort?

6. How much fiscal effort do we put into our schools nationally, statewide, and locally?

Chapter 7 begins the study of fiscal effort—or how much capacity is used to fund education services. Factors that influence effort (such as our own lack of professional public relations skills) are reviewed. The formula for determining an effort index is introduced and the various means for computing the actual figure are discussed. We also examine effort at the local, state, and national levels.

Chapter 6 introduced the idea of fiscal capacity. Chapter 7 deals with a follow-up concept to capacity—fiscal effort.[1] See Figure 6.1 (page 152) for an illustration of how these two concepts fit together.

Fiscal *effort* measures how much a locality, state, or nation spends of its resources in relation to capacity—or the ability to pay. Measuring capacity is a good place to start examining how much a nation, state, or locality can afford to spend on education. The relative *effort* of that spending—the degree of exertion or fiscal struggle a community commits to its resources for education—tells a much more robust story about what people value. It is possible for communities to have varying levels of fiscal capacity and commit varying levels of fiscal effort to fund their public educational programs and facilities. For example, poorer school districts (low capacity) may spend a greater share of their wealth on education (high effort) whereas more affluent school districts (high capacity) may spend relatively little (low effort) to support their schools to achieve the same or higher levels of services for the children.

This chapter discusses how localities and states measure fiscal effort in relation to wealth. Is it right for the state to determine a minimum local effort that is required before a community is eligible to receive state funds? Can and should states "cap" local contributions to education—in effect saying to the locality that if it levies additional taxes, those monies must go back to the state to raise the floor of educational opportunity for other localities? Is it right for the federal government to establish high academic standards that all students must meet *regardless* of a locality's capacity or effort—even if the state provides insufficient funding for education?

FACTORS INFLUENCING EFFORT

Many factors influence the fiscal effort provided to support public education. First, the public's interest and attitude about their public schools sway their effort to fund education services. In many areas, traditional attitudes about public education affect this view. Historically, some states valued public education and supported their local schools more than others did. In Chapter 2 we suggested that you examine your state in terms of its development according to what Cubberley called school conditions—good,

---

[1]We use the terms "fiscal effort" and "effort" interchangeably. Both refer to the degree of financial exertion a community commits to funding their public schools by considering the relationship between the monies available and money spent per pupil.

mixed, no action, and pauper/parochial. You may find that tradition has a great deal to do with how much your state spends on public education.

How people feel about taxes in general is another factor associated with fiscal effort to support public schools. For the past 20 years, Americans have viewed taxes as bad and have elected politicians to office on platforms of tax reduction and increased—or at least unreduced—public services. The public at large believes they pay too many tax dollars for the services they receive, and people tend to "vote with their pocketbooks." Fortunately, most politicians realize that the public does not want to reduce public education services.

Unfortunately, when legislators and councilpersons cut other public services to maintain public schools, the competition for available public dollars becomes intense. This competition can cause ill feelings among various departments if every budget but education has their monies cut. When most other public service department budgets are cut and education remains unscathed, political support from those hurt can vanish, leaving school boards and superintendents vulnerable to personnel changes. This can be the unkindest cut of all.

How citizens "feel" about their schools is another factor associated with fiscal effort. Educators are not very adept at public relations and marketing. Consider this scenario. The family sits at home on a workday evening. The phone rings, and little Johnny answers. He listens intently, covers the mouthpiece, and says, "Mommy, it's my teacher. It's for you."

What is the first question the mother asks her son? Most people say the mother would ask, "What did you do wrong in school today?" Why isn't the answer, "Oh, Johnny, your teacher must be calling to tell me another wonderful thing you did today!" Sadly, the overwhelming majority of phone calls educators make involves calling students' homes with complaints, criticisms, or bad news. Why is it that educators generally call parents with bad news, not good news? Without a doubt, it is a question of time. Most teachers and principals have more than their share to do in a very few hours. But is it any wonder that parents associate communications from school with negative feelings? If this is the case, how can educators expect parents to take the time to support requests for school funding increases with enthusiasm at budget time?[2]

Another factor related to support for education is the percentage of the population whose children are in public versus private schools. Again, this may link to tradition or how the public "feels" about schools. Where a large

---

[2]In our opinion, one action every educator could take to enhance the probability that his or her school budget would increase is to make two positive phone calls home for every one negative call.

portion of the public pays for their children to attend private schools, it is unlikely the community will garner support for large tax increases to adequately fund the public schools.[3]

The percentage of the population with children or grandchildren attending the public schools in that locality is another factor influencing support for public education. It is easier for parents and grandparents to support budget increases if they see how it benefits their family. There is less utility for individuals to support school budget increases if they do not have family members who will directly gain from school funding increases.

Leadership of the municipality and the school system also influences popular support for education programs. When the community trusts and supports its leadership and when the leadership visibly supports public education goals, the community gets a clear endorsement for education spending. When municipal and school leaders exhibit mistrust and scorn for each other, the public also gets a clear message—avoid support until both leadership positions change.

Of course, other factors influence support for education. It is difficult to pin down how much one factor contributes to the variance in spending. In fact, according to Alexander and Salmon, "No one has been able to determine, up to this time, the effects of any one factor, or the combination of factors such as these, upon the fiscal effort made by any state to support its public schools."[4]

Educators can and must do a better job of influencing fiscal effort for public education by cooperating with other agencies and gaining the public's trust and confidence. To advocate adequate education funding successfully and to collaborate effectively with other agencies, educational leaders must know the facts about education finance.

Computing Effort

The question then becomes how do we compute effort? The concept and the computation are rather simple. Effort is best described as a ratio. In its simplest form, effort can be described as the ratio of school revenue (expenditures) to the overall tax base, or

$$E = \frac{R}{TB}$$

---

[3]An interesting project to undertake would be to review municipal statistics on the total number of students in a given locality and determine the percentage of students in private schools. Comparisons could then be made among localities and the support for tax increases could be calculated. It would be relatively simple to determine comparative budget increases on a historical basis.

[4]K. Alexander and R. Salmon, *Public School Finance* (Boston: Allyn and Bacon, 1995), 174.

where E = effort, R = revenue for school budget expenditures, and TB = tax base. You can begin to see now how mills (see Chapter 5) come in handy as a constant in measurement.

Effort must be considered as a ratio for one good reason. Without comparing revenue against the available tax base, only the tax dollars *contributed* would be examined. Even if those dollars were based on a per pupil expenditure, wealthy districts—by spending just a few dollars more per pupil—would always look like they were exerting more effort than any other school district because they would present a larger budget. To get a more accurate picture of effort, these dollars must be examined in light of their *capacity* to fund education. We do that by using a ratio that takes into account the tax base available to fund services.

In addition, fiscal effort may be computed by examining the nations, states, or localities, individually, not collectively. Computing effort by summing the local, state, and national tax revenues mixes apples, oranges, and nuts. It blurs the overall picture. One purpose of state funding is to equalize for local disparities in ability to pay for education. A poor locality electing not to put many of their available tax dollars into education looks better if it includes funding received from the state when computing fiscal effort. Adding the state funding to the local budget makes the locality appear to give more money—a higher fiscal effort—to educate its children.

The same is true of localities having high capacity and electing not to put much fiscal effort into education. Computing effort including state and federal tax dollars makes this system appear to be exerting greater effort than it really is. Therefore, adding state funding to local funding to compute the effort ratio may be a flawed practice. Each level of funding must be computed individually—local, state, and federal.

Just as richer states giving the same fiscal effort to education as poorer states will always "look" better in terms of effort unless also considering capacity, the same is true when looking at nations and how they fund education relative to their capacity. That is, it is important to consider national spending relative to some measure—in this case GDP.

Relative Effort

At the state and local level, "tax effort" provides another way to consider fiscal support. One way to calculate tax effort is called the "representative tax system." This method is best described in the following passage:

> A more appropriate way to compare the relative burden of state and local taxes, or as what is often called "tax effort," is to consider what each state

| TABLE 7.1 | STATE AND LOCAL TAX EFFORT, 1996 |

State	Tax Effort %	Rank	State	Tax Effort %	Rank
Alabama	83	43	Montana	79	45
Alaska	116	4	Nebraska	99	20
Arizona	93	28	Nevada	73	50
Arkansas	92	29	New Hampshire	74	48
California	101	15	New Jersey	114	6
Colorado	82	44	New Mexico	102	12
Connecticut	115	5	New York	141	1
Delaware	90	32	North Carolina	94	27
Florida	90	32	North Dakota	89	35
Georgia	95	26	Ohio	100	16
Hawaii	104	9	Oklahoma	92	29
Idaho	92	29	Oregon	85	42
Illinois	97	25	Pennsylvania	102	12
Indiana	88	39	Rhode Island	117	2
Iowa	98	24	South Carolina	89	35
Kansas	99	20	South Dakota	79	45
Kentucky	99	20	Tennessee	79	45
Louisiana	86	41	Texas	90	32
Maine	113	7	Utah	89	35
Maryland	100	16	Vermont	100	16
Massachusetts	104	9	Virginia	89	35
Michigan	100	16	Washington	104	9
Minnesota	113	7	West Virginia	99	20
Mississippi	102	12	Wisconsin	117	3
Missouri	87	40	Wyoming	74	48
50 States	n/a				
District of Columbia	141				
United States	**100**				

Source: K. Hovey and H. Hovey, *CQ's State Fact Finder, 2002* (Washington, DC: Congressional Quarterly, Inc., 2002), 142.

would raise if it and its local governments applied national average tax rates to their own tax bases. Unfortunately, this methodology, known as the "representative tax system," is tedious and expensive to apply.[5]

This method has not been widely used since 1991 when the federal government's Advisory Commission on Intergovernmental Relations, which had historically published these data, stopped this work. In 1996 Robert Tannewald, an assistant vice president and economist at the Federal Reserve Bank in Boston, reexamined these data (latest available) and ranked the states based on his analysis (Table 7.1).

Making this type of comparison is inherently dangerous because the ability of states to raise revenues varies broadly. Some states—including Alaska and Wyoming—derive large revenues from severance taxes from oil and gas. Other states such as Nevada and New Jersey obtain large revenues from casino gambling. Most other states obtain little revenue from severance and casino gambling sources. Some, such as Delaware and New York, have a large capacity for revenue from the businesses incorporated within those states. Other states have few businesses centered within their boundaries. The representative tax method does, however, enable us to compute effort by factoring in capacity and national norms.

LOCAL EFFORT

Localities may receive education funding from a variety of sources. Table 7.2 provides capacity and effort information for two hypothetical school districts. Admittedly, this is a simplification, but it will help clarify some of the complexities and concepts involved when defining fiscal effort. When computing effort, we use the formula provided earlier in the chapter: E (effort) = R (revenues for school budgets)/TB (tax base). Note that the effort index will never be greater than 1.0 because that would mean 100% of the tax base was being spent on education, leaving no room for other agency spending.

In the first scenario, let's look at effort funded solely by a portion of the real estate tax base. School district A has $75,000 total per capita property value available (capacity) and spends $6,000 per pupil (effort). School district B

---

[5]K. Hovey and H. Hovey, *CQ's State Fact Finder, 2002* (Washington, DC: Congressional Quarterly, Inc., 2002), 163–164.

TABLE 7.2   CAPACITY AND EFFORT FOR TWO SCHOOL DISTRICTS

	School District A	School District B
Number of pupils	10,000	10,000
Per capita residential property value	$50,000	$50,000
Per capita commercial property value	$12,500	$25,000
Per capita industrial property value	$12,500	$25,000
Total per capita property value	$75,000	$100,00
Per capital income	$75,000	$60,000
Per capita sales tax	$2,500	$1,000
Per pupil spending	$6,000	$7,500

TABLE 7.3   EFFORT BASED ON PER CAPITA PROPERTY VALUE

School District A	School District B
$\dfrac{\$6,000\ (R)}{\$75,000\ (TB)} = .08\ (E)$	$\dfrac{\$7,500\ (R)}{\$100,000\ (TB)} = .075\ (E)$

has a total per capita property value of $100,000 and spends $7,500 per pupil. Using the formula for computing effort, we find that school district A expends greater effort than does school district B—.08 compared with .075—even though school district B spends more per pupil (Table 7.3). This disparity exists because school district A has one-quarter less property value than school district B yet spends only 20% less to educate each student.

We mentioned in Chapter 5 that real estate taxes, especially for home-owners in a community, may not be the fairest way to fund education. When we examine effort for these two school districts in terms of per capita income, a different view emerges (Table 7.4). Here school district A (.08) has a lower effort ratio than does school district B (.125). In terms of income available as a tax base, school district A has more capacity than school district B, but by this measure, school district B displays greater fiscal effort than does school district A.

Wealth is a measurement of many variables. Many states use a composite index of real estate, income, and sales tax on a proportional basis to calculate a locality's ability to fund education. To look at capacity with only

TABLE 7.4	EFFORT BASED ON PER CAPITA INCOME
School District A	**School District B**
$\dfrac{\$6,000\ (R)}{\$75,000\ (TB)} = .08\ (E)$	$\dfrac{\$7,500\ (R)}{\$60,000\ (TB)} = .125\ (E)$

TABLE 7.5	EFFORT BASED ON 50–50 SPLIT BETWEEN PER CAPITA PROPERTY VALUE AND INCOME
School District A	**School District B**
$\dfrac{\$6,000\ (R)}{\$75,000 + \$75,000\ (TB)} = .04\ (E)$	$\dfrac{\$7,500\ (R)}{\$100,000 + \$60,000\ (TB)} = .046875\ (E)$

one measure—real estate value or income—does not provide an accurate measurement of a locality's capacity.

Now let's measure wealth as a ratio of 50% income tax and 50% property tax (Table 7.5). In this case, school district A has an effort index of .04, and school district B has an index of .046875, the greater number indicating the greater effort. With this measure, we are using more data to determine the effort index of the two districts, leading to a more accurate picture of their effort.

If we now include another factor, sales tax collected on a per capita basis in each locality, the formula becomes 50% property, 40% income tax, and 10% sales tax (Table 7.6). Using these three measures, school district B's effort ratio is .101215, showing much more effort than school district A, with an index of .088560.

Using multiple criteria provides a better statistical measure for wealth and better comparisons of fiscal effort, although measuring these criteria can become quite complex. In the end, each state legislature determines how the state will measure wealth and apportion that wealth to the localities. Selecting the correct variables and weighting them appropriately bring personal and local values and related political agendas into the discussion.

States can use whatever multiple measures of wealth they deem appropriate. In fact, many different and complex formulae to measure wealth exist, and they vary from state to state. Educational leaders should know which formula their state uses, understand that model's strengths and weaknesses, and be able to articulate that information to the public. Table 7.7 shows how

TABLE 7.6 EFFORT BASED ON 50% PER CAPITA PROPERTY VALUE, 40% INCOME TAX, AND 10% SALES TAX

School District A	School District B
$$\frac{\$6,000\ (R)}{\$75,000(.5) + \$75,000(.4) + \$2,500(.1)\ (TB)} = .088560\ (E)$$	$$\frac{\$7,500\ (R)}{\$100,000(.5) + \$60,000(.4) + \$1,000(.1)\ (TB)} = .101215\ (E)$$

TABLE 7.7 COMPARISON OF RESULTS USING VARIOUS FACTORS TO DETERMINE WEALTH

	School District A Effort Index	School District B Effort Index
Property only	.08	.075
Income only	.08	.125
Property and income (.5 + .5)	.04	.046875
Property, income, and sales tax (.5 + .4 + .1)	.088560	.101215

much the effort indices vary depending on which of the four formulae is selected to measure wealth.

When a locality gives heavier weighting to property values as the predominant measure of wealth, the cash flow to the locality remains relatively stable over time. Property values tend to increase over time except in blighted areas. Using property values as a measure of wealth ensures relatively constant tax revenue to the locality.

In localities that use income as a primary measure of wealth, the cash flow tends to be more erratic over time. In strong economies, employed people get raises and bonuses, and the revenue from income increases rather rapidly. When the economy eventually turns down (economies always run in cycles) and salaries decrease or jobs are lost, income tax revenues tend to drop quickly. The same can be said to a lesser extent for sales tax revenue. Spending for items tends to slow when the economy slows, reducing sales tax revenue to the state and the locality.

Erratic revenue swings from the tax base make municipal planning difficult. Schools continue to need teachers, supplies, utilities, technology, buses, and other resources. Personnel costs cannot increase and decrease with every economic turn. State legislatures plan for this variable revenue stream so that monies coming into the state treasury tend to be stable rather than erratic.

STATE EFFORT

State effort can be calculated in the same way we calculated the hypothetical levels for local school districts in the previous section. The formula of determining effort by dividing the revenue or expenditures by the tax base to obtain a ratio that equalizes for capacity is still valid at the state level. All that remains is to determine the tax base structure that will be used.

"Gross state product" (as opposed to national GDP) is difficult to measure. To ensure a stable revenue stream, states typically measure relative wealth by per capita income and per capita property value, and many include sales tax generated within a given locality. Sales tax revenue can be a significant predictor of wealth—especially in tourist areas. By spreading the measures of wealth across various sources, states can protect themselves and the services they must provide from drastic swings in revenue, providing a stable tax base to fund basic services.

As you can see in Table 7.8, some states rank relatively high in terms of capacity as measured by gross state product. They may elect to spend at a level considered to be above or below their capacity for education. By computing the effort index, the relative effort among states can be determined on an equalized basis and compared fairly. One can then determine which states place a high value on the next generation's education just as one can determine what different families value by examining their spending habits.

NATIONAL EFFORT

The United States has tremendous fiscal capacity. In many ways, our country is the most powerful country on the planet. We hold undisputed influence with our military, technological, and economic strength, yet many question how much we should spend on public education. Some believe we spend too much on public education for the modest results we obtain. Others believe our moderate spending does not reflect the national priority we should place on education as an investment in human capital. The general public is not certain what to think.[6] One fact, however, remains relatively certain.

---

[6]The Phi Delta Kappa/Gallup polls on education show a somewhat confused public. For years the respondents' public schools are rated high. The rest of the country's public schools are rated lower. Obviously, people think their schools are good but others are not. This lack of information hurts our image as educators and causes confusion among the public.

TABLE 7.8   GROSS STATE PRODUCT, PER CAPITA EDUCATION SPENDING, AND COMPUTED EFFORT

State	Gross State Product Per Capita (in millions of $)	Rank Per Capita	Education Spending Per Pupil	Rank	Relative Effort $E = R/TB$	Effort Rank
Alabama	$26,333	45	$5,267	47	.2000	32
Alaska	42,539	3	9,410	4	.2212	17
Arizona	30,070	32	4,676	48	.1555	47
Arkansas	25,388	47	5,604	43	.2207	19
California	37,082	9	7,036	20	.1897	42
Colorado	37,900	8	5,333	45	.1407	50
Connecticut	46,245	1	10,163	1	.2198	20
Delaware	46,008	2	8,952	6	.1946	35
Florida	29,309	38	6,049	36	.2064	30
Georgia	35,402	15	6,869	24	.1940	37
Hawaii	34,512	17	6,570	27	.1904	40
Idaho	27,183	43	5,667	41	.2085	29
Illinois	36,746	11	7,946	10	.2162	24
Indiana	30,659	30	7,118	19	.2322	12
Iowa	29,707	33	6,362	30	.2142	26
Kansas	30,460	31	6,568	28	.2156	25
Kentucky	28,665	40	6,846	25	.2388	9
Louisiana	29,496	35	5,902	38	.2001	31
Maine	27,185	42	7,907	11	.2909	3
Maryland	33,782	20	7,469	16	.2211	18
Massachusetts	42,512	4	9,222	5	.2169	21
Michigan	31,258	27	7,458	17	.2386	10
Minnesota	36,223	14	7,830	13	.2162	24
Mississippi	23,220	49	5,301	46	.2283	15
Missouri	31,174	28	6,198	35	.1988	33
Montana	23,376	48	6,352	31	.2717	4
Nebraska	32,259	23	6,393	29	.1983	34
Nevada	38,615	7	5,600	44	.1450	49
New Hampshire	36,823	10	7,033	21	.1910	39
New Jersey	40,713	6	9,897	3	.2431	7
New Mexico	29,328	37	6,278	34	.2141	27
New York	41,469	5	10,049	2	.2423	8

TABLE 7.8 CONTINUED

State	Gross State Product Per Capita (in millions of $)	Rank Per Capita	Education Spending Per Pupil	Rank	Relative Effort $E = R/TB$	Effort Rank
North Carolina	33,799	19	6,021	37	.1781	45
North Dakota	26,814	44	4,431	49	.1652	46
Ohio	32,157	24	6,962	22	.2165	22
Oklahoma	25,724	46	5,752	39	.2236	16
Oregon	33,079	21	7,558	15	.2285	14
Pennsylvania	31,931	25	7,440	18	.2330	11
Rhode Island	32,848	22	8,392	8	.2555	6
South Carolina	27,515	41	6,346	32	.2306	13
South Dakota	29,505	34	5,680	40	.1925	38
Tennessee	31,017	29	5,616	42	.1811	43
Texas	34,288	18	6,660	26	.1942	36
Utah	29,411	36	4,425	50	.1505	48
Vermont	28,908	39	8,529	7	.2950	2
Virginia	35,243	16	6,323	33	.1794	44
Washington	36,352	13	6,913	23	.1902	41
West Virginia	22,516	50	7,859	12	.3490	1
Wisconsin	31,708	26	8,148	9	.2570	5
Wyoming	36,380	12	7,644	14	.2101	28
50 States	33,997					
District of Columbia	107,576		11,717		.1089	
United States	**34,138**		**7,095**		**.2078**	

Note: Gross state product from 1999 and per capita spending for the following year were selected because gross state product may determine state education spending for the following year. Effort is computed by dividing the spending per pupil by the gross state product per capita. For example, Alabama's effort is computed as $5,267/26,333 = .2000.

Source: The information for gross state product and per capita spending on education are from K. Hovey and H. Hovey, *CQ's State Fact Finder, 2002* (Washington, DC: Congressional Quarterly, Inc., 2002), 39 and 208. Calculations are by the authors.

Everyone wants to pay less in taxes. In reality, people tend to vote with their pocketbooks.

When examining spending as a percentage of the whole, priorities become clear. For example, if a family of four earning $60,000 were to spend 50% of their gross income on their home mortgage, one might say that having a nice home was a priority for them. If another family spent 30% of their income

FEDERAL EDUCATION SUPPORT AND ESTIMATED FEDERAL TAX EXPENDITURES FOR EDUCATION, BY CATEGORY, FISCAL YEARS 1965 TO 2002 (IN MILLIONS OF DOLLARS)

TABLE 7.9

Fiscal Year	Elementary and Secondary Funding	Spending in Constant Fiscal 2002 Dollars	CPI Adjusted from 1965 to 2002*
1965	$1,942.6	$10,625.5	$1.00
1970	5,830.4	25,498.3	1.23
1975	10,617.2	32,635.9	1.71
1980	16,027.7	33,291.0	2.62
1985	16,901.3	26,176.8	3.42
1986	17,049.9	25,771.0	3.48
1987	17,535.7	25,797.3	3.61
1988	18,564.9	26,472.4	3.76
1989	19,809.5	27,237.8	3.94
1990	21,984.4	29,240.5	4.15
1991	25,418.0	32,377.7	4.32
1992	27,926.9	34,407.1	4.45
1993	30,834.3	37,054.6	4.57
1994	32,304.4	38,032.0	4.70
1995	33,623.8	38,665.7	4.85
1996	34,391.5	38,638.9	4.98
1997	35,478.9	39,052.2	5.10
1998	37,486.2	40,746.6	5.17
1999	39,937.9	42,729.5	5.29
2000	43,790.8	45,647.6	5.47
2001	48,530.1	49,521.8	5.62
2002	53,334.6	53,334.6	5.71

Note: *Data is available at http://minneapolisfed.org/research/data/us/calc; calculation by authors.

Source: U.S. Department of Education, National Center for Education Statistics, compiled from data in U.S. Office of Management and Budget, *Budget of the U.S. Government,* Appendix, FY 1967 to 2003, available at: http://nces.ed.gov/pubs2003/digest02/tables/dt363.asp; National Science Foundation, *Federal Funds for Research and Development, FY 1965 to 2002;* and unpublished data from various federal agencies. (This table was prepared June 2003.)

on their home and gave 20% to their local church, one might say that their home and church were important parts of their value system. Moreover, if another family spent 10% of their income on dining in fancy restaurants in comparison to the first two families who prepared all family meals at home, one might say that frequently dining in fine eateries was important to the last family.

Let's look at U.S. education expenditures as a percentage of GDP, which shows the relative importance countries place on educating their children. This is perhaps the best way to examine education-related spending. The United States does not rank in the top five countries when examining spending as a portion of GDP (see Figure 1.2, page 9). In fact, Sweden, Norway, New Zealand, France, Portugal, Canada, and Switzerland all outspend the United States. This says much about national priorities. Of course, this analysis is a simplification. The U.S. defense budget is large, out of necessity and tradition. U.S. interstate highways and freedom to travel are important cultural values, probably more so than in many other countries. Reflecting on education spending as a percentage of our GDP, however, does allow us to see clearly where nations place priorities—especially the priority of developing the human capital of our children.

Looking at federal spending on education over time offers another perspective. Many of the *Digest of Education Statistics* begin with spending data in 1965. Table 7.9 shows federal spending on education beginning with that year. It also reflects spending in constant 2002 dollars. The last column shows spending adjusted by the Consumer Price Index (CPI) from 1965 using the Minneapolis Federal Reserve bank calculator for determining CPI over time.

When examining federal spending on education since 1965, it is important to remember that, for the most part, special education programs were not implemented until the mid-1970s. Millions of children were either not served or were underserved in our public schools. Neither had *Brown v. Board of Education* outlawing school segregation been implemented and would not be until 1970.[7] Both of these requirements affected federal education spending, as can be seen in Figure 7.1, the federal Department of Education's graph comparing federal spending with reading proficiency for K–12 children.

As David Rosnick points out, this graph is misleading because it suggests that federal expenditures are important in the overall achievement of students. Rosnick points out that these federal funds to elementary and secondary schools accounted for only 3.5% of all K–12 expenditures in fiscal year 1999.[8] That is hardly enough to say that federal spending has had an impact on student achievement. Although federal funding for education is valued, it is the states and localities that bear the largest burden of educating America's next generation.

---

[7]*Brown v. Board of Education II* required that schools be fully integrated by the start of school year 1970.

[8]See http://www.cepr.net/Childs_Play.PDF, citing *Statistical Abstracts of the United States,* 2002.

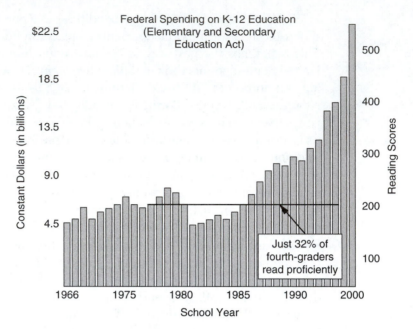

FIGURE **7.1**

Federal Government Spending on Education and Reading Scores

Source: http://www.ed.gov/images/title-one.jpg.

SUMMARY

Fiscal effort is the amount of financial exertion a community, state, or nation puts into funding public education. Effort considers the relationship between the actual revenues available and the amount spent per pupil.

The degree of fiscal effort a locality puts into education shows its values about their community and their children's future. Factors influencing a locality's fiscal effort to support public education include the public's interest and attitude about their public schools; how they feel about taxes in general; the percentage of the population whose children or grandchildren are in public schools; and the community's trust and support for its leadership that encourages public school spending. It is difficult to determine how much one factor contributes to the variance in spending.

Fiscal effort is a ratio of school revenue (expenditures) to the overall tax base, or $E = R/TB$. Viewing the effort index as a ratio—including the tax base available to fund services—considers public dollars in light of their *capacity* to fund education. The effort index is never higher than 1.0 because the nation, state, or locality cannot spend 100% of its tax base on schools, leaving no funds for other public spending.

Many different and complex formulae to measure wealth exist, and they vary from state to state. Most states use a composite index of real estate, income, and sales tax on a proportional basis to calculate a locality's ability to fund education. By spreading the measures of wealth across various sources, states can protect themselves and the services they must provide from drastic swings in revenue, providing a stable tax base to fund basic services.

The United States is not the world's largest spender for public education. When we examine spending as a percentage of gross domestic product, the United States does not even rank in the top five countries. This reflects national priorities and constitutional requirements. Federal funds to elementary and secondary schools accounted for only 3.5% of all K–12 expenditures in fiscal year 1999. By computing the effort index, the relative effort among states and their value for education can be calculated on an equalized basis and compared fairly.

CONCLUSION

Relative effort levels show how important education spending is at any given level of government. The difficulty is developing consensus as to what measure of wealth should be used to determine the tax base. An accurate measurement of this construct provides a true indicator of the real capacity to fund services. Combined with the view of human capital, it becomes obvious that education spending should be seen more as an investment than an expenditure line in the budget.

CASE STUDY

You are the superintendent of Alpha County Schools, a large suburban school district that is highly competitive with the neighboring school district, Beta County Schools. Competition for education supremacy is evidenced by such factors as teacher salaries, buildings, technology, and per pupil spending. Lately you feel as if Beta County is outspending your school district in terms of effort. You have shared this feeling with the school board, and they have asked you to present all the data possible regarding local effort of the two

TABLE 7.10   CASE STUDY DATA FOR TWO COUNTIES

	Alpha County	Beta County
Number of pupils	10,000	10,500
Per capita residential property value	$60,000	$40,000
Per capita commercial property value	$12,500	$25,000
Per capita industrial property value	$22,500	$35,000
Total per capita property value	$95,000	$100,000
Per capita income	$95,000	$84,000
Per capita sales tax	$1,000	$1,500
Per pupil spending	$7,500	$7,500

counties at the next school board meeting to support this claim. The school budgets for the coming school year will be presented to the governing bodies in the next 4 months. If Beta County is exerting more effort in their public schools, this could be a bargaining chip at budget time.

Using the data in Table 7.10, present various effort indices to the school board explaining the relative fiscal effort of both localities in funding education. Which of the tax base factors will you recommend that the school board present when making its case for budget increases to the governing body? Explain your rationale.

CHAPTER QUESTIONS

1. What is fiscal effort? Why is effort difficult to operationalize?
2. How is effort computed? What are some of the additional factors that could be considered in computing effort? Which of those factors would make your school district appear to have higher or lower effort ratios? Explain your answer.
3. What different factors should be considered in computing effort that are not included in your state? Explain your answer.
4. In the Case Study, if the school board presented to the governing body only selected data using "favorable" tax base information to compute an effort index, how would you explain other data subsequently discovered by the governing body that would lead to another conclusion?

EQUITY AND ADEQUACY

FOCUS QUESTIONS

1. What is the difference between equity and equality?

2. How does the idea of adequacy affect school finance—especially with high-stakes testing?

3. How do states equalize funding among their localities so that children from the poorest areas have access to at least a minimum level of education that the state mandates?

4. Does it cost more to educate students with disabilities, vocational students, or high school students versus elementary students? If so, how can those differences be costed out?

5. Very few educators would say that schools are funded adequately to meet the current challenges. How is adequacy of funding determined?

This chapter examines two important financial and legal concepts in education finance—equity and adequacy. Equity involves giving people what they need. Poorer communities need greater state support for education than do wealthier communities. Balancing these diverse needs is a process known as equalization. Adequacy involves providing sufficient resources to accomplish the job of educating our children. With the high-stakes testing required of NCLB legislation, adequate funding is necessary to satisfy this new level of accountability.

Chapter 7 discussed fiscal effort—how much capacity a locality, state, or nation elects to spend on education. This chapter deals with two other aspects of effort—equity and adequacy.

EQUALITY OR EQUITY IN FUNDING?

Equity should not be confused with equality. *Equality* involves treating everyone the same. *Equity* involves giving people the treatment they need. Our nation holds the idea of equality sacred—and rightfully so. The traditional view of equality as the governing principle for school spending would give everyone the same level of funding. Superficially, this sounds rather reasonable. When considering the issue more deeply, however, it becomes clear that equality cannot be the sole principle to govern school finance. In school finance treating everyone equally is not the main goal. Instead we strive for various types of equity in spending.

Here's why. No one would argue that it costs more to staff a special education classroom than a general education classroom. A special education classroom tends to have fewer students, more teachers per student, and occasionally extra resources (therapists, aides, or equipment) to facilitate learning. Inherent inequities exist within school districts, schools, and classrooms. Educational leaders must allow for those cost differentials. A medical model helps clarify further. If a patient comes to a physician with a rare cancer, it will cost more to provide medical care for that patient than for the healthy person who comes in needing only a flu shot. No one would expect both patients' bills to be the same. So it is with education. Some of our clients' needs cost more to care for than others. That is why equality cannot be the governing principle of school finance.

Consider funding for two hypothetical school systems. The first is an urban school system with 25% of its students identified as eligible to receive special education services, more than 50% of the student body reading more than 2 years below grade level, and 90% of the students eligible for free or reduced-price lunch. The second is a suburban school system with 99% of its students reading on or above grade level, 2% identified as eligible to receive special education services, and no one eligible for free or reduced-price lunch. The first school system needs more resources than the second to successfully meet the high-stakes challenges of No Child Left Behind legislation. For both to be funded equally, at some arbitrary level, is inherently inequitable because their needs are so different. The school system with greater needs incurs greater costs.

Equality is also an essential principle. When schools or school systems are considered equal, their funding should be equal. Consider the following scenario. Schools A and B are both secondary schools in the same school district. Each has 1,500 students, and the same percentage of students is on free and reduced-price lunch, eligible for special education, and going on to higher education upon graduation. Both schools have similar facilities and programs. If the funding for school A were 20% higher than for school B, there would be a fundamental unfairness in the allocation of funds.

School finance must be concerned with equity—providing what students need—as well as with equality. The concept of equity is simple, but measuring this need is complicated and requires sophisticated statistical procedures. Equity measurement has also prompted legal challenges to many states' financing formulae. We examine equity issues carefully because the concept has an important instructional impact for students' learning. School finance measures revolve around two fundamental issues of equity: horizontal and vertical equity.[1]

Horizontal Equity

Horizontal equity states that students who are alike should receive equal shares (of funding).[2] Horizontal equity is measured by calculating the dispersion, or inequality, in the distribution of funds. When there is no inequality in funding, there is perfect horizontal equity. Horizontal equity occurs when schools receive equal funding levels in areas including per pupil expenditures, student-teacher ratios, and equal teacher resources across various measures. Again, this concept applies when children or schools are considered to be alike.

Broadly applied, horizontal equity can compare large and similar subgroups of students, such as all vocational students at the high school level, all full-day kindergarten students, or all students in general education elementary classrooms. We would expect spending, or resource allocation, to be substantially similar for each of these rather large subgroups. If the resource allocations vary substantially, the criteria for horizontal equity have not been met.

---

[1]Two of the leading researchers in equity issues are Robert Berne and Leanna Stiefel. They distinguish between these two types of equity and other issues mentioned later in this chapter.

[2]This is rather easy to remember in that the word horizontal contains a Z. Take out the diagonal line between the two parallel lines and you have the = (equals) symbol. Equals should be funded equally.

Examining the national school finance research over the last 25 years reveals some interesting trends.[3] One seminal study involving 50 states revealed that between 1970 and 1975, a time of intense school finance reform, spending disparities among states increased.[4] Another important study showed that several states implementing school finance reform improved horizontal equity and fiscal neutrality measures over time in the same period.[5] More recently, a 1997 U.S. General Accounting Office study found substantial improvements in equity over time.[6] On the other hand, some studies show that significant financial disparities still remain in horizontal equity among the states.[7]

Vertical Equity

Vertical equity recognizes that students and schools are different, and that the treatment of unequals requires appropriate unequal treatment.[8] In other words, a regular education student and a special needs student are both expected to pass high-stakes tests under NCLB. These students have different learning needs, and they need to be treated appropriately, but differently.

Horizontal equity is relatively easy to quantify, but vertical equity choices are sometimes based on personal or community values. Accordingly, "appropriate treatment" varies at the macro level, from one school division to another, reflecting local priorities. What is deemed appropriate in one context, however, should be consistent across schools and districts. For example, at the micro level, two self-contained special education classrooms of emotionally disturbed students should have the same relative level of resources allocated to them. That is not to say that the two classrooms will be identical in funding

---

[3]An interesting research project for this class might be to examine horizontal equity within schools in one district over a large measure, such as per pupil expenditures at the elementary, middle, or high school, student-teacher ratios across the same levels, and equal teacher resources across various measures.

[4]Lawrence Brown, *School Finance Reform in the Seventies: Achievements and Failures* (Washington, DC: U.S. Department of Health, Education, and Welfare, Office of the Assistant Secretary for Planning and Evaluation and Killalea Associates, Inc., 1977).

[5]Allan Odden, Robert Berne, and Leanna Stiefel, *Equity in School Finance* (Denver: Education Commission of the States, 1979).

[6]General Accounting Office, *School Finance: State Efforts to Reduce Funding Gaps between Poor and Wealthy Districts* (Washington, DC: Author, 1997).

[7]Linda Hertbert, Carolyn Busch, and Allan Odden, "School Financing Inequities among the States: The Problem from a National Perspective," *Journal of Education Finance* 19 (3), 1994: 231–255.

[8]Robert Berne and Leanna Stiefel, *The Measurement of Equity in School Finance* (Baltimore: Johns Hopkins University Press, 1984).

or staffing, but differences in funding should be based on informed professional judgments and not applied indiscriminately.

Legitimate factors must be identified and used to allocate resources differently based on the characteristics of the students, the schools or school districts, and various programs. Student factors to consider include the percentage of students eligible for free and reduced-price lunch, percentage of students who are English language learners, percentage of students receiving special education services, or other valid criteria. Most educators would agree that serving these students' needs requires additional services.

Fiscal Neutrality

A third issue associated with horizontal and vertical equity is fiscal neutrality.[9] This concept can be complicated in concept and in measurement.[10] For our purposes, fiscal neutrality is funding education based on what an educated public wants to provide rather than funding based primarily on the wealth of the state or the locality. Therefore, if the public wants X level of services for all students at the state level, the lack of fiscal capacity of school district A to pay for those services should not interfere with that level of services being provided to the district.

Fiscal neutrality states that equity is achieved when the taxpayers' preferences for education—not the locality or state's fiscal capacity—determines the distribution of services. This is also known as taxpayer equity or wealth neutrality. Fiscal neutrality is an indication that the funding system provided by the state allows school districts to spend relatively equal amounts for a given tax rate, which includes state and local dollars. If this measurement is the same across districts in a state, the formula provides for fiscal neutrality.

The question then becomes, how do states impart fiscal neutrality while also accommodating equity issues? The answer is rather simple and was discussed in Chapters 3 and 5. The purpose of taxes is to redistribute wealth. States need a method to calculate a lower services cost to those who can least afford to pay for them. Likewise, states need a method that requires those who can afford to pay more to shoulder a greater share of education's costs. That concept is known as equalization of funding and will be discussed next.

---

[9]Ibid.

[10]For an excellent overview of the measurement of fiscal neutrality, see Kern Alexander and Richard Salmon, *Public School Finance* (Boston: Allyn and Bacon, 1995), chap. 9.

FISCAL EQUALIZATION

Fiscal equalization can be seen as a continuum ranging from total equalization to no equalization at all. Each state provides a method for equalizing school funding within its boundaries that fits somewhere on this continuum. Some states do this more effectively than others, and more than two-thirds of the 50 states have faced court challenges to their state funding formulae. Providing no fiscal equalization would be both immoral and illegal.

School finance scholars refer to concepts known as absolute fiscal equalization and approximate fiscal equalization. Absolute fiscal equalization is more a theoretical goal than a practical achievement. Although it is theoretically possible, it is virtually impossible to achieve politically. Alexander and Salmon say that *absolute* fiscal equalization has been achieved when three conditions are met: (1) variance in fiscal position among local school districts has been neutralized, (2) variance in fiscal effort among local school districts has been eliminated, and (3) variance in educational needs due to incidence of clients has been accommodated.[11] In other words, absolute fiscal equalization becomes possible when local school districts have equal resources, show equal effort to fund their schools, and spend what is necessary to educate students with special learning needs. Absolute fiscal equalization means that a locality has achieved fiscal neutrality and has successfully addressed horizontal and vertical equity. Although this is certainly a goal to strive for, it is rarely, if ever, achieved in the real world.

A more practical concept to work with is defined by Alexander and Salmon as *approximate* fiscal equalization. Approximate fiscal equalization has been met when (1) variance in fiscal position among local school districts has been neutralized, (2) constrained variance in fiscal effort among local school districts is permitted, and (3) variance in educational needs due to incidence of clients has been accommodated.[12] In short, approximate fiscal equalization becomes possible when local school districts have equal resources, schools have some leeway in raising and spending funds for schools, and schools spend what is necessary to educate students with special learning needs.

The two definitions are alike except for the second condition—that of constrained or controlled spending by local school districts. It is virtually

---

[11]Ibid., 193.
[12]Ibid., 194.

impossible politically to disallow variance in local spending.[13] Neutralized fiscal position and meeting clients' educational needs in spite of the local capacity are still required. This allowance for local spending makes the difference in approximate and absolute fiscal equalization. It is also the reason fiscal equalization is theoretically—but not practically—possible.

STATE AID GRANTS TO DISTRICTS

How do states provide for equalization? Each state's constitution spells out how it proposes to fund education. Basically, each state equalizes for local districts' fiscal capacity through its method for funding localities. Each state collects revenue and disperses it to districts, providing greater funding to lower capacity districts and less funding to higher capacity districts. This funding usually comes through various types of grants. Alexander and Salmon view state aid as a continuum from inequity to equity and show the types of grants as they move along the continuum (Figure 8.1).[14]

States vary in how they write equalization grants, and this affects the local districts' equity levels. Some states do not equalize as much as others. Depending on the exact legislative language, therefore, the grants may be more or less equitable. The level of equalization depends on the state's commitment to equalization. Some states are more committed to providing equity than are others. The greater the variance between the language of the state constitution and the equalization formula, the greater the likelihood that the formula will be challenged in court.

Consider this example. State A's constitution speaks to providing a *high* education level for all of its citizens despite their level of wealth. State B's constitution writes of providing an *efficient* education to its citizens. State A might then provide a method for collecting revenue sufficient to provide an excellent funding level for all localities. State B, on the other hand, might be a low-tax state, happy to provide only some limited (efficient) education level to its poorest citizens. This disparity of goals and values is apparent in each state's constitutional language. State B's grants, although referred to as equalization grants, may well be nothing more than matching or flat grants.

---

[13]The first goal of politicians is generally to be reelected. As seen in Chapter 4, the educated are wealthier and tend to vote in greater numbers than the poor and less educated. Not allowing the wealthy to supplement education funding would be political suicide for an elected official.

[14]Alexander and Salmon, *Public School Finance*, 197.

Inequity ◄───► Equity

| Nonequalization Grants | Matching Grants | Flat Grants | Equalization Grants | Full State Funding |

FIGURE **8.1**

Grants Continuum

Source: Kern Alexander and Richard Salmon, *Public School Finance* (Boston: Allyn & Bacon), 1995, p. 197. Reprinted by permission of Pearson Education, Inc., Upper Saddle River, NJ.

Nonequalization Grants

Nonequalization grants make no attempt to equalize funding for the capacity of local school districts. These grants are not designed to be inequitable, but they may have that unfortunate impact. Many times these grants provide categorical aid to school divisions, allocating a constant dollar amount on a per pupil basis based on an application process. Poorer school divisions may not have the personnel to write the grants enabling them to qualify for the funds. Higher capacity systems may have the grant-writing personnel and obtain the funds. This grant application process itself adversely impacts equalizing funding.

Flat grants provide a fixed amount of funding per pupil to each school district in the state. This funding is not based on the locality's fiscal capacity. Most states do not use flat grants as the primary vehicle for distributing funds to localities. Some states, however, have constitutional requirements for state funding regardless of the locality's capacity or position to fund education. For example, California's constitution requires $120 of state funding per pupil to each locality—regardless of the locality's fiscal position.[15] Virginia's constitution requires that regardless of the locality's capacity, the locality must fund no more than 80% and no less than 20% of state standards. In other words, California funds $120 per pupil regardless of capacity and Virginia funds 20% of the required standards for the wealthiest locality and requires the poorest locality to fund 20% of the required state standards.

Table 8.1 displays the impact of flat grant equalization. Consider four localities. Each district taxes at the rate of 10 mills (one-tenth of one cent, or $1 for $100 of property value). Each school district is awarded a flat grant in the amount of $2,000. School district A has a property tax base of $5,000 per pupil that enables it to raise $50 in revenue per pupil. The flat state grant of $2,000 brings the total spending in the locality with the least capacity to $2,050 per pupil. In comparison, School district D, the highest capacity

---

[15]But with the state's budget crisis, who knows what will happen in the future?

TABLE 8.1	FLAT GRANT IMPACT ON EDUCATION SPENDING			
School District	Local Property Value	Local Revenue	Flat Grant Amount	Total Spending per Pupil
A	$5,000	$50	$2,000	$2,050
B	50,000	500	2,000	2,500
C	250,000	2,500	2,000	4,500
D	500,000	5,000	2,000	7,000

school district, has a per pupil property value of $500,000, enabling it to exert the same effort of 10 mills and raise $5,000 per pupil. Combined with the flat grant of $2,000, School district D has a total per pupil spending of $7,000.

Obviously, the flat grant enabled school district A to spend much more than it could have on its own. It decreased the available local revenue disparity of $50 compared to $5,000 (1 to 100) to a spending disparity of $2,050 to $7,000 (1 to 3.4). The flat grant only added the grant amount to the total available local revenue. In that regard, the flat grant does little to equalize spending within a state. This also places a greater burden on the locality than on the state to provide funding for education services.

Table 8.2 shows a model with increased state support and lower local support for education. Using the same four school districts, we have increased the state's flat grant to $4,000 and reduced the local effort from 10 mills to 5 mills. Although property values have not changed—a disparity of 1 to 10 still exists—the locality has a lower tax burden, and the state has a greater burden to provide for education services. This reduces the disparity in total per pupil spending from 3.4 to 1 ($7,000 to $2,050) to 1.6 to 1 ($6,500 to $4,025). By using this method, a greater degree of equalization begins to take place. The next sections, however, show that better methods to equalize for education expenditures exist.

Equalization Grants

Many early education finance researchers laid the foundation for equalization grants.[16] These equalization grants play a role as a modern day Robin Hood, so to speak. They provide greater state funding for localities with less capacity to raise their own funds and provide less state funding for localities with greater capacity.

---

[16]The early researchers include Ellwood Cubberley, Robert Haig, Roe Johns, and others.

TABLE 8.2	FLAT GRANT WITH INCREASED STATE SUPPORT ON EDUCATION SPENDING			
School District	Local Property Value	Local Revenue	Flat Grant Amount	Total Spending per Pupil
A	$5,000	$25	$4,000	$4,025
B	50,000	250	4,000	4,250
C	250,000	1,250	4,000	5,250
D	500,000	2,500	4,000	6,500

Foundation Programs   Foundation programs are a means of providing equalization grants to school systems. A foundation program establishes some minimum level of per pupil funding that localities must meet with a combination of local and state funding. By law, no district can fall below this foundation level. Assume that the minimum foundation level is set at $10,000 per pupil. The local effort required will be lower in low-capacity school districts and higher in high-capacity districts. Once the locality meets the foundation level, districts can choose to supplement funding, called lee-way funds, to achieve a higher level of per pupil spending.

Table 8.3 provides an example of foundation program funding. Here, low-capacity school district A has a local capacity to raise only $1,000 per pupil. The state, however, has set a minimum foundation level of $10,000 per pupil.[17] In this case, the state aid would make up the difference of $9,000 so that district A can meet the state's minimum foundation level. In this scenario, district A, an economically modest community, does not have the fiscal capacity to generate any leeway funds to increase the total per pupil spending.

At the other end of the spectrum are more affluent districts D and E. District D has the local capacity to raise $7,500 per pupil. In this case, the state would offer $2,500 to meet the foundation level. District D, however, has the capacity to raise an additional $2,500 per pupil (local leeway funds), bringing their total per pupil spending to $12,500. District E has the capacity to raise the full foundation level the state prescribes. It, therefore, receives no state funding to meet the $10,000 per pupil foundation level. It raises an additional $2,500 per pupil to bring spending to $12,500 per student.

The foundation program spending approach differs from flat grants because it has the effect of equalizing funding for students on a much greater

---

[17]Admittedly this is a high level of spending; it is used only to simplify the arithmetic.

TABLE 8.3   FOUNDATION GRANTS

District	Local Capacity	State Aid	Foundation Level	Local Leeway	Total Funding
A	$1,000	$9,000	$10,000	$0	$10,000
B	$2,500	$7,500	$10,000	$500	$10,500
C	$5,000	$5,000	$10,000	$1,000	$11,000
D	$7,500	$2,500	$10,000	$2,500	$12,500
E	$10,000	0	$10,000	$2,500	$12,500

scale. In this scenario, school district E has 10 times the capacity of school district A, yet spends only 25% more on a per pupil basis. Where the fiscal capacity differential was initially 10 to 1, the spending differential due to the foundation formula is now only 1 to 1.25.

What does this means for students? The poorest school district (A) now has the financial means to provide the state prescribed minimum education foundation level—regardless of their local capacity to fund education services. This enables economically modest school district A to compete with highly affluent district E in terms of educational programs. This raises the floor level of services available to low-capacity school districts. In other words, Juan and Sally can now both receive a quality education regardless of the side of the proverbial tracks on which they live. Today, the majority of state governments use a foundation program to fund local school programs.

Unfortunately, problems with foundation funding exist. First, state legislators frequently see the word *minimum* as the spending "limits" rather than the "minimum level of funding." Too often "minimum" becomes the funding target level, and funding does not advance beyond that. Second, localities may elect not to add sufficient leeway funds (based either on values or available resources) whereas higher capacity systems may add substantially higher dollar amounts, exacerbating the per pupil spending disparity. Third, state governments may be reluctant to set adequate levels of spending for a foundation program because elected officials cannot agree on what is "adequate."

Guaranteed Tax Base Programs   Although not widely used, a second type of equalization grant is the guaranteed tax base (GTB) program. GTB programs guarantee that each locality can operate as if all school districts had an equal per pupil property tax base. Clearly, wealthier school districts have more funding available to them than do poorer school districts. GTB programs equalize for this disparity.

TABLE 8.4   GUARANTEED TAX BASED PROGRAMS

District	Local Capacity per Pupil	Local Effort @ 10 mills	Actual Effort Levied in Mills	State Aid	Local Leeway	Total Funding
A	$50,000	$500	8 = $400	$3,600	na	$4,000
B	$100,000	$1,000	9 = $900	$3,600	na	$4,500
C	$200,000	$2,000	10 = $2,000	$3,000	na	$5,000
D	$400,000	$4,000	11 = $4,400	$1,000	$400	$5,400
E	$500,000	$5,000	12 = $6,000	0	$1,000	$6,000

Table 8.4 shows five districts with an increasing capacity to fund education.[18] School district A does not have the funding available to them that school district E has. The GTB program addresses foundation levels of spending (or lack thereof) and local governments' reluctance to increase their fiscal support for an adequate educational foundation level.

In GTB programs the state determines its share of spending for the total cost of education. The formula then provides a means for deciding how much funding goes to each locality, based on a measure of its wealth. More state funding goes to low-capacity systems, and less aid goes to high-capacity systems—just as with the foundation program.

Once the state aid is calculated, the tax rates are equalized so the same tax yield is achieved for rich or poor districts. Some states use a recapture clause with the GTB formula. A recapture clause provides that the state recaptures extra funds generated by wealthy localities and dispenses them to poorer localities, effectively raising the state's floor level of services.[19]

Table 8.4 shows the hypothetical impact of a GTB program on education funding. Each district is limited to a maximum local tax levy of 10 mills to qualify for the per pupil state spending, and each district has 1,000 students (to keep the arithmetic simple). The state guarantees $5,000 per pupil funding if the locality levies a 10 mill tax rate. The locality may levy a rate higher than 10 mills, but it would receive no additional state funding.

---

[18]Thanks to Dick Salmon for helping with this table and section.

[19]Montana and Utah are two states that include a recapture clause in their funding formulae. Most programs do not include this provision.

Should a locality fund less than 10 mills, for instance, 8 or 9 mills, the state would reduce funding by the corresponding 10% or 20%.

For example, if district A levied a tax rate of only 8 mills, that would be 20% less than the required 10 mills, and state funding would decrease concomitantly from $5,000 (minus 20% or $1,000) to $4,000.

For district A, one mill generates $50 per mill per pupil, thus the state is obligated to fund $450 per mill per pupil. Because district A has set its actual effort at 8 mills, the total state aid is $3,600 per pupil. When added to the local funds of $400, this yields total funding of $4,000 per pupil.

For district B, one mill generates $100 per mill per pupil, and the state is obligated to fund $400 per mill per pupil. Because district B has set its actual effort at 9 mills, the total state aid is $3,600 per pupil. When added to the local funds of $900, this yields total funding of $4,500.

For district C, one mill generates $200 per mill per pupil, and the state is obligated to fund $300 per mill per pupil. Since district C has set its actual effort at 10 mills, the total state aid is $3,000 per pupil. When added to the local funds of $2,000, this yields total funding of $5,000.

For district D, one mill generates $400 per mill per pupil, and the state is obligated to fund $100 per mill per pupil. Because district D has set its actual effort at 11 mills (state is only obligated to fund 10 mills), the total state aid is $1,000 per pupil. When added to the local funds of $4,400, this yields total funding of $5,400.

For district E, one mill generates $500 per mill per pupil, and the state is obligated to fund $0 per mill per pupil. Because district E has set its actual effort at 12 mills (state is only obligated to fund 10 mills), the total state aid is $0 per pupil. When added to the local funds of $6,000, this yields total funding of $6,000.

Combination of Foundation and Guaranteed Tax Base Programs

Other equalization formulae exist as hybrids of foundation programs and equalization programs. These programs take the best of other formulae and apply those components to their particular conceptual framework. Harlan Updegraff proposed the basis for the percentage-equalization program.[20] Other formulae are district-power equalization and the tier program. All these programs use a hybrid of methods.[21]

---

[20]Harlan Updegraff, *Rural School Survey of New York State: Financial Support* (Ithaca, NY: Author, 1922).

[21]We will not discuss these models other than to inform the reader that such programs exist. These models are fodder for more extensive graduate study in school finance.

FULL STATE FUNDING

The full state funding model assumes that education is a state function and all the revenue raised for education should come from state—not local— sources. The federal government funds the District of Columbia, but only Hawaii has truly a full state funding model. Hawaii has a single, unified school system under the governor's and state legislature's financial control. Hawaii's funds come from the state general fund supported by state income, sales, and excise taxes. Other states have been reluctant to adopt such a model.

The full state funding concept offers a paradox. Education, by constitutional definition, is a state function. Leaving the education funding responsibility to localities gives opportunity for the rich to provide the best services and the poor to provide the least. In theory, full state funding could be an effective method to achieve fiscal equalization.[22] In reality, however, the politics of influence and resources still play a major role in funding.

Alexander and Salmon point out one healthy aspect of some local funding discretion for school districts within a state—competition.[23] When school districts compete for personnel with enhanced compensation, benefits, and professional development programs, and when they compete for students with excellent instructional programs and facilities, the entire community benefits. This competition may not exist in a full state funding model.

CALCULATING VERTICAL EQUITY

As previously described, vertical equity means providing what people need— recognizing that students and schools differ and that the treatment of unequals requires appropriate unequal treatment. Methods exist for calculating the different costs of various programs. One method is the weighted pupil approach.

Weighted Pupil Approach

This widely used method for calculating vertical equity involves determining a base cost for various categories of students. Many people think it costs

---

[22]The Fleischmann Commission in New York recommended full state funding in its 1973 report. Fleischmann Commission, *The Fleischmann Report* (New York: Viking Press, 1973).

[23]Alexander and Salmon, *Public School Finance*, 212.

TABLE 8.5   SPECIAL EDUCATION WEIGHTING FACTORS

Special Education Category	Weighting
Educable mentally retarded	2.3
Trainable mentally retarded	3.0
Physically handicapped	3.5
Physical and occupational therapy (part time)	6.0
Speech and hearing therapy (part time)	10.0
Deaf	4.0
Visually handicapped (part time)	10.0
Visually handicapped	3.5
Emotionally disturbed (part time)	7.5
Emotionally disturbed	3.7
Socially maladjusted	2.3
Specific learning disability (part time)	7.5
Specific learning disability	2.3
Hospital and homebound (part time)	15.0

Source: Richard Rossmiller, "Resource Configurations and Costs in Educational Programs for Exceptional Children," in *Planning to Finance Education,* eds. R. L. Jones, Kern Alexander, and K. Forbis Jordan (Gainesville, FL: National Educational Finance Project, 1971), chap 2.

more to operate a high school than it does to operate an elementary school. Likewise, many believe special education is more expensive than general education. Both assumptions are correct. How is the cost differential determined? Are the cost differentials sufficient to cover the additional resources needed for the students involved in various programs? The answer to these two questions is at the heart of the concept of weighting costs for various students.

History of Student Weightings

Determining appropriate costs for the construct of vertical equity is a complex process. The National Education Finance Project (NEFP) researched various education programs' costs. In one study, Richard Rossmiller examined best practices used with special education programs and used these data to establish the cost differentials for the various special education programs shown in Table 8.5.

From these weightings, many school districts established means for "costing out" related services. Later, other states established weightings that more closely reflected their actual costs. Not all of these calculations considered Rossmiller's "best practices" method. These weightings show a means for calculating the cost differences in educating individuals with varying needs.

The method used to determine "costing out" of these services varies from state to state and from district to district. How states and localities determine these cost differentials leads them to discuss community values and priorities: what constitutes an "adequate" educational program or what determines "adequate" spending. These topics are discussed later in the chapter.

Florida's Model of Pupil Weighting

Florida's Department of Education has an excellent website explaining its funding formula, including fiscal terms, concepts, and implementation.[24] Florida uses a weighted per pupil approach to address vertical equity. Basically, here is how the funding worked for the 2003–04 school year.

The state determines cost factors for operating schools at various grade levels. It establishes the basic program service level (general classroom instruction) and programs for exceptional students. Once determined, the lowest base cost is given a weight of 1.0. For example, Florida bases a weighting of 1.0 for students in basic programs in grades 4 through 8. Kindergarten and grades 1 through 3 receive weights slightly higher, with high school grades receiving even higher weights. Table 8.6 shows the various weightings for basic and exceptional student education (ESE) programs as well as students in ESL and vocational education programs.

Students in ESE programs must have an IEP, and they become eligible for funding based on the five levels of special education programs. Each student's IEP includes a matrix of services converted to a point scale. The points are then summed to determine which funding level the student receives. Level 1 is the lowest level of services, and level 5 is designed for the neediest of ESE students.

Each spring the state legislature determines funding for the Guaranteed ESE Allocation—a dollar amount that subsidizes district ESE programs. For levels 1, 2, and 3 in the 2003–04 school year, Florida allocated almost one billion dollars to school districts.[25] This form of per pupil weighting illustrates how one state compensates for equity issues.

---

[24]http://www.firn.edu/doe/fefp/pdf/fefpdist.pdf

[25]Special thanks go to Glenda Todd in Linda Champion's Office of Funding and Financial Reporting with the Florida Department of Education for her assistance.

TABLE 8.6	FLORIDA DEPARTMENT OF EDUCATION PER PUPIL COST FACTORS FOR 2003–04

Program	Cost Factor
Basic Programs	
Kindergarten, Grades 1–3	1.002
Grades 4–8	1.000
Grades 9–12	1.140
Programs for Exceptional Student Education (ESE)	
Kindergarten, Grades 1–3 with ESE Services	1.002
Grades 4–8 with ESE Services	1.000
Grades 9–12 with ESE Services	1.140
English for Speakers of Other Languages	1.298
Programs for Grades 6–12 Vocational Education	1.190

Source: http://www.firn.edu/doe/fefp/pdf/fefpdist.pdf, p. 14.

TABLE 8.7	HYPOTHETICAL FLORIDA PUBLIC SCHOOL AND FUNDING PER PUPIL

Student Demographics	Pupil Weighting
600 students grades K–3	1.002 for all in basic program
90 ESE students	Funding based on Guaranteed ESE Allocation
100 ESL students	1.298 for students in basic classes (excludes PE, art, etc.)

How does this work? Suppose you are the principal of a 600-student primary school (Grades K–3). Your district's share of state funding would be based on the number of students in each classification. Table 8.7 shows a simplified version of how the funding would work based on the per pupil expenditure model.

The Florida model attempts to provide vertical equity.[26] This is a complex, politically charged issue compounded by NCLB's high-stakes testing programs. In Florida, for example, the weightings for basic programs at grade level K–3 have decreased from 1.014 in 1992–93 to 1.002 for the 2003–04 school year. The high school weightings, grades 9–12, have decreased from

---

[26]Make yourself aware of your own state's attempts to address vertical equity.

1.225 in 1992–93 to 1.140 for the 2003–04 school year, possibly reflecting the national economic downturn and reduced state revenue of these years. Florida does, however, make an effort to quantify the vertical equity issues we have reviewed.

ADEQUACY

With the decreased relative weightings for Florida's pupil weighting model since 1992–93, educators might wonder whether the state is spending enough to meet student needs. Is the overall spending *adequate* to meet the needs? The Florida legislature put almost one billion dollars into the first three levels of special education funding for the 2003–04 school year. How much is an adequate level of spending? How is an adequate level of spending determined?

Adequacy as a fiscal concept is value driven. That is, people define adequacy subjectively according to their own priorities and opinions. Attempts have been made to quantify how much a state or school district needs to spend for its students, but the actual figure remains ambiguous. Perhaps a workable definition for adequacy is providing sufficient funds "to teach the average student to state standards, and then to identify how much each district/school requires to teach students with special needs—the learning disabled, those from poverty and thus educationally deficient backgrounds, and those without English proficiency—to the same high and rigorous achievement standards."[27] Although given these reasonable parameters, the answer to "What is adequate?" remains unclear.

As a result, this crucial yet vaguely defined concept has become the grist for court challenges since the 1990s. Recently, legal disputes have shifted from school funding disparities to adequacy issues, and fiscal adequacy may become the active focus of adjudication in coming years. Historically, in response to the case of *Rose v. Council for Better Education*, Kentucky's school finance model was the first in the United States history to be designed with an "adequate" funding base for each school and school district in the Commonwealth.[28] Several follow-up studies since its implementation

---

[27]A. Odden and L. Picus, *School Finance: A Policy Perspective*, 3rd ed. (New York: McGraw-Hill, 2004), 25.

[28]*Rose v. Council for Better Education*, 790 S.W. 2d 186 (Kent, 1989).

concluded that the new funding formula had substantially improved equity within Kentucky.[29]

How does one determine an "adequate" level of funding? School finance experts use four approaches when discussing fiscal adequacy:

- Economic cost function
- Successful school district
- Professional consensus
- State-of-the-art (or best practices)

Economic Cost Function Approach

In a nutshell, economic cost function tries to answer how much money per pupil is needed in a given school district to produce a certain level of student performance. This is a multiple regression model. Per pupil expenditure is the dependent variable, and student and school district characteristics and the desired level of student performance are the independent variables. Although no state currently uses this method, New York,[30] Wisconsin,[31] Texas,[32] and Illinois[33] have conducted research on the economic cost function approach. Businesses frequently use this complicated statistical approach, which relies on econometric techniques—cost functions—to estimate an adequate level of resources.

Results demonstrate the per pupil expenditure necessary to achieve certain levels of student performance given the student and district characteristics.

---

[29]For example, Lawrence O. Picus, Allan Odden, and Mark Fermanich, "Assessing the Equity of Kentucky's SEEK Formula: A Ten-Year Analysis." Report prepared for the Kentucky Department of Education, 2001; Verstegan Associates, "Calculation of the Cost of an Adequate Education in Kentucky," http://www.oldham.k12.ky.us/kyAdequacyStudy.pdf, 2003.

[30]W. Duncombe, J. Ruggiero, and J. Yinger, "Alternative Approaches to Measuring the Cost of Education," in *Holding Schools Accountable: Performance-Based Reform in Education,* ed. Helen F. Ladd (Washington, DC: The Brookings Institution, 1996), 327–356.

[31]A. Reschovsky and J. Imazeki, "Reforming State Aid to Achieve Educational Adequacy: Lessons from Texas and Wisconsin," in *Education Funding Adequacy and Equity in the Next Millennium: Conference Proceedings,* eds. B. Nye and G. L. Peeveley (Nashville, TN: Tennessee State University, 1999).

[32]J. Imazeki and A. Reschovsky, "Measuring the Costs of Providing an Adequate Public Education in Texas," in *Proceedings of the 91st Annual Conference on Taxation,* ed. H. Chernick (Washington, DC: National Tax Association, 1999), 275–290; and A. Reschovsky and J. Imazeki, *Let No Child Be Left Behind: Determining the Cost of Improving Student Performance* (Madison, WI: Finance Center of the Consortium for Policy Research in Education, May 2002).

[33]A. Reschovsky and J. Imazeki, "Developing a Cost Index for School Districts in Illinois." Paper submitted to the Illinois State Department of Education, 2000.

Again, this model for determining fiscal adequacy reflects personal and community values. Some group must decide how much a community is willing to spend so that some or all students can reach a certain achievement level.

What does this adequacy research tell us? For the most part, it quantifies what we may have already suspected. Some research has shown the adequate spending levels are close to the median spending levels within the state *if* the researchers selected the *average* student proficiency achievement level.[34] Most studies indicated that a wide variation exists in the average adequacy level of student performance due to student and district needs. The adequacy spending levels ranged from a low of 49% to a high of 460% of the average in Wisconsin and a low of 75% to a high of 158% in Texas.[35] In Wisconsin and Texas, the adequate expenditure level for large urban school districts was 3 to 4 times that of the average district.

Successful School District Approach

The successful school district approach is one method used to examine the adequacy concept.[36] This method bypasses some of the complicated statistical procedures of the economic cost function approach and identifies school districts that have successfully brought student performance to state proficiency standards. This approach then sets the adequacy spending level to the weighted average of the successful districts' expenditure level.

Unfortunately, this approach leaves out essential information because it omits outliers (atypical districts) from the equation. It excludes virtually all large, urban areas, very wealthy and very poor districts, as well as small, rural systems. It also may inaccurately represent the actual costs of delivering adequate services in these atypical districts.

What have we learned from the successful school district model? The districts identified as successful are generally average size and nonurban, with little student diversity. Given the atypical and excluded outliers, remaining districts also tend to spend less than the state average. Ironically, the demographics of a "successful" school district tend to distort the overall picture about what it means to be a successful school or school district. By omitting schools that must effectively address the real-world challenges

---

[34]Ibid.

[35]Reschovsky and Imazeki, "Reframing State Aid to Achieve Educational Adequacy."

[36]K. Alexander, W. Augenblick, W. Driscoll, J. Guthrie, and R. Levin, *Proposals for the Elimination of Wealth-Based Disparities in Public Education* (Columbus, OH: Ohio Department of Education, 1995); J. Augenblick, *Calculation of the Cost of an Adequate Education in Maryland in 1999–2000 Using Two Different Analytic Approaches* (Denver, CO: Augenblick and Meyers, 2001).

of educating urban, rural, and high-poverty students, the formula artificially lowers the level for achieving success.

Closely examining the successful school district model raises more questions about the validity of its use. This method and the cost function approach link educational spending levels with student performance levels, but they do not indicate what instructional strategies schools should use or how the funds should be distributed at the school level.

Professional Consensus Approach

The professional consensus approach (also known as the professional judgment approach) attempts to remedy the problems mentioned for the two previous approaches. At least nine states use the professional consensus approach. This method asks a group of educational professionals to identify the components of a "prototype" school they believe would enable the staff to teach students to some predetermined performance standard. The plan's ingredients are then "costed out" (number of professional and support staff, technology, instructional resources, and so forth) and summed to determine a school's adequate financial base. This base can then be adjusted for varying demographics.

Using the resource cost model, Jay Chambers and Tom Parrish first developed this approach.[37] Although it provides for varying demographics, the approaches identified by the professional team provide little differentiation between the average school and one with a high concentration of at-risk students. In spite of this drawback, the professional consensus approach is gaining interest at the state level.

State-of-the-Art Approach

The state-of-the-art approach takes the best of all the other methods and combines them into a new model. This approach selects research findings on student achievement frequently seen in high-achieving schools, identifies all the components needed for those research-identified teaching and learning strategies, determines a cost basis for each of the strategies, and then decides what an adequate spending base for the school should be. This model makes the decision at the school level; it does not represent the school district average.

---

[37]J. Chambers and T. Parrish, *The Development of a Resource Cost Model Funding Base for Education Finance in Illinois* (Stanford, CA: Associates for Education Finance and Planning, 1983); and J. Chambers and T. Parrish, "State-Level Education Finance," in *Advances in Educational Productivity,* ed. H. Walberg (Greenwich, CT: JAI Press, 1994).

The approach draws on research findings that link several instructional practices to increased student performance, includes some of the best thinking and data in education, and provides a funding level that allows the school to use schoolwide strategies that state-of-the-art researchers and practitioners affirm are most effective.

Allan Odden identified the costs of seven schoolwide designs created by the New American Schools and showed how resource reallocation could make these designs affordable for schools and districts spending at the average or median national expenditure level.[38]

New Jersey has used the state-of-the-art approach in response to its ongoing state Supreme Court challenge to its public education finance system. The 1998 state Supreme Court decision[39] found that the state's revised funding formula based on the state-of-the-art approach provided adequate funding because it allowed sufficient funds for schools to adopt and finance the most expensive comprehensive school design.[40] There was enough money for other schoolwide designs as well.

The fiscal adequacy issue is a dominant force in school finance and will continue to play a role in future court challenges. The issues of equity and adequacy are two sides of one coin. One side asks if we are treating children fairly. The other side asks if we are doing enough.

SUMMARY

Equality involves treating everyone the same. Equity involves giving people the treatment they need. School finance must be concerned with equity. Varying resources and student populations' factors affect the actual costs to educate all to high levels. Equity involves personal and community values, and its measurement is complicated and has prompted legal challenges to many states' finance formulae.

Three types of fiscal equity exist. Horizontal equity states that students who are alike should receive equal funding shares. Horizontal equity occurs when schools receive equal expenditures in funding levels in areas including per pupil expenditures, student-teacher ratios, and equal teacher resources across various measures.

---

[38]Allan Odden, "The Financial Side of Implementing New American Schools." Paper prepared for the New American Schools, Alexandria, Virginia, 1997.

[39]*Abbot v. Burke,* 710 A.2d 450 (1998).

[40]Success for All Foundation, 200 West Towsontown Blvd., Baltimore, MD 21204 (http://www.successforall.net).

Vertical equity recognizes that students and schools are different and that the treatment of unequals requires appropriate unequal treatment. Vertical equity choices are sometimes based on personal or community values and allocate resources differently based on the characteristics of students, schools, school districts, and various programs.

Fiscal neutrality states that equity is achieved when the taxpayers' preferences for education—not the locality or state's fiscal capacity—determine the distribution of services. Fiscal neutrality indicates that the state's funding system allows school districts to spend relatively equal amounts for a given tax rate.

The equalization concept is a continuum ranging from total equalization to no equalization. Fiscal equalization depends on addressing three conditions: (1) variance in fiscal position among local school districts, (2) variance in fiscal effort among local school districts, and (3) variance in accommodating educational needs due to incidence of clients. Each state equalizes for the local districts' fiscal capacity through its method for funding localities through various types of grants. State aid exists as a continuum from inequity to equity with different types of grants along the continuum.

Fiscal adequacy is a value-driven concept. Approaches to determining adequacy include economic cost function, successful school district, professional consensus, and state-of-the-art schoolwide best practices. These approaches to adequacy have both benefits and limitations. It is difficult for communities or state legislators to agree on how much funding is "enough" to support education to a given standard for all students, and court challenges often focus on this issue.

CONCLUSION

School financing often depends on values and other subjective factors that are determined in the political process of state government. Increasingly, these ambiguous issues are leading to legal challenges.

CASE STUDY

Assume you are the principal of Alpha High School housing grades 9 through 12. Your school serves the "blue-collar" side of town. Omega High School serves the "white-collar" side of town. Alpha High School is 45 years old;

TABLE 8.8	STUDENT POPULATIONS AT TWO SCHOOLS	
	Alpha High School	**Omega High School**
Number of students	1,200	800
Percentage of special education students	10%	5%
	• 75 LD resource students (5 classes) • 15 self-contained LD students (2 classes) • 15 ED self-contained students (2 classes) • 15 ED resource students (2 classes) • 7 EMR students (1 class) • 7 TMR students (1 class) • 1 severe autism student (1 class)	• 35 LD resource students (3 classes) • 5 self-contained ED students (1 class)
Percentage of students achieving AYP	65	70
Faculty	130	90
Assistant principals	2	2
School counselors	2	2
Number of AP classes offered	6	8
Number of vocational classes offered	8	8
Percentage of students eligible for free or reduced-price lunch	10	5
ESL students	60	20
	• 48 Spanish speaking • 6 Chinese speaking • 6 Taiwanese speaking	• 18 Chinese speaking • 2 Vietnamese speaking
Total school funding	$7,200,000	$4,800,000

Omega High School is just 4 years old. Table 8.8 lists the student populations and educational resources at both schools.

Both schools are held to the same high accountability standards under NCLB. Using the data provided, make a case that the funding for Alpha High school is inadequate to meet the challenges using the concepts of vertical and horizontal equity. Explain which method for determining adequacy might be best in arguing for increased funding for Alpha High School.

CHAPTER QUESTIONS

1. Explain the difference between horizontal and vertical equity.
2. What factors are associated with the concept of fiscal neutrality?
3. Explain the concept of absolute fiscal equalization. What conditions must be met to achieve absolute fiscal equalization? Why is this only theoretically achievable?
4. Explain the concept behind pupil cost weighting. How does your state or locality compensate for more expensive programs for students?
5. How does your state equalize funding for low socioeconomic school divisions? How would you suggest improving your state's equalization model?

THE STRUCTURE OF SCHOOL FINANCE SYSTEMS

FOCUS QUESTIONS

1. What are the federal, state, and local roles in providing, overseeing, and financing education?

2. How has the number of school districts in the United States changed over the past 100 years or so?

3. What has happened to federal, state, and local funding of school budgets in the past 100 years?

4. How are finances equalized to prevent the rich states and localities from having all the resources and the poor states and localities from having none?

5. How do states provide a fair level of funding so that equalization occurs?

This chapter examines basic concepts of how schools are structured—financially and politically. Education is a state responsibility, and states must plan for and deliver a system of free, public education. States also have the responsibility to equalize school funding based on the localities' fiscal capacity to pay for educational programs. For the most part, schools are administered at the local level.

Education is a federal interest, a state responsibility, and a local operation. As such, education is financed through three government levels. Chapter 9 integrates previously discussed topics as it reviews the political, financial, and control relationships for education among the federal, state, and local governments. Naturally, school funding has a great impact on education's direction and practice.[1] In this chapter we examine how the structure of schools and their finance systems have changed, how these changes affect funding practices, and the fiscal and political problems we must address today.

Although education is a state function, virtually every state, except Hawaii, has delegated the school systems' operation to the localities.[2] The states, for the most part, maintain an oversight and compliance role in the local school systems' functioning. Neighborhood schools and school boards once assumed local oversight, but the trend over the past 60 to 70 years (since record-keeping began) has been to decrease the number of school districts in the United States. This consolidation has accomplished greater fiscal and operational efficiency. It has also, however, depersonalized the operation and administration of our schools to some extent.

Historically, school management and operations have been primarily community based. Gradually throughout the 20th century the states have accepted more responsibility to oversee education. Federal government statistics on the number of public school districts in the United States illustrate this. In 1937–38, the first year such statistics were recorded, there were 119,001 U.S. school districts. Each succeeding year, the number of districts has decreased. In 2000–01, the total number of school districts totaled 14,859.[3]

As the number of school districts decreased, their size increased. Fewer school districts brought together more communities, representing a wider geographic area and a more diverse population. This trend decreases resource duplication and inefficiency, but it also decreases community feelings of pride and "ownership" in their local schools. Neighborhood schools gave way to larger schools made up from multiple neighborhoods with their administration more removed from local control. In fact, this ownership

---

[1]State rankings in funding programs make clear what your state is doing (or should be doing) for its students and how much fiscal effort the state deems appropriate for spending on education.

[2]Hawaii has a state-run education system that is comprised of one district—the entire state.

[3]http://nces.ed.gov/programs/digest/d02/tables/dt087.asp. Data from other sources, such as state department of education websites, NEA data, and AFT data sometimes do not match data from this source.

TABLE 9.1   TOTAL NUMBER OF SCHOOL DISTRICTS, 2002

Alabama	128	Louisiana	66	Ohio	611
Alaska	53	Maine	234	Oklahoma	544
Arizona	223	Maryland	24	Oregon	197
Arkansas	310	Massachusetts	371	Pennsylvania	500
California	989	Michigan	783	Rhode Island	36
Colorado	176	Minnesota	341	South Carolina	88
Connecticut	194	Mississippi	152	South Dakota	173
Delaware	19	Missouri	524	Tennessee	138
Florida	67	Montana	446	Texas	1,199
Georgia	180	Nebraska	545	Utah	40
Hawaii	1	Nevada	17	Vermont	287
Idaho	113	New Hampshire	163	Virginia	132
Illinois	897	New Jersey	593	Washington	296
Indiana	292	New Mexico	89	West Virginia	65
Iowa	374	New York	703	Wisconsin	426
Kansas	304	North Carolina	117	Wyoming	48
Kentucky	176	North Dakota	229	District of Columbia	34
				United States	**14,696**

issue has led to some calling for replacing school boards with individual school councils to return public school governance to the "grassroots."[4] Table 9.1 lists the number of school districts by state in 2002.

The number of students per school district has increased more than 1,400% in the 60-year period between 1940 and 2000. Table 9.2 shows that school districts averaged only 217 students in the 1939–40 school year. By the 1999–2000 school year, the number of students per district had increased to almost 3,200.

Understanding the structural changes in schools, such as consolidation of school districts, helps clarify our current school funding and educational challenges. Reviewing the shifts in school revenue sources brings additional insights about who controls and directs U.S. education.

---

[4]William G. Cunningham, "Grassroots Democracy: Putting the Public Back into Public Education," *Phi Delta Kappan* 84 (10), June 2003: 776–779.

TABLE 9.2	NUMBER OF STUDENTS PER SCHOOL DISTRICT, 1939–40 AND 1999–2000	
	1939–40	**1999–2000**
Total school enrollment	25,434,000	46,857,000
Number of school districts	117,108	14,928
Students per school district	217	3,188

Source: Data compiled from http://nces.ed.gov/programs/digest/d02_tf.asp, chap 2.

REVENUES AND EXPENDITURES

A history of public school revenue appears in Table 9.3. The federal share of public school financing has increased each decade from less than 1% in 1919 to a high of 9.8% in 1979. In the following decade, the federal share of school monies decreased by almost one-third to 6.1%. The federal share has been inching up in each subsequent decade.

In 1919 the states' contributing share of revenue was relatively low by today's standards, providing only 16.5% of the monies for public schools. That portion has increased each decade, and by 2000 the states were contributing approximately half of the average district's funding.

In the same time frame, the local share of revenue to operate public schools has steadily decreased, from 83.2% in 1919–20 to 43.2% in 1999–2000. Following the federal revenue decline from 9.8% in 1979–80 to 6.1% in 1989–90, the state and local funding sources increased to make up the difference in expanding schooling costs. Imagine the fiscal burden on local taxpayers today if the localities still produced 83% of the revenue to operate the schools!

As mentioned in Chapter 5, a good tax should be spread out over the largest number of people responsible for using the resource. In other words, the National Park Service should be funded by federal tax dollars. The state parks should be funded primarily through state tax dollars. Local and municipal parks should be funded through local tax dollars. This general concept holds true for public education. Because education is a state function with federal interests and local administration, the largest percentage of revenue should come from the state with a smaller percentage coming from localities and the smallest percentage of revenue from federal sources. Table 9.3 shows the trends in these finance percentages at a national average. Obviously, variations exist among states.

TABLE 9.3	SOURCE OF REVENUE FOR PUBLIC SCHOOLS, 1919–2000

School Year	Federal %	State %	Local %
1919–20	0.3%	16.5%	83.2%
1929–30	0.4	16.9	82.7
1939–40	1.8	30.3	68.0
1949–50	2.9	39.8	57.3
1959–60	4.4	39.1	56.5
1969–70	8.0	39.9	52.1
1979–80	9.8	46.8	43.4
1989–90	6.1	47.1	46.8
1995–96	6.6	47.5	45.9
1999–2000	7.3	49.5	43.2

Source: U.S. Department of Education, National Center for Education Statistics, "Statistics of State School Systems, Revenues and Expenditures for Public Elementary and Secondary Education," and Common Core of Data Surveys, May 2002.

Major variations in revenue sources exist for different regions. Table 9.4 shows the most current data indicating the percentage of revenue from these three major sources by region and state.

For federal revenue sources, the New England states have the lowest percentage at 5.3%, and the Southeast states have the highest at 9.1%. For state revenue sources, the mid-East states have the lowest percentage at 39.9%, and the Far West has the highest percentage at 61%. Finally, in terms of local revenue percentages, the Far West has the lowest percentage at 30.6%, and the mid-East region has the highest percentage at 55.5%.[5] One caveat should be noted. The Far West region includes Hawaii, and Hawaii's state-financed schools tend to skew the Far West's averages.

Considering federal revenue percentages, the variance ranges from a low in New Jersey of only 3% to a high of 14.1% in Mississippi. State revenue ranges from a low of 30.2% in Nevada to a high of 74.1% in New Mexico and Michigan. Local revenue ranges from a low of 12.6% in New Mexico to a high of 64.0% in Nevada. In terms of equalization, more federal funding tends to go to higher poverty states. This can be seen in Mississippi's

[5]Comparing the regional information with your state's data should provide an interesting class discussion about the elements of a good tax. Eliminating Hawaii and the District of Columbia from the mix for obvious reasons, state-by-state comparisons show rather large variations in the range of revenue sources.

TABLE 9.4	SOURCE OF REVENUE FOR PUBLIC SCHOOLS BY REGIONS AND STATES, 2001–02

Regions and States	Federal %	State %	Local %
50 states and District of Columbia	7.3%	50.2%	42.5%
New England	5.3	48.1	46.6
Connecticut	5.0	41.5	53.5
Maine	7.3	47.9	44.8
Massachusetts	5.4	45.3	49.4
New Hampshire	4.3	44.1	51.7
Rhode Island	4.1	37.4	58.5
Vermont	6.0	72.3	21.8
Mid-East	6.7	37.9	55.5
Delaware	8.2	66.9	25.0
District of Columbia	12.0	0.0	88.0
Maryland	4.8	36.9	58.3
New Jersey	3.0	37.3	59.8
New York	6.8	45.9	47.3
Pennsylvania	5.2	40.4	54.4
Southeast	9.1	55.0	35.9
Alabama	10.3	63.4	26.2
Arkansas	8.2	62.2	29.6
Florida	8.9	48.4	42.6
Georgia	6.4	47.6	46.0
Kentucky	7.7	62.9	29.4
Louisiana	11.7	48.6	39.8
Mississippi	14.1	55.2	30.7
North Carolina	7.7	70.6	21.8
South Carolina	7.9	50.5	41.6
Tennessee	9.5	46.9	43.7
Virginia	5.7	43.8	50.6
West Virginia	11.4	60.1	28.5
Great Lakes	5.7	50.9	43.4
Illinois	8.0	30.8	61.1
Indiana	5.2	52.2	42.6
Michigan	4.5	74.1	21.4
Ohio	6.0	43.3	50.8

TABLE 9.4   CONTINUED

Regions and States	Federal %	State %	Local %
Wisconsin	4.8	54.0	41.3
Plains	7.2	47.3	45.6
Iowa	4.9	52.6	42.5
Kansas	6.3	62.5	31.2
Minnesota	4.8	59.3	35.9
Missouri	7.1	37.1	55.8
Nebraska	5.5	40.7	53.8
North Dakota	11.7	38.4	50.0
South Dakota	9.8	40.3	49.9
Southwest	9.7	57.4	32.9
Arizona	6.2	52.9	40.9
New Mexico	13.2	74.1	12.6
Oklahoma	10.2	59.1	30.7
Texas	9.1	43.8	47.2
Rocky Mountains	7.9	50.6	41.5
Colorado	5.1	41.2	53.7
Idaho	7.2	60.0	32.8
Montana	11.1	44.9	44.1
Utah	7.5	58.3	34.2
Wyoming	8.4	48.8	42.8
Far West	8.4	61.0	30.6
Alaska	12.5	63.5	23.9
California	9.6	61.1	29.4
Hawaii	8.4	89.8	1.8
Nevada	4.9	30.2	66.9
Oregon	6.9	57.3	35.8
Washington	7.9	64.3	27.8

Source: http://www.nea.org/edstats/images/02rankings.pdf, summary table H.

hardship and New Jersey's wealth. Other factors, such as effort—the amount of state and local funding—also affect the percentages. Reviewing state revenue percentages, the variance ranges speak to the state funding formula's level of equalization. It may also address the level of local fiscal effort to fund schools.

Local funding, however, is at the heart of school finance. Local funding reflects a community's economic, political, and emotional investment in its children's education and the overall region's quality of life. Local revenue percentages range from a low of 12.6% in New Mexico to a high of 64.9% in Nevada. Given the high percentage of state funding in New Mexico, the lower percentage of local funding could be expected. The high range in Nevada is also associated with a low percentage of state revenue for school funding.

FEDERAL, STATE, AND LOCAL ROLES AND RESPONSIBILITIES

How do federal, state, and local structures work together in organizing and financing education for the end user—the student? As you will recall from Chapter 2, federal involvement in education preceded ratification of the first 10 amendments to the U.S. Constitution. It was not until 1867 that Congress enacted legislation to establish the United States Department of Education and coordinated education effort at a cabinet level. Later downgraded to an Office of Education, it was incorporated with two other federal departments into the Department of Housing, Education, and Welfare. President Jimmy Carter reestablished the Department of Education in 1980, and it survived threats to end its cabinet status during the Ronald Reagan years.

Federal education funding primarily provides grants and guidance for states and school systems under various programs enacted by Congress. As recently as 40 years ago, thousands of school districts reported to and communicated directly with the federal Office of Education. In 1965 Title V of the Elementary and Secondary Education Act strengthened the state Departments of Education, also known as State Education Agencies (SEA).[6]

Title V provided funding for increased State Education Agencies' personnel as well as monies for training, equipment, and research and development. With the SEAs in place and functioning, the federal office positioned itself to deal with 50 state offices instead of the thousands of local school districts they had overseen previously. This streamlining enhanced federal policy efforts toward efficiency and effectiveness in state education and reduced federal administrative and clerical expenses.

As a result, Title V afforded states the opportunity to organize and develop their state's Department of Education. Generally, state legislatures

---

[6]For example, in Virginia the organization is known as the Virginia Department of Education. In Texas that organization is known as the Texas Education Agency.

empower the SEAs to coordinate and oversee the local education agencies (LEAs). Local education agencies had already been operating schools for many years, and they had more time to develop and mature than the newer SEAs. State Boards of Education, as we know them today, date back to 1784. In 1812 New York appointed the first State Superintendent under less than desirable job security. In fact, the job did not become permanent until 1854. Once New York and Massachusetts had established and maintained a meaningful and stable State Superintendent of Public Instruction position, other states quickly followed.

State superintendents are responsible for providing educational and political leadership to the State Department of Education and carrying out the duties charged to it by the state's legislative body. In that process, state superintendents have been in the position to become eloquent education spokespersons with the general public and with the legislators, as was true with Horace Mann.[7]

In refining its role, the SEA had to define and develop its relationships with the state's legislative and executive branches. The governor is the state's chief executive, and the General Assembly is the state's legislative branch. The state Department of Education became responsible for carrying out the state's education legislation. The governor influences education through campaign platforms, individuals appointed to leadership positions, and the chief state executive's bully pulpit. These political realities come into play as the different government levels work to direct and provide education services.

Today education's political climate focuses on accountability to achieve high standards. Currently, academic achievement standards reflect the No Child Left Behind (NCLB) legislation of 2001. Although these standards and related accountability practices are not without controversy, it appears for now that most states will participate in this Elementary and Secondary Education Act grant in exchange for receiving the related funding.[8]

How does federal grant funding like NCLB flow from Washington, D.C. to the states and to the localities? What takes place at the three levels of

---

[7]For example, Massachusetts's 1837 State Superintendent for Public Instruction Horace Mann fought for nonsectarian public schools, liberal taxation to support public education, improved teaching standards and practices, introduced school libraries, and is considered one of the "founders" of the American system of free public schools. See E. Cubberley, *Public Education in the United States* (Boston: Houghton Mifflin, 1947), 226.

[8]As of this writing, Utah had announced its intention not to accept federal funds for NCLB unless it is supported with adequate funding. Other states are voicing concerns with various parts of the testing requirements. The federal Department of Education also appears to be relaxing its position on AYP and testing requirements for certain groups.

government varies depending on how Congress writes—and the federal Department of Education interprets—the grant legislation. In that light, it is informative to examine how the roles and responsibilities of the federal, state, and local agencies interact, in general.

To envision this process, let's consider a grant called the ABC Education Act. First, the federal Department of Education announces that Congress has authorized the latest version of the ABC Education Act. Following this announcement, the government makes the legislative details available to the public. The State Education Agencies are authorized to submit applications for the federal grant funding. The SEAs review the federal legislation associated with the grant and open the application process available to the Local Education Agencies. The SEA usually provides technical assistance to the local school districts in completing the grant application package. The grant will usually include a list of assurances with which the local school district must comply to obtain the funds.

Then the SEA collects all the LEA grant applications and submits the state application package to the federal Department of Education. Each state must provide an assurance to the federal Department of Education that the state and localities have met the ABC Education Act's grant provisions. Next, the federal Department of Education reviews the applications and awards the grants to the states that are in compliance with the federal grant regulations. Funds are released to flow through the SEA to the LEAs. The grant allows the SEA to take a percentage of the monies for administrative costs, and the state distributes the remaining grant funds to the localities. Finally, the localities spend the money in compliance with the grant's purpose. Occasionally, the states will audit the funds at the local level, and the federal office will audit state funds. Consequences apply if the funds are used improperly. This example oversimplifies the interrelationships among the various agencies somewhat, but it is a good overview of the process.

ADVANTAGES TO FEDERAL FINANCING

Financing educational programs through the three levels of government provides distinct advantages for meeting the public responsibilities in education.[9] First, this layered system provides for equalization due to fiscal capacity of the states and the localities. Second, it provides for equitable

---

[9]Harvey Rosen, *Public Finance*, 6th ed. (Boston: Irwin/McGraw Hill, 2001).

distribution of services. Third, it allows for a more economically efficient provision of educational services. Finally, this process gives states and localities a more decentralized decision-making method to meet their needs.

The first advantage of a federal approach to funding education initiatives is that the process allows the states to provide for equalization based on each local school district's fiscal capacity. As the Texas data in the Appendix to Chapter 6 show, significant capacity and effort disparities exist among school districts within the state. The lack of local capacity to raise revenue in some districts needs to be addressed by a higher level of government—spreading the fiscal effort over a wider base. It is impossible for a locality with little fiscal capacity to raise significant funds to service the neediest students by itself.

It is possible, on the other hand, for state or federal funding to address local disparities. When the locality simply does not have the financial resources to solve its education problems, funding can come from an expanded tax base. The "poor" locality can draw on means from the larger community. With fiscal equalization, the assets available at the local government level do not determine the quality of its students' education.

A second advantage to federal grant funding is that services can be distributed more equitably and adequately. States can determine what degree of adequate services they will mandate. With the increased government layers and funding coming from a broader tax base, states can devise different approaches to meet state and local needs. The state can decide for itself which type of minimum expenditures, programs, staffing ratios, or any other method of meeting the varied educational needs is the best approach for satisfying the grant's goal.

The third advantage to the layering of federal, state, and local services is the efficiency in producing the service. Economies of scale can cut both ways. In the multilayered approach to providing services, the state or the federal government may use its influence to consolidate school operations or the services delivered within school districts. For instance, the grant may require several smaller school districts to jointly apply and work together to develop common programs that share the grant resources. By encouraging efficiency, schools reap the economic and instructional benefit of increasing the achievement impact at a lower cost. This process, however, results in some degree of lost local control.

Finally, the fourth advantage involves the decentralized decision-making process. Allowing individuals to select the services that match what they believe they need and want is a powerful psychological dynamic that ties all three prior advantages together. Communities tend to coalesce around areas that offer public services matching their personal preferences. Localities tend to grow where young families with school-aged children want quality education services, park and recreation facilities, and safe neighborhoods and are willing to pay for them. In communities with higher concentrations of retired individuals living on fixed incomes, the desire for services may be related to other factors.[10] With fiscal layering and funding of education, the interplay of federal, state, and local resources provides distinct advantages for individuals to select the type of environment in which they wish to live and the services that are important to them. In other words, what a community spends on education tells much about that community's needs and wishes.

Keeping in mind the interplay of the three government levels, the question of how revenue is distributed begs an answer. How local and state governments equalize funding necessitates a further discussion of equity and adequacy.

LOCAL EQUALIZATION

Usually, the local level does little to equalize funding. In fact, studies show that, within the same school district, schools in wealthier locations receive a greater funding share than do poorer schools.[11] Consider this all-too-often example. Teachers tend to request transfers from "needier schools" to "less needy schools" as they build seniority within a school district. This leaves new hires right out of college to staff the transfer vacancy. A few years later, the same thing happens again. From a salary standpoint alone, the higher dollar teachers would be in the less needy schools, and the lower salaried teachers would remain in a revolving door in higher needs schools. A recent study by the Education Trust-West details this spending gap in California's teacher salaries.[12] The study shows that within the same school district spending gaps between high-minority and low-minority schools of the 10 largest school districts range from $64,291 to $522,459. Put another way, over a student's K–12 lifetime, California spends $135,000 less on teacher salaries for

---

[10]We are not saying that senior citizens living on fixed incomes are anti-education. We are saying that with limited resources people can only support those services that are most important and relevant to their particular needs.

[11]http://www.idra.org/Newslttr/1997/Mar/JAC.htm.

[12]"California's Hidden Teacher Spending Gap: How State and District Budgeting Practices Shortchange Poor and Minority Students and Their Schools." Education Trust-West, Oakland, CA, 2005.

low-income students than it does for teacher salaries for students attending wealthier schools.

As central office and building level personnel examine and use school demographic, achievement, and other data to drive the instruction process, it becomes necessary to fund schools based on their individual needs for meeting district goals. Some school systems already do this. Most do not. For that reason and others, states occasionally provide grants to individual schools based on specific, documented needs. Some researchers in school finance consider that providing for local needs will be litigated more frequently in the future.

STATE EQUALIZATION

States have a responsibility to equalize funding based on the localities' capacity to pay for services. States use a formula to establish how the equalized funds are determined. These formulae vary in complexity and effectiveness. Basically, here is how they work.

First, states determine the floor level of educational services that should be provided to all students within their jurisdiction. For the most part, this is a basic, "no frills" level of services and not what most educators would consider a program that "meets everyone's needs." This floor level funding of services usually consists of computing a dollar figure for professional education positions for a given number of students, technology, special weightings for students, and the like. The factors that states consider in this floor level of services vary.

Second, the state determines the localities' capacity to fund this floor level of services. Again, states use a wide array of variables in determining this wealth formula, and every state uses a different formula. Usually, property values, income tax, and an estimate of locally generated business revenue become proxies for determining the locality's ability to fund services. Designing a workable funding formula is an increasingly difficult process for states.

Urban locations with large business and industry tax bases tend to have more, different, and increasingly expensive social, economic, and educational problems than do suburban or rural locations. However, rural areas have problems other areas do not have, including isolation, difficulty attracting teachers, and too few students to afford many high-quality educational offerings. Coming to a consensus on community values for educational results, the relative weighting of the various factors associated with wealth, and the subsequent and varying needs within a state can "tax" even the brightest and most eloquent of politicians.

Third, once the state determines how to measure localities' wealth or capacity, it must decide the basis for distributing the funds to the localities. Some states believe the poorest localities should pay nothing toward the state-prescribed floor level of services because education is a state responsibility. These states also hold that the wealthiest localities should pay the entire cost of providing these basic services. Other states believe every locality should pay something toward the cost of providing these basic services. Likewise, these states generally hold that the wealthiest localities should receive some state assistance in paying for their educational services.

For example, Virginia has established a floor level of education services called the Standards of Quality. This document describes at a minimum level certain state-mandated requirements for services such as the number and type of positions funded per 1,000 students. It also addresses the salaries of professional teaching positions and other factors associated with the floor level of services.[13]

Virginia has established a composite index for each of its localities, indicating each locality's relative wealth or fiscal capacity to fund education services measured by the localities' property value, income tax revenue, and sales tax revenue. This composite index has a theoretical range of 0 to 1.0 and a functional range from .2 to .8. The poorer the locality is, the lower the composite index number. The higher the locality's wealth, the higher the number. Theoretically, a locality with a composite index of 0 would not be required to use any local funds to meet the Standards of Quality—the entire cost would be borne by the state. A locality with a composite index of 1.0 would be required to fund the state-mandated Standards of Quality entirely with local funds and no state funding.

Functionally, however, Virginia has decided that every locality should pay something toward its required floor level of education. It also holds that every locality should receive some state assistance in meeting this floor level of services. Using the state's functional range means that the poorest localities have a composite index of .2 and the richest have a composite index of .8. A poor locality, with a .2 composite index, would be required to raise 20% of the funding for the Standards of Quality through local sources with the state funding 80%. A mid-range locality, with a composite index of .5, would fund 50% of the Standards of Quality with local funds and 50%

---

[13]Virginia's bipartisan and independent Joint Legislative and Review Commission (JLARC) determined that the Virginia General Assembly underfunds education by approximately $1 billion in the biennial budget.

state funds. A wealthy locality, with a composite index of .8, would fund 80% of the Standards of Quality with the state paying only 20%. Virginia distributes these equalized funds through the basic aid to the localities.

CURRENT SCHOOL FINANCE STRUCTURES

Education finance giants who pioneered their ideas in the early 20th century created the foundation upon which we base all our modern school finance structures. These forward-thinking individuals who saw the need for equalizing school funding had the ability to "sell" their new ideas to progressive states and localities. These pioneers included Ellwood Cubberley, Robert Haig, Henry Morrison, Paul Mort, George Strayer, and Harlan Updegraff.[14]

A second generation of school finance scholars followed, including Roe Johns and Edgar Morphet. For 40 years, starting around 1940, Johns and Morphet refined and extended the effort to establish state equalization formulae throughout the country. The third generation of school finance scholars appeared in the 1970s and continue their efforts today. These scholars include Kern Alexander, Richard Salmon, Allan Odden, Lawrence Picus, and others who keep working to implement democratic ideals at the most basic level of education—its financing.[15]

Currently one of four major state finance systems operates to assist local school districts.[16] They include flat grants, foundation plans, district power equalizing (or guaranteed tax base), and full state funding. Refer to Chapter 8 for examples of how each of these systems affects the mix of funds at the three governmental levels. Three states use a modified version of a flat grant model. Approximately 40 states use some form of a foundation program to fund schools. Several states use district power equalizing forms of funding.[17] One state uses full state funding. Several other states use hybrid combinations

---

[14]These names are provided in alphabetical order; it would be impossible to rank their relative importance to education finance.

[15]Today we stand on these giants' shoulders. In the future, perhaps one of you will pick up the mantle as the next education finance giant and turn the nation's heart toward its greatest investment— adequately funding the next generation's education.

[16]Deborah Verstegan has written extensively on this subject. See "Financing the New Adequacy: Towards New Models of State Education Finance Systems That Support Standards Based Reform," *Journal of Education Finance* 27, Winter 2002: 749–782.

[17]See the National Center for Education Statistics, *Public School Finance Programs of the United States and Canada: 1998–99* (Washington, DC: U.S. Department of Education, 2001).

of the previous structures. What do these programs look like, and what are their advantages and disadvantages?

Flat Grants

Only three states (North Carolina, Vermont, and Delaware) use a modified form of the flat grant model, and this model does little to equalize for the districts' wealth.[18] Basically, this program distributes state aid to localities based on a flat amount of money on a per pupil basis or on a defined personnel basis (funding x number of teachers for y number of students). It does not factor in student attendance or how much additional funding the locality is able to raise independently above and beyond the flat grant; therefore, it does not have equalizing value. It strictly distributes funding to localities based on the number of students. The flat grant formula is as follows:

$$\text{State Aid per Pupil} = \frac{\text{Total State Revenue}}{\text{Number of Pupils in the State}}$$

This model does have a large percentage impact on the poorest of localities, but it does very little to equalize revenue. Despite this model's non-equalizing properties, it does have some advantages. First, it can be used in conjunction with other models. Earlier we discussed the Virginia funding model. Virginia uses a modest flat grant to each locality and adds a foundation program to equalize funding. A second advantage is that every district receives a uniform per student appropriation. Many taxpayers see this as a benefit because wealthier school districts have the autonomy to supplement these funds at the taxpayers' will. Third, *if* the state provides sufficient funding in the flat grant for a truly adequate level of education, certain advantages exist for poorer localities. All too often, however, this is not the case.

Using flat grants as the sole state funding model also brings major disadvantages. First, as noted, little provision exists for equalizing funding across the state because the grants are not based on the districts' wealth. Second, flat grants are not only unrelated to fiscal capacity, they are not related to effort either. In other words, a wealthy district could elect to use only the grant funding for the schools and choose not to exert any additional local effort. Third, the concept of flat grants assumes that the grant is sufficient to cover adequate education costs expected within the state. When the amount is

---

[18]R. A. King, A. D. Swanson, and S. R. Sweetland, *School Finance: Achieving High Standards with Equity and Efficiency*, 3rd ed. (Boston: Pearson, 2003), 179.

determined in a political process, however, the grants are usually insufficient to cover even the minimum costs.

Foundation Plans

Most states use some type of foundation plan. George Strayer and Robert Haig first proposed the foundation program in 1923.[19] The concept behind it affirms that the state has a responsibility and an interest in providing a minimum level of education. The foundation program holds that the minimum education level can be costed out, or financially apportioned, in a rational manner. The foundation plan's three-step formula is as follows:

(1) Total Foundation Guarantee = Number of Pupils × $ Guarantee of State Plan (constant)
(2) Local Share = Required Local Tax Rate (constant) × Local Assessed Valuation
(3) State Aid = Total Foundation Guarantee − Local Share

In a nutshell, here is how a foundation plan works. This program requires that a state establish a minimum local tax rate and a minimum education spending level for school districts in the state. This minimum spending level is known as the foundation amount. In some cases, this minimum tax rate will not produce a sufficient tax yield to meet the minimum spending level. In other cases, the tax revenues will be enough. The state aid makes up any shortfall in the required tax rate or yield and the spending level (the foundation amount). Localities can tax at higher rates than the state prescribes and provide even higher levels of education services.

Some early advocates of this program believed that the local leeway to increase funding would offer models for other school districts of what can be done and raise the floor of services for all school districts. Unfortunately, leeway funding did not produce the desired effect for most school districts.

The equalization impact becomes obvious when we compare the foundation plan with the flat grant model. The foundation plan has several distinct advantages. First, it has some equalizing impact toward a state-established minimum foundation level because poorer districts tend to receive more state funding. This also assumes the state has thoughtfully established a minimum education plan and has agreed to support it. Second, foundation

---

[19]George D. Strayer and Robert M. Haig, *The Financing of Education in the State of New York, Report of the Educational Finance Commission*, Vol. 1 (New York: Macmillan, 1923).

plans prescribe minimum levels of locally raised revenue requirements (taxation and spending levels) for the required local effort that must be made in meeting the state plan. Third, foundation programs allow additional spending (local leeway) that Paul Mort, a foundation plan founder, believed would encourage other localities to follow their spending leadership. Mort called these localities "lighthouse districts."[20]

Foundation plans also have some distinct disadvantages. First, the foundation level may be established at too low a level to support a realistic education plan. Second, the minimum level must be adjusted periodically to reflect changes in educational practices, state mandates, and inflation. Third, "lighthouse districts" aside, foundation plans have failed to overcome the significant variances that exist in local districts' capacity to raise revenue. Higher capacity school districts overwhelmingly spend more on education services than do lower capacity school districts. Large, wealthy school districts can raise significant revenue with lower effort whereas poorer school districts raise lower revenue from higher taxing effort. Fourth, foundation programs use local fiscal capacity, not local effort, as the variable for equalizing funding. Finally, foundation programs tend to fund a minimalist education program rather than an adequate or quality program.

District Power Equalizing

Other state funding structures include guaranteed tax yield plans, guaranteed tax base plans, and district power equalizing plans. We will treat district power equalizing (DPE) as virtually the same as guaranteed tax yield (GTY) and guaranteed tax base (GTB) programs.[21] The district power equalizing program was conceptualized by Harlan Updegraff in 1922 and further developed in 1970 by Coons, Clune, and Sugarman during the early court cases involving equalization. In fact, this concept was used as a model in the 1971 California court case of *Serrano v. Priest* discussed in Chapter 3.

The DPE program is based on the concept that ability to generate revenue should be equalized among the districts in the state. How much revenue should be generated, however, should be left to the locality. The second principle underlying this model is that variance in the localities' fiscal capacity

---

[20]Roe L. Johns and Edgar L. Morphet, *The Economics and Financing of Education*, 2nd ed. (Englewood Cliffs, NJ: Prentice-Hall, 1969), 198.

[21]For a thorough discussion of the subtle differences among the DPE, GTY, and GTB programs, see Kern Alexander and Richard Salmon, *Public School Finance* (Boston, MA: Allyn and Bacon, 1995), 200–209.

should be neutralized so that the quality of education is not a function of the locality's capacity but a function of the state's wealth—a core component of equalization formulae. The program provides for an equal yield for an equal effort. In other words, a given tax rate has the effect of producing the same amount of revenue for education regardless of the locality's wealth, or capacity. Third, the state either establishes a schedule of tax rates that guarantees a given amount per pupil for the locality, or the state provides a guaranteed tax base per pupil across the state for the localities.

This model is somewhat more complicated than the previous two models. The district power equalization formula is as follows:

State Aid = Local Tax Rate × Guaranteed Yield − (Local Assessed Valuation × Local Tax Rate)

For example, if the state has a guaranteed tax base equivalent to $100,000, the guaranteed yield at a tax rate of 5 mills will be $500, at 10 mills it will yield $1,000, at 15 mills it will yield $1,500, and so on.

There is a major difference between district power equalization and foundation programs. Foundation programs require a local effort, which does not exist in DPE programs. With DPE, a maximum mill rate is used to calculate state aid. Beyond that, the locality is free to tax at an additional rate for leeway funds. Furthermore, in DPE programs the state guarantees revenue per pupil based on the school district's fiscal capacity and the locality's chosen mill rate.

The DPE program has no single foundation level as districts are free to set their own mill rate. Those districts electing to establish the mill rate at the state determined maximum qualify for the maximum state per pupil funding. Those electing a lower mill rate qualify for reduced state per pupil funding.

A school district that elects to tax at a higher rate than 10 mills, however, will receive no additional state funding. This higher rate is called local leeway funding—as in the foundation program discussed earlier. One conceptual provision of the DPE allows the state to recapture a portion of the local funds if a locality elects to tax at a much higher rate. The state could then use those funds to increase funding for lower capacity school districts. For example, if a high-capacity school district elects to impose a 15 mill rate on taxes, the state may have a provision to recapture 20% of local funds above the 10 mill rate. In this case, the school district exceeds the 10 mill rate by 5 mills. The state could then recapture 20% of 5 mills, or one mill from this school district, which would be used to raise the base funding for lower capacity school districts. Obviously, this has political ramifications if the community believes the recapture rate is too high.

This model has advantages. First, district power equalization tends to equalize for the ability to pay for education (not spending, however). There is also a recapture provision for the state, sometimes called "negative state aid." This allows the local school districts above some determined level of fiscal capacity to levy a minimum local tax and return a portion of the tax yield to localities with lower fiscal capacity.[22] Second, it allows for the locality to set its own spending level. Third, it provides for taxpayer equity—allowing an equal yield for an equal effort. Finally, to some degree the model keeps property values equal through the aid formula.

Some disadvantages to the DPE model also exist. First, and most important, this model does not equalize for per pupil expenditures because the local districts have the autonomy to determine spending levels. Second, if a wealthy locality exceeds the guarantee, a recapture of funds goes back to the state to help poorer localities. This serves as a disincentive for localities to exceed the guarantee. Third, the locality loses a degree of autonomy if the state determines minimum and maximum mill rates.

Full State Funding

The originator of the full state funding model, Henry Morrison, developed the plan in 1930. It is similar to the flat grant model, but it has some important differences. Under this plan, the state is fully responsible for funding the schools. There is only one school district in the full state funding model of Hawaii. Local property taxes do not exist to fund education; the state collects all funding and is fully responsible for financing public education. Schools receive equally distributed state funds. Localities cannot supplement the state funding with locally generated revenue. This model, therefore, eliminates disparities and differences in funding school operations. The formula for full state funding is as follows:

$$\text{State Aid} = \frac{\text{Total Education Spending}}{\text{Number of Pupils in the State}}$$

Full state funding differs from the flat grant model in a number of ways. First, the flat grant model provides only floor funding for school districts. The full state funding model provides the funding ceiling for the schools. Second,

---

[22]Alexander and Salmon, *Public School Finance*, 207.

the flat grant model allows for spending differences. The full state model allows only equal state funds for education in all localities. Although the numerator of both formulae represents the available funding at the state level, the flat grant model does not imply that this funding is all there is. With the full state model, the numerator is all the funding that will be available to public education. For example, let's consider a state that has 500,000 pupils and is using the full state funding model. After discussion, the state decides that adequate funding should amount to $8,000 per pupil. Funding at that level would require the state to generate $4 billion for education. The political and fiscal challenge is to determine what level of spending is adequate. Educators, taxpayers, the public, and politicians all hold varied views on what that level should be.

Full state funding has advantages. First, education is a state function, and this model places the financial burden of paying for education squarely on the state. Second, this model does eliminate all variance in spending for schools and appears fair to the taxpayers and students by not making school funding a factor of local wealth or poverty. Third, local property taxes to fund education are virtually eliminated. Finally, increased efficiency is likely to result as the state administers the entire program. Overhead costs decrease as localities reduce positions for superintendents, central office staff members, and school boards. Additionally, with local politics and fighting for local funding unnecessary, more time becomes available for curriculum, instruction, and professional development.

This model does, however, have disadvantages. First, it reduces the appearance of local control. Citizens may feel that they have little or no impact on the large state operation of schools—that their local school or community is overshadowed by the education operation's large scale. As mentioned earlier, this model may make citizens feel removed from the grassroots democracy of the public schools.[23] Second, this model minimizes the appearance of local fiscal control. Wealthy areas may feel their schools are not receiving sufficient funding. At the same time, poorer communities may not feel that they have any investment in the schools. Third, the state aid may not reflect schools' diverse needs. Equal funding for a school with 5% as compared with 20% of its students receiving special education services may not provide what is actually needed. Finally, the state-set spending may not be sufficient to meet the needs of the entire educational system. This could, however, be said of any funding structure.

---

[23]Cunningham, "Grassroots Democracy."

ACCOMMODATING ADEQUATE FUNDING
WITH STANDARDS-BASED REFORM

Which, if any, of these models is appropriate for school finance today? Most of these structures were developed approximately 75 years ago. The most recent structure, district power equalization, was refined in the early 1970s. Since that time, many school district requirements have changed—not the least of which was the Special Education Law, 94-142. There are calls for finance reform.[24] As Deborah Verstegan states, "There have been no new approaches developed or used to distribute state aid to school systems since the 1920s and 1930s."[25] At that time fewer than one-third of the eligible population attended high school—much less graduated. Education needs have changed dramatically through the years. Review the statistics from Chapter 1, Figure 1.4 (page 14), which show changes in spending over a 40-year period from 1960 to 2001. Compare these figures with the variance in state spending. It becomes clear that problems exist as all students in all states move toward the eventual results of the high-stakes testing programs associated with NCLB.

In the last half century, educational demographics have changed. As late as 1950, only about one-third of the population graduated from high school.[26] The graduation rate was 12.6% for black males and 14.7% for black females.[27] Since that time, student performance accountability programs that emphasize the need for all students to achieve at high levels have taken firm root in education culture. The NCLB legislation requires all subgroups to make adequate yearly progress. Despite these overwhelming changes in educational expectations, funding formulae have not changed. Older funding models assumed that public schools provided a minimum education, not the high-quality, high-accountability programs that exist today.[28]

In addition, spending within school districts and within schools may be too varied to equitably or adequately meet students' needs in high-stakes testing climates. Studies show that spending variance among at least half of all school systems within states varies at least twofold and that in a third of all

---

[24]A. Odden, "The New School Finance: Providing Adequacy and Improving Equity," *Journal of Education Finance* 25 (4), Spring 2000: 467–487.

[25]Verstegan, "Financing the New Adequacy," 755.

[26]The figure for all races was 34.3%. http://nces.ed.gov/pubs2002/digest2001/tables/dt008.asp provides complete information for all races and sex.

[27]Ibid.

[28]Odden, "The New School Finance."

states the variance is at least threefold.[29] A more recent study by Verstegan found that variance among school districts within states was fivefold or greater.[30] In a study by Salmon and Verstegan, state spending variance between higher and lower capacity school districts in fiscal year 2000 had the following ranges: Tennessee, $3,729; Virginia $7,020; Wisconsin, $11,494; and Massachusetts, $20,437.[31]

One equity and adequacy issue involves students' needs. The neediest students tend to live in low-capacity urban areas where resources are already drained or in low-capacity rural systems where resources are nonexistent.

Another issue involves the amount of money spent per pupil per state. Table 7.8 (page 194) shows state rankings for effort and the amount of per pupil spending by state for the year 2000. Connecticut ranked number 1 in per pupil spending at $10,163. Utah ranked number 50 with per pupil spending of $4,425. That amounts to a difference of per pupil spending in the highest and lowest state of $5,738 per year per student. Examining that investment over 13 years (grade K–12), the difference per pupil is $74,594. When calculating this per pupil spending difference over one classroom of 25 children, the difference totals $143,450 each year. Examining the difference over an 800-student elementary school, the difference is $4,590,400. Further calculating this over those 800 students for their 13-year school career, the difference is $59,675,200. The difference in spending in a 5,000-student school district over 13 years totals $372,970,000. Are Utah's children's needs that much less than Connecticut's children's needs? What is the variance in district spending within your state? Is the variance equitable? More important, is spending in the lowest district adequate to meet the needs of those students? Developing appropriate school finance structures remains a 21st century challenge for all.

SUMMARY

Education is a federal interest, a state responsibility, and a local operation and receives funding through these three government levels. Historically, control over public schools has been primarily community based, but the

---

[29]W. Riddle, *Expenditures in Public School Districts: Why Do They Differ?* (Washington, DC: Library of Congress, 1990).

[30]D. A. Verstegan, "The Assessment of Equal Educational Opportunity: Methodological Advances and Multiple State Analyses," in *Optimizing Education Resources*, eds. B. S. Cooper and S. T. Speakman, Advances in Productivity Series, ed. H. Walberg (Greenwich, CT: JAI Press, 1996), 127–147.

[31]Verstegan, "Financing the New Adequacy," 757.

recent trend has been a decrease in the number of school districts and in local control but an increase in their fiscal/operational efficiency.

The proportion of school funding from each government level has changed over the years. The federal share has increased from less than 1% in 1919 to a 9.8% high in 1979. State contributions to public school funding rose from 16.5% in 1919 to approximately 50% of the average district's funding in 2000. On the other hand, the local school funding share has steadily decreased from 83.2% in 1919–20 to 43.2% in 1999–2000. Over time, state and local funding sources increased to make up the difference in expanding schooling costs.

The federal education function largely provides grants and guidance for states and school systems under various congressionally enacted programs. In 1965 Congress created the states' Departments of Education and made them responsible for coordinating and overseeing education. State superintendents provide educational and political leadership. What occurs at the federal, state, and local levels varies depending on how Congress writes—and the U.S. Department of Education interprets—grant legislation.

Financing educational programs through the three government levels provides several advantages. First, this layered system provides equalization to address local resource and population disparities. Second, it provides equitable distribution of services at the state and local levels. Third, through regional collaboration of shared resources, it delivers more economically efficient educational services. Finally, this process gives states and localities more decentralized decision making to meet their needs.

States equalize funding based on the localities' capacity to pay for services using a variety of complex formulae. First, states determine the "floor" level of educational services that should be provided to all students within their jurisdiction. Second, the state determines the localities' capacity to fund this floor level of services. Third, the state decides the basis for distributing the funds.

Currently, state school finance systems include flat grants, foundation plans, district power equalizing, and full state funding. Each has advantages and disadvantages. Flat grants distribute state aid to localities based on a predetermined, uniform amount of money on a per pupil basis or on a defined personnel basis (funding x number of teachers for y number of students) without considering impinging factors. It has no equalizing impact.

Foundation programs assume that the minimum education level can be financially apportioned in a rational manner. States establish a minimum local tax rate and a minimum education spending level—foundation amount—for their school districts. State aid makes up any shortfall in the required tax rate or yield and the spending level (the foundation amount). Localities can tax at higher rates than the state prescribes and provide more education services.

District power equalizing (DPE) programs propose that the ability to generate revenue should be equalized among the state's districts, neutralizing local fiscal capacity so the quality of education depends on the state's wealth. The program provides for an equal yield for an equal effort. The locality is free to tax at an additional rate for leeway funds.

In full state funding, the state is solely responsible for financing the schools. The state collects all monies, and schools receive equally distributed state funds. Localities cannot supplement the state funding with locally generated revenue.

Calls for finance reform recognize that no new approaches to school funding have been developed or used to distribute state aid to school systems since the 1920s and 1930s. Since then, student demographics, economic and workplace realities, and achievement expectations have markedly changed. The older funding models assumed that public schools should provide a minimum rather than an adequate education. This approach may no longer be sufficient to prepare all U.S. students for marketplace competitiveness in a global economy.

CONCLUSION

Current school spending may be too varied to equitably or adequately meet all students' needs in high-stakes testing climates or economic viability in a global economy. School funding reform is, therefore, a critical national issue.

CASE STUDY

Your state is considering a wholesale change in the state funding formula for education. As an adviser in education finance to the state legislative body, you have been asked to write an executive summary of several different types of finance systems, specifically, flat grants, foundation plans, district power equalizing plans, and full state funding. You are to state the advantages and disadvantages of each and which plan you would recommend to your state legislature. Be certain to give your "expert opinion" as to what would happen to the cost of education at the state and local levels with such a change.

CHAPTER QUESTIONS

1. What has happened to the number and size of school districts in your state over the last 100 years? In your opinion what impact has this change had?

2. Review the three sources of revenue (federal, state, and local) in your state over the past 50 years and compare the trends with the regional and national averages shown in Table 9.4. How do you explain any variances you might see? Can this information be used to demonstrate the need for increased funding at any level? How would you make that argument?

3. What has happened in your local school district over the past 20 years with local, state, and national sources of revenue? Can you identify the reasons for these changes in your school district?

4. What advantages and disadvantages would full state funding have if it were seriously considered in your state? Who would benefit and who would lose? Explain your answer.

Demographics and School Finance

Focus Questions

1. How are educators affected by demographic changes?

2. Why should students of educational finance know anything about demographics?

3. What are the major current demographic trends in the United States?

4. What are some risk factors we need to know about in the demographic trends?

5. What demographic trends affect educators as a professional group?

This chapter introduces the idea of demographics and what they mean to our profession.[1] We begin by examining what the concept involves and how it relates to education generally and school finance specifically. We review noteworthy demographic changes and their implications for the overall population, students, teachers, and administrators and their likely impact on school finance. We analyze demographic shifts in student population and examine the associated financial impact on public schools. We predict what future demographics might look like, and explore issues involved in teacher and administrator recruitment and selection related to student achievement.

---

[1]A special thanks to a good friend and professional colleague, Harold "Bud" Hodgkinson. Bud has studied and written about demographics for years. His contribution to education is profound.

"Improving student learning and ensuring that all children receive an adequate education in the 21st century will be complicated by the changing demographics of the students to be educated and the adults who must pay for education through taxes."[2] Demographics is an important consideration in finance planning for public education. As children with various family and cultural backgrounds increasingly enroll in our schools, these students bring additional learning needs that have a fiscal impact on planning, budgeting, teaching, and learning.

Demography describes statistical changes in the population. Those statistics are called demographics. Until 15 or 20 years ago, educational demographics usually referred to the number of students entering our schools each fall and showed whether they were coming from different neighborhoods than in the previous year. School enrollment numbers either went up or down, but demographics had limited implications for the way education proceeded. It also had limited fiscal impact other than the state aid that school districts received for each student in the school district.

Further, for the most part, educators were not concerned with changing racial and ethnic demographics; those factors were confined to poor, decaying urban areas. Outside center cities, educators focused more on responding to *A Nation at Risk*. Today, however, demographics have an impact on every school district tasked with assuring that all students—minority students, special education students, limited English proficient students, and students eligible for free and reduced-priced lunch—meet adequate yearly progress guidelines under the No Child Left Behind legislation.

DEMOGRAPHICS AND INSTRUCTIONAL ISSUES

The composition of our schools affects teaching, learning, and achievement. School districts must focus attention on their vision, planning, and budgeting in this new environment. Teachers need to understand their students' learning needs and develop strong relationships with them to successfully teach those with backgrounds different from their own.

Most U.S. teachers are comfortable working with upper-, middle-, and working-class students. When families from other cultures or economic

---

[2]Janet S. Hansen, "21st Century School Finance: How Is the Context Changing?" In *Education Finance in the States: Its Past, Present, and Future* (Denver, CO: Education Commission of the States, July 2001), 4.

backgrounds move into the neighborhood and enroll their children in school, teachers may be ill equipped to recognize their needs. Good teachers may be unfamiliar with these new students' cultural beliefs and practices, learning styles, and spoken languages. Unfortunately, middle-class teachers' own beliefs and behaviors do not always prepare them to understand, motivate, or instruct students from cultures different from their own.

For example, Ruby Payne, an educator and writer knowledgeable about successfully teaching students from poverty backgrounds, notes that U.S. public schools operate on middle-class norms and values.[3] Payne says that many believe wealthy people are smarter than poor people. Teachers believing this myth may not have sufficiently high expectations for students from poverty backgrounds and may be less likely to teach these students to high achievement levels. Likewise, many teachers mistakenly think "everyone wants to be middle class." Believing this, they are more likely to challenge or dismiss students' comments, attire, and behaviors that succeed at the students' homes and in their ethnic community but do not fit school norms.

In addition, Lisa Delpit describes how teachers' own experiences and values influence their choice of teaching and learning strategies for minority youth.[4] Teachers unfamiliar with poverty may stress "process" over "skills" and mistakenly encourage student writers to focus exclusively on their "voice" and expressing themselves "authentically," without concern for correct grammar, usage, development, or spelling—all qualities essential for formal language delivery expected in high school, college, or business. Although well intentioned, this misguided teaching emphasis may actually leave students without the very abilities they need to succeed outside the classroom.

Student expectations bring other demographic issues into the classroom. Students from poverty backgrounds carry their own "hidden rules" into the school, making classroom management and focus on learning difficult for naïve teachers who do not understand these behaviors. For example, Payne observes that middle-class teachers believe financial and personal security come from having a good education, a steady, well-paying job, and money in the bank. However, students from poor families are more likely to believe security comes from relationships rather than from school or work. In addition, these students may be used to functioning in an environment with higher noise levels and in receiving key information nonverbally. Their

---

[3]Ruby Payne, *Learning Structures Inside the Head* (Baytown, TX: RFT Publishing, 1997).
[4]Lisa Delpit, *Other People's Children. Cultural Conflict in the Classroom* (New York: The New Press, 1995).

teachers, on the other hand, often work best in a quiet, orderly, straight-rows environment and rely on words to communicate important ideas. Divergent expectations and learning styles between teachers and students make teaching and learning more difficult.

Furthermore, new school demographics include more special needs students, medically fragile students, second language learners, and students from other countries. Some new immigrants in today's classrooms are well educated and fluent in their own spoken and written language; others have never been to formal school and have limited oral and written facility in their native tongue. They bring extra learning (and occasionally physical) needs into the classroom. Their teachers require professional education opportunities and a specialized curriculum to learn how to work best with these students. Moreover, these students may require smaller classes, instructional assistants, special equipment and resources, family outreach, and additional school facilities to provide effective and successful learning environments. All of these add cost to the school district budget.

What is more, students in the new demographics need to learn the attitudes and behaviors to help them effectively acculturate to their new homes and communities without losing appreciation for the values and traditions they bring with them. All students need to learn the unspoken "rules" and gain the "social capital" needed to participate fully in the American mainstream. Most middle-class children learn these rules at home and in school. Students from other backgrounds, however, depend on explicit learning in schools to gain this knowledge. Mastering these rules brings students cultural power and social capital. Teachers must *teach* them. Unless teachers learn to respect the new student demographics' cultural and economic differences and use appropriate teaching strategies, they cannot bring these diverse students to high achievement levels. Without these skills, students will not have access to further education and well-paid employment, and civic responsibility will not be developed.

Similarly, until teachers recognize their personal biases and simple ignorance about students from different backgrounds and suitably adjust their views and instructional practices, new demographic students and their families may perceive such educators' attitudes as unhelpful, disrespectful, or even malicious. Results for student achievement are likely to be discouragingly self-fulfilling. Poor student attainment among students in the new demographics greatly increases community–school distrust, which may eventually require significant educator time and resources to resolve.

To be effective with students from diverse backgrounds, teachers must be able to sincerely want the same things for everyone else's children as they want for their own. Teachers need extensive, intensive, and ongoing professional education programs (such as workshops with follow-up activities in the classroom, feedback, and reflection; college courses; site-based study groups; peer coaching) to prepare them to effectively teach students different from themselves. Some students need smaller classrooms, teacher assistants, lower student-teacher ratios, a relevant curriculum, and community outreach with parent education. These programs add a variety of costs to school district budgets over many years.

Without these additional resources, teaching and learning for students in the new demographics is problematic. Budgeting and planning for extra resources is necessary. Helping school districts support their teachers' expanding understanding and repertoire of effective instructional practices for working with students from poverty, minority, and culturally diverse backgrounds has major implications for school finance.

A CASE STUDY OF DEMOGRAPHICS CHANGING FISCAL PLANNING

Consider the following scenario. Ten years ago school district A was an affluent, mostly white suburban city enclave starting to decline; large regional employers were outsourcing many local well-paying information management jobs to other countries. Many white-collar professionals moved their families to other communities where they could continue their careers. Formerly, the teaching staff mirrored the student and suburban population. In the past 10 years, however, the school district's 10,000 students has increased by 50% and changed from 98% white with 5% eligible for free or reduced-priced lunch to 48% white, 27% Hispanic, 23% black, and 2% Asian. Ninety three percent are now eligible for free or reduced-priced lunch, and 30% do not speak English as their native language. Whereas 95% of the students previously had gone on to higher education, now fewer than 25% do. The graduation rate has remained constant at 95%.

In the 10 years since outsourcing began to have an impact on the school district, the school leadership has recognized the changing student demographics, revised curriculum, provided professional development for the staff, planned for facility needs, recruited a more diverse teaching and administrative corps, and actively enacted strategies to decrease the growing achievement gap. With foresight, planning, and action, the district averted disaster. As student achievement levels changed, district schools prepared to meet the shifting student and community needs.

There are lessons to be learned from this case study. First, to teach all students to high levels in a public accountability environment, school leaders must be aware of local demographic trends. Second, school leaders must work with city, county, and state officials to predict future enrollment trends. Finally, it is vital to work with relevant government officials to develop an understanding of future business growth trends, proposed housing developments, and birth and death rates in the locality and surrounding areas.

Keeping pace with changing demographics requires higher funding levels than ever before. In addition, serving these student groups will require changes in where and how education dollars are spent. Likewise, these changing demographics require that we rethink solutions to equity and adequacy questions.

STUDENT DEMOGRAPHIC PROFILES AND TRENDS

The national school demographic profile has changed since 1980 (see Table 10.1 for these trends). In the 30 years from 1980 to 2010, our nation's public and private schools project an increase of almost 7.3 million students. Of that number, 6.68 million, an increase of more than 16%, will enter public schools, and 606,000, an increase of more than 11%, will enter private schools. Between 2005 and 2010, the total number of students is projected to decrease by some 388,000 students. In that same time period, the number of students in private schools is projected to increase by 22,000 students at the K–8 grade level and decrease by 38,000 students in grades 9–12. During the same time frame, corresponding public school enrollment is expected to decline by 71,000 students at the K–8 grade level and to decrease by 280,000 at the grade 9–12 level. In short, most school districts have experienced—and will experience—shifts in their student numbers that will likely require fiscal, facility, personnel, and resource adjustments.

Knowing generally what is happening around the country is interesting. Knowing the trends in one's own state and locality is more important. Figure 10.1 provides state-by-state enrollment trends from 1996 to 2001. Only Nevada, Arizona, and Colorado experienced school enrollment growth of more than 10%. However, 22 states and the District of Columbia experienced declining student enrollments. Two of the largest states, Texas and California, experienced student enrollment growth rates between 5% and 10%. Contiguous states, such as Nevada and Utah, may have entirely different demographic trends. For example, Utah has witnessed a decrease in student enrollment, but this decrease may not mean much to Nevada

TABLE 10.1	ENROLLMENT TRENDS, 1980–2010, IN THOUSANDS						
	1980	**1985**	**1990**	**1995**	**2000**	**2005**	**2010**
K–12	46,208	44,979	46,451	50,502	53,167	53,886	53,498
Public	40,877	39,422	41,217	44,840	47,223	47,912	47,561
Private	5,331	5,557	5,234	5,662	5,944	5,954	5,937
K–8	31,639	31,229	33,962	36,806	38,387	37,917	37,869
Public	27,647	27,034	29,878	32,341	33,709	33,315	33,244
Private	3,992	4,195	4,084	4,465	4,678	4,603	4,625
9–12	14,570	13,750	12,488	13,697	14,780	15,948	15,630
Public	13,231	12,388	11,338	12,500	13,514	14,597	14,317
Private	1,339	1,362	1,150	1,197	1,266	1,351	1,313

Source: Compiled from the National Center for Education Statistics, Digest of Education Statistics, 2002, Enrollment in Educational Institutions, tables 1 and 3. (http://nces.ed.gov/programs/digest/d02/tables/dt002.asp for table 1 and http://nces.ed.gov/programs/digest/d02/tables/dt003.asp for table 3)

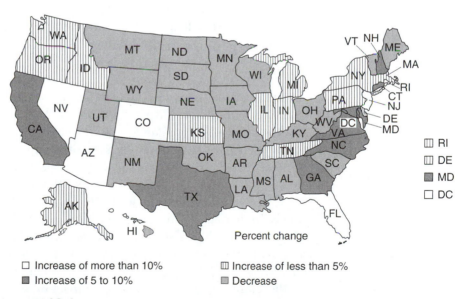

☐ Increase of more than 10%   ▥ Increase of less than 5%
■ Increase of 5 to 10%   ▨ Decrease

FIGURE 10.1

Percentage Change in Public Elementary and Secondary Enrollment, by State, Fall 1996 to Fall 2001

Source: U.S. Department of Education, National Center for Education Statistics, Common Core of Data surveys.

TABLE 10.2   RACIAL/ETHNIC BACKGROUND OF SCHOOL-AGE POPULATION

	1972	2000	2010	2020	2030	2040
White non-Hispanic	79%	65%	60%	56%	53%	49%
Black non-Hispanic	14%	15%	14%	14%	14%	14%
Asian/Pacific Islander/Other	1%	5%	6%	7%	8%	9%
Hispanic	6%	15%	20%	23%	25%	28%

Source: U.S. Census Bureau. *School Enrollment in the United States—Social and Economic Characteristics of Students: October 1999.* [20–533] Washington, DC: US Department of Commerce, March 2001.

educators and taxpayers, a state experiencing a student growth rate of more than 10%. Likewise, different cities and counties in the same geographic area may experience different demographic trends.

Furthermore, the racial/ethnic background of the school-aged population has changed. Table 10.2 highlights those changes since 1972 with projections to 2040. Although white, non-Hispanic persons will still be the racial/ethnic majority, this demographic is predicted to decrease by thirty percentage points—from 79% to 49% of the overall population. Blacks will represent approximately 14% of the population, and the Hispanic group is projected to almost double between 2000 and 2040, to 28% of the population. The Asian/Pacific Islander/Other group continues to rise by one percentage point per decade. The only group predicted to decline in enrollment is the white non-Hispanic population.

One group—illegal immigrants within the United States—is not frequently mentioned. Their numbers are difficult to obtain because these persons may fear the census taker and try to avoid catching the local or immigration authorities' attention. Estimates show that approximately 5 million illegal immigrants reside in the United States. Almost 65% of these individuals live in one of three states: California (2 million), Texas (700,000), or New York (540,000).[5] Estimating that one in five illegal immigrants is school-aged, more than 1 million such children may currently be attending U.S. schools.

Illegal immigrants have a major impact on school finance. In the early to mid-1970s, Texas spent millions of state dollars annually educating children of undocumented workers. Texas legislators argued that these students

---

[5]K. Hovey and H. Hovey, *Congressional Quarterly's State Fact Finder, 2002* (Washington, DC: CQ Press, 2002).

were in the country illegally and Texas should not have to spend its tax dollars educating lawbreakers. Subsequently, in May 1975 the Texas legislature revised its laws to withhold state education funds from school districts that enrolled children who were not legally admitted into the United States.

Responding to a legal challenge, in 1982 the United States Supreme Court in *Plyler v. Doe* determined that undocumented children of illegally immigrated parents could not be denied a public education.[6] The court reasoned that the Fourteenth Amendment provides that "No State shall . . . deprive any person of life, liberty, or property, without due process of law; *nor deny to any person within its jurisdiction* the equal protection of the laws"[emphasis added].[7] Although "illegal aliens" are not citizens, they are persons who cannot be denied equal protection of the law. The state had to pay its share of the per pupil cost for these children.

The decision had an enormous financial impact on Texas. At the time of this ruling, approximately 50,000 children of illegal immigrants attended Texas public schools. Using a low estimate, the state's share in 1975 may have been $2,000 per pupil. In that case, total yearly spending could have exceeded $100 million.[8] Clearly, demographics (along with a good understanding of school law) must be considered in planning school financing.

RISK FACTORS AFFECTING SCHOOL SUCCESS

Bud Hodgkinson, a prominent demographer and writer, describes 15 risk factors associated with young children and their school success.[9] Those risks include poverty; infant and child mortality; low birth weight; single parents; teen mothers; mothers who use alcohol, tobacco, or drugs; transience; child abuse and neglect; lack of quality day care; low-wage jobs for parents; unemployed parents; lack of access to health and medical care; low parent education levels; poor nutrition; and lack of contact with English as the primary language. Many of these factors are correlated with changing student demographics and have significant school finance implications.

---

[6]*Plyler v. Doe*, 457 U.S. 202, 102 S.Ct. 2382 (1982).

[7]The court ruled that the phrase read "any person," not any citizen.

[8]The calculation is 50,000 students × $2,000 per pupil = $100 million. This is a lot of money even by Texas standards.

[9]Harold L. Hodgkinson, *Leaving Too Many Children Behind: A Demographer's View on the Neglect of America's Youngest Children* (Washington, DC: Institute for Educational Leadership, 2003).

Understanding demographics helps schools prepare to effectively address these risk factors and other potentially expensive situations. For example, it is known that a baby's low birth weight combined with a mother's low level of education is a good predictor of a child who will have learning disabilities in school.[10] Knowing the current birth rate demographics from local hospital statistics can help educators and civic officials plan and implement strategies for projected schooling needs during the 4 or 5 years from birth until the students enter school.

Poverty

Poverty is an important risk predictor for students' learning difficulties. Poverty affects and exacerbates all other risk factors. Children of poverty are disadvantaged in more ways than economics. Although many believe the United States, the world's wealthiest country, does not have a child poverty problem, the United States actually has the highest percentage of children living in poverty of any of the 28 advanced industrial democratic countries.[11]

Table 10.3 shows poverty rates for selected countries by family type. Almost 22% of America's children live in poverty. Australia and Canada tie for second place, both with 14% of their children living in poverty. Ireland and Israel follow with 12% and 11%, respectively. Countries with the lowest percent of children living in poverty include Denmark, Switzerland, Sweden, and Finland—all tied at 3%.

Moreover, the gap between industrialized countries' poorest and richest school-aged children is also greatest in the United States. Figure 10.2 shows the wealth gap expressed in dollars of household income. Clearly, the United States has a wide range of incomes, with the poorest children experiencing difficulty in general, in society, and in school. We are a nation of economic extremes: the haves and have-nots. The household income gap between rich and poor in the United States is $54,620. Canada places second at $42,510, and Switzerland places third at $40,670.

The average wealth gap of all 18 countries is $31,442, and the U.S. gap is $23,178 larger than the average. Put another way, the gap between rich

---

[10]This is cited in many studies. For an outstanding article, see C. Blair and K. Scott, "Proportion of LD Placements Associated with Low Socioeconomic Status: Evidence for Gradient?" *Journal of Special Education* 36 (1), 2002: 14–22.

[11]Lee Rainwater and Timothy Smeeding, "Doing Poorly: The Real Income of American Children in a Comparative Perspective," Working Paper 127, Luxembourg Income Study (Syracuse, NY: Maxwell School of Citizenship and Public Affairs, Syracuse University, 1995).

TABLE 10.3	POVERTY RATES FOR CHILDREN OF SELECTED COUNTRIES, BY FAMILY TYPE		
Country	**All Children**	**Children in Two-Parent Family**	**Children in Single Parent/Solo Mother Family**
United States	21.5	11.1	59.5
Australia	14.0	7.7	56.2
Belgium	3.8	3.2	10.0
Canada	13.5	7.4	50.2
Denmark	3.3	2.5	7.3
Finland	2.5	1.9	7.5
France	6.5	5.4	22.6
Germany	6.8	2.9	42.7
Ireland	12.0	10.5	40.5
Israel	11.1	10.3	27.5
Italy	9.6	9.5	13.9
Luxembourg	4.1	3.6	10.0
The Netherlands	6.2	3.1	39.5
Norway	4.6	1.9	18.4
Sweden	2.7	2.2	5.2
Switzerland	3.3	1.0	25.6
United Kingdom	9.9	8.4	18.7

Source: Lee Rainwater and Timothy Smeeding, "Doing Poorly: The Real Income of American Children in a Comparative Perspective," Working Paper 127, Luxembourg Income Study (Syracuse, NY: Maxwell School of Citizenship and Public Affairs, Syracuse University, 1995).

and poor in the United States is more than 1.7 times larger than the average gap of all 18 countries. U.S. schoolchildren at the lower end of the wealth gap are at particular risk. Fully 22% of all U.S. school-aged children—more than one in five—grow up in poverty, placing them at educational risk.

Localities with increasing rates of children qualifying for free and reduced-priced lunch programs—a proxy for poverty—need to plan proactively and provide early intervention programs. Preschool programs, expanded Head Start opportunities, parent education activities, quality day care options, and the associated professional development programs can help states and school districts lessen the financial impact from the risk factor of poverty.

Clearly, poverty has a negative impact on school achievement, and school leaders must recognize and address this issue proactively. One-third of black and Hispanic children live in poverty, but only one-tenth of white

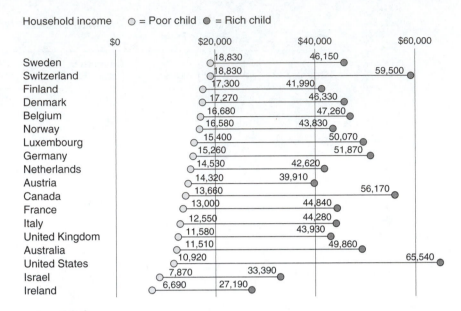

Household income   ○ = Poor child   ● = Rich child

FIGURE **10.2**

Gap between Rich and Poor Children of Industrialized Nations

Source: Data from Timothy Smeeding, "No Child Left Behind?" *Indicators* 1(3): 6–30. 2002, as appeared in *The Progress of Nations 1996,* UNICEF. Reprinted by permission.

children are raised in poverty. In terms of sheer numbers, however, 14 million school-aged U.S. children were living in poverty in 2000.[12] Of those 14 million, 9 million were white children and 4 million were black children. Four million were Hispanic children who were included in the black and white totals.[13]

Interestingly, the poorest families (those with income of less than $10,000 per year) have yearly birth rates of 73 per 1,000 females.[14] Families with incomes greater than $75,000 per year have yearly birth rates of 50 per 1,000 females. If local poverty rates are increasing, it may be safe to predict greater student enrollment growth in coming years. It may also be a wise fiscal investment to adequately meet poorer children's educational needs through proven programs because education appears to be the only intervention that may break the poverty cycle.

As schools and school divisions measure and publish adequate yearly progress reports for minority and special needs groups, increasing student

---

[12]Hodgkinson, *Leaving Too Many Children Behind.*

[13]Hispanic is not a race but an ethnic classification.

[14]Hodgkinson, *Leaving Too Many Children Behind,* 2.

TABLE 10.4   **PERCENTAGE OF HISPANIC SCHOOL-AGED CHILDREN**

Racial/Ethnic Group	1972	2000	2010	2020	2030	2040
Hispanic	6%	15%	20%	23%	25%	28%

Source: U.S. Census Bureau. *School Enrollment in the United States—Social and Economic Characteristics of Students: October 1999.* [20–533] Washington, DC: U.S. Department of Commerce, March 2001.

achievement becomes even more critical for the locality's future. Planning for the school year's needs cannot begin in September of the same year. Demographics must be considered early in the planning process and include interventions for students and families before children begin the formal schooling process. Without these interventions, these students will arrive at public school already significantly behind their peers in learning readiness, vocabulary, and social skills, and they will fall farther behind each year.

Second Language Learners

Students who do not speak or understand fluent English have a difficult time adjusting and learning in English-speaking schools. Most school districts have experienced increases in students who are native Spanish speakers. In fact, Hispanic is the fastest growing racial/ethnic group in the United States. Table 10.4 shows the rapid school enrollment increase for this group.

In 2005, 47,912,000 children attended public schools in the United States (see Table 10.1). If a low estimate of 15% of these students are Hispanic, 4,791,200 children fall into this category. If only 10% of these children need special classroom assistance for English for Speakers of Other Languages (ESOL), the Florida model of pupil weighting discussed in Chapter 8 (at 1.298) yields a national yearly additional cost to educate these children of $10,742,598,662.[15] This applies only to Hispanic children—not students who come to U.S. schools from other countries. In school districts where enrollments of non-native speakers of English are increasing, educational leaders cannot afford to play "catch up" with financial planning and recruiting for ESOL teachers. The students' academic success and the school district's reputation as successful educators are at risk.

---

[15]The calculation is: 4,791,200 × $7,524 = $36,048,988,800. Multiply that figure by the .298 for the total additional spending required each year.

Transience

Population transience is another risk indicator for learning difficulties. Forty-three million Americans move to a home in a new location each year.[16] In fact, the United States has the highest migration level of any developed country. What does this mean for school-aged students? Every year 22% of students under the age of 5 move into a different house: 14% stay within the same county, 4% within the same state but to a different county, and 4% to a different state.[17] Additionally, low-income children move more frequently than their higher income peers, compounding the impact of poverty on school performance.

States vary within these averages. For example, Pennsylvania has a rather low transience rate. Approximately 80% of those who live in Pennsylvania were born there. Florida, on the other hand, has a relatively high transience rate. Only 30% of Florida residents were born in the state. This has serious implications for the classroom. Teachers in Pennsylvania and Florida may each start and end the year with 25 students, but at the end of the year the Florida teacher, unlike the Pennsylvania teacher, may have 20 students who were not among the original 25. Educational leaders need to plan programs that ease the educational disadvantages of transience for students and provide professional development for those teachers and staff who deal with those students. In areas with a high concentration of military personnel, this risk factor may be pronounced although the military does have an extensive support system for its personnel.

Transience can be a factor in family stress and conflict, leading to feelings of alienation on the part of children and parents. This condition has been linked to psychiatric disorders and behavior problems for preschool children,[18] who have a high probability of being placed in special education programs when they enter public schools. In areas with known transience issues such as military base areas, high-poverty areas, and areas with concentrations of migrant workers, educators should be aware of the concomitant emotional problems and implement programs for these families and their children.

---

[16]U.S. Census Bureau, *Statistical Abstract of the United States, 2001* (Washington, DC: U.S. Department of Commerce, November 2001).

[17]Hodgkinson, *Leaving Too Many Children Behind,* 4.

[18]J. Lavigne, R. Gibbons, K. Christoffel, R. Arend, D. Rosenbaum, H. Binns, N. Dawson, H. Sobel, and C. Isaacs, "Prevalence Rates and Correlates of Psychiatric Disorders among Preschool Children." *Journal of the American Academy of Child and Adolescent Psychiatry* 35 (2), 1996: 204–214.

Low Birth Weight

According to the U.S. Census Bureau, about 7% of newborns have low birth weights, which is in line with statistics that predict that 7 to 12% of the school-aged population may be eligible for special education services.[19] Low birth weight tends to be associated with learning difficulties starting in early elementary grades. For infants born to black mothers, the percentage of low-birth-weight babies is 13%—almost double the national average.

Studies link low birth weight and other risk factors with learning disabilities.[20] Blair and Scott found that low birth weight alone increases by 39% the risk of being identified as eligible for special education services as learning disabled. The additive effect of an unmarried mother's low education level, late prenatal care, and low birth weight increase that same risk by 341% for girls and 233% for boys. According to Lewit and Baker, more than half of the 4.6 million students receiving special education services in 1996 were identified as learning disabled. Because special education services cost approximately 2.3 times more than general education services, this growth in learning disabilities identification and placements strains the financial and personnel resources of public school systems.[21]

Infant Mortality Rates

High infant and child mortality rates are another risk factor for increased school costs. The United States has a surprisingly high infant mortality rate. Table 10.5 shows infant mortality rates for 30 countries. The United States ranks 25th, with only Hungary, Mexico, Poland, the Slovak Republic, and Turkey having higher infant mortality rates than those in the United States.

In 1998 the United States experienced 681 deaths per 100,000 babies under the age of 1. For the next several years, the mortality rate dropped off precipitously. Disaggregating the data, however, reveals that the infant mortality rate for white babies in the first year of life is 571 per 100,000, whereas the rate for black babies is 1,363 per 100,000. In other words, for every 1 white infant death, 2.4 black infants die. Infant mortality is associated with family stress and conflict. As is the case with transience, this can lead to feelings of alienation on the part of children and parents and to learning difficulties in school.

---

[19]U.S. Census Bureau, *Statistical Abstract of the United States, 2001.*

[20]C. Blair and K. G. Scott, "Proportion of LD Placements Associated with Low Socioeconomic Status," *Journal of Special Education,* Spring 2002, 31(1): 14–22.

[21]E. Lewit and L. Baker, "Children in Special Education." *The Future of Children* 6, 1996: 139–151.

TABLE 10.5   INFANT MORTALITY RATES PER 1,000 LIVE BIRTHS

Country	2000	Country	2000
Australia	5.2	Korea	na
Austria	4.8	Luxembourg	5.1
Belgium	4.8	Mexico	23.3
Canada	5.3	Netherlands	5.1
Czech Republic	4.1	New Zealand	na
Denmark	5.3	Norway	3.8
Finland	3.8	Poland	8.1
France	4.6	Portugal	5.5
Germany	4.4	Slovak Republic	8.6
Greece	6.1	Spain	3.9
Hungary	9.2	Sweden	3.4
Iceland	3	Switzerland	4.9
Ireland	6.2	Turkey	39.7
Italy	4.5	United Kingdom	5.6
Japan	3.2	United States	6.9

Source: OECD Health Data, 2003, www.oecd.org/dataoecd2/0/2957156.xls (latest year available).

Infant mortality has been linked to psychiatric disorders and behavior problems for preschool children.[22] Children of families who have experienced infant mortality have a higher probability of being placed in special education programs as they enter public schools—especially in LD and DD (learning disabled and developmental delay) programs.[23] In areas with a known incidence of high infant mortality, high poverty, and related factors, educational leaders should be aware of the concomitant emotional problems that impede learning and implement programs for these families. The Florida weighted pupil cost of a learning disabled student receiving part-time services is equal to 2.914 (there was no cost factor identified for DD services); this is clearly more expensive than the 1.656 weighted cost for at risk students.

---

[22]Lavigne et al., "Prevalence Rates and Correlates of Psychiatric Disorders among Preschool Children."

[23]It is interesting to note that the Lavigne et al. study did not find these factors associated with the condition of ED (emotionally disturbed).

Single Parenthood

Single parenthood presents another risk factor for children and schools. In the United States, about one-third of all births are to unmarried parents. Again, this risk factor is associated with poverty and education level. Of births to unwed mothers, 26% were white, 68% black, 42% Hispanic, 58% Native American, and 5% Asian. For every ethnic/racial group, a child raised by a single mother is 2 to 3 times as likely to be raised in poverty as a child raised in a two-parent home.[24]

As discussed in Chapter 4, higher education levels are associated with a lower incidence of premarital births. Moreover, higher education levels usually relate to significantly increased early prenatal care. Educational leaders in high-poverty areas must plan to meet these challenges with highly qualified teachers and an array of meaningful programs that address the real at-risk behaviors facing students while building community support for the direction taken. Otherwise, the poverty cycle remains intact, with attendant social, educational, and economic costs.

Grandparents as Parents

In recent years, more and more grandparents are raising their grandchildren. Four million school-aged children live with their grandparents, and grandparents have sole custody of approximately 1 million school-aged children.[25] There are several reasons for this trend, including parents in jail or drug rehabilitation centers and parents who—for whatever reason—are simply incapable of caring for their own children. As mentioned earlier, children losing one or both parents—even to live with grandparents—can stress the child and may lead to problems in school.

Little is known about how these grandparents support school funding. Suffice it to say, in school districts where this situation occurs frequently, school leaders need to provide educational support mechanisms for grandparents raising their grandchildren as well as offer professional development for staff members who interact with them. Raising a child as a 30-year-old parent is difficult enough. Meeting those challenges at age 65 takes physical vitality as well as financial and emotional resources.

School leaders could garner popular backing among this population by providing school and community programs that fit grandparents' time, energy, and limited income demands. Scheduling daytime activities and

---

[24]Hodgkinson, *Leaving Too Many Children Behind.*
[25]Ibid.

meeting with teachers for conferences, plays, and concerts instead of having grandparents come out at night shows educators' concern and understanding. A changed approach here would not cost more but could gain vital community academic and economic collaboration.

Premarital Pregnancy

The lower the mother's educational attainment, the more likely she is to conceive a child premaritally. Women without a high school diploma have a premarital birth rate of 63.6% as opposed to the high school graduate with a premarital birth rate of 38.9%. Women with a bachelor's degree or higher have a premarital birth rate of only 7%.[26] Teenaged mothers and their children face many challenges, not the least of which is schooling.

Mothers who have not completed their own basic education often have difficulty encouraging their children's academic success. Frequently these parents do not enjoy reading and do not regularly read to their infants and young children. Studies find that reading frequently to young children increases their vocabulary, increases their ability to learn how to read themselves, and improves their readiness to learn in school.

Furthermore, many single parents are working and have little time to engage their young children in exploring and understanding the world, to supervise after school time when students should be practicing school learning through homework or study, or to quickly get involved with the school if the student's achievement lags. Coupled with poverty and other risk factors, single parenthood often requires the schools to provide additional resources—and the expenses they incur—to help these children succeed.

School districts with a high percentage of dropouts, especially female dropouts, should plan programs to deal proactively with this issue. Involvement from community leaders and politicians to secure funding for such research-based programs is necessary and cost effective in the end.

Child Abuse and Neglect

Child abuse and neglect are serious risk factors for students. Abuse drains emotional, physical, and intellectual energy from any school-aged child. The achievement toll on abused children is large. To put this in perspective, a recent report indicates that in 2002 alone local or state Child Protective

---

[26]U.S. Census Bureau, *Current Population Reports*, http://landview.census.gov/prod/2001pubs/statab/ section02.pdf, p. 41. Also, see Chapter 4 and especially Table 4.9 for more information on this trend.

Services (CPS) received an estimated 2.6 million referrals for investigation involving nearly 4.5 million children. Of this number, investigations found approximately 896,000 children to be abuse or neglect victims.[27] Of those children, approximately 1,400 died.

Child abuse and neglect has important school finance implications. Virtually all of these referrals involved school-aged children. In addition, educational personnel generate the largest percentage of referrals (16.1%) of all the professional groups reporting child abuse and neglect. That translated to 418,600 referrals to CPS by educational personnel in the 2002 school year alone. In terms of workers' time, if each referral involved only a total of one hour of school officials' listening to students, investigating, contacting CPS and arranging for on-site interviews, and subsequent calling and visiting with parents, educators' child abuse and neglect referrals consume more than 200 years of work time, assuming a 40 hour workweek for 52 weeks each year.[28] The resulting loss of educators' work productivity—although addressing an important and legal aspect of an educator's role—remains very costly.

In addition, abused and neglected children's resulting emotional problems take a more direct toll on school finances. The weighted pupil approach discussed in Chapter 8 shows the increased cost associated with various student classifications. Using the Florida finance model, the lowest weighting, socially maladjusted, has a factor of 2.3. In other words, the cost for educating a child diagnosed as socially maladjusted costs 2.3 times the base cost per student. If only one-tenth of the 418,600 children referred for child abuse or neglect are eventually diagnosed with emotional problems, these 41,860 students would add yearly personnel costs of $724,395,672 to address child neglect and abuse alone.[29]

Toddlers and Television

A recent report in the journal *Pediatrics* cites learning problems associated with children under the age of 2 watching television.[30] Examining data involving 1,278 children, researchers compared the rates of television

---

[27]Department of Health and Human Services, Administration for Children and Families, Administration on Children, Youth, and Families, "Child Maltreatment," www.acf.hhs.gov/programs/cb/publications/cmreports.htm. These are the latest data set available.

[28]The calculation is 418,600 hours/2080 (40 hours per week × 52 weeks per year) = 201.25 years of work to process the CPS referrals.

[29]The calculations is $7,524 × 2.3 × 41,860 students = $724,395,672.

[30]D. Christakis, F. Zimmerman, D. DiGiuseppe, and C. McCarty, "Early Television Exposure and Subsequent Attentional Problems in Children." *Pediatrics* 113, 2004: 708–713.

watching during children's first 3 years of life and the presence of attention deficit problems in school at age 7. Research findings indicate that each additional hour watching TV per day increased attention problems by approximately 10%. The study also found that toddlers who watched 8 hours of TV per day have an 80% increased risk of attention problems over a child who watched no TV.

Furthermore, IDEA specifically lists attention deficit hyperactivity disorder (ADHD) as a qualifying condition for special education services. ADHD identified students may be eligible for special education services under the category Other Health Impaired (OHI). Moreover, if parents consider the school's assessment to be inadequate or inappropriate, the law allows parents to require the school to conduct and pay for an independent evaluation of the child's possible learning needs.

In addition, school districts with increasing enrollment percentages of children eligible to receive free or reduced-price lunch can expect increased costs from this demographic. According to the Economic Policy Institute's *Inequality at the Starting Gate*, important differences exist between students from the wealthiest 20% of families and the poorest 20%.[31] Findings show that students in the poorest group watched TV 18 hours per week whereas top income group students watched only 11 hours per week. Considering that day care practices may involve television watching as a part of the children's routine, educators need to be aware of the number of students coming from day care and prepare for rising ADHD rates and related expenses.

TEACHER DEMOGRAPHICS AND SCHOOL FINANCE

Student achievement is the ultimate goal of education. The previous sections reviewed risk factors for student achievement and their financial impact on public schools. Teacher quality, however, is a variable that may outweigh all other variables associated with student achievement. Although student demographics such as poverty, minority status, and language background are strongly related to student outcomes in reading and math at the state level, Linda Darling-Hammond found that these factors appear less important in predicting individual achievement levels than do variables

---

[31]V. Lee and D. Burkam, *Inequality at the Starting Gate* (Washington, DC: Economic Policy Institute, 2002).

associated with teacher quality.[32] Teacher variables such as holding full certification and having a major in the field in which the teacher is assigned can make a significant difference in whether and how much students learn.

Teacher Turnover

Teacher demographics also have an impact on school finance. The U.S. Department of Education estimates that schools will have to replace more than 2 million teachers over the next 10 years, an average of 200,000 new teachers annually.[33] Teacher shortages are most pervasive in math, science, special education, and bilingual and ESL classes.

The National Center for Education Statistics (NCES) reports that 28% of former public school teachers and 33% of private school teachers left the classroom and went to work for private businesses in 2000, attracted by better salaries or commission.[34] In addition, only 60% of newly prepared teachers actually enter classrooms as full-time teachers.[35] It is not surprising, therefore, when Ingersoll states,

> Rather than insufficient supply, the data indicate that school staffing problems are primarily due to excess demand, resulting from a "revolving door"—where large numbers of teachers depart their jobs for reasons other than retirement.[36]

Today's teacher "revolving door" shortages reflect more than those retiring or increased student enrollments. Job dissatisfaction or the desire to pursue a career outside of education drives many out of the classroom.[37] Approximately 40% of all beginning teachers leave the profession within their first 5 years; more than 10% of beginning teachers leave before the end

---

[32]L. Darling-Hammond, "Teacher Quality and Student Achievement: A Review of State Policy Evidence." *Education Policy Analysis Archives*, www.epaa.asu.edu/epaa/v8n1, January 1, 2000.

[33]Tyrone C. Howard, "Who Receives the Short End of the Shortage? Implications of the U.S. Teacher Shortage on Urban Schools." *Journal of Curriculum and Supervision* 18 (2), Winter 2003: 142–160; and L. Kaplan and W. Owings, *Teacher Quality, Teaching Quality, and School Improvement* (Bloomington, IN: Phi Delta Kappa Educational Foundation, 2002).

[34]J. Thomas, "Educating Our Future Work Force," *Women in Business* 50 (6), 1998: 26–28.

[35]American Association for Employment in Education, *Teacher Supply and Demand in the United States* (New York: National Commission on Teaching and America's Future, 2000).

[36]Richard M. Ingersoll, "Teacher Turnover and Teacher Shortages: An Organizational Analysis." *American Education Research Journal,* 38 (3), Fall 2001: 449–534, quote at 501.

[37]Ibid.

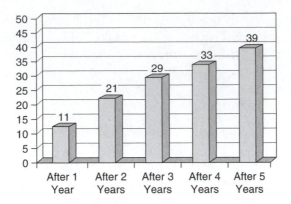

FIGURE 10.3

Cumulative Percentage of Teachers Leaving the Profession Each Year

Source: Richard Ingersoll, "The Teacher Shortage: A Case of Wrong Diagnosis and Wrong Prescription." *NASSP Bulletin* 86, June 2002, p. 23. Reprinted by permission.

of their first school year. Salary looms large as one relevant factor in this attrition, with one-quarter to one-third of departing teachers stating this reason.

Figure 10.3 shows the cumulative percentage of teachers who leave the profession in years 1 through 5. High teacher turnover costs significant amounts of money. Business models cost out employee turnover expenses at 25% of the employee's salary and benefits. Estimates place teacher turnover's entire organizational costs of termination, recruitment, hiring substitutes, and new training expenses to U.S. public education at approximately $2.1 billion each year.[38]

Furthermore, education concentrates teacher induction, mentoring, and training costs in the early years of employment. One study estimates that a teacher who quits after 1 year costs the school district $13,500 in lost recruitment and training. The expenses jump to $50,000 for a teacher who quits after 3 years.[39]

The attrition rate for new teachers participating in induction programs is 15%, compared to 26% for those who had no induction support. Faculty stability has been shown to enhance student achievement, so it makes

---

[38]B. Berry, "Rationalizing the Why and How of Teacher Education: The Need for Large-Scale Data." Paper presented at the Holmes Partnership Annual Meeting, Washington, DC, February 22, 2003.

[39]Tom Carroll, President of the National Commission on Teaching and America's Future, http://www .cnn.com/2004/EDUCATION/03/25/teacher.turnover.ap/.

financial common sense to provide quality induction programs to minimize personnel costs.[40]

Ironically, the problem of retiring teachers may provide part of a solution. Teachers with many years' experience and advanced degrees likely will be replaced with newer, less experienced, and less credentialed teachers. These replacements may cost less than the retiring teachers at the top of the salary scale. This cost-saving factor has enormous implications for school finance as well as for student achievement. School districts could use these newly available monies to increase master teacher salaries and stem the turnover of high-quality teachers into better paying fields. At the same time, increasing high-quality teachers' compensation and responsibilities to more equitable professional levels would also attract high-quality educators into this career. Students and educators both would benefit from these redirected funds.

For example, we know that 200,000 teachers must be replaced annually. If only half of those vacancies are filled by applicants with fewer years of experience (and subsequently lower on the salary scale) earning $10,000 less per year, the national yearly savings to school districts would be $1 billion.[41] That money could be redirected into salary and benefits enhancements to attract and retain high-quality teachers without increasing local and state tax expenditures.

If this $1 billion in annual savings to school districts were combined with a only 50% reduction of the $2.1 billion organizational costs to school systems, more than $2 billion annually could be redirected to teacher salary and benefits enhancements to attract and retain high-quality teachers, again without an increase in local and state taxes.[42]

Teacher Turnover, Teacher Quality, and Student Achievement

Teacher quality has a major impact on student learning as well as on school operations. Much research indicates that low-income and urban schools experience higher degrees of teacher turnover and greater teacher shortages than do other schools.[43] As a result, urban and low-income students

---

[40]Berry, "Rationalizing the Why and How of Teacher Education."

[41]One-half of the 200,000 teachers is 100,000. That number multiplied by a $10,000 savings equals $1 billion.

[42]Eventually this would increase expenditures as superintendents and CFOs plan for this attrition through retirement and retraining costs. Keeping higher level salaried professionals on staff for longer periods of time will eventually increase costs.

[43]Richard Ingersoll, "Teaching Quality," *Policy Briefs* (Denver, CO: Center for the Study of Teaching and Policy, January 2001).

are nearly twice as likely to be assigned to underprepared and uncertified teachers than their more affluent, white counterparts.[44] Other research indicates that poor black students are less likely than poor white students to have a well-qualified teacher.[45] Research also shows that these shortages are more severe at the secondary than at the elementary level.[46]

Unfortunately, urban, high-poverty students are those most in need of highly qualified teachers to help them redress the "achievement gap" between their own measured achievement and that of suburban peers. Moreover, these high-needs school districts incur the greatest turnover costs even though they can least afford it.

High-quality teachers make a measurable difference in student achievement. An Educational Testing Service (ETS) study examined eighth grade students' math and science scores on the National Assessment of Educational Progress (NAEP), also known as the Nation's Report Card.[47] When teachers had strong content knowledge, had learned to work with students from other cultures, and had learned to work with special needs students, their students tested more than a full grade level above their peers.

Perhaps the most important teacher quality and student achievement studies come from Texas and Tennessee.[48] These value-added studies show that students who are placed over consecutive years with high-quality teachers instead of lower quality teachers make significantly higher achievement score gains. In fact, after 3 consecutive years with either a highly effective teacher or a very ineffective teacher, students initially scoring at approximately the same level had a 35 percentile point difference in reading scores and a 49 percentile point difference in math scores. Students with less

[44]See K. Haycock, "No More Settling for Less." *Thinking K–16* 4, Spring 2000: 3–22; and D. Reeves, "Standards Are Not Enough: Essential Transformations for School Success." *NASSP Bulletin* 84, December 2000: 5–13.

[45]J. Kain and K. Singleton, "Equality of Educational Opportunity Revisited." *New England Economic Review*, May-June 1996: 87–114.

[46]Recruiting New Teachers, Inc. Council of the Great City Schools, and Council of the Great City Colleges of Education, *The Urban Teacher Challenge: Teacher Demand and Supply in the Great City Schools* (Washington, DC: Author, January 2000).

[47]See J. Blair, "ETS Study Links Effective Teaching Methods to Test-Score Gains." *Education Week*, October 25, 2000: 24–25; and H. Weglinsky, *How Teaching Matters: Bringing the Classroom Back to Discussions of Teacher Quality*, Policy Information Center Report (Princeton, NJ: Milken Family Foundation, Educational Testing Service, October 2000).

[48]H. Jordon, R. Mendro, and D. Weerasinghe, "Teacher Effects on Longitudinal Student Achievement." Paper presented at the CREATE Annual Meeting, Indianapolis, IN, July 1997; and W. Sanders and J. Rivers, *Cumulative and Residual Effects of Teachers on Future Student Academic Achievement* (Knoxville: University of Tennessee, Tennessee Value Added Assessment System, November 1996).

effective teachers may not only fail to grow academically at the same rate as peers but may even lose ground in terms of achievement scores.[49]

Alternatively Licensed Teachers

With increasing need for teachers, many states have enacted alternative licensure programs for those seeking entry into teaching. In response to this opportunity, more than 250 higher education institutions offer alternative routes to teacher licensure for people with a baccalaureate in a field other than education.[50] Barnett Berry estimates that 80,000 teachers entered the teaching profession in the last 10 years through nontraditional means, and in the school year 1998–99 alone more than 24,000 teachers received their certification through alternative means in the 28 states that record such data.[51]

These alternative teacher licensure programs vary in quality and rigor—in other words, they are not all equal.[52] As a result, some alternatively certified teachers do not fare well in the classroom and, therefore, do not stay in the profession as long as their traditionally trained peers. One study found that 60% of those who entered teaching through "short-cut" programs left teaching in the first 3 years—as opposed to the 30% who leave in the same time frame from traditional programs and the 10 to 15% who leave from 5 year preparation programs.[53]

High teacher turnover increases school districts' costs, and some alternative licensure programs have high turnover rates. It is fiscally and instructionally wise for the educational leader to know what to look for in alternative licensure programs when hiring teachers. Generally, high-quality alternative teacher preparation programs have the following characteristics:[54]

- Sufficient preparation time, generally from 9 to 15 months, and professional learning experiences before entering the classroom as an independent teacher.

---

[49]Public education is attacked at its weakest point: many poor, urban schools with large concentrations of high-needs students do fail. To staff these high-needs schools with lower quality teachers exacerbates the problems that education has not yet successfully addressed.

[50]J. Basinger, "Colleges Widen Alternative Routes to Teacher Certification." *Chronicle of Higher Education*, January 14, 2000: A18–A19.

[51]B. Berry, "No Shortcuts in Preparing Good Teachers." *Educational Leadership* 58, May 2001: 32–36.

[52]For a full explanation of programs, see Kaplan and Owings, *Teacher Quality, Teaching Quality, and School Improvement*.

[53]Kain and Singleton, "Equality of Educational Opportunity Revisited."

[54]Kaplan and Owings, *Teacher Quality, Teaching Quality, and School Improvement*, 20.

- Strong academic and pedagogical coursework.
- Intensive field experiences with internships or student teaching under the direct daily supervision of an expert teacher.
- The expectation that all new teachers meet all the state's teacher quality standards.
- The expectation that all new teachers gain full state teacher certification within a specified time.

Knowing whether or not applicants have these experiences in their alternative path to licensure can assist in selecting wisely at the time of hiring. A wise choice costs less in terms of time for the principal and money for the school district in the long run.

The National Council on Teacher Quality (NCTQ) evaluates states' teacher quality standards and grades each state on the quality of the standards they set to assess whether teachers have adequate subject knowledge.[55] To be deemed a highly qualified teacher under NCLB, teachers must hold a teaching license and demonstrate that they know the subject they teach. Experienced teachers may, under certain states' provisions, forgo tests or coursework to prove their competency under certain NCLB provisions. Teachers applying for positions with school systems from other states may have weak or no documentation of their professional skills and content knowledge for the subject they are applying to teach.

School leaders interviewing teaching candidates can better judge the quality of the applicants' professional preparation by knowing the standards of their prior locale. The 20 states randomly selected for the 2004 NCTQ report and their grades are shown in Table 10.6.

The teacher shortage—whether from teacher turnover, insufficient candidates, retirement, or increased student enrollments—has an impact on student learning and school finance. Some outcomes include increased class size, fewer teachers available in specialized subjects, an overall lack of teacher quality, and an increase in teachers teaching subjects in which they have insufficient preparation.[56] Although increased class size may reduce personnel costs, it may have a negative impact on student achievement and harm public relations, thus affecting budget support by the community at large.

---

[55]C. Tracey and K. Walsh, "Necessary and Insufficient: Resisting a Full Measure of Teacher Quality." National Council for Teacher Quality, http://www.nctq.org/nctq/images/nctq_report_spring2004.pdf, Spring 2004.

[56]Kaplan and Owings, *Teacher Quality, Teaching Quality, and School Improvement.*

TABLE 10.6 **GRADES ASSIGNED TO STATES FOR TEACHER-QUALITY STANDARDS**

Grade of A	Grade of B	Grade of C	Grade of D	Grade of F
Illinois	Oregon	New Mexico	Tennessee	Michigan
	Alabama	Oklahoma	West Virginia	Virginia
	Ohio	Georgia	New York	California
	Kentucky	New Hampshire	Louisiana	South Carolina
		Maryland		
		North Carolina		

Note: Idaho received an Incomplete on this grading.

Source: Adapted from http://www.nctq.org/nctq/images/nctq_report_ spring2004.pdf, 2004, 9–12.

Moreover, when specialized subjects either are not offered or are taught by individuals with inadequate professional preparation at a reduced salary level,[57] the school system may save money on personnel costs but reduce teachers' incentive to work toward securing specialty knowledge and licensure. Furthermore, teaching in academic disciplines or special education without sufficient academic preparation may fill vacancies without aiding student learning and reduce the community's trust in their educational leaders and institutions. This, too, holds negative outcomes for school finance.

ADMINISTRATOR DEMOGRAPHICS AND SCHOOL FINANCE

Most superintendents think that a high-quality principal is the key to a successful school. As principals become increasingly accountable for student achievement, providing a sufficient number of high-quality principal candidates to meet current and future school leadership needs becomes a vital community concern. Quality, however, not quantity, is the core issue.

Regrettably, as with teachers, a growing shortage of qualified people willing to take on the principal's job is becoming evident. The "graying" of school administrators linked with the increased job complexity, rising standards, and greater accountability demands have led to increased numbers of school leadership vacancies nationwide. The National Association of

---

[57]Many teacher salary scales pay reduced earnings to those not yet endorsed in their teaching area.

Elementary School Principals (NAESP) estimates that approximately 40% of the country's 93,200 current principals will retire by 2008.[58] The recruitment and retention of qualified principals has become one of the greatest challenges facing school systems across the United States.[59]

Table 10.7 shows some demographic information about principals. Approximately 22% of all principals are eligible to retire now. They have 14.1 years of principal experience and had 15.5 years of classroom experience prior to their administrative assignment. In addition, blacks and Hispanics appear to be underrepresented in the administrative population.

Attracting and retaining high-quality principals can be an expensive proposition for school districts competing for high-quality, underrepresented racial/ethnic groups. Table 10.8 shows that for the same number of years' experience, salaries vary for racial/ethnic groups with blacks and Hispanics earning higher salaries than whites for fewer years' total experience.

These salary variances may reflect school district attempts to recruit and retain underrepresented minorities as school leaders. Simple arithmetic shows that Hispanics with fewer years of experience earn $2,637 more than whites and almost $900 more than blacks. Hispanics are the most underrepresented ethnic group and may be recruited more vigorously. The American Indian/Alaska Native racial/ethnic group has the highest salary and lowest average years' experience. In this case, other factors may be influencing salary such as the high cost of living (and subsequent salaries) in Alaska.

Principal Quality and School Finance

Although many education experts predict a nationwide shortage of school administrators, few superintendents (except those in large urban districts) and principals say this is currently a pressing worry in their own district.[60] In a 2001 Public Agenda survey, 61% of superintendents in large urban districts admitted to experiencing at least a somewhat serious shortage of principals.[61]

---

[58]J. L. Doud and E. P. Keller, "The K–8 Principalship in 1998." *Principal* 78 (1), 1998: 5–6, 8, 10–12.

[59]For a fuller discussion of this issue, see Michael DiPaola and Megan Tschannen-Moran, "The Principalship at a Crossroads: A Study of the Conditions and Concerns of Principals." *NASSP Bulletin* 87 (634), March 2003: 43–63.

[60]L. D. Mitgang, *Beyond the Pipeline: Getting the Principals We Need, Where They Are Needed Most* (New York: Wallace Foundation, 2003), estimates that educational administration positions will increase by as much as 20% in the next 5 years, and 40% of the current school leaders will be eligible to retire in the next 6 years.

[61]Public Agenda, "Trying to Stay Ahead of the Game. Superintendents and Principals Talk about School Leadership." A report prepared for the Wallace-Readers Digest Funds. (New York: Author, 2001), 22.

TABLE 10.7 PRINCIPALS IN PUBLIC SCHOOLS BY SELECTED CHARACTERISTICS, 1999–2000

	Highest Degree Earned					Years of Experience as a		Average Salary
	Total	B.A.	M.S.	Ed.S.	Doctorate	Teacher	Principal	
Total Gender	$83,790							$66,504
Men	56.25%	1.9%	57.1%	31.7%	9.4%	13.1	10.6	$66,463
Women	43.75%	1.8%	50.6%	36.4%	11.2%	15.2	6.9	$66,557
Race/Ethnicity								
White	82.27%	1.6%	53.8%	34.8%	9.7%	13.8	9.2	$66,198
Black	11.03%	0.8%	51.5%	35%	12.8%	15.2	7.9	$68,044
Hispanic	5.16%	6.1%	64%	18%	11.9%	13.9	7.9	$68,835
Asian/ Pacific	0.8%	4.7%	58%	31.6%	5.7%	13.6	9.1	$56,986
American Indian or Alaska Native	0.8%	4.5%	69.8%	9.1%	16.5%	15.8	5.1	$71,396
Age								
<40	10%	5.6%	64%	25.2%	5.2%	8.4	2.9	$57,328
40–44	12.54%	1.4%	60.1%	31%	7.6%	12	5.3	$62,513
45–49	24%	1.8%	54.2%	35.2%	8.7%	14.3	7.4	$66,549
50–54	32.37%	1.6%	49.8%	37.7%	10.9%	15.4	9.9	$68,625
>55	21.63%	0.7%	53%	31.9%	14.4%	15.5	14.1	$69,867
Type of School								
Elementary	71.74%	1.8%	53.9%	34.6%	9.7%	14.1	9.1	$66,002
Secondary	24.41%	1.4%	55.8%	31.3%	11.6%	13.8	8.6	$68,554
Combined	3.85%	4.4%	51%	33.6%	11%	13.4	8.1	$62,880

Note: Totals may not equal 100% due to reporting, rounding, or survey processing procedures.

Source: Adapted from http://nces.ed.gov/programs/digest/d02/tables/dt076.asp.

Superintendents do, however, express concern about their current principals' skills, and many acknowledge difficulties in finding effective, well-qualified principal applicants. Nationwide, just over half (52%) say they are "happy" with the overall job their current principals are doing. Only 41% of large urban district superintendents, however, say they are "happy" with their current principals' performance. When it comes to specific principal behavior, barely one in three superintendents says he or she is "happy" with the district's principals when it comes to recruiting talented teachers (36%), knowing how to make tough decisions (35%), delegating

TABLE 10.8 AVERAGE SALARIES PAID TO RACIAL/ETHNIC GROUPS BY AVERAGE YEARS OF EXPERIENCE

Racial/Ethnic Group	Total Years Experience	Average Annual Salary
White	23	$66,198
Black	23.1	$68,044
Hispanic	21.8	$68,835
Asian/Pacific Islander	22.7	$56,986
American Indian/ Alaska Native	20.9	$71,396

Source: Michael DiPaola and Megan Tschannen-Moran, "The Principalship at a Crossroads: A Study of the Conditions and Concerns of Principals," *NASSP Bulletin,* Vol. 87 (634), March 2003: 43–63.

responsibility and authority (34%), involving teachers in decisions (33%), and using money effectively (32%).[62]

Although principal quality is undoubtedly related to student achievement, few recent empirical studies clearly demonstrate this relationship. In one study that does, Owings and Kaplan find that elementary school principals rated highly by supervisors using the ISLLC professional standards related to specific behaviors have significantly higher achieving students than those principals who were rated lower. Middle and high school principals' ratings were in the expected direction although not statistically significant.[63]

A meta-analysis by Waters, Marzano, and McNulty examined the effects of leadership responsibilities on student achievement over a 30-year period.[64] Clearly, not all leaders or leadership practices have a positive impact on student achievement, but the study identified 21 leadership areas that are positively associated with increased levels of student achievement (those with an effect size of .25).[65] Knowing how to use precious (and limited) school resources effectively—including educational leadership

---

[62]Ibid., 23.

[63]William A. Owings, Leslie S. Kaplan, and John Nunnery, "Principal Quality, Student Achievement, and ISLLC Standards. A Virginia Study." *Journal of School Leadership,* January 2005: 99–119.

[64]T. Waters, R. Marzano, and B. McNulty, "Balanced Leadership: What 30 Years of Research Tells us about the Effect of Leadership on Student Achievement." A working paper by McREL, http://www.mcrel.org/PDF/LeadershipOrganizationDevelopment/5031RR_BalancedLeadership.pdf, 2003.

[65]An effect size is the change in standard deviation units. An effect size of 1.0 indicates that the experimental group, on average, scored one standard deviation higher than the control group. Because standard deviations are easily translated into percentile gains and losses (remember the normal distribution curve?), the effect size is rather useful in making comparisons of student achievement.

personnel—to maximize student learning and develop and maintain a high-quality teaching staff and principal leadership can make a measurable difference in the value taxpayers get for their school support.

Principal Quality, Salaries, and School Finance

School finance plays an important role in attracting and keeping high-quality school leadership candidates. The varied and enormous demands on school leaders' time and energies force serious compromises in principals' personal and family lives. Two-thirds of elementary and secondary principals cite broadened accountability and focus on test scores as the most significant changes over the last 5 years.[66] Issues including community respect, adversarial working conditions, prestige, and salary also make being principal less attractive to promising high-quality candidates. In some cases, principals earn less per diem than senior teachers.[67] These factors often dissuade talented educators from applying for school leadership positions.

Given principals' greatly increased burdens without a comparable increase in compensation, administrative salaries are becoming a source of dissatisfaction. In one state study, 51.3% of administrators indicated they were dissatisfied or very dissatisfied with their salary.[68] As with teacher turnover and organizational costs, administrative turnover costs to the organization are also high. To reasonably accomplish the task of implementing and succeeding with the NCLB standards, additional resources may have to be allocated to school leadership. A 10% increase in the number of administrators, or 9,320 new positions at an average salary of $50,000 per year, would cost the nation $466 million annually.

Professional turnover costs could create a means to address this underlying problem as well. According to the National Center for Education Statistics, the average salary for school administrators in the 1999–2000 school year (latest data available) was $66,504.[69] If 10% of the nation's 93,200 principals retire each year at a savings to the school district of $15,000 per year, the annual national savings would be almost $140 million. This personnel cost savings, as with teachers, could be redirected to administrator salary and benefit enhancements to attract and retain high-quality principals in the schools.

---

[66]Doud and Keller, "The K–8 Principalship in 1998."

[67]DiPaolo and Tschannen-Moran, "The Principalship at a Crossroads," 58.

[68]Ibid.

[69]Public Agenda, "Trying to Stay Ahead of the Game."

School Budgets

School finances play an important role in principals' day-to-day work. For many school leaders, existing budgets have not kept pace with new spending demands. A majority of superintendents (66%) and principals (53%) say insufficient funding is a more pressing problem for them than lack of parental involvement, ineffective administrators, or poor teacher quality.[70] Not only have responsibilities increased but additional mandates have been assigned to school leaders without the corresponding funds to enact them.

Superintendents' and principals' top-rated ideas to improve leadership have fiscal implications for school districts' budgets. These ideas include improving school administrators' pay and prestige, improving the quality of principals' professional development, making it easier for principals to remove ineffective teachers, and creating initiatives that encourage teachers to consider school leadership careers. Improving the quality of principals already on the job while making the profession attractive to retaining and attracting excellent leaders takes planning, action, and money.

SUMMARY

Demographic changes in student populations affect teaching, learning, and achievement and have significant implications for school finance. Most communities are witnessing an influx of students with backgrounds, cultures, and learning needs different from those with which most current educators are familiar. Without vision, planning, and budgeting by administrators and teachers, many new students' language, values, traditions, and behaviors will likely separate otherwise effective teachers from understanding their students' learning needs, developing strong relationships with these students, and successfully teaching them.

New student demographics include more special needs and medically fragile students, second language learners, students with different racial/ethnic backgrounds, and students from other countries. By 2040 the white, non-Hispanic student majority will decrease from 79% to 49% of the overall population. Blacks will represent approximately 14% of the student population, and Hispanics will represent 28%. If current income patterns

---

[70]Ibid., 19.

continue, 33% of black and Hispanic children will live in poverty, whereas only 10% of white children will be raised in poverty.

Most students in the new demographics bring extra learning (and occasionally physical) needs to the classroom. Their teachers may require professional education opportunities and occasionally a specialized curriculum to learn how to teach these students. Moreover, these students may require smaller classes, instructional assistants, special equipment and resources, family outreach, and additional school facilities to provide successful learning environments. All of these dimensions add costs to school district budgets.

Students from poverty backgrounds represent a demographic with critical school needs. Poverty is an important risk predictor for students' learning difficulties. Although noted as a single risk predictor, poverty exacerbates all other risk factors. Localities with increasing rates of children qualifying for free and reduced-price lunch programs—a proxy for poverty—need to plan proactively and provide early intervention programs dealing with school-related issues.

Related demographic factors that increase students' learning difficulties and schooling costs include transience, not speaking fluent English, low birth weight, infant mortality rates, single parenthood, grandparents raising grandchildren, premarital pregnancy, and child abuse and neglect.

Finally, high-quality teachers and principals are the keys to increased student achievement. Research affirms that effective teachers make a marked difference in measured student achievement. Principals have responsibility for hiring and developing effective teachers and creating the working and learning conditions that support increased student achievement. With increasing shortages of high-quality educators, especially in poor and urban areas, the U.S. public schools cannot effectively address the achievement needs of its most challenging students. Adequate professional compensation is required to develop and retain committed and knowledgeable school leadership—inside and outside the classroom.

CONCLUSION

Demographic changes in students and educators have significant impacts on school finance. School leaders who understand these trends and are willing to consider new solutions need adequate funding to fulfill their mandate. Full awareness of local demographic changes in both populations linked with thoughtful and innovative planning may lead schools to use school finance to effectively address many of these challenges.

TABLE 10.9 DEMOGRAPHIC CHANGES IN ALPHA CITY PUBLIC SCHOOLS, 1975–2005

	1975	1985	1995	2005
Student enrollment	8,000	8,800	10,500	15,000
Number of schools	15	17	20	26
Race/ethnicity	White 98% Asian 1% Black 1%	White 89% Asian 6% Black 5%	White 72% Asian 10% Black 8% Hispanic 10%	White 55% Asian 10% Black 15% Hispanic 20%
Students eligible for free or reduced-price lunch	<1%	8%	23%	58%
Students eligible for special education services	2%	9%	11%	15%
Graduation rate	99%	96%	78%	72%
Graduates attending college	95%	89%	70	51%
Per pupil funding (in 2005 constant dollars)	$9,000	$8,800	$8,600	$8,000
Teacher retention rate (from previous year)*	96%	88%	81%	72%
Average teacher salary (in 2005 constant dollars)	$39,000	$38,700	$37,350	$37,100
School district measure of wealth†	21/100	23/100	25/100	23/100
School district standardized test scores, national norms	95th percentile	85th percentile	74th percentile	60th percentile

Note: *New teacher turnover rates are 75% in the first 4 years of service. Older teachers tend to retire from Alpha City Public Schools. Once teachers have worked in the system for 10 years, they tend to remain for the rest of their career.

†Used for equalizing state funding. The percentage shows the relative wealth ranking of the 100 school districts in the state. The higher the number, the wealthier the school district: 1/100 would be the wealthiest school district; 100/100 would be the poorest.

CASE STUDY

You are the new superintendent for Alpha City Public Schools. The previous superintendent had been in that position for 27 years. Over the last 30 years the community has changed from a small city with a suburban upper-middle-class community to a connected part of two cities. As the communities grew together to form one large urban area—a megalopolis—problems associated with urban settings entered the community. Table 10.9 shows the demographic changes in the school system and the community over the last 30 years.

TABLE 10.10	REVENUE SOURCES FOR ALPHA CITY PUBLIC SCHOOLS			
	1975	**1985**	**1995**	**2005**
Federal	8%	9%	11%	12%
State	45%	46%	49%	53%
Local	47%	45%	39%	32%
Grants	0	0	1%	3%

The city has a strong tax base, but some industries have talked about moving to the cities directly to the north or south for the better school systems. Such a move would have a severe negative impact on the local economy. The local governing body is evenly split about additional funding to the local schools.

You know that the previous superintendent was a manager who maintained the status quo; he believes his legacy is the nine new schools built in his tenure. The central office staff has almost no leadership capacity. Virtually no new curricular programs have been initiated in the past 20 years. Staff development consisted of a motivational speaker at the beginning of the school year. Half of the school board and half of the governing body members want you to lead the campaign to improve the schools and save the local economy. The other half is complacent, believing that everything is fine the way it is.

Moreover, you have received information from the local health department that the incidence of teenage pregnancy has increased from virtually zero in 1975 to more than 8% of your female students grades 8–12 for the past 2 years.

Given these data and your knowledge of school finance and demographics, what plan of action would you pursue as the new superintendent? Specifically, as you examine the revenue sources for the school system in Table 10.10, what trends do you see? Has the local revenue share been maintained appropriately?

CHAPTER QUESTIONS

1. What has happened to the demographics in your state over the past 10 years? What population shifts have occurred? Are there at-risk signs in the demographics? Is what you are seeing reflected in Figure 10.1? Explain.

2. What demographic changes have taken place in your school district in the past 10 years? What at-risk signs in the demographics have you seen? What would you do to plan proactively to meet these needs?
3. What proactive planning has taken place in your school district to meet the changing demographics? Has the planning been effective? Explain. What would you do differently?
4. What has been happening with teacher and administrator turnover in your state and in your school district? Where are the teacher vacancies occurring in your district, and what is the major cause of the turnover?

BUDGETING: APPLYING POLICY VALUES

FOCUS QUESTIONS

1. How does a budget indicate what policy ideals a school system holds most valuable?

2. How do states differ in allocating education funds to instruction versus administration or operations and maintenance?

3. What percentage of overall state spending goes to education as opposed to funding for other public programs?

4. Has federal funding for education kept pace with federal spending in other areas?

5. How do states and localities keep track of their spending? Which budgeting model is most effective?

6. Has the accountability movement had an impact on education budgets?

This chapter reviews budgeting and how what we spend reflects factors that are important to us. We examine how state education budgets vary and how spending within other state function categories vary. Budgeting models are then examined.

A budget is a plan for spending one's financial resources, and no one likes being constrained by a budget. Think of your family's budget. Most people think their family's budget is too small. Too frequently funds supposedly devoted to savings are used to meet the rising costs of living: another pediatrician's visit for a child's ear infection, replacing a broken air conditioner, or fixing the car, again. Some costs in our family budgets are constant, or fixed, such as the mortgage (assuming you have a fixed-rate mortgage) and the car payment. These payments remain the same year after year. Other parts of our budget are variable, such as the pediatrician's visit or the car repair. Those parts that we establish for ourselves, such as how much we choose to spend each month on a mortgage payment or a car payment, represent what is important to us.

If a family of four earning $60,000 spent 50% of its gross income on a home mortgage, one might say that having a nice home was a priority for this family. If another family spent 30% of its income on a home and gave 20% to the local church, one might say that both home and church were important parts of this family's value system. And a family that spends 10% of its income on dining in fancy restaurants rather than mostly eating at home clearly values fine dining experiences.

How we spend our financial resources represents what is important to us. A budget is a "snapshot" of what we spend and where we spend it, and this snapshot reflects our priorities at the time. The same can be said of all budgets, family, corporate, or educational. The difference between personal budgets and educational budgets is that the former is private with varying levels of organization whereas the latter is well-organized public information.

"The management of resources is one of the most important and one of the most controversial areas of educational administration."[1] Education budgets are controversial as they are public information and because great variance exists in how the public believes public monies should be spent— for roads, government, or on education. The public process of establishing the education budget reflects and confirms what our elected officials value. That process involves economics, politics, and the moral standards we hold as a community and society.

---

[1]R. Johns, E. Morphet, and K. Alexander, *The Economics and Financing of Education* (Englewood Cliffs, NJ: Prentice Hall, 1983), 346.

BUDGETS DETERMINE EDUCATION PRIORITIES

Examining how public monies are budgeted, society's priorities for education and other public services become clear. This can be seen at the federal, state, local, and building levels. Roe defined education budgets as "the translation of educational needs into a financial plan which is interpreted to the public in such a way that when formally adopted it expresses the kind of educational program the community is willing to support, financially and morally, for a one-year period."[2] Studying educational budgets, therefore, reveals a community's beliefs and values.

A Hypothetical Example

Let's consider the two school district budgets shown in Table 11.1. Funds have been divided into six distinct categories with the percentages of the budget shown beside each category. Both school districts have roughly the same number of students from relatively similar geographic and socio-economic backgrounds. The communities have been stable and have not changed demographically for more than 30 years. All of the school buildings in both districts were built within the last 10 years. The budget allocations in the various categories make it possible for us to infer each district's priorities.

A cursory examination reveals that both school districts have similarities. They have the same number of pupils and the same total budget (12,000 students × $7,800 = $93,600,000). Both spend the same on a per pupil basis ($7,800). All of the schools were built around the same time, and the debt service on the school buildings comprises an identical 3% of the budgets. In addition, the budget for instruction (at 75%) is also the same for both school districts.

Distinct differences between the two school districts' budgets also exist. Most obviously, school district A has 17 schools whereas school district B has 22 schools. Knowing that none of the schools is more than 10 years old, and recognizing that the demographics of these communities have not changed in 30 years, school district B chose to serve the community with smaller schools. As a result, school district B has five more schools than school district A. Five additional schools means five additional principals,

---

[2]William H. Roe, *School Business Management* (New York: McGraw Hill, 1961), 61.

TABLE 11.1   BUDGET COMPARISON OF TWO DISTRICTS

	School District A	School District B
Total Budget	$93,600,000	$93,600,000
Number of students	12,000	12,000
Number of schools	17	22
Elementary schools	10 (500 students each)	12 (400 students each)
Middle schools	5 (800 students each)	7 (600 students each)
High schools	2 (1,500 students each)	3 (1,000 students each)
Budget Categories		
Administration	4%	7%
Health services	2%	3%
Instruction	75%	75%
Transportation	4%	6%
Operations and maintenance	12%	6%
Debt service for buildings	3%	3%
Per pupil expenditure	$7,800	$7,800

librarians, guidance counselors, secretaries, and custodians. The community's value for smaller schools has clear implications for the district's education budget. For example, the additional principals in school district B will mean that administration costs will be higher. It is also safe to assume that transportation costs may be somewhat higher for school bus runs to the district with more schools.

The similarities and differences are rather obvious to this point. Looking at the operations and maintenance budgets reveals rather large differences between the two districts. School district A spends twice as much (12%) on operations and maintenance as school district B (6%). A discerning observer might note a yellow warning flag: school district B may not be maintaining its buildings as well as school district A.

There is an odd phenomenon associated with facilities maintenance. Delaying roof repairs costs exponentially more the following year than it does right now.[3] Repair costs inevitably increase, as do costs due to damages

---

[3]Some of you may remember the 1960s Fram oil filter commercial, "You can pay me now or you can pay me later." The mechanic was saying that you could pay for a good oil filter now or you could defer regular maintenance and pay me to replace your engine later. The same general concept is true for maintenance on buildings.

caused by the faulty maintenance and the enduring burden of employees and customers' frayed nerves. In the meantime, the public forms opinions about school quality based on how well the buildings are maintained. A poorly maintained building may have excellent teachers and administrators, but if the public sees leaking roofs and broken windows, they assume that the quality of instruction is declining. Deferring maintenance costs on two fronts: increased costs later and a community relations' cost today. Studying school districts' budgets is a complex task that requires understanding not only of the sums but also of what these sums mean in relationship to each other. Analyzing an educational budget requires that we read both the fine print and between the lines.

State Data

States too have varying priorities, which can be seen in how they allocate resources within education budgets. Table 11.2 shows the budget priorities for 14 states and the District of Columbia, which reflect total per pupil expenditures for the top five, bottom five, and five middle-of the-road states and the District of Columbia. By comparing the proportion of total spending across three categories, we can discover what each community values.

Per pupil spending ranges from a low of $5,278 in Utah to a high of $11,510 in the District of Columbia (a difference of $6,232). The average per pupil spending in the United States is $8,032. Stated another way, the District of Columbia spends more than twice the amount Utah spends per pupil. Moreover, the *combined* per pupil spending of Utah and Mississippi does not equal the per pupil spending of Connecticut. Although the cost of living in Washington, D.C., or Connecticut is significantly higher than it is in Utah or Mississippi and educators' salaries and operational expenses will likely be higher, the level of per pupil spending also speaks to the community's value of education.

The way each entity allocates funding among the three categories speaks to its civic values without the confounding cost of living variable. For example, the variance in state percentage spending on instruction ranges from a low of 36% in the District of Columbia to a high of 61% in New York. Spending on administration varies from a low of 5% in three states to a high of 8% in four states. Spending on operations and maintenance ranges from a low of 7% in two states to a high of 11% in the District of Columbia. These differences reflect where the elected officials believe their tax dollars are best spent.

TABLE 11.2 **EDUCATION BUDGET CATEGORICAL PERCENTAGES FOR SELECTED STATES, 1999–2000**

		Per Pupil Spending and % of Budget for		
	Total Per Pupil Spending*	Instruction	School and General Administration	Operations and Maintenance
United States	$8,032	$4,267 (53%)	$535 (6%)	$665 (8%)
District of Columbia	$11,510	$4,201 (36%)	$730 (6%)	$1,283 (11%)
New Jersey	$11,471	$6,088 (53%)	$867 (7%)	$1,064 (9%)
Connecticut	$11,196	$6,185 (55%)	$729 (6%)	$879 (7%)
New York	$10,819	$6,707 (61%)	$620 (5%)	$886 (8%)
Alaska	$10,344	$4,933 (47%)	$926 (8%)	$1,181 (11%)
Pennsylvania	$9,160	$4,876 (53%)	$582 (6%)	$785 (8%)
Vermont	$8,837	$5,379 (60%)	$777 (8%)	$660 (7%)
Virginia	$7,896	$4,255 (53%)	$474 (6%)	$670 (8%)
Texas	$7,743	$3,828 (49%)	$462 (5%)	$676 (8%)
California	$7,284	$3,947 (54%)	$489 (6%)	$607 (8%)
Idaho	$6,076	$3,280 (53%)	$452 (7%)	$495 (8%)
Arkansas	$5,922	$3,210 (54%)	$495 (8%)	$481 (8%)
Oklahoma	$5,837	$3,120 (53%)	$488 (8%)	$594 (10%)
Mississippi	$5,818	$3,061 (52%)	$436 (7%)	$483 (8%)
Utah	$5,278	$2,858 (54%)	$306 (5%)	$397 (7%)

Note: *Total spending includes all current expenditures, capital expenditures, and interest on school debt.

Source: From Digest for Education Statistics, http://nces.ed.gov/programs/digest/d02/tables/PDF/table167.pdf.

Moreover, state budgets must balance education spending against other public service spending. For anyone living in a congested area, traffic is a major problem. Traffic speaks to a transportation budget. New England's first settlers thought it important to erect a jail. Today the corrections budget remains a state's budget priority. Higher education is another important state budget category.

Table 11.3 shows six major budget categories for the states: Public Education (K–12), Higher Education, Public Assistance, Medicaid, Corrections, and Transportation. Other categories not specifically mentioned here are summed in the "All Other" section. The chart groups the regions and notes the average public education state budget percentages. Most regional education budgets are similar, in the 20% range. However,

TABLE 11.3 STATE SPENDING AS A PERCENTAGE OF TOTAL STATE EXPENDITURES, FISCAL 2002

	Elementary and Secondary Education	Higher Education	Public Assistance	Medicaid	Corrections	Transportation	All Other	Total
New England (20.73%)†								
Connecticut	13.2%	9.5%	2.5%	24.1%	2.9%	6.4%	41.4%	100%
Maine	18.5	3.9	2.7	25.2	2.0	8.1	39.5	100
Massachusetts	17.9	4.3	4.8	19.6	2.2	7.5	43.6	100
New Hampshire	28.3	4.3	1.3	26.3	2.0	12.2	25.5	100
Rhode Island	15.6	11.2	4.8	26.1	2.6	4.7	34.9	100
Vermont	30.9	2.8	2.2	22.6	2.9	12.5	26.2	100
Mid-Atlantic (20.58%)†								
Delaware	24.0	5.1	1.3	11.3	3.4	8.4	46.6	100
Maryland	17.9	15.8	0.6	17.9	5.0	13.2	29.6	100
New Jersey	22.3	7.1	0.8	20.5	3.6	7.9	37.8	100
New York	20.3	6.8	2.2	25.7	3.1	5.2	36.8	100
Pennsylvania	18.4	5.1	2.2	28.5	3.7	10.6	31.6	100
Great Lakes (22.46%)†								
Illinois	20.2	7.6	0.5	22.5	3.6	10.4	35.2	100
Indiana	24.2	8.0	0.8	21.6	4.5	8.4	32.6	100
Michigan	31.1	6.3	1.2	19.1	4.8	8.3	29.2	100
Ohio	18.9	6.2	0.8	21.4	4.0	7.7	41.1	100
Wisconsin	17.9	11.2	0.9	11.7	3.1	6.8	48.5	100
Plains (20.97%)†								
Iowa	18.6	24.5	1.0	18.9	2.3	8.8	25.9	100
Kansas	27.0	17.4	0.6	15.0	3.4	11.8	24.9	100
Minnesota	24.7	7.7	2.0	20.4	2.0	9.9	33.4	100
Missouri	25.4	5.6	1.1	31.1	3.0	10.7	23.1	100
Nebraska	16.4	21.9	0.9	18.9	2.8	8.5	30.8	100
North Dakota	16.7	11.7	0.6	18.1	1.9	14.6	36.5	100
South Dakota	18.0	15.5	0.5	22.9	2.8	16.7	23.6	100

Continued

TABLE 11.3 CONTINUED

	Elementary and Secondary Education	Higher Education	Public Assistance	Medicaid	Corrections	Transportation	All Other	Total
Southeast (20.93%)†								
Alabama	23.3	24.0	0.2	19.6	2.1	7.4	23.5	100
Arkansas	17.3	16.0	2.3	19.0	1.8	8.6	35.0	100
Florida	18.8	11.4	0.5	20.0	3.5	12.2	33.6	100
Georgia	28.6	16.0	0.0	22.5	3.6	6.5	22.9	100
Kentucky	20.1	17.9	1.1	21.5	2.7	10.9	25.8	100
Louisiana	20.0	13.5	0.8	26.8	3.6	5.7	29.6	100
Mississippi	20.9	17.3	0.7	26.0	2.5	9.1	23.6	100
North Carolina	25.1	14.2	2.1	24.9	3.4	12.6	17.6	100
South Carolina	20.2	17.1	0.3	22.6	3.3	6.9	29.6	100
Tennessee	16.9	12.2	0.7	32.9	2.5	7.0	27.7	100
Virginia	18.0	13.5	0.5	13.8	4.1	9.3	40.7	100
West Virginia	22.0	16.0	2.6	19.8	1.3	12.7	25.7	100
Southwest (22.98%)†								
Arizona	18.0	12.5	0.7	19.0	3.6	10.4	35.8	100
New Mexico	24.1	14.6	1.8	19.4	2.3	9.0	28.8	100
Oklahoma	22.0	17.6	1.1	17.9	3.4	8.4	29.6	100
Texas	27.8	14.2	1.5	22.0	6.2	9.2	19.2	100
Rocky Mountain (26.16%)†								
Colorado	20.9	13.6	0.9	17.0	4.0	9.9	33.7	100
Idaho	26.8	9.4	0.3	17.7	4.2	11.8	29.9	100
Montana	20.4	10.1	1.0	16.7	3.3	14.2	34.4	100
Utah	27.4	12.4	1.5	13.7	3.7	12.1	29.2	100
Wyoming	35.3	14.9	1.2	18.0	4.7	25.9	0.0	100

TABLE 11.3 CONTINUED

	Elementary and Secondary Education	Higher Education	Public Assistance	Medicaid	Corrections	Transportation	All Other	Total
Far West (21.38%)*†								
Alaska	—	—	—	—	—	—	—	—
California	23.0	11.9	6.4	18.5	4.1	4.4	31.8	100
Hawaii	21.7	11.4	1.8	8.9	2.0	9.2	45.0	100
Nevada	23.1	13.0	1.4	17.6	4.8	6.5	33.6	100
Oregon	16.2	10.6	1.3	13.3	4.1	4.4	50.0	100
Washington	22.9	16.1	4.8	13.1	2.9	7.6	32.5	100
All states	21.6%	11.2%	2.1%	20.8%	3.6%	8.1%	32.6%	100%

Note: * Due to the missing variable of Alaska, the regional average computation omits this state.
†Regional percentages calculated by the authors.

Source: National Association of State Budget Officers, 2002 *State Expenditure Report*, p. 10. available at www.nasbo.org. Reprinted by permission of the National Association of State Budget Officers.

the range in individual state budgets for public education is much broader, from a low in Connecticut of 13.2% to a high of 35.3% in Wyoming.

Like most families, states have limited income. Some states may decide to spend more on roads, responding to the political necessity of appeasing voting commuters. Others may choose to have fewer institutions of higher education and concentrate on funding a single flagship university. Still other states may choose to deal more generously with the poor through expanded public assistance or Medicaid funding. Regardless of the choices made, where states place their monies shows what their people value.

Let's examine some of the priorities different states have chosen. For higher education, the average state percentage expenditure is 11.2%, with a high of 24.5% in Iowa to a low of 2.8% in Vermont. For Medicaid, the average state percentage expenditure is 20.8%, with a high of 32.9% in Tennessee and a low of 8.9% in Hawaii. For corrections, the average state percentage is 3.6%, with a high of 6.2% in Texas and a low of 1.3% in West Virginia. Transportation ranges from a high of 25.9% in Wyoming to a low of 4.4% in California and Oregon. Reasons for these variances are complex as needs differ from state to state. However, we believe education needs are paramount to the state's economic health both now and in the future. Shortchanging education is shortsighted.

Federal Data

The federal government also allocates funding according to its priorities. With changes in political parties come changes in those priorities. With limited resources, elected officials must make decisions as to where to place those resources. Just as with the local and state budgets, our national values reflect where and how we structure our federal budget.

Table 11.4 shows that only 3% of the federal budget was allocated for education in 2003. In part this is due to the fact that education is a state function, a local responsibility, and only a federal interest. As such, the federal government is not primarily responsible for education's fiscal support. However, the combined percentage total of education, the environment, and international affairs is less than the percentage the federal government spends on interest owed.[4] Put another way, the percentage of federal

---

[4]Arguably, spending more on education could reduce other budget categories in the long run, thereby saving federal dollars for the next generations.

TABLE 11.4   FEDERAL BUDGET SPENDING, FISCAL YEAR 2003

Budget Category	2003 Spending (in billions)	% of Total Spending
Social Security	$475	22%
Health	493	23
Defense	404	19
Income security	336	16
Interest	153	7
Other	190	9
Education	57	3
Environmental	28	1
International affairs	21	1
Total spending	2,157	100

Notes: Health includes Medicare, Medicaid, National Institutes of Health, health-related research support, safety-health inspections, and veterans health programs. *Income security* includes unemployment compensation, housing assistance, food stamps, nutrition programs, general retirement and disability insurance (excluding Social Security), and other income security programs. *Education* includes all Department of Education outlays. *International affairs* includes international development and humanitarian assistance, international security assistance, conducting foreign affairs, foreign information and exchange programs, and international financial programs. *Other* includes science, space, and technology; energy; agriculture, commerce, and housing credits, postal service, and deposit insurance; transportation, community/regional development, and disaster relief; job training and social services; veterans benefits and services (except health benefits); justice; and general government. Figures may not add up precisely due to rounding.

Source: Final Monthly Treasury Statement, September 2003, http://www.rci.rutgers.edu/~gpomper/Budget.htm.

spending on interest the government pays is more than twice what it spends on education.

Knowing what percentage of revenue the federal government allocates to education is one matter. Knowing the historical trend data puts the information into a different perspective. Figure 11.1 shows the three main sources of revenue for public education over time. Notice that the federal percentage appears relatively flat since 1970 whereas state and local percentage shares have converged at least three times since the 1970–71 school year. That controversy is being played out in courts across the country as localities force states to reconsider their funding levels in response to high-stakes testing and adequacy issues.

One factor remains relatively constant. Education needs more money—an issue that will be addressed in Chapter 12. Obtaining increased funding will require political influence—something with which most educators are unfamiliar.

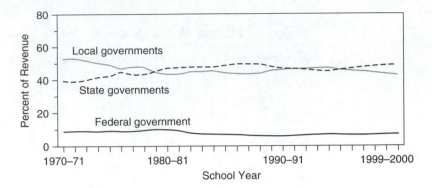

FIGURE 11.1

Sources of Revenue for Public Elementary and Secondary Schools, 1970–71 to 1999–2000

Source: U.S. Department of Education, National Center for Education Statistics, "Statistics of State School Systems; Revenues and Expenditures for Public Elementary and Secondary Education"; and Common Core of Data surveys.

The Budget Process

Budgets have driven business decisions for a thousand years, but governmental budgets are a much more recent phenomenon.[5] As early as 1314, the British Parliament insisted that the King spend tax revenue for the purpose for which the taxes had been levied. After the revolution of 1688 and fully effective in 1742, the authority to levy taxes was taken from the King and his Ministers and placed with the Parliament. The Cabinet held the responsibility for preparing the budget and presenting it to the House of Commons. By law, the English people controlled their country's finances through a popularly elected legislative body.[6] In fact, Britain implemented the first full-fledged government budget in 1822.

Today, virtually all democratic governments use a budget process similar to the one the British developed. In that process, the executive branch develops the budget and gives it to the legislative branch, which amends and approves it. The legislature then levies taxes to support the budget. The executive branch then administers the budget. The budget is more

---

[5]For an interesting history of budgeting and finance, see Henry Adams, *The Science of Finance* (New York: Holt, Rinehart, and Winston, 1899).

[6]Ibid., 109.

than a document with many figures in columns. It is ultimately a process by which people govern themselves.

In the United States, however, it was not until 1921—after years of rivalry and petty jealousy between the House of Representatives and the Senate—that the first law requiring a national budget was passed. In fact, in 1920 Congress passed a national budget law, but President Woodrow Wilson vetoed it. President Warren G. Harding signed the legislation the following year.

School boards also moved slowly to adopt a formal budgeting process. Accurate historical records of school budgeting are not available. But today every school district employs some form of budgeting process with varying levels of effectiveness, efficiency, and understandability.

Budget Defined

It may seem awkward to define "budget" this late in the chapter; however, with the background information presented, the definition can be more readily appreciated. A budget is a comprehensive financial plan that involves four distinct essential elements:

1. Planning for the needs of the school district
2. Seeking adequate funding for the program
3. Spending the received funds
4. Evaluating the results of the process and program

Figure 11.2 shows this budget process, with the evaluation component cycling throughout the process and the program. Both the process and the program are evaluated to refine the figures and the effectiveness of the program.

Educational Planning

Roe defined the budget as "the translation of educational needs into a financial plan . . . that when formally adopted it expresses the kind of educational program the community is willing to support."[7] As such, the budget reflects community values. Planning with and for the community is a vital stage of the budgeting process. People cannot value what they do not know or what they do not understand. Developing this value for education requires educating the public about the importance of what educators do.

---

[7]Roe, *School Business Management*, 81.

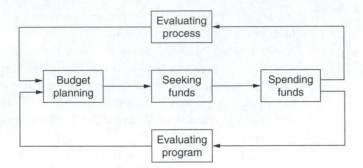

FIGURE **11.2**

The Budget Process

Developing these values into a budget involves a four-step process of identifying needs in the school district, establishing goals and organizing objectives to obtain those goals, building a program to meet the objectives, and costing out the programs.[8] Figure 11.3 illustrates this four-step process.

Identifying schools' and school districts' needs involves data analysis. In today's world, it is impossible to examine programs without using student achievement data in the decision-making process. Effective principals and superintendents obtain relevant data and have a wide group of constituents involved in analyzing and interpreting what these data mean. Parents, business and community leaders, teachers, administrators, clergy, and other vested groups come together to determine educational needs. They seek patterns and meaning from the data and work to achieve a consensus, identifying the school or school district's urgent requirements.

Once the needs have been determined through this extensive and collaborative data analysis process, goals can be established and objectives can be organized. In this step, it is important to maintain community involvement. Constituent groups need to be "kept in the loop" so they understand the linkage between determining needs, establishing goals, and organizing objectives.

For example, data may show that students in grades 3, 5, and 8 are performing below state and national norms. Increasing achievement means improving students' skills in reading comprehension. The schools need both a new reading series and ongoing, intensive staff development for teachers to improve reading in all content areas. This promising intervention has a

---

[8]This is based Vern Brinkley and Rulon Garfield, *Financing Education in a Climate of Change,* 8th ed. (Boston: Allyn and Bacon, 2002), 294.

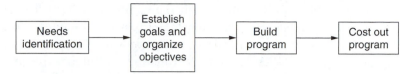

FIGURE **11.3**

The Budget Planning Process

price tag. When constituent groups do not participate in this complete process, all too often a disconnect occurs between understanding the school or district needs and the goals and objectives (that is, the programs, practices, and related fiscal requirements) to meet the needs. This lack of coherent connections ultimately leads to the community's failure to support adequate school funding.

When consensus has been achieved concerning the goals and objectives, it is time to build a program that meets these goals and objectives. This program may be developed in house by school district staff or purchased from an outside vendor. Available resources and local priorities affect these choices and actions. For example, a choice may have to be made either to purchase a new reading series in the elementary grades, and prepackaged science experiments in middle school, or have the science teachers develop the experiments in summer workshops. It is vital to maintain community involvement in this stage. Various programs should be explored until the best fit for the educational needs and fiscal means is identified.

The final stage in this phase is to "cost out" the program. Given all the relevant data, what will the final cost be? Maintaining community input increases the probability that support for the required funding will increase. The constituent groups involved at the beginning of the planning process should continue in the phase of costing out the program. This is the final step of the budget construction process wherein various program budgets are combined to form a total dollar value for the planned programs.

Seeking Adequate Funding

Once the total dollar value for the educational plan has been determined, the school district must seek funding from the appropriate authority. Funding sources vary from district to state. In some areas the school board must gain budget approval from the municipal authority or the governing body. In other areas the community approves the budget. In some locations the school board sets the school budget funding when the locality sets the tax rate (sometimes called a school tax). Regardless, a majority of the public must support the budget. Nothing is more important in seeking funding than open and honest communication with the community. Integrity matters.[9]

Sufficient public sentiment will influence the governing body to approve the school budget. The first rule of elected officials is to be reelected. Siding with a vocal majority supporting a school budget virtually assures reelection for the official and passage for the school budget.

Maintaining community support and momentum from the planning stages of the budget will help in the efforts to secure adequate funding. When school officials and those on the budget planning team speak in local civic, service, and religious gatherings, the public has the opportunity to see the community involvement in the budget process. Involving interested citizens from the start of budget planning saves time and energy; these people do not need to be "brought up to speed" on the educational issues or the budgeting process. They can answer questions knowingly and publicly, assuring their neighbors and legislators that the funding is necessary. Moreover, seeing other influential community members actively supporting the school budget brings credibility to the process as well as to the product.

Once a critical mass of the community has established support for the school budget, the role of the school board and the superintendent changes from "selling" to "closing the deal." Put another way, it is difficult to close the budget deal if the public has not bought the need for the budget. Once the budget has been approved and the new fiscal year begins, it is time to spend the new budget's funds.

APPROPRIATING SCHOOL FUNDS

States and localities have various methods for appropriating funding to local school boards. In some cases the school board receives a "lump sum" appropriation. Even though the school board budget may be divided into categories (instruction, administration, transportation, and the like), the funding is a total amount and not assigned to various categories. In this case the school board is usually free to transfer funds between categories to meet various needs as they may arise during the year.

---

[9]In light of accounting scandals involving WorldCom, Enron, Tyco, and others, the community does not necessarily trust the budgeting and accounting process. This has a direct impact on school budgeting and accounting.

In other localities funding may be appropriated by category. In that case the governing body may either allow or not allow the school board to transfer funds from one category to another. This tends to be restrictive in meeting the needs of the school district.

In a worst case of funding, the governing body may appropriate funds by category on a monthly basis. This would require the superintendent or designee to attend a monthly meeting of the governing body and request that the funds already approved be appropriated by category to the school board so the bills can be paid. This tends to be highly restrictive and inflexible in meeting the needs of the school district.

It is important that educational leaders be aware of their school division's funding status. Perhaps this brief story will illustrate this point.

> A superintendent fired a long-standing high school principal on appropriate grounds: the principal played golf each Friday during school time and did not use vacation time. Unaware that the principal was best friends with the City Council Chairman and was playing golf with this same City Council Chair, the superintendent received a phone call from the principal's golfing partner warning of the principal's long-standing ties in the community and the backlash that might occur from the firing. The superintendent dismissed the warning and proceeded with the dismissal.
>
> This superintendent's budget was appropriated on a monthly basis by category. At the last City Council meeting of the fiscal year, the superintendent attended the meeting to request appropriation of the school board's funds by category as had been the practice. The Chair told the superintendent that it would be a long meeting and asked if he were in attendance only for the school board's appropriation. When the superintendent responded that there were no other agenda items, the Chair told him, "I will take care of you."
>
> The superintendent left the meeting, and the City Council Chair intentionally never brought the appropriations forward for a vote. Meanwhile, the superintendent did not check to make certain that the City Council made the appropriation and proceeded to authorize spending funds that were not officially appropriated to the school district. The Chair later called the State Police to report that the superintendent had expended funds he did not have—a felony. The superintendent was arrested, and a deal was struck behind the scenes for the superintendent to be fired in exchange for the charges being dropped. The principal was rehired, and the golfing continued.

This story shows how important it is to know and follow the spending procedures in a school division. Failure to do so can be very costly.

SPENDING THE RECEIVED FUNDS

Once the new fiscal year begins, the new budget cycle starts. The purpose of administering the budget is not to save money and see how much will be left at the end of the year. The purpose is to spend the funds wisely in accordance with the education plan. To have a surplus at the end of the year can make the school board and the superintendent appear less than trustworthy and competent in the budget process.

On the other hand, no amount of budget planning will anticipate everything that could happen or be needed during the course of a school year. For instance, it is impossible to know that a bus engine will have to be replaced just after it goes out of warranty or that a boiler in the high school will not last the 2 more years your maintenance people told you it should. Superintendents and school boards do not want to go back to their funding bodies and request more money for these unexpected occurrences.

There are two other ways to handle these situations. First, a line item in the budget can be inserted called "contingencies." This provides funds for unexpected situations that might arise. The problem with a contingency line item, however, is that the public may see this as "padding" or "putting fat" into the budget. The public may also negatively interpret this as the school board's and superintendent's insufficient thought into the overall operation of the school system.

The second way to handle unanticipated expenses is to discretely "expand" another budget area. Frequently, the budget may "overestimate" the fringe benefit factor for employees' wages. For example, if the total cost of fringe benefits (employer's share of FICA, health insurance, life insurance, retirement, and other benefits) comes to 24% of the wages, some school leaders budget for a factor of 26%—a spread of 2% on the entire wage line. To illustrate this, every 2% pad on a $10 million salary and fringe benefit factor budget allows for an additional $200,000 to be used at the school district's discretion.

Naturally, it would be unethical to advocate "hiding" funds in the budget.[10] The superintendent and the school board will have to determine an acceptable manner for dealing with unanticipated expenses. One principle is clear: The funds must be spent appropriately. It is important to know that not all school districts and states have identical spending procedures.

---

[10]Our aim is simply to provide educational leadership candidates with general principles for spending money and staying out of trouble.

EVALUATING THE RESULTS OF THE PROCESS AND PROGRAM

With No Child Left Behind legislation, schools are more and more likely to be evaluating their spending patterns to determine overall value. In business circles, this is akin to analyzing the *return on investment*. Superintendents, as the Chief Executive Officers (CEO) of the school system, are responsible for ensuring that the funds allocated in developing the education plan, and spent in accordance with the plan, effectively and efficiently met the budget goals. This involves evaluating the results of the budget's process and spending program.

Superintendents provide the school board with periodic budget updates—usually monthly. This update lists budget line items in major categories and the amount and percentage of those funds expended to date. Additionally, the board should be kept informed about anticipated problems with over- or underfinanced budget categories in the event that steps need to be taken to shift funds from one category to another. Some school systems have the authority to transfer funds from one category to another. Others must have these actions approved by the governing body.

Over time the budget should improve in accuracy and effectiveness in meeting student achievement needs. Each year's budget should build on the previous year's data and allow for refinements in forecasting needs. One problem with achieving this refining is the relatively short tenure length of superintendents on the job. When leadership changes are made in a school system, the new leader reassesses all the budget practices of the previous superintendent and implements a new system for budgeting that disturbs the refinement process.

An accountant or business manager can evaluate the spending process. Instructional leadership is required in evaluating the spending program. It takes an instructional leader to be able to determine if spending $1 million on middle school science labs is making an achievement difference for students. It will be necessary initially to demonstrate to the school board that the expenditure is wise and subsequently to show that the purchase made a positive difference in student achievement. The same can be said of other equipment purchases, such as textbook series, technology, manipulatives, as well as salary increases.

In light of NCLB requirements that all students (including those in special education, those receiving free or reduced-price lunches, English language learners, and minorities) make adequate yearly progress (AYP), it is increasingly incumbent on instructional leaders to make certain that all children benefit from the educational program. Good leaders will not only evaluate programs in light of overall student achievement but also of achievement in these four subgroup populations. Currently, most principals and superintendents disaggregate student achievement data to determine which students are not progressing satisfactorily. The planning process involves the achievement (or lack thereof) of these students and determines programs that may improve achievement. Plans are put into place, funds are solicited, monies are spent, and school personnel wait for the accountability test results to return. More and more frequently, educational leaders assess the impact of their programs on the four NCLB subgroups to determine whether spending interventions are making a difference. If they are making a difference, how much cost is associated with the academic increase?

TYPES OF BUDGETS

Education professionals are facing accountability for student achievement like never before. Budgeting systems provide the public with an explanation of where their monies go and what the achievement results entail. It is vital for educational leaders to explain the evaluation results of the budgeting process to the community so those who fund the education programs know their investment has made a difference.

Various types of budgets exist, and each school district has a formally adopted budgeting process. A few of the most commonly used budgets are reviewed in the following sections.

Percentage Add-On Budgeting

Adding a percentage to the previous year's funding level is the most common budgeting method. If the school district had a local contribution of $50 million and the local increase for the next year were 5%, the local increase in revenue would be $2.5 million. If the governing body granted a 5% increase over last year's funding, the superintendent would ask staff to make recommendations about what programs should receive additional funding.

The advantage of a percentage add-on budget is its simplicity for the governing body and the school board. The percentage is determined and funded. Other budget types demand much more time. The disadvantage is that it may be removed from the school district's real needs. For example, if the school district made large technology purchases in one year and anticipates a substantial state funding increase, a 5% local increase may not reflect real needs.

Zero-Base Budgeting

Zero-base budgeting (ZBB) has existed for more than a hundred years. However, it was not until Jimmy Carter declared he would implement zero-base budgeting for the federal budget if elected president that ZBB gained widespread interest. Basically, ZBB requires that the budget start from zero each year—unlike a percentage add on. It makes no reference to the previous year's funding. Nothing in the budgeting process is sacred—everything is reevaluated each year. Each budget inclusion must be justified.

The advantage of ZBB is the staff involvement in ranking and selecting alternatives in resource allocation. Additionally, ZBB requires program evaluation as a criterion for future budget inclusion. This tends to foster more public confidence in the budgeting process. The disadvantage is the time and level of complexity involved in administering ZBB. Most school districts do not have the staff and time to adequately address this type of budgeting process.

Planning, Programming, Budgeting, Evaluation System

Originally developed by the U.S. Department of Defense as the Planning, Programming, Budgeting System (PPBS), an evaluation component was later added (PPBES). Although similar to other budget planning processes, it was designed to be a more flexible and fluid process that extended beyond the 1 year budget cycle, often lasting at least 5 years. PPBES has five goals—as its name suggests:

1. Planning and establishing goals
2. Determining the cost and alternative plan's costs for achieving the goal
3. Evaluating the results of the plans
4. Modifying and improving the goals
5. Establishing and improving alternative plans to achieve the modified and improved goals

The advantage of PPBES is its flexibility. This approach recognizes that goals and objectives are not met in a single fiscal year and that modifications may be needed during a fiscal year's cycle. The disadvantage is that few school district and governing body budgets are flexible enough to accommodate this budgeting approach.

Site-Based Budgeting

Site-based budgeting (SBB) decentralizes the process; district budgets are developed at each building level with staff and community input. The principal is not given a fixed amount of money to manage the school's operation. Instead, a grassroots collection of ideas from community members, staff, and administrators are evaluated to address the needs of a particular school in meeting district objectives. Effective SBB requires that the school budget address student needs with financial resources.

This approach allows the school site decision-making latitude for aligning goals with resources. For example, if the site deemed professional development a priority, it might decide to forgo substitute teacher costs by having regular teachers use planning periods to cover classes when teachers are ill, saving the cost of a substitute. These unspent substitute teacher funds would then be rerouted to a professional development account for the teachers. This particular arrangement may not be possible in some areas where strict contracts are in place with various professional associations.

The advantage of site-based budgeting is that it involves community input in building support for the budget. Done correctly, SBB generates public support for the budget. The disadvantage involves the time and skills necessary to manage the process. Education staffs are overworked already. Moreover, few principals are trained in how to manage site-based budgeting. Adding more to their plate in times of high-stakes testing and accountability is unduly burdensome.

COMMENTS ON ACCOUNTABILITY

Whatever its flaws, NCLB has forced educators to examine all students' achievement—and not just the averages. A good educational leader promotes the success of all students by understanding, responding to, and influencing the larger political, social, economic, legal, and cultural context.[11]

---

[11]This comes from ISLLC Standard 6, but in truth all the ISLLC standards apply. ISLLC Standards are available through the Educational Testing Service, Teaching and Learning Division, P.O. Box 6051, Princeton, New Jersey, 08541-6051.

By comprehending this accountability movement and addressing the budgeting process as described in this chapter, educational leaders demonstrate that they understand, respond to, and influence the larger contexts.

Accountability is not new to education. A study in 1976 cited the political nature of accountability in education:

> Our examination of the accountability movement has led us to conclude that it is not an educational but rather a political movement fueled by economic concerns. Economic and political forces provide the main thrust behind the movement that has attracted many who really believe that it will improve education.[12]

As education is increasingly politically driven toward a business management model, good budgeting knowledge—especially in the area of program evaluation—can establish a professionalism about our practices and encourage community support for education funding. "GOB budgeting" is not playing by the new rules.[13] The budgeting process requires ethical and professional treatment. Not doing so will not only show a lack of understanding about the larger educational context; it will show a disregard for it.

SUMMARY

Resource management is one of the most important and most controversial areas of education administration. School budget information is public, and great variance exists in how the public believes it should spend public monies. Education budgets translate educational needs into a financial plan. Creating education budgets is a process that reflects a community's and society's economics, politics, and moral values.

States and localities differ greatly on the amount and in the ways they spend education dollars. In addition, states have other public funding responsibilities—such as transportation, corrections, higher education, and Medicaid—that compete with elementary and secondary education for tax dollars. The average per pupil spending in the United States is $8,032, but the variance alone between the high and low state is $6,232. Likewise, the

---

[12]D. Martin, G. Overholt, and W. Urban, *Accountability in American Education: A Critique* (Princeton, NJ: Princeton Book Company, 1976), 75.

[13]GOB (Good Old Boy) funding refers to the practice of the governing body and selected school board members working out in a back room how much funding the schools will receive for the year and how much the school board will be expected to return to the governing body at the end of the fiscal year.

variance in state percentage spending on instruction ranges from a low of 36% to a high of 61%. Spending on administration varies from a low of 5% in three states to a high of 8% in four states.

Likewise, our national values reflect where and how we structure our federal budget. Only 3% of the federal budget is allocated for education. Because education is a state function, a local responsibility, and only a federal interest, the federal government is not primarily responsible for education's fiscal support.

The process of developing, amending, approving, and providing tax monies to support and administer a budget is a uniquely democratic process. A budget is a comprehensive financial plan that involves planning for the needs of the school district; seeking adequate funding for the program; spending the received funds; and evaluating the results of the process and program. Planning with and for the community is a vital stage of the budgeting process. Once the total dollar value for the educational plan has been determined, the school district must seek funding from the appropriate authority. Funding sources vary from district to state. Maintaining community support and momentum during the planning stages of the budget will help to secure adequate funding for the budget. Over time the budget should improve in accuracy and effectiveness in meeting student achievement needs.

CONCLUSION

With school budgets, you either pay now or pay later in increased expenses and lost community trust in educational quality. Studying school districts' budgets is a complex task that requires understanding not only of sums but also of what they mean in relation to each other.

CASE STUDY

Review your school district's budget for the current school year. Determine the major spending categories and reduce them to percentages of the overall budget. What does your budget say about your school district's priorities? Examine the budget of a neighboring school district and determine their major spending categories by percentages. What does their budget say about their priorities in comparison with those of your school district?

CHAPTER QUESTIONS

1. Describe the budget process in your school district.
2. Who is involved in the budget planning process in your district? Explain how this process works.
3. Who approves the budget in your locality? What is the approval process and time line?
4. How is your budget appropriated? On a monthly, yearly lump sum, categorical, or other basis?
5. Describe how your superintendent and school board evaluate the budget process and product.
6. What are your school district's priorities as seen in the budget that was adopted last year? Do you believe the spending priorities fit with the needs of the district? Defend your answer.

SPENDING AND STUDENT ACHIEVEMENT

FOCUS QUESTIONS

1. Have you studied the relationship between the amount of money spent on a child's education and how well he or she achieves in school?

2. What do we know about the effects of spending on student achievement? Why is there any controversy on the issue?

3. Is there a relationship between teachers' salaries and student achievement?

4. Where is money best spent in the classroom to improve student achievement?

5. In what other areas does spending improve student achievement?

This chapter examines the relationship between spending and student achievement. To be sure, there is a great deal of controversy on the subject, which was brought about by the Coleman Report and other production function research. In this chapter we review the foundational issue of education—how to enhance student achievement. Research can help us understand how spending can enhance student learning, and we present information on this from a variety of perspectives including teacher quality, professional development, reduced class and school size, teacher salaries, and school facilities. This information will allow educational leaders to knowledgeably advocate investing budget monies in areas research has shown are connected to student achievement gains. Where we spend our educational dollars does make a difference in accomplishing our goals.

Alexander and Salmon believe questions about the impact of school funding on education lie at the heart of national education reform. Publication of *A Nation at Risk* prompted some conservative politicians to advocate educational reform, and they seriously questioned the value of public schools if educational interventions could not overcome the destiny of children's backgrounds. Currently, a wave of school finance litigation seeks to distribute school funding on a more equal—and less equitable—basis.[1]

Does public education make a difference in student achievement apart from family influences? Where should educators spend money in schools to get the biggest "bang for the instructional buck"? The third Interstate School Leaders Licensure Consortium (ISLLC) Standard states that a school administrator is an educational leader who promotes the success of all students by ensuring management of the organization, operations, and resources for a safe, efficient, and effective learning environment.[2] It is vital that educational leaders know how to assign resources for effective and efficient teaching and learning. Knowing the history behind the current school spending and student achievement debate provides a context for informed decision making about school finance allotments.

RECENT HISTORY INVOLVING FUNDING AND ACHIEVEMENT

In 1966 the Coleman Report changed the public's attitude about education spending.[3] Funded by the federal government as a part of the Civil Rights Act of 1964, the Coleman study focused on questions of racial segregation and educational inequality by examining the adequacy of physical facilities, curriculum, teacher characteristics, and student achievement as measured by standardized test scores. The study also factored in student self-attitudes and academic goals, socioeconomic status, and parent education levels.

In addition, the methodology of the Coleman study was an important factor. The project was designed as a production function study, also called an input-output study. Production function studies attempt to show the

---

[1] K. Alexander and R. Salmon, *Public School Finance* (Needham Heights, MA: Allyn and Bacon, 1995).

[2] For a complete review of these standards and rubrics, see K. Hessel and J. Holloway, *A Framework for School Leaders: Linking the ISLLC Standards to Practice* (Princeton, NJ: Educational Testing Service, 2002).

[3] James Coleman et al., *Equality of Educational Opportunity* (Washington, DC: U.S. Government Printing Office, 1966).

maximum output that can be expected from a combination of inputs. In the education context, the question was stated as: How much student learning and achievement (outputs) would result from a given number of resources (inputs)?

Politicians and social scientists originally interpreted the Coleman study findings as showing that schools had little impact on student achievement when compared to the impact of family background. Coleman's study seemed to say that the educational inputs (such as student-teacher ratio, funding resources, teaching practices, quality of school facilities) did not contribute much to student achievement (outputs). Parental education and affluence had more influence on students' learning in school than anything the schools or teachers did in the classroom. In brief, the affluent students of well-educated parents became smarter in school but the economically disadvantaged students of poorly educated parents did not. This important finding made the report particularly influential in some educational and political circles.[4]

Other concurrent studies, however, indicated positive connections between school spending and student outcomes. Instead of using student achievement on a standardized test as the output variable, these economists examined individuals' later earnings in the labor force and found a significant association between adult earnings and school spending.[5] Verstegan states that these positive findings have been strong and consistent over time.[6] Unfortunately, Coleman's study seriously overshadowed the others, relegating them to political obscurity.

For the most part, educators reacted to the Coleman Report with cautious silence, but researcher Eric Hanushek and education writer and political activist William Bennett both spoke up. Hanushek continued the education production function studies and came to similar conclusions as had James Coleman.[7] Hanushek published meta-analyses of existing studies and found

---

[4]Most public educators, K–16, reacted to the Coleman Report's findings with stunned incredulity, believing that their contributions made a difference in student achievement. Many conservative politicians, on the other hand, saw the findings that school had little impact on learning as justification for reducing taxes to support public education.

[5]F. Welch, "Measurements of the Quality of Schooling," A.E.R. Papers and Proc. 56 (Evanston, IL: American Economic Association, May 1966); and G. Johnson and F. Stafford, "Social Returns to Quantity and Quality of Schooling," *Journal of Human Resources,* 8, Spring 1973: 139–155.

[6]D. Verstegan and R. King, "The Relationship between School Spending and Student Achievement: A Review and Analysis of 35 Years of Production Function Research," *Journal of Education Finance,* 24 (2), Fall, 1998: 243–262.

[7]E. A. Hanushek, "The Economics of Schooling: Production and Efficiency in Public Schools," *Journal of Economic Literature,* 24 (3), 1986: 1141–1177.

that the relationship between spending and student achievement was neither strong nor consistent given the way the government currently funded education. With titles such as *Throwing Money at Schools* and *The Quest for Equalized Mediocrity: School Finance Reform without Consideration of School Performance,* Hanushek incited public and policy opinion against increased education funding.[8]

When William Bennett became Secretary of Education (1985–1988), the political climate was ready for the nation's chief education advocate to openly challenge public education funding. Bennett cited his own study of per pupil spending and SAT scores as a reason to believe that education spending was unrelated to student achievement.[9] He concluded that the states with the highest SAT scores—Iowa, North and South Dakota, Utah, and Minnesota—spent low amounts on a per pupil basis. Students could show high academic achievement, Bennett argued persuasively, without high levels of school funding. Public education did not need more money, he logically avowed, to assure students' learning gains.

Unfortunately, Bennett's argument did not tell the whole story. He omitted the fact that these five Midwestern states had a very low percentage of students taking the SAT. Most students living in this region take a different college admissions test, the ACT. Only those few elite students interested in attending highly competitive, prestigious Ivy League schools in the East take the SAT. They would, necessarily, have high SAT scores and test well above the mean. In other words, these SAT students did not accurately represent the normal population distribution, and drawing such conclusions on that basis was invalid at best.

The education and political debate about money and students' educational achievement continues. On one hand, educators envision what additional funds could do to support student achievement—especially in this era of high-stakes testing for all students. On the other hand, politicians increasingly seek reelection on platforms of tax reduction, citing limited public resources and a lack of research showing that increased school funding produces higher student achievement.

---

[8]Hanushek's articles include "Throwing Money at Schools," *Journal of Policy Analysis and Management* 1, 1981: 19–41; and "The Quest for Equalized Mediocrity: School Finance Reform without Consideration of School Performance." In *Where Does the Money Go?* L. Picus and J. Wattenbarger, eds. (Thousand Oaks, CA: Corwin Press, 1996): 20–43.

[9]W. Bennett, *Report Card on American Education* (Washington, DC: American Legislative Exchange Council, 1993).

The Value of Production Function Studies in Education

According to Thompson and Wood, the conclusions about the seeming lack of relationship between spending and student achievement are "both incomplete and unsatisfying."[10] Intuitively, it makes sense to believe that increased spending on education will produce better student achievement or at least *not decrease* it—that spending less money will certainly *not increase* student achievement. On the other hand, it seems logical that if spending more money does not guarantee better student achievement, spending less can certainly harm it. Carrying Secretary Bennett's faulty logic to an extreme, the best education would cost nothing—a conclusion no reasonable person could reach. Unfortunately, the answers surrounding the relationship between spending and student achievement do remain incomplete and confusing. The problems with researching such a complicated issue are legion.

For example, some argue that production function studies are inappropriate models for education.[11] Such economic models for study in industry applications are quite precise. For instance, an industrial application might legitimately examine the following question: Given a productivity rate per line worker of 15 widgets[12] per hour (where P is the productivity rate), what would happen to daily output (where O is the daily output) if working conditions changed by lowering summer air-conditioning temperatures on the factory floor from 80 degrees to 75 degrees (where t is the temperature)?

The equation might look like this:

$$P = (t)O$$

In this case, the workplace temperature would be adjusted, and the increased utilities cost would be measured against the anticipated increase in widget production. If the increased cost resulted in increased profit, the temperature change would be effected.

In this example and in most industrial situations, the factory's supply of widget parts undergoes a systematic, rigid quality control check. Defective

---

[10]D. Thompson and C. Wood, *Money and Schools* (Larchmont, NY: Eye on Education, Inc., 2001).

[11]See C. F. Edley, "Lawyers and Education Reform," *Harvard Journal on Legislation,* 28 (2), Summer 1991: 293–305; also see Alexander and Salmon, *Public School Finance,* chap. 15, for an in-depth review of the systemic problems associated with production function studies.

[12]"Widget" is a commonly used manufacturing term to signify a key part of the production process of some item, alternately called a thingamajig, doohickey, or doodad.

widgets are not accepted in the production line. Through many studies, all widget assembly processes are known to take the same average time. All widget workers work at approximately the same rate. Workers who produce significantly more widgets per hour may receive higher pay rates. Widget workers who produce significantly fewer widgets per hour are fired. But can this model be transferred to education?

Education uses no quality control factors (other than student's age and home address) for the supply of students (product) entering the schooling process. Parents send us the best children they have. Students enter school with varying levels of readiness to get along well with others in an extended social (classroom or playground) situation, with different degrees of reading and math preparedness and ability, with varying beliefs about the value of school in their lives, and with varied family backgrounds. Some children come to school loved and nurtured. Others come to school abused and neglected. Some arrive daily, prepared to learn; others arrive late or are absent frequently, unable to benefit from classroom instructional activities.

Moreover, in education not only does the "product quality" vary but the production process in schools also varies. Unlike industry, education's production process is not standardized, and all students do not move through the same production process. School cultures differ in their philosophical beliefs concerning teaching and learning. Teacher quality varies from classroom to classroom, school to school, and district to district. Professional development varies in quality and frequency. The physical plant conditions vary, class size fluctuates, teacher experience and education levels differ, and educators' financial compensation varies and is not related to students' achievement gains.[13] Most important, per pupil spending varies significantly from state to state and from district to district, and how those funds are applied varies as well.

This is not to say that examining the inputs and outputs of education (production function studies) cannot be useful in our profession. But the methods, variables, and outputs examined are complicated and do not lend themselves to political "sound bite" answers.

What reasonable basis exists for making judgments about education spending inputs and outputs? What valid and reliable information is available that equates spending public monies and student achievement gains? How can public funds be best spent to promote student achievement? Are better outputs than student achievement on a one-time end-of-course test

---

[13]Educators' salaries typically depend on their job responsibilities and titles, years of service, and advanced degrees completed rather than quality or quantity of their work output.

available for scrutiny? Some recent studies prove valuable in answering these questions and addressing issues of money and student achievement.

WHAT THE RESEARCH SHOWS ABOUT MONEY AND STUDENT ACHIEVEMENT

As mentioned earlier, a reanalysis of Hanushek's work concluded that money does matter to student achievement.[14] Hedges et al. reexamined Hanushek's data and came to the opposite conclusion. Hedges states that upon reviewing the data "most often used to deny that resources are related to achievement, we find that money does matter after all."[15] In addition, another study conducted at the same time as Coleman's determined that per pupil expenditures, controlling for other factors, were significantly related to student outcomes.[16] Verstegan writes that "this body of work provides further evidence that school resource inputs make a difference in improving the educational outcomes of students."[17]

Many other studies show positive relationships between increased spending on education and student achievement. One Virginia Tech study, using an improved model for examining production function studies, found significant increases in student achievement with increases in instructional expenditures.[18] Verstegan found that overall school revenue accounted for about one-third of the variance in school achievement scores.[19]

The data show that increased spending focused on delivery of quality instruction directly to students produces the greatest achievement return for the dollars spent. In the following sections we provide evidence that increased spending on teacher quality, professional development for staff,

---

[14]See K. Baker, "Yes, Throw Money at Schools." *Phi Delta Kappan*, 72 (8), 1991: 628–630; and L. Hedges, R. Laine, and R. Greenwald, "Does Money Matter? A Meta-Analysis of Studies of the Effects of Differential School Inputs on Student Outcomes," *Educational Researcher*, 23, 1994: 5–14.

[15]Hedges et al., "Does Money Matter?" 13.

[16]B. Cooper and Associates, "Making Money Matter in Education: A Micro-Financial Model for Determining School-Level Allocations, Efficiency, and Productivity," *Journal of Education Finance*, 20, 1994: 66–87.

[17]Verstegan and King, "The Relationship between School Spending and Student Achievement," 1–2.

[18]J. Fortune and J. O'Neil, "Production Function Analyses and the Study of Educational Funding Equity: A Methodological Critique." *Journal of Education Finance* 20, 1994: 21–46.

[19]D. Verstegan, "Efficiency and Equity in the Provision and Reform of American Schooling." *Journal of Education Finance*, 20, 1994: 107–131.

reduced class size and school size, increased teacher salaries, and improved school facilities produce a significant return on investment for fostering student achievement gains.

Teacher Quality

"We know what constitutes good teaching, and we know that good teaching can matter more than students' family backgrounds and economic status."[20] Parents have long known that the quality of teachers matters.[21] Concerned, involved, and informed parents request certain teachers for their children where this practice is permitted. Research now supports what many have known intuitively for years—that the quality of the teacher and teaching are the most powerful predictors of student success. In fact, Minner states, "Teacher quality is not just an important issue facing the nation's schools: It is *the* issue."[22]

Darling-Hammond found that teacher quality variables, such as full certification and completing a major in the teaching field, are more important to student outcomes in reading and math than are student demographic variables such as poverty, minority status, and language background.[23] Formal teacher preparation accounts for 40 to 60% of the total variance in student achievement, controlling for students' demographic background.[24]

Darling-Hammond identified the following teacher quality factors related to increased student achievement:

- Verbal ability
- Content knowledge
- Education methods coursework related to their discipline
- Licensing exam scores that measure basic skills and teaching knowledge
- Skillful teaching behaviors
- Ongoing professional development
- Enthusiasm for learning

---

[20]Baker, "Yes, Throw Money at Schools," 1.

[21]For an excellent resource on Teacher Quality see L. Kaplan and W. Owings, *Teacher Quality, Teaching Quality, and School Improvement* (Bloomington, IN: Phi Delta Kappa Education Foundation, 2002).

[22]S. Minner, "Our Own Worst Enemy. Why Are We So Silent on the Issue That Matters Most?" *Education Week,* 20 (38), May 30, 2001: 33.

[23]L. Darling-Hammond, "Teacher Quality and Student Achievement: A Review of State Policy Evidence." Education Policy Analysis Archives, www.epaa.asu.edu/epaa/v8n1, January 1, 2000.

[24]Ibid., 27.

- Flexibility, creativity, and adaptability
- Teaching experience (those with fewer than 3 years' experience tend to be less effective, but there is little evidence that more than 3 years produces greater student achievement)
- Asking higher order questions (application, analysis, synthesis, and evaluation as opposed to recognition and recall questions) and probing student responses

Moreover, value-added studies in Texas and Tennessee indicate explicitly how much of an achievement difference teacher quality makes in student achievement as measured by standardized test results.[25] The Texas study indicates that when students are assigned to effective teachers for 3 consecutive years, reading scores rise from the 59th percentile to the 76th percentile from grades 4 to 6. Conversely, scores for students assigned to ineffective teachers for 3 consecutive years drop from the 60th percentile in grade 4 to the 42nd percentile by grade 6.[26] This reflects a 35 percentile point decline for students who started at approximately the same achievement level 3 years earlier.

The Tennessee value-added study provides similar results.[27] Again, dramatic differences appeared after students studying 3 consecutive years with effective versus ineffective teachers. In this case, math scores were examined. No significant differences existed among the groups at the start of the fourth grade level, but by the end of sixth grade the group assigned to 3 consecutive years with effective teachers had math scores at the 83rd percentile whereas the group with 3 consecutive years with ineffective teachers scored at the 29th percentile.

With NCLB requirements, the value of teacher quality is increasingly crucial. Data from the 1998 National Assessment of Educational Progress (NAEP) indicate that effective teachers make a difference in minority achievement.[28] For example, on the NAEP writing test, in grade 8 Texas

---

[25]Value-added studies look at students' own academic progress over several consecutive years with teachers identified as either highly effective or highly ineffective; future scores are predicted by a numerical formula.

[26]H. Jordan, R. Mendro, and D. Weerasinge, "Teacher Effects on Longitudinal Student Achievement." Paper presented at the CREATE Annual Meeting, Indianapolis, IN, July 1997.

[27]R. Sanders and J. Rivers, *Cumulative and Residual Effects of Teachers on Future Student Academic Achievement* (Knoxville: University of Tennessee, Tennessee Value Added Assessment System, November 1996).

[28]K. Haycock, C. Jerald, and S. Huang, "Closing the Gap: Done in a Decade." *Thinking K–16*, 5, Spring 2001: 3–22.

African American students scored 146 points whereas Arkansas African American students scored 121 points, a 25 point difference worth 2.5 years of learning. Likewise, Latino students in Virginia scored 146 points on the NAEP writing test whereas Latino students in Mississippi scored 106 points, a 40 point difference worth 4 years of learning.

At testing time, both Texas and Virginia had been high-stakes testing states for several years with clear and public sanctions for schools and students who did not achieve at predetermined levels. Arkansas and Mississippi were not. One can assume that Texas and Virginia teachers felt explicit pressures to assure that even traditionally lower achieving students mastered the "standard curriculum" and used those effective practices in their classrooms to bring more children across the bar.

Similarly, analyses of the 1996 NAEP data for eighth grade math and science scores determined that students whose teachers either majored or minored in the subjects they taught outperformed their peers by approximately 40% of a grade level.[29] Eighth graders scored 39% higher in math than their peers when taught by teachers who stressed critical thinking skills, such as writing about math.[30] Haycock suggests that teacher content knowledge in English and social sciences may be just as meaningful to student achievement.[31]

Actual teaching performance—not just courses taken—makes a significant difference in student achievement, and teacher education accrediting bodies are now recognizing this. "Receiving an endorsement from a public or private accrediting body is one way in which teacher education programs show their worth."[32] Since 2001 the National Council for Accreditation of Teacher Education (NCATE) has been using a performance-based accreditation system that looks more closely at the teacher candidate's work, subject knowledge, and demonstrated teaching skills rather than at inputs and processes not directly related to classroom practice.[33] By refocusing attention on actual teaching practices, this national standards organization affirms that teachers' pedagogy with students inside the classroom is essential to teacher effectiveness.

---

[29]H. Weglinsky, *How Teaching Matters: Bringing the Classroom Back into the Discussions of Teacher Quality.* Policy Information Center Report (Princeton, NJ: Milken Family Foundation. Educational Testing Service, October 2000).

[30]Ibid.

[31]K. Haycock, "Good Teaching Matters . . . A Lot." *Thinking K–16,* 3, Summer 1998: 3–14.

[32]Ibid., 14.

[33]National Council for Accreditation of Teacher Education (NCATE). "NCATE 2000: Performance-Based Accreditation." *NCATE Making a Difference* (Washington, DC: Author, September 2000).

Given this information and knowing how much high-quality teachers and teaching contribute to student achievement, education dollars appear best spent in hiring and keeping the highest quality teachers and most effective candidates possible. Interviewing and hiring practices that include looking for the characteristics mentioned earlier, providing a professional work environment that includes a focus on improved classroom practices that reach all students, and implementing salary structures designed to maximize hiring and retaining teachers who produce the most student learning may be the best use of limited education dollars.

Professional Development

Once employed, professional development plays an important role in retaining the highest quality teachers. New teachers can get better, marginal teachers can improve, and successful teachers can continue to strengthen their expertise through well-designed professional development programs. Quality professional development programs can have a positive impact on student achievement. Every extra factor that provides teachers with techniques for individualizing instruction increases student achievement. Studies of the 1996 NAEP data indicate that professional development in cultural diversity, teaching techniques for addressing needs of students with limited English proficiency, and teaching students identified with special education needs are linked to higher student achievement in math.[34]

Not all professional development programs are equally effective. Professional development that describes specific teaching behaviors and constructs provides a faculty with a common language to address teaching and learning collaboratively. Once teachers receive a systematic study of learning processes that allow them to reflect and address their own teaching and learning beliefs and practices, they can analyze and improve what they do in the classroom. Given this opportunity, faculty can then address students' learning needs from a variety of strategies with a common language to help all students learn and achieve more effectively.[35]

Teachers who believe that their instructional practices have a direct impact on student achievement are more likely to seek out and implement

[34]See J. Blair, "ETS Study Links Effective Teaching Methods to Test-Score Gains." *Education Week*, 25, October 2000: 24–25; and Weglinsky, *How Teaching Matters.*

[35]J. Monroe, "Learning More about Learning Improves Teacher Effectiveness." *School Effectiveness and School Improvement*, 10, June 1999: 151–171.

new teaching and learning techniques.[36] Armed with new information and invested in their ongoing professional development, teachers gain confidence about their teaching skills, reflect on their practices, and seek professional colleagues' advice to maximize student achievement. In short, professional development can help create a systemic culture of teaching for learning within the school.

Effective professional development programs foster professional confidence by providing ongoing, collaborative, collegial programs that are highly connected to what teachers actually do in their classrooms—in other words, the activities are job imbedded.[37] When principals design professional development learning activities, they should ask, "Do these practices enhance student learning?" and "Do these instructional practices produce student achievement and positive school culture results that are measurable and observable?"

Other research finds that when professional development is sustained over time and based on curriculum standards, teachers are more likely to adopt new and reform-based teaching practices. Subsequently, their students achieve at higher levels on standardized tests.[38] Having motivational speakers address the faculty at the start of the school may be good for short-term morale, but such practices should not be confused with a professional development program for a lasting impact.

Reduced Class Size

Teachers and parents have long known that, all else being equal, smaller class size allows teachers to spend more time meeting individual student needs. California's legislature appropriated $1 billion starting in the 1996–97 school year to lower class size in grades K–3 from almost 30 to 20. New York followed suit, and in 1999 President Clinton's budget included $12 billion to states to reduce K–3 class size.

Salaries consume the lion's share of education budgets. Hiring more qualified teachers to reduce overall class size, building additional classrooms for the extra teachers, and providing the resources associated with each

---

[36]J. P. Scribner, "Teacher Efficacy and Teacher Professional Learning: Implications for School Leaders." *Journal of School Leadership*, 9, May 1999: 209–234.

[37]P. K. Anderson, "But What If . . . Supporting Leaders and Learners." *Phi Delta Kappan*, 82, June 2001: 737–739.

[38]E. Hirsh, J. E. Koppich, and M. S. Knapp, *What States Are Doing to Improve the Quality of Teaching. A Brief Review of Current Patterns and Trends* (Seattle, WA: Center for the Study of Teaching and Policy, December 1998).

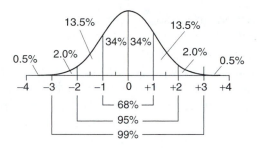

FIGURE **12.1**

The Normal Distribution

additional teacher and classroom pose difficult policy questions for district administrators. Does the increased cost of decreasing class size produce enough achievement gain to warrant spending limited resources toward that end, or do other more cost-effective measures exist to increase student achievement? Does the research reveal the effect size of reducing class size?

To understand the answer, it is important to understand the concept of "effect size."[39] Effect size measures the change in the experimental group in standard deviation units. An effect size of 1.0, therefore, means that students in the experimental group would score one standard deviation above those in the control group. Figure 12.1 shows the normal distribution, or bell-shaped curve, and illustrates how much difference an effect size of 1.0 makes. If control group students were scoring at the 50th percentile, experimental group students would be scoring one standard deviation higher, or 34 percentile points higher. That would make them score at approximately the 84th percentile. Marzano and colleagues point out how easily effect size translates into percentile point gains.

The impact of class size on student achievement has been studied for many years. Tennessee's study successfully controlled experiments of class size reduction in primary grades and showed positive results. The teacher-student achievement ratio, or STAR, program involved more than 12,000 students over 4 years using fully qualified, experienced teachers and a relatively homogeneous student population. This highly controlled longitudinal study indicates that attending small classes for 3 consecutive years in grades K–3 is associated with sustained academic benefits in all school subjects through grade 8.[40] Consecutive years in small classes had the most effect

[39]Effect size is also known as a Z-score. For an excellent overview of effect size, see R. Marzano, D. Pickering, and J. Pollock, *Classroom Instruction That Works: Research-Based Strategies for Increasing Student Achievement* (Alexandria, VA: ASCD, 2001), 4–6.

[40]B. Stecher, G. Bohrnstedt, M. Kirst, J. McRobbie, and T. Williams, "Class-Size Reduction in California: A Story of Hope, Promise, and Unintended Consequences." *Phi Delta Kappan*, 82, June 2001: 670–674.

on minority and urban students.[41] An AERA report indicates that even when students return to "normal sized" classrooms in fourth grade, achievement gains were maintained.[42]

In addition, a review and synthesis of more than 100 class-size studies suggests that the most positive effect of small classes appears in kindergarten to third grade for mathematics and reading test scores, with results consistent across schools.[43] Unfortunately, findings in several studies indicate that the advantages of small classes, defined as 13 to 19 pupils, may not continue in later school years.[44] Likewise, several cost-effectiveness studies of various strategies for improving student learning indicate that reducing class size has a small positive effect on achievement compared to many less costly strategies.[45] Decreased class size is, at times, associated with an increase in the cost of additional teachers and, frequently, additional classrooms.

It is important to note that lowering licensure regulations to attract additional candidates of lower quality could negate the impact of class size. California's class-size reduction experience increased the teacher workforce by 38%, but the drop in teacher quality disproportionately affected urban districts already challenged by poverty, overcrowding, and language barriers.[46]

The earlier studies seem to cast doubt on the efficacy of spending money to reduce class size; monies might better be spent elsewhere to better effect. One early review examined 27 alterable variables associated with student achievement and found class size to be an ineffective means of improving student achievement—ranking 25th of the 27 variables with an estimated effect size of only 0.09.[47] Robinson and Wittebols also reviewed

---

[41]Ibid. Also G. E. Robinson, "Synthesis of Research on the Effects of Class Size." *Educational Leadership,* 47, April 1990: 80–90; and L. Jacobson, "Wisconsin Class-Size Study Yields Advice on Teachers' Methods." *Education Week,* 24, January 2001: 15.

[42]http://www.aera.net/gov/archive/r0699-01.htm

[43]B. Nye, L. V. Hodges, and S. Konstantopoulos, "The Effects of Small Class Sizes on Academic Achievement: The Results of the Tennessee Class Size Experiment." *American Educational Research Journal,* 37, Spring 2000: 123–151; and Robinson, "Synthesis of Research on the Effects of Class Size."

[44]Jacobson, "Wisconsin Class Size Study"; and Robinson, "Synthesis of Research on the Effects of Class Size," 82.

[45]Robinson, "Synthesis of Research on the Effects of Class Size."

[46]Stecher et al., "Class-Size Reduction in California."

[47]H. Walberg, "Improving the Productivity of America's Schools," *Educational Leadership,* 1984: 19–27.

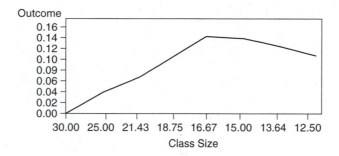

FIGURE **12.2**

Cumulative Effect Size at Various Resource Levels

Source: M. Addonizio and J. Phelps, "Class Size and Student Performance: A Framework for Policy Analysis," *Journal of Education Finance,* 26, Fall 2000: 153.

the literature on class size. They state that from a policy standpoint reducing class size may be a prohibitively expensive method of increasing student achievement.[48] Researchers from this early time began looking to "programs that work" ideas for improving student achievement.

Despite these findings, class size has decreased rather consistently since 1960. Research, however, does not support the expectation that reducing class size alone results in greater academic gains. Class size effects vary by grade level, pupil characteristics, subject areas, teaching methods, and other variables. Recent research affirms that class size appears to matter most for reading and math at the early elementary years for all students, and especially for at-risk students. One study reviews the benefits and costs of class size reduction of several well-researched studies;[49] the cost effectiveness of class size on the effect size of student performance is shown in Figure 12.2.

As policy makers examine the role of decreased class size and achievement, it is important to understand that other variables may well come into play. Reducing class size without simultaneously improving teaching quality appears to be both expensive and often ineffective.

---

[48]G. E. Robinson and J. H. Wittebols, *Class Size Research: A Related Cluster Analysis for Decisionmaking* (Arlington, VA: Educational Research Service, 1986).

[49]M. Addonizio and J. Phelps, "Class Size and Student Performance: A Framework for Policy Analysis," *Journal of Education Finance,* 26, Fall 2000: 135–156.

Reduced School Size

Recent substantial grant awards from the Bill and Melinda Gates Foundation to large urban school districts to create smaller schools would lead one to believe that reduced school size is associated with increased student achievement. These grant awards are fueled by recent research.

In fact, a 2002 study by Ohio researchers for the Rural School and Community Trust (founded as the Annenburg Rural Challenge) found in a seven-state study (Alaska, California, Georgia, Montana, Ohio, Texas, and West Virginia) that smaller schools reduce the harmful effects of poverty on student achievement and help students from less affluent communities narrow the academic achievement gap between them and students from wealthier communities. The implication is that the less affluent a community, the smaller the school and school district serving that community should be to maximize student achievement. The present study conducted by Ohio University researchers extends this analysis to Arkansas.[50]

An Education Commission of the States (ECS) report details the benefits of reduced school size.[51] Although the report finds no consensus on the optimal size of a small school, four conclusions are drawn. First, as schools get smaller they produce better student performance in terms of student attendance, test scores, graduation rates, and participation in extracurricular activities. Second, parents like the communication and participation levels in smaller schools, thereby increasing parent satisfaction ratings. Third, teachers like smaller schools and reporting feeling that they can make a real difference in student learning. Finally, smaller schools tend to produce a safer learning environment for students.

It is true that smaller schools are more expensive to operate on a per pupil basis, thereby reducing efficiency, but smaller schools may be more cost effective when evaluated on a cost per graduate basis. With fewer dropouts, smaller schools graduate more of their students. Furthermore, another study shows that it is possible to construct smaller schools on a cost-effective basis with real economic and social advantages for the community.[52]

---

[50]J. D. Johnson, C. B. Howley, and A. A. Howley, *Size, Excellence, and Equity. A Report on Arkansas Schools and Districts* (Athens, OH: Ohio University, College of Education, Educational Studies Department, 2002). ERIC Document Reproduction Service (forthcoming).

[51]http://www.ecs.org/html/issue.asp?print=true&issueID=105&subIssueID=0

[52]http://www.ecs.org/html/offsite.asp?document=http%3A%2F%2Fwww%2Ekwfdn%2Eorg%2FProgramAreas%2FFacilities%2Fdollars%5Fsense%2Epdf

A 2004 ECS report cites 11 studies dealing with school size.[53] One report explores the reform efforts associated with reducing school size.[54] Smaller high schools, in this study defined as 600 or fewer students, had higher traditionally calculated per pupil costs but higher graduation rates and lower dropout rates. Again, considering cost per graduate, the operating costs were less than those of larger schools.

Stiefel and colleagues examined more than 140 schools and 50,000 students in the New York City Public Schools. Their findings are consistent with other positive student achievement results:

> In this study, we found that a combined output and cost measure, budget per graduate, shows that small academic high schools have budgets per graduate similar to those of large high schools (greater than 2,000). For small academic high schools, this result is due to their vastly lower dropout rates. Smaller medium-sized vocational schools (600–1,200 students) and small alternative transfer high schools have the highest budgets per graduate.
>
> These are interesting findings because they seem to support the arguments of both advocates of small schools and advocates of large schools. Our results indicate that small schools are cost-effective, but so are large schools in New York City. . . . For now, using graduates as outcomes, this study suggests that the city might do well to continue to encourage the formation and continuing support of small high schools.[55]

Certainly the apparent size of a large school can be reduced by implementing a "school-within-a-school" concept. Smaller schools organized within a larger school may be a way to achieve the benefits of smaller schools.[56] This school-within-a-school approach establishes a smaller educational unit with a separate educational program within the larger school; it has its own staff and students, and its own budget. Several cities, including New York City, Philadelphia, and Chicago, have experimented with this concept as a method for downsizing larger schools to reap the benefits of smaller schools.

---

[53]http://www.ecs.org/html/IssueSection.asp?issueid=105&s=Selected+Research+%26+Readings

[54]http://www.ecs.org/clearinghouse/34/31/3431.pdf

[55]L. Stiefel, R. Berne, P. Iatarola, and N. Fruchter, "High School Size: Effects on Budgets and Performance in New York City." *Educational Evaluation and Policy Analysis,* 22 (1), Spring 2000: 27–39, at 36–37.

[56]http://www.ericfacility.net/databases/ERIC_Digests/ed438147.html

The school-within-a-school must negotiate the use of common space such as the gym, auditorium, and playground with a "host" school and defer to the building principal on matters of safety and building operation. The school-within-a-school often reports to a district official instead of being responsible to the building principal. Ideally, the school-within-a-school teachers and students are affiliated with the school-within-a-school as a matter of choice.

There are many methods to achieve this concept, and many distinctions without differences. Some are known as house plans, mini-schools, learning communities, or clusters. All share the same purpose—to downsize and personalize the learning environment for students and to increase achievement. The distinction in effectiveness, however, comes from the program implementation. "The major challenge to schools-within-schools has been obtaining sufficient separateness and autonomy to permit staff members to generate a distinctive environment and to carry out their own vision of schooling."[57] This involves professional development and time to develop and enact their educational vision.

Teacher Salaries

To be sure, controversy surrounds the issue of teacher salaries and student achievement.[58] Virtually no one doubts the common belief that higher salaries will attract brighter individuals into a profession. Unfortunately, this may not be possible in the near term. The Education Policy Institute notes that teachers' salaries have slipped 15% since 1993 and 12% since 1983 after adjusting for inflation.[59] Teacher salaries are now well below those of comparable professions, complicating efforts to attract and keep highly qualified educators. Although teachers tend to receive benefits, their health insurance and pensions are not valuable enough to offset the wage differential. Nor do teachers receive paid leave, bonuses, or overtime available in other professions.

Low education salaries are nothing new to our profession. Johns, Morphet, and Alexander discuss Adam Smith's attribution of low teachers' salary to supply and demand factors as far back as 1776.[60] Smith stated that

---

[57]M. A. Raywid, "Family Choice Arrangements in Public Schools: A Review of the Literature." *Review of Educational Research*, 55 (4), 1985: 435–467, at 455.

[58]To exacerbate this dilemma, most school finance textbooks do not address this issue.

[59]Kathleen Kennedy Manzo, "Study Finds Teachers Are Losing Ground on Salary Front." *Education Week*, 24 (1), 2004: 12. Available at www.edweek.org/links.

[60]R. Johns, E. Morphet, and K. Alexander, *The Economics and Financing of Education*, 4th ed. (Secaucus, NJ: Prentice Hall, 1983), 305.

low teacher compensation was due to an oversupply of individuals trained to enter the clergy who were unable to find ministerial positions. These people subsequently entered teaching, creating a virtual flood of those trained and willing to teach. Supply and demand ruled; with oversupply of labor, wages fell. A tradition of low pay and the fact that public coffers pay teacher salaries keeps pay artificially low today even during a teacher shortage.

It is difficult to link empirical evidence of increased teacher quality with higher teacher salaries because most school districts have salary schedules that are functions of years of experience and degrees. Salaries are not based on student achievement. It is logical to surmise that increased salaries will, however, expand the potential teacher applicant pool. Even Hanushek states that "nobody doubts that increasing teacher salaries will expand the pool of potential teachers from which a district can choose. But the influence on students depends directly on the ability of districts to choose the best teachers from the expanded pool. Research shows that the typical school district does poorly in these choices. The combination of these factors implies there is virtually no relationship between teacher salaries and student achievement."[61]

Although some school districts do not do a good job in selecting the highest quality teachers, it is a false assumption that there is no relationship between salary and student achievement. The evidence is overwhelming that teacher quality is related to student achievement. Salary is a proven method of attracting a larger applicant pool, and selecting the highest quality teachers from that pool is key. Linda Darling-Hammond has determined that teacher quality issues related to teacher preparation and certification affect student achievement.[62] In fact, the Teaching Commission, a nonprofit group formed in 2003 to improve teaching, has recommended raising base salaries to make teachers' pay more competitive and attract higher quality teachers.[63]

School Facilities

The overall impact of the school building's design features and environmental conditions affects student achievement and teacher effectiveness. In Earthman's study, a 5 to 17 percentile point difference in standardized test scores was shown for students in good facilities (well-maintained buildings

---

[61]www.hoover.stanford.edu/publicaffairs/we/current/hanushek_0400.html

[62]Darling-Hammond, "Teacher Quality and Student Achievement."

[63]See http://www.cnn.com/2004/EDUCATION/01/14/teacher.salaries.ap/.

The commission includes former IBM Chair Louis Gerstner, former Department of Education Secretary Richard Riley, and former First Lady Barbara Bush.

with comfortable room and hall temperatures, satisfactory lighting, appropriate noise levels, good roofs, sufficient space) compared with those in poor facilities (poorly maintained, too cold or hot rooms, inadequate lighting, high noise levels, leaky roofs, overcrowding) controlling for the socioeconomic status of the students.[64]

Earthman logically concludes that a school's acoustic quality that permits students' to hear clearly and understand what is being spoken, their presence in rooms maintained within the temperature and humidity tolerances of 67 degrees to 73 degrees and 50% relative humidity (to reduce incidence of illness), and above standard school buildings that provide the appropriate learning environment conditions are all prerequisites for effective learning. Many of the building factors necessary for proper learning environments are absent in older buildings, and student achievement in older buildings is lower than that of students in newer ones.

In a study of elementary schools in the District of Columbia, Berner found that if a school district were to improve conditions of its schools from poor to excellent, student achievement scores would increase an average of 10.9 percentile points.[65] The percentage of students on free or reduced-price lunch, mean income in the census tract, and the percentage of white students in the census tract were used as a control for socioeconomic status.

Furthermore, perception often influences (and perhaps creates) reality. Teachers in buildings in poor condition stated that the facility's design and appearance had a negative impact on the learning climate whereas teachers in buildings in good condition report that the building had a positive influence on the learning climate.[66] Working in substandard buildings or in newer buildings that are poorly maintained or repaired harms teachers' morale and increases their work frustration; these attitudes likely transfer negatively into their classroom expectations and practices, reducing student achievement.

Likewise, students in overcrowded schools and classrooms do not score as high on achievement tests as students in schools and rooms that were not overcrowded. Corcoran and colleagues report that overcrowding results in

[64]G. Earthman, "School Facility Conditions and Student Academic Achievement." Williams Watch Series: Investigating the Claims of *Williams v. State of California* (Los Angeles, CA: UCLA Institute for Democracy, Education, and Access, 2002).

[65]M. Berner, "Building Conditions, Parental Involvement, and Student Achievement in the District of Columbia Public School System." *Urban Education*, 28 (1), April 1993: 6–29.

[66]J. Lowe, "The Interface between Educational Facilities and Learning Climate in Three Elementary Schools." Unpublished doctoral dissertation, Texas A&M University, College Station, Texas.

high absentee rates for students and teachers.[67] Additionally, overcrowded schools are often noisier and create more paperwork. Stressful and unpleasant learning and working conditions and related negative attitudes and lower attendance reduce learning opportunities and measured achievement.

Frustrating efforts to improve school facilities is the rapidly rising cost of steel, concrete, and other construction materials—often between 15 and 30%—which are forcing some districts building new schools to seek additional funds, delay, or redesign projects. Prices for nearly every construction material have been rising at double-digit percentages, making serious difficulties for the $29 billion school construction industry.[68]

With research clearly affirming that school funding carefully targeted on enhancing teaching quality, designing appropriate school organization, and providing comfortable facilities makes a measurable difference in student achievement, communities and school leaders face serious challenges in acquiring additional resources to support public education.

SUMMARY

Questions about the impact of school funding on student achievement lie at the heart of national education reform. The 1966 Coleman Report influenced some to think that schools had little impact on student achievement. Similarly, some researchers found that the relationship between spending and student achievement was neither strong nor consistent, and they incited public and policy opinion against increased education funding.

On the other hand, many studies, and a reanalysis of negative studies, show positive relationships between increased spending on education and student achievement and outcomes. Overall school revenue accounted for about one-third of the variance in school achievement scores, and increased spending focused on delivery of high-quality instruction directly to students produces the greatest achievement return for the dollars spent.

The quality of the teacher and teaching effectiveness are the most powerful predictors of student success. Value-added studies indicate a significant achievement difference on standardized achievement tests for students working with effective teachers (as compared with ineffective teachers) over

---

[67]T. B. Corcoran, L. J. Walker, and J. L. White, *Working in Urban Schools* (Washington, DC: Institute for Educational Leadership, 1988).

[68]Joetta L. Sack, "Costs Climb on Materials for Schools. Construction Projects Delayed, Scrapped." *Education Week*, 24 (1), 2004: 1, 24.

3 consecutive years. Similarly, studies comparing students on 1996 NAEP standards show that certain effective teaching practices led to significantly higher student achievement.

Additional links exist between school finance and student achievement. Class size sometimes affects student achievement but may not be cost effective. Small classes (13 to 19 pupils) show the most positive effects in kindergarten to third grade for mathematics and reading test scores, especially for at-risk students, but the advantages may not continue in later grades. Moreover, smaller schools (under 600 students) may have a positive impact on student achievement but may be more expensive to operate on a per pupil basis. Smaller schools organized within a larger school may achieve the benefits of smaller schools with increased efficiency. Moreover, the overall impact of the school building's design features and environmental conditions affect students' measured achievement and teacher effectiveness.

CONCLUSION

The relationship between spending and student achievement remains incomplete and confusing, but education dollars appear to be best spent in hiring and keeping the highest quality teachers, providing meaningful professional development, and maintaining school facilities to permit comfortable and safe learning environments. Maintaining low teacher-student ratios in the early grades also has a positive impact on student achievement but at a rather high cost.

CASE STUDY

You have been hired as a consultant to the Alpha School District, a neighbor of Omega School District. Twenty years ago Alpha School District was known as the premiere school system in the state. Omega School District is a suburban area on the outskirts of Alpha. Test scores have been declining in Alpha for the past 10 years or so—very little at first, but somewhat noticeably in the last 2 or 3 years. In fact, Omega School District is now written up in the papers as the best school district in the state whereas Alpha failed to make AYP last year.

Both Alpha and Omega school districts have adequate capacity, but effort has been declining in Alpha while increasing in Omega. Omega's

TABLE 12.1 **DATA SHEETS FOR ALPHA AND OMEGA SCHOOL DISTRICTS**

	Alpha School District	Omega School District
Student enrollment	25,000	25,000
Percentage of students on free or reduced-price lunch	15%	15%
Number of schools	2 high schools, 3,800 students each	3 high schools, 2,500 students each
	4 middle schools, 1,450 students each	5 middle schools, 1,150 students each
	14 elementary schools, 825 students each	20 elementary schools, 575 students each
Starting teacher salary	$34,000	$36,500
Midpoint teacher salary: 13 years and master's degree	$45,000	$45,500
Maximum teacher salary: 25 years and master's degree	$55,000	$55,000
Student teacher ratio:		
Grades K–3	23:1	16:1
Grades 4–5	23:1	22:1
Grades 6–8	22:1	22:1
Grades 9–12	20:1	20:1
Per pupil expenditure	$9,000	$12,000
Per capita property value	$225,000	$175,000

starting teacher salary now outpaces Alpha's starting salary. Alpha School District is willing to spend money on its schools if they have a good, research-based plan. Given the data in Table 12.1, what suggestions would you offer the new superintendent of Alpha School District to improve achievement? Justify your answers.

CHAPTER QUESTIONS

1. Describe a production function study. How does this type of study work in manufacturing? What are some of the difficulties in performing production function studies in education?
2. What does the research say about spending and student achievement?

3. What positive, proactive steps can school districts take to make certain they hire and retain the highest quality teachers possible?
4. What does the research say about class size and student achievement?
5. How do school facilities affect student achievement?
6. What are some specific advantages to small high schools? How can costs be calculated so that small high schools are more cost effective?
7. Examine your school district budget over the last 3 years. To what extent is the budget putting money in areas that increase student achievement? How would you change the budget to make it more effective in terms of having a positive impact on student achievement?

CRITICAL AND EMERGING SCHOOL FINANCE ISSUES

FOCUS QUESTIONS

1. What is the overall physical condition of school facilities in the United States? Are maintenance programs and new construction keeping pace with school district needs?

2. What health issues must be addressed to provide a safe indoor environment in our schools?

3. How is school construction financed? Are there ways to reduce interest costs?

4. Are salaries and benefits adequate to retain experienced educators? How does your state compare with other states?

5. What impact do alternative licensure standards have on the quality of educators in our schools today?

6. If voucher programs increase and taxes continue to be reduced, what is the future of public education?

In this chapter we examine some of the critical and emerging issues in school finance. Critical issues include maintaining adequate school facilities, funding human resources for education, and measuring student achievement. Emerging issues that could change the financial base of public education include voucher programs and federal, state, and local support for public education. We need to begin to think about the long-term impact of underfunding public education and what that means to our democratic way of life.

School districts face major challenges as communities address critical and emerging issues in school finance. Many of our nation's schools are in serious disrepair and pose major health risks for students and teachers. In addition, although a 30-year-old building is relatively new, it was built before computers became an essential part of daily business, leisure, and education. Many existing school facilities require upgrades to wiring and cabling infrastructure for computer use. Finding ways to fund these necessary improvements in the physical plants of education is a critical issue now and in the future.

Human resources are the largest portion of every school budget, and hiring and retaining high-quality teachers is a critical need throughout the nation. The most needy school districts have the most difficult time hiring quality teachers due to salary disparities and working conditions between these districts and more affluent districts. In addition, all districts face steeply rising health care costs that have a severe impact on employee benefits, and benefit packages are becoming another dimension in the competition for quality educators. We begin by examining these two critical issues for the future of public education.

MAINTAINING ADEQUATE SCHOOL FACILITIES

In times of tight budgets, limiting building maintenance and repairs rarely results in a public outcry. But the public quickly grows agitated and vocal when athletics or driver education programs or band uniforms face similar curtailment. As a result, deferred maintenance of school facilities has grown to far-reaching proportions.

In 1965 the U.S. Department of Education completed a survey of school facility conditions, and 30 years later the General Accounting Office (GAO) completed the next school facilities study.[1] This 1995 report found that $112 billion was needed to repair or upgrade America's public schools to "good overall condition." This report contains pictures of decaying school facilities that defy belief and leave us to question the credibility of state or local school building safety inspections.

In 1999 the National Center for Education Statistics report added these facts to the list:[2]

---

[1]To view the entire report, go to http://www.gao.gov/archive/1995/he95061.pdf.

[2]U.S. Department of Education, National Center for Education Statistics, *Condition of America's Public School Facilities: 1999* (NCES 2000-032), http://nces.ed.gov/fastfact/display.asp?id=94, 2000.

- Approximately 25% of American schools report at least one type of on-site building in "less than adequate" condition.
- Fifty percent of American schools have at least one building feature in "less than adequate" condition.
- Nearly 40% of American schools have at least one unsatisfactory environmental condition.
- The oldest buildings are most in need of repair, but most of these schools have no plan for improvements.
- At least 10% of American school buildings have enrollments that exceed designed capacity by more than 25%.

Congress failed to pass capital-outlay legislation that would have begun to address these needs, denying both a 1995 budget request for $5 billion and a 1999 scaled-down request of under $1 billion.

In 2000 the NEA school facility needs study, using a more comprehensive set of criteria than the GAO, found it would cost $322 billion to repair and modernize America's public schools and provide the necessary technology.[3] The NEA report shocked and embarrassed Congress and state legislatures by releasing press statements such as these:[4]

- America's schools are in disrepair. The average public school is 42 years old. Twenty-eight percent of the public schools in America are over 50 years old.
- Record enrollments and growing communities are leading to severe overcrowding in our nation's public schools. Putting students in trailers and going to school in shifts is not the answer.
- America's schools can't support today's technology. Forty-six percent of the public schools in America lack the electrical and communication wiring to support today's computer systems.

Table 13.1 lists the NEA report's state-by-state breakdown of unmet public school facility needs. The unmet facility needs for the nation as a whole total a whopping $321,955,416,998.

Similarly, in 2002 the *Digest of Education Statistics* indicated that 39% of American schools have building deficiencies and have plans to fix them.[5] Those renovations will not be inexpensive. The total U.S. population in 2004

---

[3]National Education Association, *Modernizing Our Schools: What Will It Cost?* at www.nea.org/nr/ ne000503.html, 2000.

[4]"Testimony Too Profound to Ignore," *NEA Today*, May 2000: 14–15.

[5]http://nces.ed.gov/programs/digest/d02/tables/dt102.asp

TABLE 13.1   UNMET STATE SCHOOL FACILITY NEEDS, 2000

State	Unmet Need	State	Unmet Need
Alabama	$2,310,853,117	Montana	1,077,299,591
Alaska	868,794,867	Nebraska	$1,922,603,928
Arizona	5,669,527,982	Nevada	5,573,977,712
Arkansas	2,256,405,911	New Hampshire	620,317,062
California	32,901,183,414	New Jersey	22,029,345,313
Colorado	4,543,245,163	New Mexico	1,750,185,035
Connecticut	5,555,226,320	New York	50,675,796,800
Delaware	1,166,375,768	North Carolina	7,525,524,823
Florida	5,487,697,936	North Dakota	545,223,536
Georgia	8,536,952,027	Ohio	24,977,840,000
Hawaii	955,443,168	Oklahoma	2,874,081,833
Idaho	967,791,137	Oregon	2,986,932,022
Illinois	11,328,098,880	Pennsylvania	10,408,541,747
Indiana	3,537,737,613	Rhode Island	1,583,941,627
Iowa	3,898,924,833	South Carolina	3,268,063,360
Kansas	2,296,811,280	South Dakota	650,174,846
Kentucky	3,127,235,884	Tennessee	3,244,784,824
Louisiana	3,941,071,195	Texas	13,654,055,206
Maine	684,775,372	Utah	9,003,985,557
Maryland	4,785,427,084	Vermont	333,386,471
Massachusetts	9,942,061,620	Virginia	6,892,107,208
Michigan	9,924,079,040	Washington	6,541,506,697
Minnesota	5,423,822,916	West Virginia	1,322,390,064
Mississippi	1,580,245,504	Wisconsin	5,718,119,395
Missouri	4,451,022,957	Wyoming	634,421,353

Source: National Education Association, *Modernizing Our Schools: What Will It Cost?*, Table 1, p. 11. Used with permission of the National Education Association. Copyright © 2000. All rights reserved.

was 294,202,058 persons.[6] Dividing the national unmet school facility need by the total population reveals an astonishing statistic: To address this need would cost every man, woman, and child in the country almost $1,100.[7]

---

[6]U.S. Census Bureau at http://www.census.gov/main/www/popclock.html, table 102.

[7]To put this in perspective, the cost of the war in Iraq reached $207.5 billion on September 30, 2005, or 64% of the cost of bringing all of America's school buildings to good condition.

TABLE 13.2   SCHOOL CONSTRUCTION, 1993 THROUGH 2002

Year	Construction (in billions of dollars)
1993	$10,778
1994	$10,687
1995	$10,417
1996	$10,964
1997	$12,394
1998	$17,095
1999	$16,039
2000	$21,567
2001	$26,777
2002	$24,343

Source: Adapted from Joe Agron, American School and University, Overland Park, Kansas, May 1, 2003. (http://asumag.com/ar/university_strong_showing_2/)

Although many unmet needs in school facilities continue, some school construction has been under way. Table 13.2 lists the public school construction project dollar amounts undertaken between 1993 and 2002.

For the school years 2003 through 2005, American School and University provides estimates of expenditures for U.S. public school districts, which are shown in Table 13.3.

The expenses for school facilities renovation and construction are mind boggling, but they cannot be postponed indefinitely without considerable risk to employee and student health and student achievement.

Health Issues in School Facilities

Older or poorly designed school facilities have health issues, including radon gas, lead paint and solder, poor indoor air quality, and mold. Radon gas, a naturally occurring gas formed from decomposing uranium found in most soils, is the second leading cause of lung cancer in the United States, responsible for between 15,000 and 22,000 deaths each year.[8] Radon detection and treatment are important in schools as younger lungs are thought to be more susceptible to damage.

---

[8]http://www.epa.gov/radon/pubs/citguide.html

TABLE 13.3	ESTIMATED PUBLIC SCHOOL CONSTRUCTION EXPENDITURES, 2003 THROUGH 2005
New school construction	$51,162,337,000
Additions	$15,352,273
Modernizations	$27,208,060,000
Total	$93,722,670,000

Source: Adapted from Joe Agron, American School and University, Overland Park, Kansas, May 1, 2003. (http://asumag.com/ ar/university_strong_showing_2/)

In addition, lead paint and lead solder in older plumbing joints hold particular health risks for young children. Almost 1 million children ages 1 to 5 have elevated lead levels in their blood.[9] Lead combines with hemoglobin instead of the necessary oxygen, depriving the brain of oxygen and replacing it with lead. This leads to neurological impairments and learning problems. As with radon gas, lead in the environment can be dealt with in a straightforward manner, but cleanup is not without costs.

Poor indoor air quality is another issue facing school facilities. Most recently constructed school buildings were designed to be energy efficient. That is, they were built to avoid letting air-conditioned and heated air (depending on the season) out of the building. When a building is too energy efficient and does not let fresh air into the system, trouble occurs. Today 6.3 million school-aged children suffer from asthma, a number that has been increasing for at least 20 years.[10] Asthma results in students missing more than 14 million school days each year.

Mold is also related to indoor air quality. Molds exist where water and oxygen conditions encourage spore growth. Many molds can trigger allergens causing asthma and other allergic reactions, and molds can produce lethal toxins. The Environmental Protection Agency publishes *Mold Remediation in Schools and Commercial Buildings* to help school officials understand and deal with mold threats in school facilities.[11] Children and many adults are susceptible to the harmful effects of molds, and remediation is a costly and time-consuming process.

---

[9]http://www.epa.gov/lead/leadinfo.htm#health

[10]http://www.epa.gov/iaq/

[11]http://www.epa.gov/mold/intro.html

TABLE 13.4   **APPROXIMATE COST OF PRINCIPAL AND INTEREST**

Construction Cost	Interest Rate	Interest	Total Building Cost
$1,000,000	3%	$517,774	$1,517,774
$1,000,000	4%	$718,694	$1,718,694
$1,000,000	5%	$932,559	$1,932,559
$1,000,000	6%	$1,158,383	$2,158,383

An Interest in Interest

To address these varied health and learning issues, school districts often try to reduce the fiscal impact on the local community by borrowing money from outside sources rather than increasing the tax load for education. Borrowing money for school construction, however, brings an additional expense. If a locality or state borrows funds at 5% interest for 30 years, every $1 million borrowed will cost an additional $932,000—almost doubling the cost of construction. Borrowing the same amount at 3% interest for 30 years increases the total cost of construction by approximately 50%. The total cost of principal and interest at various interest rates is shown in Table 13.4. Unfortunately $1 million does not buy a lot of school building today.

Schools are municipal entities. As such, financing them is a safe investment with certain tax advantages. Safer investments with tax advantages usually bear a lower interest rate than do riskier investments. So one method to reduce interest rates for school construction is to take advantage of this situation through *arbitrage.* Webster defines arbitrage as "purchasing in one market for immediate sale in another at a higher rate." In business the term is relatively well known. In education, however, it is rather obscure. Arbitrage is one way to reduce interest costs in financing school facilities. Table 13.5 shows how it works.

Let's say that the Alpha School District needed $25 million for a new school. The school system or governing authority can issue bonds or certificates for up to $25 million per year. Bonds or Certificates of Participation (COPs) for the municipal project would be drawn up for sale at a rate of 2% interest, free of state taxes, for 30 years. Alpha School District can then invest those proceeds at a higher rate of interest for 18 months and keep the interest difference, or spread.

Here is how a simplification of the arbitrage figures would look. The difference is a little less than half a million dollars. Out of that profit would

TABLE 13.5   ARBITRAGE SIMPLIFICATION

Amount Borrowed	Interest Rate (30 years)	Payments	Total of Payments (18 months)
$25,000,000	2%	$92,404.87	$1,663,287.66

Amount Loaned	Interest Rate (30 years)	Payments Received	Total of Payments (18 months)
$25,000,000	4%	$119,353.82	$2,148,368.76

Net Difference

$485,081.10

come the cost of issuing the bonds or COPs. The amount of money available either to buy down the cost of the building project or add to it depends on the spread of the interest rates. Currently, the limit is $25 million per calendar year. If the building project is larger, one series of bonds (or COPs) could be issued on December 31st and another on January 1st. Issuing two series in close proximity virtually doubles the return.

Some states have public authorities to assist in the arbitrage process. Virginia, for example, has Virginia SNAP (State Non-Arbitrage Program) to assist with such initiatives. Professional advice is essential for effectively using these resources to address school facilities' needs.

FUNDING HUMAN RESOURCES FOR EDUCATION

Public education's largest cost is paying its people for the services they provide. Employee compensation consumes 70 to 80% of school budgets. The purpose of compensation is to attract and retain high-quality staff. Community values and policy decisions about human resources affect this process. When decision makers consider compensation, basic salary schedules, fringe benefits, professional development, and licensure or certification requirements all come into play.

Salary Schedules

In earlier days, professional pay scales for men and women teachers varied. Married heads of households received higher salaries than did single men. Elementary teachers received lower salaries than did high school teachers.

Political affiliation and loyalty frequently were rewarded with teaching, coaching, or administrative jobs. Now virtually all school systems have an objective, structured salary scale. The progress is obvious, but questions concerning salary schedules remain.

The Fair Labor Standards Act was amended to become the Equal Pay Act in 1963. The Equal Pay Act was designed to "eliminate pay or wage discrimination based on sex where equal work, equal skills, and equal effort are performed under the same working conditions."[12] The Equal Pay Act became part of Title VII of the Civil Rights Act of 1964, which outlawed discrimination based on sex, race, color, religion, and national origin.

A typical educator salary scale today is based on years of work experience and earned academic degrees. Many scales provide for a step increase each year for up to 40 years. Stipends are usually provided for graduate degrees. Table 13.6 shows the salary schedule for Lynchburg, Virginia, a medium-sized city in Central Virginia, about 3 hours south of Washington, D.C.

Lynchburg schools compute teacher salaries based on a bachelor's degree, with stipends added to the base salary for master's, specialist's, or doctoral degrees. Under this plan, a teacher with 20 years' experience and a master's degree would earn $43,216.

Three hours to the north, in Fairfax County, Virginia, is a school district with a different approach to teachers' salaries. Fairfax County lies just southwest of the Metropolitan D.C. area and is currently the 10th largest school system in the United States. Table 13.7 shows the salary scale for Fairfax County, Virginia.

It takes 5 fewer years to reach the maximum teacher salary in Fairfax than in Lynchburg. The Fairfax scale is based on a bachelor's degree, a bachelor's degree plus 15 graduate credits or 30 credits, a master's degree, a master's degree plus 30 credits, and the doctorate. A teacher with 20 years' experience and a master's degree in Fairfax County would earn $75,502 compared with Lynchburg's $43,216.

Some salary schedules contain steps that are constant percentage increases. For example, each step on the bachelor's scale would increase by the same percentage. Alternatively, some scales have a constant dollar amount of increase between steps. Making a pay scale decision of this nature has fiscal as well as policy implications. Table 13.8 shows a hypothetical salary scale based on both percentage and dollar step increases and the difference between these two methods.

---

[12]K. Alexander and M. D. Alexander, *American Public School Law*, 5th ed. (Belmont, CA: Wadsworth, 2001), 825.

TABLE 13.6   **LYNCHBURG, VIRGINIA, 2004–05 SALARY SCHEDULE**

Experience Level (years teaching)	Base Salary
0	$31,300
1	31,620
2	32,306
3	32,358
4	32,569
5	32,779
6	33,199
7	33,409
8	33,724
9	33,934
10	34,460
11	34,880
12	35,300
13	35,615
14	36,036
15	36,975
16	38,084
17	38,767
18	39,187
19	39,713
20	40,133
21	40,868
22	41,604
23	42,234
24	42,759
25	43,516
26	44,608
27	53,581
28	53,581
Degree Supplements	
Master's degree	$3,083
Education specialist	4,161
Educational doctorate	4,770

Source: http://www.lynchburg.org/jobs/pay/teacher.htm.

TABLE 13.7   FAIRFAX COUNTY, VIRGINIA, SALARY SCHEDULE, 2004–05

Degree Step	BA	BA +15	BA +30	MA	MA +30	Ph.D.
1	$36,887	$38,251	$39,612	$41,593	$42,213	$45,034
2	37,460	38,825	40,187	42,167	43,786	45,608
3	38,960	40,324	41,687	43,667	45,287	47,108
4	40,516	41,881	43,244	45,223	46,843	48,664
5	42,138	43,503	44,866	46,845	48,465	50,286
6	43,821	45,185	46,548	48,528	50,148	51,969
7	45,576	46,940	48,303	50,282	51,902	53,723
8	47,400	48,764	50,127	52,106	53,726	55,547
9	49,296	50,660	50,023	54,002	55,622	57,443
10	51,070	52,434	53,798	55,777	57,397	59,218
11	52,909	54,273	55,636	57,616	59,235	61,056
12	54,814	56,178	57,541	59,520	61,140	62,961
13	56,787	58,151	59,514	61,493	63,113	64,934
14	58,604	59,968	61,331	63,310	64,930	66,751
15	60,479	61,844	63,207	65,186	66,806	68,627
16	62,415	63,779	65,142	67,121	68,741	70,562
17	64,412	65,776	67,139	69,119	70,738	72,559
18	66,473	67,837	69,201	71,180	72,799	74,621
19	68,600	69,965	71,328	73,307	74,927	76,728
20	70,796	72,160	73,523	75,502	77,122	78,943
Long 1*			74,939	76,918	78,538	80,359
Long 2*			76,383	78,362	79,982	81,803
Long 3*			77,856	79,836	81,455	83,276

Note: * Eligibility for Long 1 (Longevity step) is two years on step 20 plus a BA +30. Eligibility for Long 2 (Longevity step) is two years on step 1. Eligibility for Long 3 (Longevity step) is two years on step 2.

Source: http://www.fcps.k12.va.us/DHR/salary.htm.

The sum of all salaries is virtually the same over 20 years, but those having the $1,500 step increase earn $10,194 more than those with the 3% step increase. The impact for taxpayers is almost identical if all teachers stay in the system for 20 years. Teachers on the 3% step increase make less per year until the 17th year when they earn $188 more per year.

The policy questions are these: What factors does the system wish to reward? and What teacher demographics are most affected by the differences

TABLE 13.8   HYPOTHETICAL SALARY SCALE WITH PERCENTAGE AND DOLLAR INCREASES

Step	3% Step Increase	$1,500 Step Increase	Difference
1	$40,000	$40,000	0
2	41,200	41,500	($300)
3	42,436	43,000	(564)
4	43,709	44,500	(791)
5	45,020	46,000	(980)
6	46,370	47,500	(1,130)
7	47,761	49,000	(1,239)
8	49,194	50,500	(1,306)
9	50,670	52,000	(1,330)
10	52,190	53,500	(1,310)
11	53,756	55,000	(1,244)
12	55,369	56,500	(1,131)
13	57,030	58,000	(970)
14	58,741	59,500	(759)
15	60,503	61,000	(497)
16	62,318	62,500	(182)
17	64,188	64,000	188
18	66,114	65,500	614
19	68,097	67,000	1,097
20	70,140	68,500	1,640
Total after 20 years	$1,074,806	$1,085,000	(10,194)

in salary scales? In the Lynchburg salary scale (Table 13.6), the 1 to 2.5% step increase concept must have been thoughtfully discussed by planners, administrators, school board members, and teacher representatives. Yet why does the step from 26 to 27 involve a 20% increase of almost $9,000? Is there a relationship between teacher longevity and student achievement, or does loyalty itself deserve a reward? Why did Fairfax County (Table 13.7) decide on five graduate credit stipends instead of one larger stipend for the completed degree? Could the planners' and teachers' intention be to foster teacher motivation for further graduate study by providing a financial incentive to do so?

Salary schedules show what the school district culture values and rewards. In education, salaries show how much the community appreciates its teachers. Educational policy makers and planners must visit these ideas. Nationally, the years of experience for U.S. teachers are as follows:[13]

- Less than 3 years   12.9%
- 3–9 years   28.8%
- 10–20 years   28.5%
- More than 20 years   29.8%

As you can see, the greatest percentage of the teaching force has more than 20 years of full-time teaching experience. But keep in mind that these figures are exacerbated by the fact that up to 50% of all new teachers leave the profession in the first 5 years of teaching. To attract teachers in sufficient numbers to replace those eligible to retire, incentives must be sufficient to draw young, talented, mature people into the field.

In a business where 70 to 80% of all expenditures are salaries, it is vital to know how the funds should be best expended. Does the salary structure attract and retain the highest quality educators? What does the salary schedule reward? Finally, who should the salary schedule reward? Each community and school district must thoughtfully consider these demographic and fiscal issues as they design their salary packages.

Salary schedules are the product of a political process. Former President Clinton says in his book, *My Life*, "You can have a good policy without good politics, but you can't give people good government without both."[14] A salary structure may have the best goals and foster the best policy for attracting and retaining quality people, but it will not succeed without involving those whom the schedule affects. Gaining their understanding and agreement is a political necessity.

Interstate Salary Trends

Salary trends among the states for 2001 are shown in Table 13.9. Column 2 reports average salary and state ranking. Some states report retirement benefits as a part of the salary, others report health benefits in salary figures, and some report estimated average salaries. The average salary of all 50 states and the District of Columbia is $43,250. Column 3 shows each state's average salary as a percentage of the national average of $43,250. For example, Alabama's salary of $37,606 is 87% of the national average. Column 4 lists each state's average beginning salary along with its relative national ranking.

---

[13]Adapted from http://nces.ed.gov/programs/digest/d02/tables/dt069.asp, table 69.
[14]William Jefferson Clinton, *My Life* (New York: Knopf, 2004), 268.

TABLE 13.9   INTERSTATE TEACHER SALARY COMPARISONS 2001

State	Average Salary (rank)	Average Teacher Salary as a % of the U.S. Average (rank)	Average Beginning Salary (rank)	Average Salary Adjusted by Cost of Living Index (adjusted rank)	Teacher Salaries as a % of State Education Expenses (rank)
Alabama	$37,606 (31)	87.0% (31)	$28,649 (19)	$41,325 (23)	41.2% (8)
Alaska	$48,123 (9)	111.3% (9)	$36,293 (1)	$39,124 (32)	31.9% (48)
Arizona	$36,502 (35)	84.4% (35)	$26,801 (27)	$38,044 (36)	38.2% (18)
Arkansas	$34,729 (42)	80.3% (42)	$24,469 (44)	$38,980 (33)	42.7% (3)
California	$52,480 (2)	121.3% (2)	$33,121 (2)	$43,061 (16)	40.3% (12)
Colorado	$39,184 (25)	90.6% (25)	$26,479 (28)	$36,241 (41)	37.4% (25)
Connecticut	$53,507 (1)	123.7% (1)	$32,203 (5)	$49,244 (4)	39.9% (13)
Delaware	$47,047 (12)	108.8% (12)	$32,281 (4)	$48,492 (6)	35.1% (36)
Florida	$38,230 (29)	88.4% (29)	$25,786 (36)	$40,604 (26)	35.1% (36)
Georgia	$42,141 (20)	97.4% (20)	$31,314 (7)	$44,919 (12)	42.2% (4)
Hawaii	$40,536 (23)	93.7% (23)	$29,204 (18)	$30,899 (51)	37.1% (29)
Idaho	$37,109 (33)	85.8% (33)	$23,386 (47)	$39,560 (29)	39.0% (16)
Illinois	$47,865 (10)	110.7% (10)	$31,222 (8)	$48,275 (7)	41.9% (6)
Indiana	$43,000 (16)	99.4% (16)	$27,311 (23)	$46,516 (10)	33.5% (44)
Iowa	$36,479 (36)	84.3% (36)	$26,058 (33)	$39,591 (28)	37.4% (26)
Kansas	$35,766 (40)	82.7% (40)	$26,010 (34)	$38,830 (34)	37.0% (30)
Kentucky	$36,688 (34)	84.8% (34)	$25,027 (37)	$40,299 (27)	35.1% (35)
Louisiana	$33,615 (45)	77.7% (45)	$26,124 (32)	$35,919 (43)	38.1% (19)
Maine	$36,373 (38)	84.1% (38)	$23,689 (46)	$36,678 (39)	37.8% (20)
Maryland	$45,963 (13)	106.3% (13)	$30,321 (12)	$45,548 (11)	37.2% (28)
Massachusetts	$47,789 (11)	110.5% (11)	$31,115 (10)	$41,773 (22)	42.0% (5)
Michigan	$50,515 (5)	116.8% (5)	$29,401 (16)	$51,868 (2)	35.0% (38)
Minnesota	$42,212 (18)	97.6% (18)	$27,003 (26)	$42,677 (18)	33.0% (45)
Mississippi	$31,954 (49)	73.9% (49)	$23,292 (48)	$35,652 (45)	37.3% (27)
Missouri	$35,091 (41)	81.1% (41)	$27,173 (25)	$37,712 (37)	41.7% (7)
Montana	$33,249 (47)	76.9% (47)	$21,728 (50)	$33,975 (48)	34.4% (40)
Nebraska	$34,258 (44)	79.2% (44)	$24,356 (45)	$36,967 (38)	35.5% (34)
Nevada	$44,234 (15)	102.3% (15)	$29,413 (15)	$47,384 (9)	41.1% (9)
New Hampshire	$38,301 (27)	88.6% (27)	$25,020 (38)	$36,077 (42)	34.9% (39)
New Jersey	$51,955 (3)	120.1% (3)	$30,937 (11)	$49,173 (5)	36.2% (32)
New Mexico	$33,531 (46)	77.5% (46)	$25,999 (35)	$34,873 (46)	32.9% (46)
New York	$51,020 (4)	118.0% (4)	$32,772 (3)	$47,681 (8)	38.7% (17)

TABLE 13.9   **CONTINUED**

State	Average Salary (rank)	Average Teacher Salary as a % of the U.S. Average (rank)	Average Beginning Salary (rank)	Average Salary Adjusted by Cost of Living Index` (adjusted rank)	Teacher Salaries as a % of State Education Expenses (rank)
North Carolina	$41,496 (21)	95.9% (21)	$29,786 (14)	$44,559 (13)	43.7% (1)
North Dakota	$30,891 (50)	71.4% (50)	$20,675 (51)	$33,437 (49)	29.5% (51)
Ohio	$42,892 (17)	99.2% (17)	$24,894 (39)	$44,495 (14)	39.1% (15)
Oklahoma	$32,545 (48)	75.2% (48)	$27,016 (25)	$36,261 (40)	36.9% (31)
Oregon	$44,988 (14)	104.0% (14)	$27,903 (22)	$43,424 (15)	31.2% (49)
Pennsylvania	$49,528 (7)	114.5% (7)	$31,127 (9)	$52,832 (1)	37.7% (23)
Rhode Island	$50,400 (6)	116.5% (6)	$29,265 (17)	$51,042 (3)	37.7% (21)
South Carolina	$37,938 (30)	87.7% (30)	$26,314 (29)	$40,808 (25)	39.5% (14)
South Dakota	$30,265 (51)	70.0% (51)	$22,457 (49)	$33,020 (50)	35.9% (33)
Tennessee	$37,413 (32)	86.5% (32)	$28,074 (21)	$40,888 (24)	41.1% (10)
Texas	$38,359 (26)	88.7% (26)	$29,823 (13)	$42,444 (20)	40.9% (11)
Utah	$36,441 (37)	84.3% (37)	$24,553 (43)	$35,824 (44)	37.7% (22)
Vermont	$38,254 (28)	88.4% (28)	$26,152 (31)	$38,279 (35)	37.6% (24)
Virginia	$40,247 (24)	93.1% (24)	$28,139 (20)	$42,194 (21)	43.1% (2)
Washington	$42,143 (19)	97.4% (19)	$27,284 (24)	$39,276 (31)	32.9% (47)
West Virginia	$35,888 (39)	83.0% (39)	$24,889 (40)	$39,554 (30)	33.8% (42)
Wisconsin	$40,939 (22)	94.7% (22)	$26,232 (30)	$42,469 (19)	34.2% (41)
Wyoming	$34,678 (43)	80.2% (43)	$24,651 (41)	$34,779 (47)	33.7% (43)
District of Columbia	$48,488 (8)	112.1% (8)	$31,889 (6)	$42,758 (17)	30.0% (50)
U.S. Average	$43,250	$43,250	$43,250	$43,250	38.4%

Source: Data compiled from various sources within the AFT Survey and Analysis of Teacher Salary Trends, 2001, the latest data available (http://www.aft.org/salary/ 2001/download/salarysurvey01.pdf).

The average teacher salary adjusted by the cost of living index for the state is shown in column 5. For example, Alabama has a cost of living index of 91.0, which is below the national average. Using that figure as an index, the salary is adjusted upward by $3,719 for a total of adjusted salary of $41,325, which reflects this increased purchasing power. Alabama's average salary rank was 31, but its moves up to 23 when the cost of living index is considered.

Column 6 lists teacher salaries as a percentage of the total public school expenditures for the state. This percentage has declined in every state since the 1964–65 school year, and the average decline of teacher salaries as a percentage of total state education expenditures for public education has been 15%. North Dakota has had the largest percentage decline in that time frame of 28.7 percentage points and New York has had the smallest decline of 9.4 percentage points.

These salary trends are important in attracting and retaining high-quality teachers. States that do not keep their salaries competitive will have difficulty employing excellent teachers—and increasing student achievement. For example, South Dakota has an average teacher salary of $30,265, the lowest of those states in the Plains region. The three contiguous state average salaries, compared with South Dakota, are all higher—Nebraska by $3,993, Iowa by $6,214, and Minnesota by $11,947. Even when adjusted for cost of living, all three remain higher—Nebraska by $3,947, Iowa by $6,571, and Minnesota by $9,657. If a high-quality teacher with experience raising student achievement is moving to the upper Midwest, where will he or she most likely look for employment?

The salary issue places policy concerns before each state legislature and locality. Paying higher teacher salaries alone is not sufficient, however, for increasing student achievement. Darling-Hammond points out that linking higher salaries with increased teacher education and licensing standards can make a positive gain in student achievement.[15] States that have invested in higher salaries linked with intensive recruitment efforts to improve preservice teacher education programs, strong licensing requirements, beginning teacher mentoring, and ongoing professional development show gains in student achievement over states where these initiatives are not carried out.

Licensing and Certification

Licensing and certification are teacher quality issues. Licensure and certification are a state's method for approving teachers for professional practice.[16] Certification serves as a professional benchmark for teacher quality. All 50 states have a teacher certification process. When facing teacher shortages, however, some states have decided that it is faster and less expensive to change the certification requirements than to raise teacher salaries to attract more high-quality candidates. Alternative certification usually shortens the traditional pathway into the classroom by reducing or eliminating required professional courses and internship hours.

---

[15]L. Darling-Hammond, "Teacher Quality and Student Achievement: A Review of State Policy Evidence." *Education Policy Analysis Archives,* 8 (1), January 2000. (http://epaa.asu.edu/epaa/v8n1/ index.html#note1)

[16]Frequently the terms *licensure* and *certification* are used interchangeably. For the purpose of this text, we will use the term *certification.*

Current standards for "highly qualified teachers" in the NCLB legislation include the following requirements:

- Bachelor's degree
- Full state certification or licensure
- Proof that teachers know the subjects they will teach

States must show the extent to which all students have highly qualified teachers. Although the first two requirements are clear, proof of subject matter competence can be demonstrated in a number of ways:

- A college major in the subject
- Credits equivalent to a major in the subject
- Passing score on a state-developed test to measure knowledge
- Demonstrating high, objective, uniform state standard of evaluation (HOUSSE) by some state-approved combination of teaching experience, professional development, and knowledge gained in the subject over time in the profession

NCLB's definition of a highly qualified teacher allows states to determine what "highly qualified" means. States may make this professional determination based on efficiency rather than effectiveness, on politics rather than professional standards, or on expediency and cost issues rather than on what is best for either student learning or cost effectiveness in the long run. This would be an unintended and unfortunate consequence.

All 50 states recognize the National Board of Professional Teaching Standards (NBPTS) rigorous professional certification process, and many states provide additional monetary incentives to NBPTS certification holders.[17] Recent research findings from three national studies demonstrate that elementary grade students working with teachers holding National Board Certification outperform peers whose teachers are not certified on standardized achievement tests in reading, math, and language arts.[18] A study of

---

[17]For more information on NBPTS, see http://www.nbpts.org/.

[18]L. Bond, T. Smith, W. Baker, and J. Hattie, *The Certification System of the National Board for Professional Teaching Standards: A Construct and Consequential Validity Study* (Greensboro, NC: University of North Carolina at Greensboro, Center for Educational Research and Evaluation, 2000); and L. G. Vandevoort, A. Amrein-Beardsley, and D. C. Berliner, "National Board Certified Teachers and Their Students' Achievement." *Education Policy Analysis Archives, 12* (46), September 8, 2004; and D. Goldhaber and E. Anthony, *Can Teacher Quality Be Effectively Assessed?* (Seattle, WA: Center on Reinventing Public Education, University of Washington, 2004).

Arizona's National Board Certified teachers (NBCT) found that this certification influenced student achievement in a positive direction.[19] Policy questions are as follows: Should schools pay higher salaries to those who hold NBPTS certification? How can school districts place more board certified teachers in high-needs schools? What action should be taken for those who do not have appropriate certification for the jobs they now hold?

North Carolina has supported NBPTS efforts by reimbursing teachers for application fees and providing a 12% salary increase upon successful certification. As a result, North Carolina has the highest concentration of NBPTS certified teachers in the nation at an annual cost of $25 million.[20] The question is not if, but "How big of a stipend should states pay their NBCTs who we now know demonstrate excellence in the performance of their duties . . . and whose teaching yields significantly higher productivity?"[21]

Linking higher salaries to higher levels of licensure and certification are policy issues that pay off in student achievement. States and localities would do well to consider these issues before adopting relaxed licensure and certification requirements in times of teacher shortages.

Benefits

The Bureau of Labor Statistics defines "benefits" as non–wage compensation provided to employees.[22] Typically, these benefits fall into the five categories shown in Table 13.10. Paid leave includes sick leave, vacations, and holidays. Supplementary pay includes overtime pay for work on holidays, weekends, or hours beyond 40 per week. Retirement pay includes both defined benefit and defined contribution plans. A defined benefit is the amount the organization promises to pay as part of the retirement plan. A defined contribution is the amount the organization promises to pay as a match into a retirement annuity, for example. Insurance benefits include life, health, and disability. And finally, some benefits are legally required of the employer, such as Social Security, workers' compensation, and federal and state unemployment taxes.

---

[19]Ibid., 37.

[20]Vandevoort, Amrein-Beardsley, and Berliner, "National Board Certified Teachers and Their Students' Achievement," 18.

[21]Ibid.

[22]www.bls.gov/bls/glossary.htm

TABLE 13.10 TYPES OF BENEFITS

Paid leave	Sick leave	Most school systems provide sick leave and sick leave accrual for employees.
	Vacation	Vacation leave is usually associated with 12-month contract employees.
	Holidays	Paid holidays are not usually figured into pay although they may be seen as a benefit.
Supplementary pay	Overtime	Governed by the Fair Labor Standards Act, new refinements may have implications for extracurricular activities and stipends and for educational support personnel.
Retirement	Defined benefit	Usually associated with what the school system will provide for employees upon retirement. May cover health insurance, prescription drugs, vision care, dental care, and so forth. Defined benefits may be reduced over time in many states.
	Defined contribution	Usually associated with the contributions the school system will make for the employee for retirement. May include matching percentages into a tax-sheltered annuity or contributions to the state retirement system.
Insurance	Life	Provided in most states as a percentage of annual salary. This is a relatively inexpensive benefit.
	Health	An increasingly expensive benefit for employers as health care costs rise. Trends include increasing deductibles, copayments for physicians, and prescription drug plans.
	Disability	Provided in most states to educators as a part of the state retirement provisions.
Legally required	Social Security	Employer and employee pay 7.65% each for a total of 15.3% of salary up to a level of $90,000.
	Workers' compensation	Usually required by state to provide for risks of employment. Not required in all states.
	Unemployment insurance	Usually required by state to provide for risks of employment. Benefits vary from state to state.

Benefits rank second only to salary and good working conditions in motivating employees to work to high levels.[23] Benefits are important to employees because they are not taxed, and they provide services that employees would not or could not provide for themselves without employer assistance. The benefits provided to educators vary widely across the United States.

The U.S. Department of Labor's Bureau of Labor Statistics 2004 statement reports an average hourly salary for public school teachers of $33.47.[24] Fringe benefits total $11.61 per hour, for a total hourly compensation of $45.08. Benefits are not included in the paycheck; if the hourly wage of $33.47 is calculated for 40 hours per week for 40 weeks, the average annual teacher salary would be $53,552.[25] Furthermore, fringe benefits total almost 35% of total wages and salaries. Retirement costs account for employers' largest benefit cost, and health insurance is the second largest cost.[26]

In addition, employers are legally required to pay Social Security benefits, known as FICA (Federal Insurance Contributions Act), and workers' compensation programs are required in most states to insure risk from injuries sustained during employment. The cost of these programs varies and may depend on an incidence rate over time. The last legally required benefit, unemployment insurance, pays a stipend for a defined period of time to workers who lose their jobs. A school district's employees, therefore, cost their employers much more than their salaries.

Retirement benefits also vary widely. For example, North Carolina provides fully paid health insurance benefits for retired teachers after only 5 years of service. Some districts allow retired employees to purchase health insurance at the full rate plan; others do not provide this service after the defined COBRA period of severance ends in an effort to keep insurance costs low as determined from experience rates. The area of employer-sponsored health benefits is becoming one of the most difficult in school finance.

---

[23]V. Brimley and R. Garfield, *Financing Education in a Climate of Change,* 6th ed. (Boston: Pearson, 2005), 389.

[24]http://www.bls.gov/news.release/ecec.t04.htm

[25]http://www.educationnext.org/20033/71.html, p. 1. Teacher salary was calculated at less than 38 hours per week. We all know that teachers spend additional time grading papers, planning lessons, and contacting parents. According to the American Federation of Teachers' study, the average annual teacher salary was $43,250. This possibly explains the variance in salary calculations.

[26]Ibid.

Health Care

Providing health care benefits is emerging as a critical and contentious factor in school finance. In 2004 workers' health care premiums in 35 states rose at least 3 times faster than their earnings, despite reductions in coverage.[27] The U.S. health care industry has placed substantial economic pressure on all employers, including school systems, that make fringe benefits available to employees. As a result, educators' insurance programs increasingly want to reduce benefits, increase copayments, and limit the number of "family" members eligible to receive these expensive compensations. Unless school divisions place limits on benefits, the financial burden threatens to overwhelm available resources.

Nationwide, workers' costs for employer-sponsored health insurance have risen by 36 percent since 2000, overshadowing the average 12.4 percent earnings increase. Employee contributions have increased 57% since 2001 for individual coverage and 49% for family coverage.[28] Employer-sponsored insurance premiums jumped 11.2% in 2004.[29] In addition, employers estimate that health care costs will rise almost 13% on average each year if they make no changes in their health plans.[30] Recently, a survey of 900 businesses by Mercer Human Resource Consulting projects a 9.6% increase in health care spending per employee in 2005—4 times the rate of general inflation.[31] A disturbing interrelated trend results as costs rise and coverage falls. Decreased coverage and the resulting shifting of costs to the insured increases the pressure on the entire system's ability to deliver high-quality care.

Likewise, from 1965 to 1990 the total costs of hospitalization increased more than 350%, even after controlling for general inflation. During the same period, physicians' payments increased almost 250%, and costs for dentists, drugs, appliances, and vision care went up 150 to 200%. In the same time period, the real gross national product rose by 94%.[32]

---

[27]D. Colaiacova, "Health Care: Are You Better Off?" The Civil Rights Coalition for the 21st Century, www.civilrights.org/issues/labor/deteails.cfm?id=25306, September 28, 2004.

[28]L. B. Benko, "Cost of Coverage: Premiums on the Rise by an Average of 11.2%: Kaiser Study." *Modern Healthcare*, 34 (36), September 13, 2004: 8.

[29]C. Connolly, "Higher Costs, Less Care. Data Shows Crisis in Health Insurance." *Washington Post*, September 28, 2004: A 01.

[30]A. N. Crenshaw, "Health Insurance Costs Keep Rising. Premiums for Employer-Sponsored Plans Grew by 11.2%, Survey Finds." *Washington Post*, September 10, 2004: E 01.

[31]Connolly, "Higher Costs, Less Care."

[32]S. Liebowitz, "Policy Analysis. Why Health Care Costs Too Much." Cato Policy Analysis No. 211, www.cato.org/pubs/pas/pa211.html, 2004.

As a result, workers' average monthly contributions to premiums for family coverage have more than quadrupled, rising from $52 in 1988 to $222 in 2004.[33] The current health insurance cost for a typical family of four is more than $10,000. Family health costs have increased at 5 times the rate of inflation[34] and 3 times faster than average earnings in the past 4 years.[35] Today's family health insurance premium represents 21% of the national median household income.[36]

Employers are urgently seeking ways to manage their employees' health care costs. Many companies are dropping medical coverage entirely or trimming their benefits packages.[37] From 2001 to 2004, the proportion of workers and their dependents receiving health coverage through an employer fell from 65% to 61% and continues dropping—5 million fewer jobs provide health benefits.[38] Other employers are sharing more of the expense with employees through larger payroll contributions or higher out-of-pocket expenses. In a recent survey of nearly 200 major national employers, 80% said they planned to increase copayments or cost sharing compared with 65% who answered that way in 2001. If employers reduce their contributions to premiums, however, many workers will drop their health insurance because they will not be able to afford their share of the higher premiums.

Increased health care costs result from traditional and demographic factors, including patients' overuse of medical resources because they do not pay the full costs, administrative and paperwork costs of overseeing the provision of health care, and the fear of malpractice suits that lead doctors and hospitals to administer medically unnecessary tests and procedures to insulate them from litigious patients or relatives. The medical needs and demands of 77 million baby boomers, the escalating prices of prescription drugs, and consumer expectations for easier and broader access to care also increase health care costs.[39]

---

[33]National Coalition on Health Care, "Health Insurance Cost," www.nchc.org/facts/cost.shtml, 2004.

[34]Ibid.

[35]W. M. Welch, "Health Costs Rising Faster Than Incomes, Study Says." *USA Today,* September 27, 2004.

[36]National Coalition on Health Care, "Health Insurance Cost."

[37]B. Martinez, "As Health Costs Increase, Workers Must Pay More," *Wall Street Journal,* June 16, 2003: 1.

[38]Connolly, "Higher Costs, Less Care."

[39]J. E. Miller, *Deja Vu All Over Again: The Soaring Cost of Private Health Insurance and Its Impact on Consumers and Employers* (Washington, DC: National Coalition on Health Care, May 2000).

In addition, Wall Street pressure on for-profit health plans to raise premiums to increase profits also plays an important role.[40] HMOs showed combined net profits of $10.2 billion in 2003, up 87% from $5.5 billion in 2002, and 345% from $2.3 billion in 2000. Blue Cross and Blue Shield plans alone saw their total profits reach $5.4 billion in 2003, up 63% from 2002, and 164% from 2000.[41]

Furthermore, the underwriting cycle affects health insurance prices. During the fall underwriting cycle, insurers compete aggressively for market share, but this is followed by an increase in prices as insurers attempt to recover lost profits. Currently, a longer and deeper insurance underwriting cycle is increasing costs.[42]

Patients overuse medical resources because of increased third-party payments (insurance companies and government). A RAND Corporation study in the late 1970s investigated the relationship between coinsurance rates and 2,500 families' use of medical resources for 3 to 5 years and found pronounced changes in the use of medical resources depending on the extent of third-party payments.[43] Families with no copayments used 53% more hospital services and 63% more doctor visits, drugs, and other medical services than did families who paid 95% copayments. Overall, the total use of medical resources was 58% greater for the group who had no copayments. The study notes that consumers do not begin to overuse medical resources seriously until they pay less than half the cost, and the high costs associated with excessive use of medical resources do not materially improve the health of those receiving that care.

In 1990 third parties paid 77 cents of each medical expense dollar. Because patients pay an average of only 23 cents on each medical expense dollar, only a weak linkage exists between the consumer's use of medical resources and the consumer's medical payments. Medical resources appear to be free or almost free. Because patients pay so little of their own health care costs, it seems rational for them to consume medical services even when the value of those medical services is less than the value of the resources used to provide them. As a result, consumers lose their incentive to economize on their use of medical resources.

No single solution exists to medical care's high price, and policy makers disagree on the best ways to address these serious problems. Policy analysts

---

[40]Ibid.

[41]Benko, "Cost of Coverage."

[42]Ibid.

[43]For more information, see Liebowitz, "Policy Analysis. Why Health Care Costs Too Much."

believe patients need to again become the central actors in the medical marketplace. That is, they need to be given the same motivation to economize on medical care that they have to economize in other markets. Consumers cannot buy a Cadillac health care program on a Chevrolet's willingness to pay, and increasingly low medical copayments lull medical consumers into a false, and wasteful, sense of economy.[44]

As health care insurance costs to employers increases, school districts look for economically viable ways to respond: significantly reduce benefits, significantly increase patient costs (premiums, deductibles, copayments, and changing out-of-pocket limits), slow salary growth, limit hiring, increase outsourcing, or drop insurance coverage altogether. Some employers plan to levy surcharges in 2005 on employees who sign up for family benefits when their spouse is eligible for health coverage through a separate job.[45] Cost shifting to employees is inevitable as employers redesign their benefits packages to protect their "financial exposure."

Same-Sex Benefits

One of today's most contentious human resources issues involves "domestic partner benefits." This controversy has significant economic aspects. Because health care benefits—including medical, dental, and vision coverage—are an increasingly important part of employees' compensation and because such benefits are usually only available to spouses and family members, homosexual employees believe they are undercompensated unless they receive similar benefits for a designated "domestic partner."

A few states, cities, and major companies provide domestic partner benefits to their employees. California is leading the United States in instituting protections for gay and lesbian couples without a court mandate. In Hawaii and Vermont, state courts compelled legislatures to extend equal benefits to same-sex couples. Religious groups and social conservatives who believe this policy constitutes a social endorsement of homosexuality as an acceptable alternative lifestyle actively oppose this trend. Congress recently rejected a provision that would have banned the establishment of domestic partner health benefits for workers in the District of Columbia. The domestic partner concept has recently been expanded in California to include

---

[44]Ibid.

[45]Welch, "Health Costs Rising Faster Than Incomes."

many governmental rights normally provided to spouses. Nevertheless, public opinion has shifted to the extent that most Americans support domestic partner benefits.

At present, most public school districts do not offer benefits to same-sex couples. Exceptions, however, exist. For example, the Chicago Public Schools has provided same-sex health benefits for many years.[46] Similarly, a number of larger high school districts in Illinois provide health coverage for same-sex employees. Brookline also extends this benefit to same-sex partners, but Massachusetts law does not require same-sex benefits. And the Thomas More Law Center sued the Ann Arbor Public School District, claiming the district violated state law by giving its employees same-sex health benefits.[47]

Public universities appear more willing to provide health benefits to same-sex partners. For example, three of Ohio's four publicly supported universities recently announced that they would offer full paid benefits, including health and dental care and free tuition, to their employees' same-sex domestic partners.[48] Ohio's recently enacted ban on same-sex marriage does not forbid the 13 state-sponsored universities and two medical schools from extending financial benefits such as health insurance to its employees' unmarried domestic partners. Another state where a public university extends insurance benefits to same-sex partners is Michigan (Wayne State University).

The issue of providing benefits to same-sex partners remains controversial and will likely be a source of active discussion and litigation for many years. "Marriage" is traditionally considered a religious commitment whereas "civil unions" are considered secular, although the term "marriage" is popularly used to describe both. When the courts carefully separate religion and government practices, the ban on same-sex insurance benefits may be clearly seen as a religious rather than a civic objection, and school human resources practices will adjust. The sharply escalating and burdensome health care costs to school districts for employees, however, may make the move toward same-sex partner benefits moot.

---

[46]M. Kiefer, "Benefits for Same Sex Partners Are Turned Down by District 214." *The Journal & Topics Newspapers*, www.journal-topics.com/ph/04/ph040901.7.html, September 1, 2004.

[47]"Schools Sued over Same-Sex Benefits," *Michigan News*, www.freep.com/news/mich/part23_20030923.htm, September 23, 2003.

[48]G. McClanahan, "Benefits for Same-Sex Partners," *WTAP News*, http://www.wtap.com/news/headlines/85827.html, September 19, 2004.

MEASURING STUDENT ACHIEVEMENT

The Bush administration's No Child Left Behind Act requires stringent accountability for student achievement.[49] Some of the requirements are that states develop approved student achievement testing programs, that schools make adequate yearly progress toward 100% of their students passing those tests by school year 2013–14, and that highly qualified teachers be placed in every classroom by 2005–06. Compliance failure involves various sanctions for schools and transfer opportunities for students.

The dollar cost of implementing NCLB may be higher than most have calculated. The NCLB implementation costs for states and localities have not been fully researched. Ohio, Minnesota, and New Hampshire have studied the implementation costs. Ohio alone estimates the outlay to be as high as $1.447 billion in addition to the already existing programs for its 1.8 million students.[50] That amounts to an additional expense in Ohio of more than $800 per student per year. Additional expenditures and financial sanctions face failing schools: Should failing schools be reconstituted, closed, or punished financially? or Should they be provided with additional resources and support? These policy issues must be discussed.

Opening an innovative dialogue, Stiefel and Schwartz have examined the idea of academic achievement standards and consequences from a financial efficiency—rather than sanctions—perspective.[51] They posit that examining efficiency with student performance data is the key to resource distribution for troubled schools. Efficiency is defined as using the resources in a manner that maximizes student achievement outputs. Using production function studies, a dual metric graphic using academic performance and efficiency describes four types of schools.

High-performing, efficient schools would be left alone to serve as models. They are using their resources wisely to gain maximum student achievement for dollars spent. High-performing, inefficient schools would be required either to increase achievement or to give up some of the financial or support services. Low-performing, efficient schools would be given

---

[49]For more information on NCLB, see http://www.ed.gov/nclb/landing.jhtml?src=pb and the Education Commission of the States report at http://nclb2.ecs.org/Projects_Centers/index.aspx?issueid=gen&IssueName=General.

[50]http://www.ode.state.oh.us/legislator/COST_OF_NCLB/COST%20OF%20IMPLEMENTING%20NCLB-012104.pdf

[51]L. Stiefel and A. Schwartz, "Efficiency: The Missing Metric." *Education Week*, 24 (2), September 8, 2004: 42.

additional resources. They are using their fiscal resources well but need additional funds to support even higher student achievement. Finally, low-performing, inefficient schools would be reconstituted. They are making poor fiscal and instructional decisions and have little to show for their spending. If schools were distributed evenly across these four quadrants, the cost of implementing NCLB from an efficiency metric would reduce the overall implementation costs. Such an approach might save even more from a financial standpoint in terms of human resource costs and public relations capital to correct problems.

Regardless of the approach used, NCLB's overall additional cost to localities, states, and the nation must be considered. If the $800 additional cost per pupil in Ohio is typical of expenditure for other states, the expenses would be staggering. According to the U.S. Census Bureau, 53.8 million students enrolled in school for the 2004-05 school year.[52] At an additional $800 per pupil, the additional cost to education would be $43,040,000,000 each year.

EMERGING ISSUES

It is difficult to predict the future. Presidential elections come every four Novembers and can redirect the flow of events. However, predict we must. Voucher programs and federal, state, and local support for public education are areas of concern that could reshape public education and public school finance in the coming years. Let's look at each of these areas in more detail.

Vouchers

As NCLB legislation currently stands, parents of the lowest scoring students attending schools that have not made adequate yearly progress over time may request vouchers to attend other schools—private, parochial, or public. Additionally, the local school system would be responsible for providing transportation for those students.

Vouchers have been a political battle cry for opposing sides since Milton Friedman first proposed them in 1955.[53] Using vouchers or public

---

[52]http://www.census.gov/Press-Release/www/releases/archives/facts_for_features_special_editions/002263.html

[53]M. Friedman, "The Role of Government in Education." In *Economics and the Public Interest*, Robert Solo, ed. (New Brunswick, NJ: Rutgers University Press, 1955), pp. 127–128.

school monies for students to attend private, parochial schools was addressed by the U.S. Supreme Court in June 2002 when it ruled 5–4 in favor of Cleveland's program in the *Zelman* case.[54] Many commentators took a broad-brush approach in describing the impact of this decision. Newspapers declared that the Supreme Court had approved vouchers.

The Supreme Court was asked to determine if the voucher program established to help parents with children in failing Cleveland schools, known as CSTP (Cleveland's Scholarship and Tutoring Program), violated the First Amendment's Establishment clause. Basically, the program provided alternatives of attending private schools and tutoring to the lowest scoring students with certain income limitations. In August 1999 a federal district court rejected the program as favoring religion, therefore, violating the Constitution. In September 2001 the United States Supreme Court agreed to review the case's constitutionality. On June 27, 2002, the Court ruled that CSTP "is a program of true private choice . . . neutral in all aspects to religion." In this decision, the Court leaned toward approving privatization in education with First Amendment protections. Privatization is a continuum ranging from totally secular to completely religious, and the Court found that, in this case, vouchers fell at an acceptable place on that expanse. The essential separation of church and state, however, will prevail. In addition, the few people interested in voucher plans will keep this political topic alive for debate.

Following the *Zelman* ruling, Florida tried to enact its own voucher law. A Florida appeals court ruled on August 16, 2004, that this voucher law was unconstitutional in that it violated state constitutional provisions by providing funds to private, sectarian schools. The Florida Supreme Court is scheduled to hear arguments on June 7, 2005.[55] If the Florida voucher law passes, voters will have to amend Florida's state constitution.

A 2004 PDK/Gallup poll shows the public opposes vouchers by 54% to 42% (with 4% who "do not know"). With that level of public sentiment opposing vouchers, it is unlikely that legislation will pass to support such court rulings. In fact, Gerald Bracey writes that "People predicted that the *Zelman* decision would open the sluices for a flood of state voucher programs. But vouchers continued to be a nonevent."[56] Nevertheless, any program that would take monies out of public education must be of concern to all educators now and in the future.

---

[54]*Zelman v. Simmon-Harris,* 000 U.S. 00-1751 (2002).

[55]http://www.macon.com/mld/miamiherald/news/breaking news/11316604.htm

[56]G. Bracey, "The 14th Bracey Report on the Condition of Public Education." *Phi Delta Kappan,* 86 (2), 2004: 149.

Federal Support for Education

As discussed in previous chapters, schools have only four funding sources: federal, state, and local taxes and grants. Funding at all three levels of government has remained fairly constant over the past 30 years. Federal revenue has been flat with some downturn in the early 1980s. State revenue has had a moderate positive slope, and local revenue has had a somewhat negative slope (see Chapter 11, Figure 11.1).

Without a major alteration in Washington's political makeup, no major changes in federal education funding appear imminent. Federal politicians seem content to let the states bear the major burden of funding schools. Overall spending cuts to provide tax cuts may mean that long-standing programs become subject to "recissions."[57] Funds will likely be shifted or eliminated from other programs and placed in ESEA funding.

This fiscal activity will produce the appearance of increased federal funding, but it is a shell game. If $1 million is cut from Program A and moved to Program B, the net change is zero. One politician is likely to say, however, that funding for Program B was increased by $1 million. Another politician is likely to say that funding for Program A was cut by $1 million. All three statements are correct. Two are misleading.

Federal interest in standards and accountability will remain for the foreseeable future, but it is unlikely that federal funding will match the rhetoric. The public at large favors accountability without noticing that educators are being asked to make bricks without straw.

State Support for Education

The primary responsibility for funding education lies with the state. As such, states have to pay larger and larger percentages of their education budgets toward NCLB accountability—especially as federal revenue remains flat or declines slightly. Increasing revenue for education will cause political and financial problems in low-capacity, low-effort states with a history of not supporting education.

Moreover, 20 states began legal contests at the state supreme court level in 2004 regarding their funding formulae.[58] This assigns to the courts what

---

[57]The term "recission" was used by Newt Gingrich and the Republican's Contract with America as a euphemism for cutting programs and services.

[58]Plaintiffs lost at the state supreme court level but still have complaints without final determination in Alaska, Colorado, Florida, Idaho, Kansas, Maryland, Minnesota, North Carolina, and Pennsylvania. Decisions are still pending on cases in Delaware, Hawaii, Indiana, Iowa, Mississippi, Missouri, Nevada, New Mexico, South Dakota, and Utah.

politicians should have been doing for the public welfare. This legislative tactic to increase state funding on adequacy issues in the courts appears to be a back door approach to finding increased state revenue. These partisan state politics may well increase as federal dollars remain flat and accountability levels increase.

Education associations (at the local, state, and national levels), educators, administrators, and higher education personnel need to work for a unified method to increase funding for the good of all students. Public education supporters, teachers, and association representatives must avoid divide and conquer strategies that fragment the support base for increased education funding. Unfortunately, divide and conquer strategies are increasingly visible at the state level. Bills to augment funding for teachers' salaries while not naming school counselors, administrators, and support staff as salary increase recipients are blatant attempts to divide a sincere effort to help public education succeed in times of crisis.

Local Support for Education

Local support for education is likely to increase in high-capacity, high-effort areas. There is also a growing resentment of state equalization efforts from these areas. More frequently, equalization is being referred to as "Robin Hood" laws. The clear meaning is that states are engaged in stealing funds from the rich localities to give to the poor localities.

Low-capacity localities will experience increased stress to meet NCLB requirements for adequate yearly progress. These high-needs areas are suffering from higher teacher turnover and teacher shortages from retiring baby boomers. Localities need state policy assistance to help in recruiting highly qualified teachers.

Connecticut enacted a strategy to help in this regard. The state's 1986 Educational Enhancement Act spent more than $300 million to boost minimum beginning teacher salaries in such a way that it made it possible for low-wealth districts to compete in the job market for highly qualified teachers. Concurrently, Connecticut raised teacher licensing standards by requiring a major in the discipline to be taught and extensive knowledge of teaching and learning as part of preparation; instituted performance-based examinations to test subject matter and knowledge of teaching as a basis for receiving a license; created a state-funded mentoring program to support trained mentors for first-year teachers; and created an elaborate assessment program using state-trained assessors to determine which first-year teachers could continue in teaching. Analysis of the outcomes found that it eliminated teacher shortages and emergency hiring in high-poverty cities and created surpluses of teachers within 3 years of its passage.[59]

If high-needs localities are to be successful, such programs will need to become commonplace. If states do not provide increased equalization programs to attract high-quality teacher applicants to low-capacity localities, the achievement gap will increase, resulting in even greater economic disparity between high- and low-capacity localities. Support to localities can be a major source of contention for state legislatures and local politicians. Should problem solving break down and animosity take over with publicly traded criticisms, the general public may become polarized and split in their support for education.

SUMMARY

School districts face major finance challenges as communities address contemporary critical and emerging issues. Critical issues include capital outlay investments to repair decaying school facilities and human resources issues involving salaries and benefits. Emerging issues comprise vouchers and privatization associated with NCLB, and federal, state, and local support for public education.

Deferred school facilities maintenance has grown into a sizeable dilemma. National studies from 1995 to 2000 report that it would take $112 billion to $322 billion to repair or modernize America's public schools to "good overall condition." From 2003 to 2005, new school construction additions and modernizations are expected to cost $93,722,670,000. Borrowing money for school construction can virtually double the cost.

Older school facilities often place students in environmentally hazardous situations. Radon gas causes lung cancer. Lead paint and lead solder in older plumbing joints lead to neurological impairments and learning problems. Poor indoor air quality results in students missing more than 14 million school days each year. Many molds existing in older schools can trigger allergens causing asthma, allergic reactions, and lethal toxins. Removing all of these dangerous substances is expensive.

---

[59]Connecticut State Department of Education Division of Research, Evaluation, and Assessment, *Research Bulletin, School Year 1990–91,* No. 1 (Hartford, CT: Bureau of Research and Teacher Assessment, 1991).

Salaries comprise 70 to 80% of school expenditures, and it is vital to decide how to best spend the funds. To attract and retain the highest quality educators, human resources policies must be based on thoughtful, value-based decisions about how educators are paid through basic salary schedules, fringe benefits, professional development, and licensure and certification requirements—deciding whom to pay and what factors to reward. At the same time, current steeply rising health care costs are making serious demands on school financial resources and are adversely affecting employee benefits. Current research on teacher quality and student achievement as well as upcoming approaches to address the health care situation can help localities make more informed salary and benefits decisions.

Other expenses also compete for school finance dollars. Although NCLB implementation costs have not been fully researched, estimates suggest that this legislation may cost $43 billion annually. In 2002 the U.S. Supreme Court found that using vouchers or public school monies for students to attend private, parochial schools was acceptable in certain situations. Federal education spending continues to require that states and localities pay the lion's share of education bills.

Conclusion

Schools face varied and competing demands for limited fiscal resources. Devastating student health and achievement issues lie at the heart of school finance, and local school districts face wrenching decisions about how to best spend their inadequate education dollars for the maximum return.

Case Study

How does your state compare to other states in Table 13.9? What does this say about how your state values education? What policy implications do you see for your state legislators who want to improve education quality? List the top three implications and justify their inclusion. How would you go about implementing change? What data would you use to convince legislators who do not support public education to vote for these changes?

Compare your locality to other localities in your state in relation to salary and benefits. What is the impact on teacher recruitment and retention of highly qualified personnel? What is the most needed change as you examine the comparisons? What would be the cost of making that change to the locality?

CHAPTER QUESTIONS

1. What is the overall condition of school facilities in your school district? How old are the buildings? Are they in need of repair? Is there a disparity in overall building conditions (are some air conditioned while others are not, do roofs leak in some and not in others, are there issues with air quality in some and not others)? How do the facilities in your district compare with facilities in surrounding districts? If there is a difference, please explain it.
2. Has your district ever used arbitrage to finance school facilities? If so, what were the results? If not, what were the reasons for not using it?
3. Review your district's salary schedule. What does the schedule appear to value? What does it appear not to value? Explain your answer.
4. Review your state and school district's policy regarding licensure and certification. Does it assure high levels of training and quality, or have there been trends to relax requirements? What are the provisions for National Board Certified Teachers? Document and explain your answers.
5. How do your district's health insurance costs and benefits compare to those of neighboring districts?
6. Looking at several years of data, what are the trends for federal, state, and local funding of your budget? Knowing what you know now about determining effort indices ($E = R/TB$, or Effort equals Revenue divided by the Tax Base), what trends can you see in terms of local effort and the budget? Has local effort been increasing, remaining relatively constant, or decreasing?

Name Index

Adams, Henry, 300nn5–6
Addonizio, M., 329n49
Agron, Joe, 343n, 344n
Alexander, Kern, 55n14, 65n, 68n10, 77n31, 82n38, 86n45, 89nn56–57, 121n5, 137n21, 157, 157n, 186n4, 205n10, 206nn11–12, 207n14, 214, 214n23, 220n36, 241, 244n21, 246n, 290n, 316, 316n1, 319n11, 332, 332n60, 347n
Alexander, Lamar, 5–6
Alexander, M. David, 55n14, 65n, 68n10, 82n38, 86n45, 89nn56–57, 347n
Amrein–Beardsley, A., 355n18, 356nn20–21
Anderson, P. K., 326n37
Anthony, E., 355n18
Archer, J., 28n
Arend, D., 266n18
Arnold, S. E., 104n12
Augenblick, W., 220n36

Baker, K., 26n43, 321n14, 322n20
Baker, L., 267, 267n21
Baker, W., 355n18
Banko, L. B., 359n28, 361nn41–42
Barnes, L. L., 104n12
Basinger, J., 277n50
Bennett, D. A., 104n12
Bennett, William, 12, 12n25, 17, 26, 36, 317, 318n9, 319

Berliner, D., 3nn5–6, 11n24, 18, 18n32, 27, 27n47, 355n18, 356nn20–21
Berne, Robert, 203n1, 204n5, 204n8, 205n9, 331n55
Berner, M., 334, 334n65
Berry, Barnett, 274n38, 275n40, 277, 277n51
Biddle, B., 3nn5–6, 11n24, 18, 18n32, 27, 27n47
Bienias, J. L., 104n12
Binns, H., 266n18
Blair, C., 262n10, 267, 267n20
Blair, J., 276n47, 325n34
Bohrnstedt, G., 327n40, 328n41
Bond, L., 355n18
Books, Sue, 146, 146n24
Bracey, Gerald W., 3n6, 4n14, 5, 5n, 16n28, 17, 17n, 38, 38n, 366, 366n56
Brandon, D., 38–39, 39n
Brimley, Vera, 141n, 358n23
Brinkley, Vern, 302n
Brown, Lawrence, 204n4
Burkam, D., 272n
Busch, Carolyn, 204n7
Bush, George H. W., 88
Bush, George W., 3, 61, 364

Campbell, E. Q., 27nn45–46
Carroll, Tom, 274n39
Carter, Jimmy, 3, 234, 309
Cavasos, Lauro, 5–6
Chambers, Jay, 221, 221n

Champion, Linda, 216n25
Christakis, D., 271n30
Christoffel, K., 266n18
Clinton, William Jefferson "Bill," 90, 326, 351
Clune, William H., III, 244
Colaiacova, D., 359n27
Cole, G. D. H., 47n7
Coleman, J. S., 27nn45–46, 316n3, 317, 317n4, 321
Connolly, C., 359n29, 359n31, 360n38
Coons, John E., 244
Cooper, B., 249n30, 321n16
Corcoran, T. B., 334–335, 335n67
Crenshaw, A. N., 359n30
Cubberley, Ellwood, 46, 46n1, 46nn3–4, 47nn5–6, 48nn8–9, 49–50, 49nn10–11, 64, 72n, 85, 85nn42–44, 86nn46–49, 156, 156n5, 184, 209n, 241
Cunningham, William G., 229n, 247n

Darling–Hammond, Linda, 30, 30nn55–56, 33, 272–273, 273n32, 322, 322nn23–24, 333, 333n62, 354, 354n15
Dawson, N., 266n18
Delpit, Lisa, 255, 255n4
DiGiuseppe, D., 271n30
DiPaola, Michael, 280n59, 282n, 283nn67–68

Doud, J. L., 280n58, 283n66
Doyle, D., 6n
Driscoll, W., 220n36
Duncombe, W., 219n30

Earthman, G., 333–334, 334n64
Edley, C., 84n41, 319n11
Eisenhower, Dwight D., 56
Evans, D. A., 104n12

Ferguson, R., 26n42, 30n53
Fermanich, Mark, 219n29
Finn, Chester, 6
Fortune, J., 321n18
Friedman, Milton, 64, 64n, 87,
    87n52, 365, 365n53
Friedman, Rose, 64n
Fruchter, N., 331n55

Garfield, Rulon, 141n, 302n,
    358n23
Gates, Bill, 330
Gates, Melinda, 330
Gerstner, Louis, 6, 6n, 333n63
Gibbons, R., 266n18
Gingrich, Newt, 367n57
Goldhaber, D., 355n18
Greenwald, R., 321n14
Guthrie, J., 220n36

Haig, Robert, 209n, 241, 243,
    243n
Hamilton, Alexander, 68
Hansen, Janet S., 254n
Hanushek, Eric, 12, 12n25, 26,
    27, 27n48, 317–318, 317n7,
    318n8, 321
Harding, Warren G., 301
Hattie, J., 355n18
Hawkins, Augustus F., 59
Haycock, K., 19n35, 20n, 28n,
    276n44, 323n28, 324nn31–32
Hedges, Larry, 27, 27nn49–50,
    321, 321nn14–15
Hertbert, Linda, 204n7
Hessel, K., 316n2
Hirsh, E., 326n38

Hobson, C. J., 27nn45–46
Hodges, L. V., 328n43
Hodgkinson, Harold "Bud," 253n,
    261, 261n9, 264n12, 264n14,
    266n17, 269nn24–25
Hodgkinson, Virginia, 106n
Holloway, J., 316n2
Hovey, H., 33nn60–61, 130n,
    131n17, 132n, 134n, 136n,
    188–189, 188n, 189n, 195n,
    260n5
Hovey, K., 33nn60–61, 130n,
    131n17, 132n, 134n, 136n,
    188–189, 188n, 189n, 195n,
    260n5
Howard, Tyrone C., 273n33
Howley, A. A., 330n50
Howley, C. B., 330n50
Huang, S., 19n35, 20n, 28n, 323n28
Hugo, Victor, 110

Iatorola, P., 331n55
Imazeki, J., 219nn31–33,
    220nn34–35
Ingersoll, Richard M., 273nn36–37,
    275n43
Irving, Washington, 2
Isaacs, C., 266n18

Jackson, Andrew, 51
Jackson, Howell, 74
Jacobson, L., 328n41
Jerald, C., 19n35, 20n, 323n28
Johns, R., 209n, 241, 244n20, 290n,
    332, 332n60
Johnson, G., 317n5
Johnson, J. D., 330n50
Johnson, Lyndon, 55, 161
Johnston, W., 6n
Jordan, H., 276n48, 323n26

Kain, J., 276n45, 277n53
Kaplan, Leslie S., 28n51, 273n33,
    277n52, 277n54, 278n56,
    282n63, 322n21
Keller, E. P., 280n58, 283n66
Kiefer, M., 363n46

King, R., 138n, 141n, 242n, 317n6,
    321n17
Kirst, M., 327n40, 328n41
Knapp, M. S., 326n38
Konstantopoulos, S., 328n43
Koppich, J. E., 326n38
Kozol, Jonathan, 24n
Ladd, Helen F., 219n30
Laine, R., 27nn49–50, 321n14
Lee, V., 272n
Levigne, J., 266n18, 268n22
Levin, R., 220n36
Levine, Daniel U., 10n
Lewit, E., 267, 267n21
Liebowitz, S., 359n32, 361n43,
    362n44
Lochner, L., 110, 110n, 111,
    111nn16–19
Lockwood, R., 26n41
Lowe, J., 334n66

Madison, James, 68
Mann, Horace, 86, 235n7
Manzo, Kathleen Kennedy,
    332n59
Martin, D., 311n12
Martin, George, 46
Martinez, B., 360n37
Marzano, R., 57, 282, 282n64,
    327n39
McCarty, C., 271n30
McClanahan, G., 363n48
McLean, J., 26n41
McLoughlin, M., 27nn49–50
McLuhan, Marshall, 2–3, 3n3
McNulty, B., 282, 282n64
McPartland, J., 27nn45–46
McRobbie, J., 327n40, 328n41
Mendes de Leon, C. F., 104n12
Mendro, R., 276n48, 323n26
Miller, J. E., 360n39, 361n40
Minner, S., 322, 322n22
Mitgang, L. D., 280n60
Monroe, J., 325n35
Mood, A. M., 27nn45–46
Moretti, E., 110, 110n, 111,
    111nn16–19

Morphet, Edgar, 241, 244n20, 290n, 332, 332n60
Morrison, Henry, 241
Mort, Paul, 241, 244
Moynihan, Patrick, 88

Nunnery, John, 282n63
Nye, B., 219n31, 328n43
Odden, Allan, 78n33, 204n5, 204n7, 218n27, 219n29, 222, 222n38, 241, 248n24, 248n28
O'Neil, J., 321n18
Overholt, G., 311n12
Owings, William A., 28n51, 273n33, 277n52, 277n54, 278n56, 282, 282n63, 322n21

Packwood, Robert, 88
Parrish, Tom, 221, 221n
Payne, Ruby, 255, 255n3
Peeveley, G. L., 219n31
Perkins, Carl, 59
Peterson, George E., 128n14
Phelps, J., 329n49
Pickering, D., 327n39
Picus, Lawrence O., 78n33, 218n27, 218n29, 241, 318n8
Pollock, J., 327n39
Poppink, S., 8nn18–19, 35nn63–64
Powell, Lewis, 76, 80

Rainwater, Lee, 262n11, 263n
Raywid, M. A., 332n57
Ready, T., 84n41
Reagan, Ronald, 3, 5, 88, 234
Rebell, M. A., 84n41
Reeves, D., 276n44
Reich, Robert, 59n19, 168, 168n7
Reschovsky, A., 219nn31–33, 220nn 34–35
Riddle, W., 249n29
Riley, Richard, 333n63
Rivers, J., 29n, 323n27
Robinson, G., 38–39, 39n, 328–329, 328n41, 328nn44–45, 329n48
Roe, William H., 291n, 301n

Rosen, Harvey, 236n
Rosenbaum, D., 266n18
Rosnick, David, 197
Rossmiller, Richard, 215–216, 215n
Rousseau, Jean Jacques, 47, 47n7
Ruggiero, J., 219n30

Sack, Joetta L., 335n68
Salmon, Richard, 77n31, 121n5, 137n21, 157, 157n, 186n4, 205n10, 206nn11–12, 207n14, 212n18, 214, 214n23, 241, 244n21, 246n, 249, 316, 316n1, 319n11
Sanders, R., 323n27
Sanders, W., 29n
Saxon–Harrold, S. K. E., 105n, 106n
Schneider, J. A., 104n12
Schultz, Theodore W., 96–97, 96n2, 97n3, 115
Schwartz, A., 364n51
Scott, K., 262n10, 267, 267n20
Scribner, J. P., 326n36
Semerat, R., 6n
Shannon, John, 128n14
Shen, J., 8nn18–19, 35nn63–64
Singleton, K., 276n45, 277n53
Smeeding, Timothy, 262n11, 263n
Smith, Adam, 95, 96, 96n2, 168n7, 332–333
Smith, T., 355n18
Snow, C. E., 84n41
Sobel, H., 266n18
Solo, Robert, 87n52, 365n53
Speakman, S. T., 249n30
Stafford, F., 317n5
Stafford, Robert T., 59
Stecher, B., 327n40, 328n41, 328n46
Stephens, Robert, 81–82, 84
Stiefel, Leanna, 203n1, 204n5, 204n8, 205n9, 331n55, 364, 364n51
Strayer, George, 241, 243, 243n
Sugarman, Stephen D., 244

Swanson, A., 138n, 141n, 242n
Sweetland, S., 138n, 141n, 242n
Tannewald, Robert, 189
Thomas, J., 273n34
Thompson, D., 319, 319n10
Todd, Glenda, 216n25
Tracey, C., 278n55
Tschannen–Moran, Megan, 280n59, 282n, 283nn67–68

Updegraff, Harlan, 213, 213n20, 241, 244
Urban, W., 311n12

Vandevoort, L. G., 355n18, 356nn20–21
Verstegan, Deborah A., 241n16, 248n25, 249, 249nn30–31, 317, 317n6, 321, 321n17, 321n19

Walberg, H., 328n47
Walker, L. J., 335n67
Walsh, K., 278n55
Walsh, Mark, 115n, 120n1
Waters, T., 282, 282n64
Wattenbarger, J., 318n8
Weerasinge, D., 276n48, 323n26
Weglinsky, H., 276n47, 324nn29–30, 325n34
Weinfeld, F. D., 27nn45–46
Weitzman, Murray, 105n, 106n
Welch, F., 317n5
Welch, W. M., 360n35, 362n45
White, Byron, 89
White, J. L., 335n67
Will, George, 13, 17
Williams, T., 327n40, 328n41
Wilson, R. S., 104n12
Wilson, Woodrow, 301
Wittebols, J. H., 328–329, 329n48
Wood, C., 319, 319n10

Yinger, J., 219n30
York, R. L., 27nn45–46

Zimmerman, F., 271n30

Subject Index

Abbot v. Burke (1998), 222n39

ABC Education Act, 236

Absolute fiscal equalization, 206

Abuse, and student achievement, 270–271

Accountability
    budgeting and, 310–311
    of schools, 61

Achievement. *See* Student achievement

ACT college admissions test, 318

Act to Provide for Further Educational Facilities (1919), 52

Ad valorem tax, 124, 127

ADA (Americans with Disabilities Act of 1990), 59–60

Adequacy, 218–222, 223
    defined, 201
    economic cost function approach to, 219–220
    equity and, 82–84
    professional consensus approach to, 221
    state-of-the-art approach to, 221–222
    successful school district approach to, 220–221
    of yield, 141

Adequate yearly progress (AYP) guidelines, 19, 61, 139, 235n8, 248, 254, 307

ADHD (attention deficit hyperactivity disorder), 272

Administrators. *See* School administrators

Advisory Commission on Intergovernmental Relations, 189

African Americans
    in administrative population, 280, 281
    free lunch program and, 257
    low birth weights among, 267
    poverty among, 263, 284
    salaries of, 282
    in school-age population, 260, 284
    segregation of, 2
    single parenthood among, 269
    test scores of, 18, 19n34, 20, 323–324

Agricultural Adjustment Act of 1935, 53

Air quality, indoor, 344, 369

Alabama
    early public education in, 50
    "no action" groups in, 49
    spending vs. student achievement in, 26
    teacher salaries in, 351, 352

Alabama Department of Education study, 26

Alaska
    severance taxes in, 137, 189
    study of school size in, 330

Alaskan Natives
    in administrative population, 281
    salaries of, 280, 282
    test scores of, 18

Alcohol, sumptuary taxes on, 138

Alternative schools, 85–86

Alternatively licensed teachers, 277–279

American Association for Employment in Education, 273n35

American Federation of Teachers, 358n25

American Indians. *See* Native Americans

Americans with Disabilities Act of 1990 (ADA), 59–60

America's Teacher Profile, 4n9

Ann Arbor Public School District, 363

Appalachian Education Laboratory, 57

Approximate fiscal equalization, 206–207

Arbitrage, 345–346

Arizona
    school enrollment growth in, 258, 259
    teacher certification in, 356

Arkansas, test scores in, 324

Articles of Confederation, 48

Asian Americans
    in administrative population, 281
    free lunch program and, 257
    salaries of, 282

Asian Americans (*Cont.*)
  in school–age population, 260
  single parenthood among, 269
  test scores of, 18, 19nn33–34
Assessment, of home, 128,
    128n13, 129
Attention deficit hyperactivity
    disorder (ADHD), 272
Augustus E. Hawkins–Robert T.
    Stafford Elementary and
    Secondary School Improve-
    ment Amendments of 1988, 59
Australia
  education spending in, 9, 11
  infant mortality rates in, 268
  poverty in, 262, 263, 264
  test scores in, 21, 22
Austria
  education spending in, 11
  infant mortality rates in, 268
  poverty in, 264
  test scores in, 21, 22

Bagley v. Raymond (1999), 87,
    87n50
Baker v. Carr (1962), 74n24
Belgium
  education spending in, 9
  infant mortality rates in, 268
  poverty in, 263, 264
*Bell's Gap Railroad Co. v.
    Pennsylvania* (1890),
    74nn20–21
Benefits, 356–358
  defined, 356
  legally required, 356, 357, 358
  same–sex, 362–363
Bilingual education, 58
Bill and Melinda Gates
    Foundation, 330
Bill of Rights, 66, 79
Birth weight, and student
    achievement, 267
Blacks. *See* African Americans
Blue Cross and Blue Shield, 361
*Board of Education of Central
    School District No. 1 v. Allen*
    (1968), 89n56

Bonds, 345
Britain. *See* England
Brookline, Massachusetts, 363
*Brown v. Board of Education of
    Topeka* (1954), 58, 66, 76–77,
    76n28, 80, 197, 197n7
Brown v. Board of Education II
    (1970), 2, 66
*Brushhaber v. Union Pacific R.R.
    Co.* (1916), 131n16
Budget(s)
  comparing, 291–293
  defined, 290, 301
  education priorities and,
    291–304
  examples of, 291–293
  principals and, 284
Budgeting, 289–313
  accountability and, 310–311
  appropriating funds and, 304–305
  categories in, 294
  evaluating results of, 307–308
  federal data on, 298–300
  percentage add–on, 308–309
  planning and, 301–303
  Planning, Programming,
    Budgeting System (PPBS) of,
    309–310
  process of, 300–308
  repair costs in, 292–293
  site–based (SBB), 310
  spending and, 306
  state data on, 293–298
  for unanticipated expenses, 306
  zero–base (ZBB), 309
Bureau of Labor Statistics, 101n,
    356, 358
Bureau of the Census. *See* U.S.
    Census Bureau
Burruss v. Wilkerson (1970),
    75n25, 91

California
  class size in, 326, 328
  cost of living in, 143
  illegal immigrants in, 260
  property taxes in, 120–121
  same–sex benefits in, 362–363

school enrollment growth in,
    258, 259
  school funding in, 75–76, 80
  study of school size in, 330
  teacher salaries in, 238–239
  transportation spending of, 298
Canada
  education spending in, 9, 197
  income gap in, 262
  infant mortality rates in, 268
  poverty in, 262, 263, 264
  test scores in, 21, 22
Capacity. *See* Fiscal capacity
*Cardiff v. Bismark Public School
    District* (1978), 120n3
Career Education Implementation
    Incentive Act of 1977, 58
Carl Perkins Vocational Education
    Act of 1984, 59
Center for Culture and Technology,
    3n3
Certificates of Participation (COPs),
    345–346
Certification, of teachers, 351–354
Charitable contributions, 105–107,
    105n
Charter schools, 85, 89–90, 92
"Cherish clause," 81, 81n35
Chicago
  same–sex health benefits
    in, 363
  school size in, 331
Child abuse and neglect, and
    student achievement, 270–271
Child Protective Services (CPS),
    270–271
Childbirth, and education,
    109–110, 111
Children's Internet Protection Act
    of 2000, 61
Church of England, 48
Civil Rights Act of 1964, 55, 74,
    74n22, 80, 91, 316, 347
Civil War
  education legislation during,
    51–52
  end of, 73
  taxes following, 131

Class size, and student achievement, 326–329, 336

Cleveland (Ohio) Scholarship and Tutoring Program (CSTP), 366

CMA (comprehensive market analysis), 129

COBRA, 358

Coinsurance rates, 361

Coleman Report, 13, 27, 27nn45–46, 316–317

Colonies, education in, 46–50, 63, 64

Colorado, school enrollment growth in, 258, 259

Commerce clause, 69

Commonwealths, 66n2, 218

Comprehensive market analysis (CMA), 129

Concentration grants, 56

Connecticut
  budget for, 298
  legal gambling in, 133
  per capita income in, 131, 132, 162, 163, 164, 166, 167
  per pupil spending in, 293, 294
  percent of spending on education in, 295, 298
  progressive education in, 49
  sales taxes in, 133, 134
  school laws of, 47
  severance taxes in, 137, 137n19
  teacher licensing standards in, 368

Consolidated Appropriations Act of 2001, 61

Constitutions, state, 81–82. *See also* U.S. Constitution

Continental Congress, 50

Contract With America: Unfunded Mandates (1996), 60–61

COPS (Certificates of Participation), 345–346

Corporate income taxes, 137–138

Corporation for Public Broadcasting (CPB), 58

Corrections, state spending on, 294, 295–297, 298

Cost(s)
  misconceptions about, 12, 24–25, 39

student enrollment vs., 13–15
student needs and, 15–16
test scores vs., 12–13, 16–24

Cost of living, and per capita income, 143, 144–145, 166–167

"Costing out," 303

Council of Organizations of Others for Education about Parochiaid v. Governor (1997), 90n59

CPB (Corporation for Public Broadcasting), 58

CPS (Child Protective Services), 270–271

Crime victimization, 112–113

CSTP (Cleveland, Ohio Scholarship and Tutoring Program), 366

Cultural activities, 108–109

Cyprus, test scores in, 21, 22

Czech Republic
  education spending in, 6
  infant mortality rates in, 268
  test scores in, 21, 22

Data analysis of education needs, 302

Declaration of Independence, 48

Defined benefit, 356

Defined contribution, 356

Delaware
  flat grant model in, 242
  minimal education in, 49
  pauper education in, 49
  revenue from business incorporated within, 189
  severance taxes in, 137n19

Demographics, 253–288
  changes in, 248, 251, 254, 258–261, 285–287
  cultural beliefs and practices and, 255
  defined, 254
  fiscal planning and, 257–258
  illegal immigrants and, 260–261, 261n8
  instructional issues and, 254–257

in racial/ethnic backgrounds, 260–261

risk factors and, 261–272

of school administrators, 279–284

special needs students and, 256

of teachers, 272–279

trends in, 258–261

Denmark
  education spending in, 11
  infant mortality rates in, 268
  poverty in, 262, 263, 264
  test scores in, 21, 22

Depression, 52–53

Development delay (DD) programs, 268

Digest of Education Statistics, 197, 341–342

Diminishing marginal utility, 140–141

Disabilities, students with
  education costs and, 15–16
  legislation involving, 55, 58, 59–60

Disability insurance, 356, 357

District(s). *See* School district(s)

District of Columbia
  authority for education in, 67
  budget for, 293, 294
  domestic partner health benefits in, 362
  elementary school study in, 334
  federal funding in, 214
  per capita income in, 163, 164, 167
  per capita spending in, 166, 167, 293, 294
  school enrollment trends in, 258, 259
  size of school districts in, 159
  teacher salaries in, 351, 353

District power equalizing (DPE), 244–246, 250, 251

Domestic partner benefits, 362–363

DPE (district power equalizing), 244–246, 250, 251

Dropout(s)
  charitable contributions of, 107
  childbearing and, 109, 110, 111
  earning potential of, 99, 100
  employability of, 100, 101
  health insurance of, 103
  incarceration rates of, 110,
    111, 112
  volunteerism among, 105
  voting behavior of, 103
Dropout prevention, 60
Drug Abuse Education Act of
  1970, 58, 69
Due process, 261
Dwight D. Eisenhower
  Mathematics and Science
  Education Act of 1965, 56

EAHCA. See Education for All
  Handicapped Children Act
  of 1975 (EAHCA)
Earning potential, 98–100
Economic cost function approach
  to adequacy, 219–220
Economic Policy Institute, 272
ECS (Education Commission of
  the States), 330–331, 364n49
Education
  as big business, 4
  bilingual, 58
  budget for, 3–4. See also
    Budget(s); Budgeting
  career, 58
  crime victimization and, 112–113
  cultural activities and, 108–109
  disappointment in, 2
  earning potential and, 98–100
  employability and, 100–102
  federal contribution to, 70–71
  health and, 104
  importance of, 3
  incarceration rates and, 110,
    111, 112
  as investment in human capital,
    95–116
  leisure activities and,
    107–108, 109
  of migrant workers, 116–117

misconception about U.S.
  spending on, 5–12, 39
number of professionals in, 4, 14,
  35–39
quality of life and, 102–113
vocational, 52
volunteerism and, 104–105
as wise investment, 114–115
Education Amendments of 1974, 58
Education Commission of the States
  (ECS), 330–331, 364n49
Education Consolidation and
  Improvement Act of 1981, 59
Education for All Handicapped
  Children Act of 1975
  (EAHCA), 15–16, 32, 55,
  58, 61
Education for Economic Security
  Act of 1984, 59
Education of Mentally Retarded
  Children Act of 1958, 55
Education Policy Institute, 332
Education revenues. See
  Revenue(s)
Education Trust–West, 238
Educational Enhancement Act
  (Connecticut, 1986), 368
Educational planning, 301–303
Educational Testing Service (ETS),
  17, 276
Effort. See Fiscal effort
Elementary and Secondary
  Education Act of 1965
  (ESEA), 55–57, 60, 198,
  234, 235, 367
Elementary and Secondary
  Education Assistance
  Programs Extension, 58
Elementary schools
  enrollment in, 14
  expenditures in, 14
  number of teachers in, 14
  per pupil expenditures for, 25
  pupil–teacher ratios in, 14
  salaries of teachers in, 15, 31
  state spending on, 294, 295–297
ELL (English language learners),
  61, 261, 265

Employability, 100–102
Employee benefits. See Benefits
Energy efficiency, and indoor air
  quality, 344
England
  budgeting in, 300
  religious persecution in, 48, 49
  test scores in, 21, 22
English for Speakers of Other
  Languages (ESOL), 265
English language learners (ELL),
  61, 261, 265
Enrollment. See Student enrollment
Environmental Education Act of
  1970, 58
Environmental Protection
  Agency, 344
Equal Pay Act of 1963, 347
Equal Protection clause, 73–81,
  91, 146
  standards of equal protection
    under, 77–81, 91–92
  taxation and, 73–77
Equality, vs. equity, 82, 146–147,
  148, 201, 202–203, 222
Equalization
  defined, 201
  fiscal, 206–207, 223
  for fiscal capacity, 153,
    154, 161
  local, 238–239
  state, 239–241, 250
Equalization grants, 207,
  209–213, 223
Equity, 82, 83, 146–147, 201–218
  adequacy and, 82–84
  defined, 201
  equality vs., 82, 146–147, 148,
    201, 202–203, 222
  horizontal, 83, 203–204,
    204n3, 222
  vertical, 83, 204–205,
    214–218, 223
ESE (exceptional student education)
  programs, 216
ESEA. See Elementary and
  Secondary Education Act
  of 1965 (ESEA)

ESOL (English for Speakers of Other Languages), 265
Ethnicity, demographic trends in, 260–261
ETS (Educational Testing Service), 17, 276
Even Start program, 61
Exceptional student education (ESE) programs, 216
Expenditures. *See* Spending

Fair Labor Standards Act, 347
Fair market value, 128n13, 129
Fairfax County, Virginia, 347, 349, 350
Far West Lab, 57
Federal government
  advantages to federal financing, 236–238, 250
  budget data for, 298–300
  control of state's education function, 68–70
  decentralization of, 51
  education legislation of, 3, 52–62
  guidelines for states accepting federal grants, 69
  history of education funding by, 50–51, 56–62, 63
  roles and responsibilities of, 234–236
  as source of public school revenues, 231–233, 250
  support for education, 70–71, 367
  taxes levied by, 124, 125–126, 125n11, 129, 131–133
Federal Insurance Contributions Act (FICA), 125–126, 125nn10–11, 358
Federal Reserve Bank, 189, 197
Ferris Bueller's Day Off (film), 2
FICA. *See* Federal Insurance Contributions Act (FICA)
Finance. *See* School Finance
Finance systems. *See* School finance systems

Finland
  infant mortality rates in, 268
  poverty in, 262, 263, 264
Firearms, law concerning, 69, 69n13
First Amendment, 89
Fiscal adequacy. *See* Adequacy
Fiscal capacity, 151–181
  defined, 143, 148
  determining, 154–155, 156, 161, 171, 172
  equalization for, 153, 154, 161
  GDP and, 168
  GNP and, 168
  local issues, 156–161
  national issues, 168–171
  relative, 152–153, 160
  state issues, 161–168, 173–181
Fiscal effort, 143, 145–146, 183–199
  computing, 186–187
  defined, 143, 145, 184
  factors influencing, 184–186
  international comparisons, 197, 199
  leadership and, 186
  local, 188, 189–192
  national, 193, 195–198
  relative, 152–153, 187, 189
  state, 188, 193, 194–195
  wealth and, 190–192
Fiscal equalization, 206–207, 223
Fiscal neutrality, 205, 223
Fiscal planning, and demographics, 257–258
Flat grants, 209, 210, 242–243, 250
Fleischmann Commission, 214n22
Florida
  emotional problems of pupils in, 271
  Hispanic American students in, 265
  model of pupil weighting in, 216–218
  ratio of students to overall population in, 161
  school taxes in, 71–72
  school vouchers in, 366

  size of school districts in, 159
  transience rate in, 266
Florida Department of Education v. Glasser (1993), 71n18
Foundation programs, 210–211, 213, 243–244, 250
Fourteenth Amendment, 73–77, 146
France
  education spending in, 9, 197
  infant mortality rates in, 268
  poverty in, 263, 264
  test scores in, 21, 22
Fringe benefits, 358. *See also* Benefits
Full state funding, 214, 246–247, 250, 251
Fundamental rights, 79
Funding
  appropriating, 304–305
  federal, advantages of, 236–238, 250
  federal, history of, 50–51, 56–62, 63
  full state, 214, 246–247, 250, 251
  of human resources for education, 346–363
  recent history involving, 316–318
  seeking, 303–304
  of teacher salaries, 346–354, 370
  See also Property Taxes; Revenue(s)

Gallup Organization, 105n, 106n, 193n, 366
Gambling, legal, 133, 135–136
GDP. *See* Gross Domestic Product (GDP)
General Accounting Office (GAO), 204, 340
General Court, 46
General Welfare clause, 68, 91
Georgia
  minimal education in, 49
  pauper education in, 49
  severance taxes in, 137n19
  study of school size in, 330

Germany
    comparison with U.S. education
        system, 66
    education spending in, 9
    infant mortality rates in, 268
    poverty in, 263, 264
    test scores in, 21, 22
GI Bill, 53–54
GNP. See Gross National Product
    (GNP)
Goals, in budget process, 303
Goals 2000: Educate America Act
    of 1994, 60
"Good school conditions," 49
Goss v. Lopez, 69n11
Graduation rates, and race, 2
Grandparents, as parents, 268–269
Grant(s)
    concentration, 56
    equalization, 207, 209–213, 223
    federal, guidelines for states
        accepting, 69
    flat, 209, 210, 242–243, 250
    foundation, 210–211, 213,
        243–244, 250
    land, 51
    nonequalization, 208–209
    state aid, 207–213
Great Britain. See England
Great Depression, 52–53
"Great Society" legislation, 55
Greece
    education funding in, 72
    infant mortality rates in, 268
    test scores in, 21, 22
Griffin v. Illinois (1956), 74n24
Gross Domestic Product (GDP)
    computing, 168
    defined, 8
    fiscal capacity and, 168
    GNP vs., 8n20, 168, 172
    gross state product vs., 193
    international comparisons of
        education spending and, 7,
        8–12, 8n20, 152
    for poorest countries, 169–171
    school spending as portion of, 4,
        7, 8–12, 197

Gross National Product (GNP)
    computing, 168
    fiscal capacity and, 168
    GDP vs., 8n20, 168, 172
    spending comparisons and, 8n20
Gross state product, vs. GDP, 193
GTB (guaranteed tax base)
        programs, 211–213, 244
GTY (guaranteed tax yield), 244
Guaranteed ESE Allocation, 216
Guaranteed tax base (GTB)
        programs, 211–213, 244
Guaranteed tax yield (GTY), 244
Gun–Free School Zone Act of
    1990, 69, 69n13

Handicapped Children's Early
    Education Assistance Act
    of 1968, 58
Handicapped Children's Protection
    Act of 1986, 59
Hartzell v. Connell (1984), 120n3
Harvard study, 26
Hawaii
    authority for education in, 67
    full state funding in, 214
    Medicaid spending of, 298
    revenue sources in, 231
    same–sex benefits in, 362
    severance taxes in, 137n19
    single school district in, 67, 159,
        228n2
Head Start program, 70
Health
    education and, 104
    school facilities and, 343–344
Health insurance, 103–104, 356,
    357, 359–362
High schools. See Secondary schools
Higher education spending, 294,
    295–297, 298
Hispanic Americans
    in administrative population,
        280, 281
    equal protection of, 76
    free lunch program and, 257
    poverty among, 263, 264, 284
    salaries of, 280, 282

in school–age population, 260,
    265, 284
single parenthood among, 269
test scores of, 17, 18, 19nn33–34,
    20, 324
History, 45–64
    of alternative schools, 85–86
    colonial education in, 46–50,
        63, 64
    of federal education funding,
        50–51, 56–62, 63
    federal legislation in, 51–62
    of public school revenues,
        230–231
    of regional evolution of schools
        and school financing, 48–50
    of student weightings, 215–216
    of tax funding for public schools,
        47, 123
    war years' legislation in, 51–54
Home(s)
    assessment of, 128, 128n13, 129
    fair market value of, 128n13, 129
    See also Property taxes
Home improvement, 107, 107n
Hong Kong, test scores in, 21, 22
Hoover Institution (Stanford
    University), 26
Horizontal equity, 83, 203–204,
    204n3, 222
Human capital
    school finance as investment in,
        95–116
    taxing to support, 113–114
Hungary
    education spending in, 6, 11
    infant mortality rates in,
        267, 268
    test scores in, 21, 22
Iceland
    infant mortality rates in, 268
    test scores in, 21, 22
IDEA (Individuals with Disabilities
    Education Act of 1990), 61, 272
IEP (individual education plan),
    36–37, 216
Illegal immigrants, 260–261,
    261n8

Illinois
  economic cost function approach
    in, 219
  Equal Protection clause in, 75
  funding practices in, 75
Immigrants, illegal, 260–261, 261n8
Imprisonment, and education,
    110–112
Improving America's Schools Act
    of 1994, 60
In personam tax, 124
In rem tax, 124
Incarceration rates, 110–112
Income, per capita, 143, 168
  adjusted for cost of living,
    144–145, 166–167
  adjusted for inflation, 164–165
  effort based on, 191
  number of residents and, 159
  relative capacity by, 159–160
  by state, 131, 132, 162–163
Income taxes
  corporate, 137–138
  personal, 124, 126, 129, 131–133
Individual education plan (IEP),
    36–37, 216
Individuals with Disabilities
    Education Act of 1990
    (IDEA), 61, 272
Individuals with Disabilities in
    Education Act Amendments
    of 1997, 61
Inequality at the Starting Gate
    (Lee and Burkam), 272, 272n
Infant mortality rates, 267–268
Inflation–adjusted per capita
    personal income, 164–165
Input–output (production function)
    studies, 316–317, 319–321
Insurance
  disability, 356, 357
  health, 103–104, 356, 357,
    359–362
  life, 356, 357
  unemployment, 356, 357, 358
Interagency Task Force on
    Literacy, 60
Interest rates, 345–346

Intermediate test, 78–79, 92
Internal Revenue Service, 126n
International comparisons
  cultural differences and, 23–24
  of education spending, 6–12
  of fiscal capacity, 168–171, 172
  of fiscal effort, 197, 199
  of test scores, 20–24
  See also individual countries
Interstate School Leaders Licensure
    Consortium (ISLLC)
    Standards, 310n, 316
Iowa
  higher education spending of, 298
  SAT scores in, 13, 17, 318
  severance taxes in, 137n19
  teacher salaries in, 352, 354
Iran, test scores in, 21, 22
Ireland
  education spending in, 9
  infant mortality rates in, 268
  poverty in, 262, 263, 264
  test scores in, 21, 22
Islamic Republic (Kuwait),
    test scores in, 21, 22
ISLLC Standards, 310n, 316
Israel
  poverty in, 262, 263, 264
  test scores in, 21, 22
Italy
  education spending in, 9
  infant mortality rates in, 268
  poverty in, 263, 264
  test scores in, 21, 22

Jackson v. Benson (1998), 87n53
Japan
  education spending in, 9
  infant mortality rates in, 268
  per capita GNP in, 168,
    168n8, 169
  test scores in, 12, 21, 22
Judicial standards, 77–81, 91–92
  intermediate test, 78–79, 92
  in practice, 80–81
  rational relationship test,
    77–78, 92
  strict scrutiny test, 79–80, 92

Juvenile Justice and Delinquency
    Prevention Act of 1974, 58

Kansas, school taxes in, 71n17
Kentucky
  as commonwealth, 66n2, 218
  early public education in, 49
  education clause in, 81–82, 83–84
  "no action" groups in, 49
  school finance model in, 218–219
Kentucky Education Reform Act
    (KERA), 66, 82
Korea
  infant mortality rates in, 268
  test scores in, 21
Kuwait, test scores in, 21, 22

Land Ordinance of 1785, 50
Lanham Act of 1940, 53
Latinos. *See* Hispanic Americans
Latvia, test scores in, 21, 22
Law(s), 65–92
  on alternative schools, 85–86
  on construction, maintenance,
    and operation of schools, 53, 61
  on dropout prevention, 60
  on economically disadvantaged
    students, 56
  on equal protection, 73–81,
    91, 146
  establishing Department of
    Education, 52
  on firearms in school, 69, 69n13
  GI Bill, 53–54
  legislation during war years,
    51–54
  post–World War II, 54–62
  on Public Broadcasting, 58
  "Robin Hood," 368
  on special education, 248
  on students with disabilities, 55,
    58, 59–60
  on taxation, 67–68
  on tuition tax credits, 85,
    88–89, 92
  on vouchers, 84, 86–88, 92,
    365–366
  See also specific laws

LEA. *See* Local Education Agencies (LEAs)
Lead paint and lead solder, 344, 369
Learning disabled (LD) programs, 268
Legally required benefits, 356, 357, 358
Legend of Sleepy Hollow, The (film), 2
Leisure activities, 107–108, 109
Levittown, New York, 54
Licensing
   alternative, 277–279
   of teachers, 277–279, 354–356
Life insurance, 356, 357
Lithuania, test scores in, 21, 22
Local Education Agencies (LEAs), 67, 234–236
Local equalization, 238–239
Local sources of public school revenues, 231, 232–233, 234, 250
Local support for education, 368–369
Lotteries, 133
Louisiana
   minimal education in, 49
   pauper education in, 49
   severance taxes in, 137
Low birth weight, 267
Lunch programs, 53, 70, 257, 263, 307
Luxembourg
   infant mortality rates in, 268
   poverty in, 263, 264
Lynchburg, Virginia, 347–348, 350

Magnet schools, 58
Maine
   progressive education in, 49
   severance taxes in, 137n19
   tuition statute in, 87
Marginal utility, 140–141
Marion and McPherson Railway Co. v. Alexander (1901), 71n17
Maryland
   minimal education in, 49
   pauper education in, 49

per capita income in, 167
severance taxes in, 137n19
size of school districts in, 159
Massachusetts
   "cherish clause" in, 81n35
   as commonwealth, 66n2
   cost of living in, 143
   progressive education in, 49
   school laws of, 46, 47, 64, 86
   severance taxes in, 137n19
   spending variance between higher and lower capacity school districts in, 249
   State Superintendent of Public Instruction in, 235, 235n7
   taxes for education in, 67
Massachusetts Act of 1642, 46, 64
Massachusetts Act of 1827, 86
Massachusetts Law of 1647 (Ye Olde Deluder Satan law), 46, 47, 67, 72, 120, 120n4, 123
Mathematics
   laws involving education in, 54–55, 59
   student achievement vs. spending, 28–29
   U.S. students of, compared to other countries, 20–24
McInnis v. Shapiro (1968), 75nn25–26, 78n32, 91
Medicaid, state spending on, 294, 295–297, 298
Medicare, 126
Mercer Human Resource Consulting, 359
Merchant Marine Academy, 51
Mexican Americans
   equal protection of, 76
   test scores of, 17, 18, 19nn33–34
Mexico
   education spending in, 6, 8, 8n17, 9, 11
   infant mortality rates in, 267, 268
Michigan
   charter school concept in, 90
   domestic partner benefits in, 363
   revenue sources in, 231

Mid–Continent Research for Education and Learning (MCREL) labs, 57
Middle class, assumptions about, 255–256
Middle schools. *See* Secondary schools
Migrant workers, educating, 116–117
Millage rate, 127–128, 212–213, 245
Mills v. Board of Education of District of Columbia (1972), 16, 16n27, 55, 55n16
"Minimum," defined, 211
Minnesota
   NCLB implementation in, 364
   SAT scores in, 13, 17, 318
   teacher salaries in, 352, 354
Misconceptions, 1–42
   about educator salaries, 32–35, 40
   about number of school administrators, 35–39, 40
   about skyrocketing costs of education, 12, 24–25, 39
   about spending vs. achievement results, 25–32, 40
   about test scores, 12–13, 16–24, 39
   about U.S. spending on education vs. other countries, 5–12, 39
Mississippi
   early public education in, 50
   legal gambling in, 133
   "no action" groups in, 49
   per capita income in, 131, 132
   per pupil spending in, 293, 294
   revenue sources in, 231, 233
   sales taxes in, 133, 134
   severance taxes in, 137
   test scores in, 324
Missouri, severance taxes in, 137
"Mixed conditions," 49
Mold problems, 344, 369
Montana
   average number of pupils in school districts, 159
   cost of living in, 143

recapture clause in funding
   formulae, 212n19
study of school size in, 330
Morrill Act of 1862, 51–52
Morrill Act of 1890, 52, 63
Mortality rates, infant, 267–268
Mueller v. Allen (1983), 89,
   89n55

NAEP scores. *See* National
   Assessment of Educational
   Progress (NAEP) scores
NAESP (National Association of
   Elementary School Principals),
   279–280
Nation at Risk, A, 4–5, 4n14, 120,
   120n2, 254, 316
National Adult Literacy Survey, 29n
National Assessment of
   Educational Progress (NAEP)
   scores, 12, 19, 20, 60, 276,
   323–324, 325
National Association of Elementary
   School Principals (NAESP),
   279–280
National Board Certification,
   355, 371
National Board Certified teachers
   (NBCT), 356
National Board of Professional
   Teaching Standards (NBPTS),
   355–356
National Center for Education
   Statistics (NCES), 4nn7–8,
   4n11, 4n13, 7n, 10n, 11n23,
   14n, 21n, 37n, 58, 71, 100n8,
   101n, 103n, 196n, 231n, 273,
   283, 340–341
National Church, 48
National Commission on Excellence
   in Education, *A Nation at Risk,*
   4–5, 4n14, 120, 120n2,
   254, 316
National Commission on School
   Finance, 58
National Council for Accreditation
   of Teacher Education
   (NCATE), 324, 324n33

National Council on Teacher
   Quality (NCTQ), 278
National Defense Education Act of
   1958 (NDEA), 54–55
National Education Association
   (NEA), 15n, 55n17, 341,
   341n3, 342n
National Education Finance
   Project (NEFP), 215
National Education Goals
   Panel, 60
National Institute Board, 60
National Institute for Literacy, 60
National Literacy Act of 1991, 60
National School Lunch Act of
   1946, 53
Nation's Report Card, 276. *See also*
   National Assessment of
   Educational Progress (NAEP)
   scores
Native Americans
   in administrative population, 281
   salaries of, 282
   single parenthood among, 269
   test scores of, 18
Naval Academy, 51
NBCT (National Board Certified
   teachers), 356
NBPTS (National Board of
   Professional Teaching
   Standards), 355–356
NCATE (National Council for
   Accreditation of Teacher
   Education), 324, 324n33
NCES. *See* National Center
   for Education Statistics
   (NCES)
NCLB. *See* No Child Left Behind
   Act of 2001 (NCLB)
NCTQ (National Council on
   Teacher Quality), 278
NDEA (National Defense
   Education Act of 1958), 54–55
NEA (National Education
   Association), 15n, 55n17, 341,
   341n3, 342n
Nebraska, teacher salaries in,
   352, 354

Needs
   data analysis of, 302
   of school facilities, 342
   of students, 15–16
NEFP (National Education
   Finance Project), 215
Neglect, and student achievement,
   270–271
Netherlands
   infant mortality rates in, 268
   poverty in, 263, 264
   test scores in, 21, 22
Neutrality, fiscal, 205, 223
Nevada
   legal gambling in, 133, 189
   revenue sources in, 231,
      233, 234
   school enrollment growth in,
      258, 259
New England
   "cherish clause" in, 81, 81n35
   early education in, 47
   revenue sources in, 231
   Virginia compared to, 48–49
New Hampshire
   NCLB implementation in, 364
   progressive education in, 49
   severance taxes in, 137n19
New Jersey
   legal gambling in, 133, 189
   minimal education in, 49
   pauper education in, 49
   revenue sources in, 231, 233
   salaries in, 8
   SAT scores in, 17
   severance taxes in, 137n19
   Supreme Court on public edu-
      cation finance system, 222
New Mexico
   revenue sources in, 231,
      233, 234
   severance taxes in, 137
New York
   class size in, 326
   economic cost function
      approach in, 219
   illegal immigrants in, 260
   per pupil spending in, 293, 294

New York (*Cont.*)
  progressive education in, 49
  revenue from business
    incorporated within, 189
  severance taxes in, 137n19
  State Superintendent of Public
    Instruction in, 235
  teacher salaries in, 352, 354
New York City, school size in, 331
New Zealand
  education spending in, 9, 197
  infant mortality rates in, 268
  test scores in, 21, 22
"No action" groups, 49–50
No Child Left Behind Act of 2001
    (NCLB)
  academic expectations and, 10,
    224, 235, 310
  on accountability for student
    achievement, 224, 364,
    365, 367
  achievement testing and, 19,
    38, 122n8, 139, 202, 204,
    217, 248
  adequate yearly progress (AYP)
    guidelines and, 19, 61, 139,
    235n8, 248, 254, 307
  costs of, 26, 370
  federal control and, 66, 69, 122
  mandates in, 3
  origin of, 55, 61
  state standards and, 30,
    153, 159
  teacher quality and, 323, 355
Nonequalization grants, 208–209
North Carolina
  cost of living in, 143
  early public education in, 49
  flat grant model in, 242
  "no action" groups in, 49
  retirement benefits in, 359
  teacher certification in, 356
North Dakota
  SAT scores in, 13, 17, 318
  severance taxes in, 137
  teacher salaries in, 353, 354
Northwest Ordinance of 1787,
    50–51

Norway
  education spending in, 9,
    23–24, 197
  infant mortality rates in, 268
  poverty in, 263, 264
  test scores in, 21, 22

Objectives, in budget process, 303
OECD. *See* Organization for
    Economic Cooperation and
    Development (OECD)
Office of Education Appropriation
    Act of 1970, 58
Ohio
  domestic partner benefits in, 363
  educational assistance programs
    in, 88
  land grants in, 51
  NCLB implementation in, 364
  progressive education in, 49
  study of school size in, 330
Oregon
  percent of spending on
    transportation in, 298
  transportation spending of, 298
Organization for Economic
    Cooperation and
    Development (OECD), 9, 9n,
    11, 11n22, 97
Overcrowding, 334–335
Pacific Islanders
  in administrative population, 281
  salaries of, 282
  in school–age population, 260
  test scores of, 18, 19n33
Paid leave, 356, 357
Parent(s)
  grandparents as, 268–269
  single, 269
Parental Choice program
    (Milwaukee), 87–88
Parochial schools, 49, 85–86, 89, 90
Pauper schools, 49
Pediatrics, 271–272
Pennsylvania
  as commonwealth, 66n2
  minimal education in, 49
  pauper education in, 49

  school taxes in, 72
  severance taxes in, 137n19
  transience rate in, 266
*Pennsylvania Association of
    Retarded Citizens v.
    Commonwealth*, 55, 55n15
Percentage add–on budgeting,
    308–309
Phi Delta Kappa/Gallup polls, 193n
Philadelphia, school size in, 331
Planning, educational, 301–303
Planning, Programming, Budgeting,
    Evaluating System (PPBES),
    309–310
Planning, Programming, Budgeting
    System (PPBS), 309–310
Plenary power, 66, 66n4
Plyler v. Doe (1982), 261, 261n6
Poland
  education spending in, 6, 11
  infant mortality rates in, 267, 268
*Pollock v. Farmers' Loan and Trust
    Co.* (1895), 131n15
Portugal
  education spending in, 9, 197
  infant mortality rates in, 268
  test scores in, 21, 22
Poverty
  assumptions about, 255–256
  "hidden rules" and, 255
  student achievement and, 256,
    262–265
PPBES (Planning, Programming,
    Budgeting, Evaluating
    System), 309–310
PPBS (Planning, Programming,
    Budgeting System), 309–310
Pregnancy, premarital, 269
Prenatal issues, and education,
    109–110, 111
Princeton Review, 86
Principals
  attracting and retaining, 280
  characteristics of, 281
  demographics of, 279–284
  duties of, 36–37
  number of, 37, 38, 40
  quality of, 280–284

ratio to students, 38
salaries of, 8, 280, 281, 283
school budgets and, 284
turnover among, 283
Priorities, and budgets, 291–304
Production function (input–output)
    studies, 316–317, 319–321
Professional consensus approach to
    adequacy, 221
Professional development, of
    teachers, 325–326
Progressive taxes, 124, 125–126,
    126n, 127
Property and Administrative
    Services Act of 1949, 54
Property taxes, 72–73, 127–130, 148
    administration of, 129
    in history of education funding,
        47, 123
    per capita by state, 130
    public rejection of, 120–121,
        121n5, 128–129
Proportional taxes, 124–125,
    126, 127
Proposition 13 (California),
    120–121, 121n5
Public Agenda survey, 280, 280n61
Public assistance, state spending
    on, 294, 295–297, 298
Public Broadcasting Act of 1967, 58
Public Education Network, 2n1
Public school finance. *See* School
    Finance
Puerto Ricans, test scores of, 18
Pupils. *See* Student(s)

Quality of life, 102–113
    charitable contributions, 105–107,
        105n
    childbirth and prenatal issues,
        109–110, 111
    crime victimization, 112–113
    cultural activities, 108–109
    health insurance, 103–104
    incarceration rates, 110–112
    leisure activities, 107–108, 109
    volunteerism, 104–105
    voting frequency, 102–103

Race
    demographic trends in, 260–261
    graduation rates and, 2
    test scores and, 17, 18,
        19nn33–34, 20
    See also African Americans
Radon gas, 343, 344, 369
RAND Corporation, 361
*Randolph County Board of
    Education v. Adams* (1995),
    120n3
Rational relationship test, 77–78, 92
Reading, and student achievement
    vs. spending, 28–29
Recruiting New Teachers, Inc.,
    276n46
Redistribution of wealth, 113,
    121–122
Regressive taxes, 124, 125, 126, 127
Reinventing Education (Gerstner,
    Semerat, Doyle, & Johnston),
    6, 6n
Religion, and education, 48, 49,
    85, 86
Religious persecution, 48, 49
Repair costs, 292–293
Retirement, 275
Retirement benefits, 356, 357, 358
Revenue(s)
    history of, 230–231
    sources of, 70–71, 231–234,
        299, 300
    See also Funding
Rhode Island
    early public education in, 49
    "no action" groups in, 49
    severance taxes in, 137n19
Risk factors, 261–272
    child abuse and neglect, 270–271
    grandparents as parents, 268–269
    infant mortality rates, 267–268
    low birth weight, 267
    poverty, 262–265
    premarital pregnancy, 269
    second language learners, 261, 265
    single parents, 268
    toddlers and television, 271–272
    transience, 266

"Robin Hood" laws, 368
Rome, education funding in, 72
*Rose v. The Council for Better
    Education, Inc.* (1989), 81,
    81n36, 83–84, 84n40, 218,
    218n28
Rural School and Community
    Trust, 330
Russian Federation, test scores in,
    21, 22

Safe Schools Act of 1994, 60
Salaries
    education costs and, 8, 13, 15
    entry–level, 34
    of principals, 8, 280, 281, 283
    student achievement and, 320,
        320n, 332–333
    of teachers. *See* Teacher salaries
Sales taxes, 124–125, 133, 134
Same–sex benefits, 362–363
*San Antonio Independent School
    District v. Rodriguez* (1973),
    76, 76n29, 77, 77n30, 79,
    80–81, 81n34, 91, 92
SAT scores. *See* Scholastic Achieve-
    ment Test (SAT) scores
SBB (site–based budgeting), 310
Scholastic Achievement Test (SAT)
    scores, 12–13, 17–19, 29n, 318
School(s)
    accountability of, 61
    alternative, 85–86
    budget for, 3–4
    charter, 85, 89–90, 92
    disappointment in, 2
    effectiveness of, 3
    magnet, 58
    number of professionals in, 4,
        14, 40
    parochial, 49, 85–86, 89, 90
    pauper, 49
    regional evolution of, 48–50
    size of, 330–332, 336
    See also Elementary schools;
        Secondary schools
School administrators
    in budget process, 305, 307

School administrators (*Cont.*)
  demographics of, 279–284
  ISLLC Standard on, 316
  misconceptions about number of, 35–39, 40
  school budgets and, 284
  See also Principals
School district(s)
  fiscal capacity of, 154–155, 156, 159–160, 189–193
  fiscal effort of, 189–193
  number of, 158, 228, 229, 230
  size of, 158, 228–229, 230
  spending variance among, 248–249
  state aid grants to, 207–213
  successful, as approach to adequacy, 220–221
School District Administrators, number of, 37, 38
School Dropout Prevention and Basic Skills Improvement Act of 1990, 60
School facilities
  acoustic quality of, 334
  construction of, 4n12, 53, 61, 343, 344, 369
  health issues in, 343–344
  interest rates and, 345–346
  maintaining, 53, 61, 340–346, 369
  overcrowding of, 334–335
  student achievement and, 333–335
  temperature of, 334
School finance
  administrator demographics and, 279–284
  employee benefits and, 356–358, 362–363
  federal government and, 50–51, 56–62, 63, 70–71
  health care and, 359–362
  history of. *See* History
  as investment in human capital, 95–116
  involvement of federal government in, 50–51, 56–62
  issues in, 339–371

misconceptions about. *See* Misconceptions
  regional evolution of, 48–50
  state constitutional language and, 81–82
  teacher demographics and, 272–279
  teacher licensing and certification and, 354–356
  teacher salaries and, 346–354, 370
School finance systems, 227–251
  advantages to federal financing of, 236–238, 250
  current structures in, 241–247
  district power equalizing (DPE) in, 244–246, 250, 251
  flat grants in, 242–243
  foundation plans in, 243–244, 250
  local equalization, 238–239
  revenues and expenditures in, 230–234
  standards–based reform in, 248–249
  state equalization, 239–241, 250
School Lunch programs, 53, 70, 257, 263, 307
School success. *See* Student achievement
Science
  laws involving education in, 54–55, 59
  U.S. students of, compared to other countries, 20–24
Scotland, test scores in, 21, 22
SEAs. *See* State Education Agencies (SEAs)
Secondary schools
  enrollment in, 14
  expenditures in, 14, 25, 294, 295–297
  number of teachers in, 14
  pupil–teacher ratios in, 14
  salaries of teachers in, 15, 31
  state spending on, 294, 295–297
Self–employed individuals, FICA taxes on, 125nn10–11

Serrano v. Priest (1974), 75–76, 75n27, 80, 91, 92, 146, 146n25, 244
Service(s), equalizing, 121–122, 148
Servicemen's Readjustment Act of 1944, 53–54
Severance taxes, 136–137, 137n19, 189
Shaffer v. Carter (1970), 68nn8–9
Simmons–Harris v. Zelman (1999), 88
"Sin" taxes, 138–139
Singapore, test scores in, 21, 22
Single parents, and student achievement, 269
Site–based budgeting (SBB), 310
Sixteenth Amendment, 131
Slovak Republic, infant mortality rates in, 267, 268
Slovenia, test scores in, 21, 22
Smith–Bankhead Act of 1920, 52
Smith–Hughes Act of 1917, 52, 63
SNAP (State Non–Arbitrage Program), 346
Social Security, 125–126, 125n11, 356, 357, 358
South Africa, test scores in, 21, 22
South Carolina
  minimal education in, 49
  pauper education in, 49
  severance taxes in, 137n19
South Dakota
  SAT scores in, 13, 17, 318
  teacher salaries in, 8, 353, 354
Spain
  education spending in, 9
  infant mortality rates in, 268
Special education
  low birth rate and, 267
  student weighting in, 215
Special Education Law, 248
Special needs students, and demographics, 256
Spending
  in budget process, 306
  comparison of U.S. vs. other countries, 6–12
  in elementary schools, 14

misconception about U.S. spending on education, 5–12, 39

per student, 7, 25, 41, 293, 294, 311

in secondary schools, 14

student achievement and, 25–32, 40, 315–338

studies of, 316–317, 319–321

test scores and, 28–30

for unanticipated expenses, 306

See also Budget(s)

Sporting Goods Market in 1999, The, 108n

Sports, involvement in, 107, 108

Standards–based reform, 248–249

Standards of Quality, 240–241

State(s)

    acceptance of federal grant by, 69

    budget data for, 293–298

    comparing teacher salary trends in, 351–354

    federal control of state's education function, 68–70

    fiscal capacity issues in, 161–168, 173–181

    fiscal effort, 188, 193, 194–195

    grades assigned for teacher–quality standards in, 279

    income taxes of, 131–133

    "no action" groups in, 49–50

    number of school districts in, 158

    pauper education in, 49

    per capita personal income in, 132, 162–163, 164–165, 166–167

    property taxes per capita, 130

    pupils per school district in, 158

    roles and responsibilities of, 234–236

    sales taxes in, 134

    school spending by, 24, 295–297

    as source of public school revenues, 231–234, 250

    taxing prerogatives of, 71–72

    trends in student enrollment in, 258–260

    See also individual states

State aid grants, 207–213

    equalization, 207, 209–213, 223

    nonequalization, 208–209

State constitutions, 81–82

State Education Agencies (SEAs), 56, 57, 67, 234–236

State equalization, 239–241, 250

State funding, full, 214, 246–247, 250, 251

State Non–Arbitrage Program (SNAP), 346

State Superintendent of Public Instruction, 235

State–of–the–art approach to adequacy, 221–222

Statistical Abstracts of the United States, 197

Strict scrutiny test, 79–80, 92

Strout v. Albanese (1999), 87, 87n51

Student(s)

    disabled. *See* Disabilities, students with

    earning potential of, 98–100

    employability of, 100–102

    future quality of life of, 102–113

    per capita spending on, 7, 25, 41, 293, 294, 311

    ratio of principals to, 38

    ratio of teachers' aides to, 38

    ratio of teachers to, 14, 32, 38

Student achievement

    child abuse and neglect and, 270–271

    effective teaching and, 28–30

    grandparents as parents and, 268–269

    infant mortality rates and, 267–268

    low birth weight and, 267

    measuring, 364–365

    poverty and, 256, 262–265

    premarital pregnancy and, 269

    professional development of teachers and, 325–326

    recent history involving, 316–318

    reduced class size and, 326–329, 336

reduced school size and, 330–332, 336

    risk factors affecting, 261–272

    school facilities and, 333–335

    of second language learners, 261, 265

    spending and, 25–32, 40, 315–338

    student enrollment vs., 31–32

    studies of, 316–317, 319–321

    teacher quality and, 275–277, 322–325, 335–336

    teacher salaries and, 320, 320n, 332–333

    teacher turnover and, 275–277

    television and, 271–272

    transience and, 266

    See also Test scores

Student enrollment

    education costs vs., 13–15

    in elementary schools, 14

    in secondary schools, 14

    student achievement vs., 31–32

    trends in, 258–260

Student needs, and education costs, 15–16

Success for All Foundation, 222n40

Successful school district approach to adequacy, 220–221

Sumptuary taxes, 138–139

Superintendents. *See* School administrators

Supplementary pay, 356, 357

Supreme Court. *See* U.S. Supreme Court

Surplus Revenue Deposit Act of 1836, 51

Suspect classification, 79–80

Sweden

    education spending in, 9, 197

    infant mortality rates in, 268

    poverty in, 262, 263, 264

    test scores in, 21, 22

Switzerland

    education spending in, 9, 11, 197

    income gap in, 262

    infant mortality rates in, 268

    poverty in, 262, 263, 264

    test scores in, 21, 22

Taxation, 119–148
  ad valorem, 124, 127
  administration costs of, 141–142
  convenience of payment, 142
  corporate income taxes, 137–138
  "double," 138
  earning potential and, 98–100
  Equal Protection clause and,
      73–77
  in equalizing resources and
      services, 121–122, 148
  fairness of, 142
  federal, 131–133
  of flow of production, 123–124
  indicators of a good tax, 141–142
  from legal perspective, 67–68
  measuring impact of, 139–142
  personal income taxes, 124, 126,
      129, 131–133
  in personam, 124
  progressive, 124, 125–126,
      126n, 127
  proportional, 124–125, 126, 127
  redistribution of wealth and, 113,
      121–122
  regressive, 124, 125, 126, 127
  in rem, 124
  sales taxes, 124–125, 133, 134
  severance taxes, 136–137,
      137n19, 189
  "sin" taxes, 138–139
  state perogatives involving, 71–72
  of stock of wealth, 123–124
  sumptuary taxes, 138–139
  to support human capital,
      113–114
  tax brackets and, 126
  tuition tax credits and, 85, 92
  understanding, 121–127
  visibility of benefit of, 142
  See also Property taxes
Teacher(s), 272–279
  aging of, 31
  alternatively licensed, 277–279
  degrees held by, 347–349
  demographics of, 272–279
  effectiveness of, vs. student
      achievement, 28–30, 40

  experience of, 349–351
  licensing and certification of,
      277–279, 354–356
  number of, 4, 14, 37, 38
  professional development of,
      325–326
  quality of, 275–277, 322–325,
      335–336
  ratio to students, 14, 32, 38
  retirement of, 275
  school finance and, 272–279
  shortage of, 278
  turnover among, 273–277
  workday of, 32–33
Teacher salaries
  funding of, 346–354, 370
  increased education expenses
      and, 13, 15
  interstate comparisons of,
      351–354
  misconceptions about, 31,
      32–35, 40
  spending gaps involving,
      238–239
  student achievement and, 320,
      320n, 332–333
Teachers' aides
  number of, 37
  ratio to students, 38
Teaching Commission, 333
Television
  academic results and, 23
  student achievement and,
      271–272
Tennessee
  early public education in, 49
  math achievement vs. effective
      teaching in, 29
  Medicaid spending in, 298
  "no action" groups in, 49
  spending variance between
      higher and lower capacity
      school districts in, 249
  study of class size in, 327
  teacher quality and student
      achievement studies in, 276
  value–added study of, 323
Tenth Amendment, 66–67

Test scores, 29n, 318
  costs vs., 12–13, 16–24
  misconceptions about, 12–13,
      16–24, 39
  race and, 17, 18, 19nn33–34, 20
  spending and, 28–30
Texas
  corrections spending of, 298
  economic cost function approach
      in, 219
  Education Agency in, 234n
  fiscal capacity in, 159–160,
      173–181
  illegal immigrants in, 260–261,
      261n8
  per capita income in, 168
  per capita tax base in, 157
  reading achievement vs. effective
      teaching in, 29
  school enrollment growth in,
      258, 259
  school funding in, 76, 77, 79,
      80–81, 92
  State Education Agency in, 57
  study of school size in, 330
  teacher quality and student
      achievement studies
      in, 276
  test scores in, 324
  value–added study of, 323
Thailand, test scores in, 21, 22
Third International Math and
      Science Study (Trends in
      International Mathematics
      and Science Study), 20–22
Thomas More Law Center, 363
TIMSS (Trends in International
      Mathematics and Science
      Study), 20–22
Tinker v. Des Moines Independent
      Community School District
      (1969), 69, 69n14
Title Programs, 45, 46, 55–57,
      66, 234
Tobacco, sumptuary taxes on,
      138–139
Toddlers, and television, 271–272
Transience, 266

Transportation spending, 294, 295–297, 298

Trends
  in demographics, 258–261
  in student enrollment, 258–260
  in teacher salaries, 351–354

Trends in International Mathematics and Science Study (TIMSS), 20–22

Tuition tax credits, 85, 88–89, 92

Turkey, infant mortality rates in, 267, 268

Turnover
  among principals, 283
  among teachers, 273–277

Unemployment insurance, 356, 357, 358

United Kingdom
  comparison with U.S. education system, 66
  education spending in, 9
  infant mortality rates in, 268
  poverty in, 263, 264

United States
  budget process in, 301
  education spending in, 6–12, 197, 199
  fiscal capacity issues in, 168–171
  fiscal effort in, 193, 195–198, 199
  infant mortality rates in, 267–268
  misconception about spending on education, 5–12, 39
  national budget of, 301
  poverty in, 262, 263–264
  test scores compared to other countries, 20–24

U.S. Bureau of Justice Statistics, 112n

U.S. Census Bureau, 99n, 104n, 110n, 266n16, 267, 270n26, 342n6, 365

U.S. Congress, power to tax and spend, 67–68

U.S. Constitution
  Bill of Rights in, 66, 79
  on Congress's right to tax and spend, 68

First Amendment to, 89
Fourteenth Amendment to, 73–77, 146
  freedoms guaranteed in, 66, 69, 79
Sixteenth Amendment to, 131
  on states and public education, 48, 50, 63, 114n
  suspect classifications in, 80
Tenth Amendment to, 66–67

U.S. Department of Commerce, 99n, 136

U.S. Department of Defense, 309

U.S. Department of Education
  contributions to education spending, 70
  establishment of, 52, 59, 234
  interpretation of grant legislation by, 236
  National Center for Education Statistics, 4nn7–8, 4n11, 4n13, 7n, 10n, 11n23, 14n, 21n, 37n, 58, 71, 100n8, 101n, 196n, 231n, 340–341
  Office of Special Education and Rehabilitative Services, 16n
  position on AYP and testing requirements, 235n8
  survey of school facility conditions, 340
  on teacher turnover, 273
  on tuition payments, 87

U.S. Department of Health, Education, and Welfare (HEW), 52, 59, 204n4, 234

U.S. Department of Health and Human Services, 271n27

U.S. Department of Labor, 33, 101n, 358

U.S. General Accounting Office, 204, 340

U.S. Military Academy, 51

U.S. National Center for Health Statistics, 111n

U.S. National Endowment for the Arts, 107n, 109n

U.S. Office of Management and Budget, 196n

U.S. Supreme Court
  on charter schools, 89, 90
  on equal protection, 74, 75, 76–77
  on gun–free zones, 69, 69n13
  on income taxes, 131
  on judicial standards, 79, 80–81
  on power to tax and spend, 68
  on school vouchers, 366

United States v. Butler (1936), 68n7

United States v. Lopez (1995), 69, 69n11

University of Wisconsin–Milwaukee, 32–33

Utah
  education spending in, 24, 293, 294
  nonacceptance of federal funds for NCLB, 235n8
  recapture clause in funding formulae, 212n19
  SAT scores in, 13, 17, 318
  school enrollment trends in, 258, 259

Value–added studies, 323, 335–336

Vermont
  average number of pupils in school districts in, 159
  flat grant model in, 242
  higher education spending of, 298
  progressive education in, 49
  same–sex benefits in, 362
  severance taxes in, 137n19
  tuition statute in, 86–87

Vertical equity, 83, 204–205, 214–218, 223

Victimization, 112–113

Virginia
  as commonwealth, 66n2
  Department of Education in, 234n
  Equal Protection clause in, 75
  flat grants in, 242
  funding practices in, 75
  Joint Legislative and Review Commission in, 240n
  minimal education in, 49

New England compared to, 48–49

number of schools, districts, and pupils per district, 158

pauper education in, 49

per capita income in, 163, 164

per capita tax base in, 157, 159

sales tax in, 124–125

SNAP program in, 346

spending variance between higher and lower capacity school districts in, 249

Standards of Quality in, 240–241

teacher salaries in, 347–351

test scores in, 324

underfunding of education in, 240n

Vocational education, 52

Vocational Rehabilitation Act of 1918, 52

Vocational Rehabilitation Act of 1943, 53

Volunteerism, 104–105

Voting frequency, 102–103

Vouchers, 84, 86–88, 92, 365–366

War years, education legislation during, 51–54

Washington Post, 13

Wealth

determining, 191–192

fiscal capacity and, 190–191

fiscal effort and, 190–192

redistribution of, 113, 121–122

taxing, 123–124

Wealth of Nations, The (Smith), 96, 96n2

Weighted pupil approach to calculating vertical equity, 214–218

West Virginia

corrections spending of, 298

study of school size in, 330

White students, test scores of, 18, 19nn33–34

"Widgets," 319–320, 319n12

Wisconsin

economic cost function approach in, 219

income taxes in, 137

Parental Choice program in, 87–88

spending variance between higher and lower capacity school districts in, 249

Women

in administrative population, 281

childbearing and education, 109–110, 111

earning potential of, 98, 99

education of, 46, 63

Work of Nations, The (Reich), 168, 168n7

Workers' compensation, 356, 357, 358

World Bank, 97, 97n4

World War I, 52, 63

World War II, 53–54

Wyoming

budget for, 298

education spending in, 296, 298

severance taxes in, 189

transportation spending in, 298

Ye Olde Deluder Satan Law of 1647, 46, 47, 67, 72, 120, 120n4, 123

Zelman v. Simmon–Harris (2002), 366, 366n54

Zero–base budgeting (ZBB), 309